PENGUIN CLASSICS

THE HISTORY OF THE CHURCH

EUSEBIUS (A.D. *c.* 260–339) was a Greek Christian writer, often called the 'Father of Ecclesiastical History'. He was born in Palestine and educated at Caesarea, the city of which he later became bishop.

Eusebius' voluminous literary remains may be grouped into four categories: the historical, the apologetic, the Biblical and the dogmatic. *The Ecclesiastical History* comprises ten books, covering the period from the foundation of the Church to the defeat of Licinius in 324. *A Preparation for the Gospel*, in fifteen books, shows that Christians rightly prefer Judaism to paganism, and its continuation, the *Proof of the Gospel*, shows how the Christian religion is the fulfilment of the Old Testament. Among Eusebius' other works are the *Onomasticon*, a gazetteer of Bible sites, *Commentary on the Psalms*, of which only fragments remain, and the two books *Against Marcellus*.

Sometimes termed the 'Christian Herodotus', Eusebius has earned legitimate fame as *the* historian of Christian antiquity.

G. A. WILLIAMSON was born in 1895 and was a Classical Exhibitioner at Worcester College, Oxford, graduating with a First Class Honours degree. He was Senior Classics Master at Norwich School from 1922 to 1960. He also translated *Josephus: The Jewish War* (1959) and *Procopius: The Secret History* (1966) for the Penguin Classics. He died in 1982.

ANDREW LOUTH, born in Lincolnshire and brought up in the north of England, studied Theology at the universities of Cambridge and Edinburgh. From 1970 to 1985 he was Fellow and Chaplain of Worcester College, Oxford, and University Lecturer in Theology, teaching principally Patristics. Since 1985 he has been at Goldsmiths' College, London where he is now Reader in History. He is the author of *The Origins of the Christian Mystical Tradition* (1981), *Discerning the Mystery: An Essay on the Nature of Theology* (1983) and *Denys the Areopagite* (1989). He has also edited *Early Christian Writings* for the Penguin Classics.

Contents

FOREWORD TO THE REVISED EDITION   vii

INTRODUCTION   ix

NOTE ON THE TEXT   xxxvi

TRANSLATOR'S NOTE   xxxvii

1 THE NATURE AND WORK OF CHRIST: HIS
CONTEMPORARIES: HIS CHOICE OF FOLLOWERS:
CORRESPONDENCE WITH ABGAR   1

2 TIBERIUS TO NERO: THE WORK OF THE APOSTLES
FROM THE CHOICE OF MATTHIAS TO THE DEATHS
OF PAUL AND PETER   35

3 VESPASIAN TO TRAJAN: THE DISTRIBUTION AND
WRITINGS OF THE APOSTLES AND THEIR
SUCCESSORS: ENEMIES WITHIN THE CHURCH:
PERSECUTIONS   65

4 TRAJAN TO MARCUS AURELIUS: THE SUCCESSION
OF BISHOPS: THEIR WRITINGS AND MARTYRDOMS   105

5 MARCUS AURELIUS TO SEVERUS: THE SUCCESSION
OF BISHOPS: THEIR REFUTATION OF MARCION AND
MONTANUS: THEIR SETTLEMENT OF THE DATE OF
THE EASTER FESTIVAL   138

6 SEVERUS TO DECIUS: THE WORK OF ORIGEN AND
HIS CONTEMPORARIES: WIDESPREAD PERSECUTION   179

7 GALLUS TO GALLIENUS: THE WORK OF CYPRIAN
AND DIONYSIUS: THE HERESIES OF SABELLIUS,
NOVATUS, NEPOS, PAUL, AND THE MANICHEES   221

The History of the Church

8 DIOCLETIAN TO MAXIMIAN: PERSECUTIONS:
THE IMPERIAL RECANTATION   256

9 MAXIMIN'S RENEWED ATTACKS ON THE CHURCH:
THE END OF PERSECUTION   282

10 PEACE AND RECOVERY OF THE CHURCH: VICTORY
OF CONSTANTINE   303

BIBLIOGRAPHY   334

MAP   338

WHO'S WHO IN EUSEBIUS   339

APPENDICES   428

Foreword to the Revised Edition

The translation given here is that of the first edition, G. A. Williamson's clear and readable version, altered only in a very few places, mainly for editorial reasons. As is (or was) normal, Greek names are Latinized in their translation from Greek to Latin script (e.g., Eusebius, not Eusebios). Hebrew names, when they refer to Old Testament figures, are given in the form (often based on the Hebrew) familiar from English Bibles (e.g., Joshua, not Jesus).

The footnotes simply contain (mainly biblical) references, except for a few cases where it is necessary to identify to whom Eusebius is referring, or to explain a point of translation. All other commentary (apart from that in the appendices) is to be found in the 'Who's Who in Eusebius' (pp. 339–427), as most of what the reader will want to know concerns the people who appear in Eusebius' pages. The 'Who's Who' also contains a few items on such matters as Easter, the Septuagint and so on, to which the reader is directed by cross-references; otherwise the value of cross-referring is taken for granted.

The introduction, 'Who's Who' and appendices are intended for the general reader and student: no elaborate justification is given of the opinions stated. The bibliography lists works that will take the reader further (as do the entries in the 'Who's Who'). For further commentary, the reader is referred to the notes to A. C. McGiffert's translation of Eusebius in *Nicene and Post-Nicene Fathers*, Second Series, vol. 1 (1904), and to Lawlor and Oulton's commentary in vol. 2 of their translation of Eusebius' *The History of the Church* and *Martyrs of Palestine* (London, 1927–8). Much information, supplementary to the 'Who's Who', is to be found in the *Oxford Dictionary of the Christian Church*, ed. F. L. Cross and E. A. Livingstone (2nd rev. edn, Oxford, 1983) and in the much older, but still very valuable, *Dictionary*

The History of the Church

of Christian Biography, ed. W. Smith and H. Wace, 4 vols. (London, 1877–87).

Finstock   Andrew Louth
September, 1988

Introduction

Eusebius' life

Eusebius was born in the early 260s, probably in Caesarea, which was to be the scene of his activities for most of his long life. Originally a small town on the Palestinian coast of the Mediterranean with a fortified harbour, known as Strato's Tower after the dynast of Sidon who had built it, it became a Greek city during the struggles for Palestine between the Seleucid and Ptolemaic kings. About 100 B.C. it became part of the Hasmonean kingdom and probably received a large influx of Jewish settlers, but forty years later Pompey made the city once again a Gentile city. Strato's Tower then came under the rule of Herod the Great, who ruled as king of Judaea 37–4 B.C.: he rebuilt the city on a grandiose scale as a Hellenistic capital and Roman metropolis and renamed it after Augustus Caesar. Henceforth he was regarded as its founder. When Judaea became a Roman province, Caesarea became its capital. It was raised to the status of a Roman colony by Vespasian, who settled veterans there. The importance of Caesarea was further enhanced by Jerusalem's decline in significance after the Jewish wars (A.D.66–73 and 132–5): in 135 Jerusalem became a pagan city, Aelia Capitolina, from which Jews were banned on pain of death. The growing importance of Persia in the third century made Caesarea even more important to the Romans as a focal point for campaigns against Persia. In the fourth century it was even deemed worthy to be, briefly, the residence of one of the Roman Emperors, Maximin Daia.[1]

By the third century Caesarea had a population of 100,000. A pagan city under the protection of the goddess Tyche (Fortune), it had a cosmopolitan population with a large Jewish community, an almost equally large Samaritan community, and a growing

1. See Timothy Barnes, *Constantine and Eusebius* (Cambridge, Mass., and London, 1981), p. 81 ff., and the whole of chapter VI.

Christian presence. Origen the great Christian theologian had spent the last twenty years of his life there and had established a kind of Christian academy that had attracted Christian pupils from all over the East. This academy, with its library, was consolidated by Pamphilus, a great admirer of Origen (though he had never known him), who settled in Caesarea and set about preserving Origen's heritage by making copies of all his voluminous works and continuing his labours on the text of the Scriptures. This Pamphilus was Eusebius' adored mentor: Eusebius became Pamphilus' pupil and collaborated with him on his last work, the *Apology for Origen*, composed while Pamphilus was in prison awaiting martyrdom during the Great Persecution at the beginning of the fourth century. Eusebius preserved Pamphilus' memory after his death, both in his account of his martyrdom in *Martyrs of Palestine* and in his (lost) *Life of Pamphilus*, and, more personally, by adding Pamphilus' name to his own so that he was known as *Eusebius Pamphili*, 'Pamphilus' Eusebius'.

Eusebius was born after a decade that had seen the first attempts by the Roman Emperors to persecute the Christian Church on an imperial scale. By the time of his birth, the successive waves of that persecution had come to an end and from the time of the Emperor Gallienus (who ruled as sole Emperor 260–68) the Church knew a period of settled peace and an officially recognized right to its places of worship. Eusebius thus grew up in a Church that seemed to have seen the back of persecution, both the imperial persecution of the immediate past and the sporadic local persecution the Church had always known. Such conditions of peace were conducive to scholarship and Eusebius was, more than anything else, a scholar. During these years he acquired the massive learning he was to put to use in the great works of his maturity. This period of peace came to an abrupt end with the Great Persecution, initiated by the Emperor Diocletian in 303, which continued spasmodically in the East until 313.

In fact we know little in detail about Eusebius' life: his date of birth has to be deduced from hints in *The History of the Church* (from which it transpires that he was born during the very last years of the life of Dionysius, bishop of Alexandria, who died *c.*264); he became bishop of Caesarea in about 313 (probably in succession to Agapius, who had ordained him priest and seems to have survived the persecution), and died on 30 May 339. His successor in the see of Caesarea, Acacius, wrote a life of Eusebius, but this has been lost. The loss of the *Life* and the obscurity about the details of his life are both probably due to one factor: his involvement in the great theological controversy of the 320s, the Arian controversy, among the supporters of the heresiarch Arius. The Church never canonized him, and though many of his works have been preserved, the memory of the man has been largely lost. Further, what can be gleaned of Eusebius does not endear him much to modern scholars. When the Arian controversy blew up, Eusebius was one of those condemned at the council of Antioch, presided over by Bishop Ossius of Cordova (Constantine's religious adviser), in early 325. (We learn of this from a document preserved only in Syriac.) He therefore arrived at the council of Nicaea (originally arranged for Ancyra – modern Ankara – but moved to Nicaea on account of the climate: apparently a credible reason) as a condemned heretic, which is hard to square with the prominent role in which Eusebius casts himself in his letter about the Council of Nicaea to his Church back home in Caesarea. Eusebius, however, emerged from that council among the orthodox majority, having signed the creed and condemned Arius. At the council, too, he met the Emperor, Constantine the Great, and conceived a great admiration for him. Eusebius would like us to think that this admiration was mutual, and that he became the confidant of the Emperor. We may feel that he was deceiving himself; none the less he was chosen by the Emperor to deliver an oration on the occasion of his *Tricennalia* (the celebration of Constantine's first thirty years as Emperor, which he celebrated 335–6) and after the death of Constantine wrote his *Life*, on which he was still working when he died himself. The oration in praise of the Emperor and the *Life* are works of flattery (which we, anachronistically, find tasteless) and give expression to a theology of the place of the Christian Emperor in the Christian Empire, which, while foreshadowing the political ideas of 'Christendom' that were to hold sway in the Middle Ages and later, both in the East and the West, seems irrelevant, or worse a betrayal of the essential nature of the Gospel, to most modern Christians living in a secular society and holds little appeal for non-Christians. According to Eusebius, the (Christian) Emperor is God's representative on earth, and as the Word of God expressed God's will in the creation of the world, so the Emperor expresses the will of God in the government of the civilized world (the *oikoumene*), and fulfils this role by his imitation of the Word (or *Logos*), by his *logomimesis*. Such an understanding of the Emperor's role in relation to the Word, who is God's agent in creation and who became incarnate in Christ, not only gives the Emperor's position a religious aura (which it had always had for pagans) but also affects the way in which Christ's religious significance is seen. As A. N. Whitehead provocatively put it (thinking more specifically of the culmination under the Emperor Justinian of the process initiated by Constantine):

> When the Western world accepted Christianity, Caesar conquered; and the received text of Western theology was edited by his lawyers. The code of Justinian and the theology of Justinian are two volumes expressing one movement of the human spirit. The brief Galilean vision of humility flickered throughout the ages, uncertainly. In the official formulation of the religion it has assumed the trivial form of the mere attribution to the Jews that they cherished a misconception about their Messiah. But the deeper idolatry, of fashioning God in the image of the Egyptian, Persian, and Roman Imperial rulers, was retained. The Church gave unto God the attributes which belonged exclusively to Caesar.[1]

The Arian controversy and Eusebius' 'Constantinian theology' do not much affect *The History of the Church*: its latest edition dates from 324/5, and most of it was written about a decade (or more) earlier. Most of what we can glean about Eusebius otherwise – from his books – is, however, directly relevant to an understanding of *The History of the Church*. His literary output was enormous and

1. A. N. Whitehead, *Process and Reality* (Cambridge, 1929), p. 484f. For Eusebius' political theology, see Norman Baynes's important essay, reprinted in his *Byzantine Studies and Other Essays* (London, 1955), pp. 168–72. More generally on Eusebian political theology and its influence, see Erik Peterson, 'Der Monotheismus als politisches Problem', reprinted in *Theologische Traktate* (Munich, 1950), pp. 45–147.

he continued writing, as we have seen, right up to his death in his late seventies. They are all the works of a scholar who delights in displaying his massive erudition, rather than the works of an original thinker. Eusebius knew an awful lot; it is less clear how much he really understood. His works are full of endless citations from the works of others; rarely does Eusebius allow himself to speak with his own voice. Such writing is enormously valuable to have, though tedious to read. As Photius, the great ninth-century scholar and Patriarch of Constantinople, remarked, 'his style is neither agreeable nor brilliant, but he was a man of great learning'.[1] But it is probably as well. Eusebius the theologian was the Arian-sympathizer, the opponent of Athanasius: later generations would not have preserved the works of such. But Eusebius the great repository of learning was *useful*; even in his own century his works were being used as a more convenient source for the writings of others than the original texts:[2] as such he was valued and his works preserved.

Eusebius' works

The History of the Church was not Eusebius' only work of history. Earlier he had composed a *Chronicle*. This is in two parts: the first consists of brief epitomes of the history of the Chaldaeans, the Assyrians, the Hebrews, the Egyptians, the Greeks and the Romans, based on appropriate historical sources; the second part consists of tables of dates arranged in columns, the columns corresponding to Hebrew history, Greek history, and so on, so that events that took place at the same time are next to one another. These columns begin with the year of Abraham's birth (2016/15 B.C., though it

1. Photius, *Bibliotheca* 13 (ed. W. Henry, Paris, 1959, vol. 1, p. 11).
2. See, for instance, the anthology of Origenian material put together by St Basil the Great and St Gregory of Nazianzus in 358: *Philocalia*, xxiv (ed. J. A. Robinson, 1893, pp. 212–26). The selection of this passage, incidentally, tells a cautionary tale, the moral of which is the importance of 'verifying one's references'. It is certainly not by Origen; in his *Preparation for the Gospel*, whence Basil and Gregory cite it, Eusebius ascribes it to Maximus (q.v.). On this see, most recently, T. D. Barnes, 'Methodius, Maximus and Valentinus' in *Journal of Theological Studies*, New Series, 30 (1979), pp. 47–55.

must be remembered that the B.C./A.D. system that we are familiar with was not invented for a couple of centuries after Eusebius' time) and continue (subdivided into five sections) up to Eusebius' own time. It is clear that the *Chronicle* was revised and brought up to date from time to time. Part of the purpose of the *Chronicle* was to demonstrate the superior antiquity of the Hebrew religion (of which, for Eusebius, Christianity was the continuation or, rather, recovery) over any other. The system of tables was accompanied by notes. As we shall see, Eusebius' *The History of the Church* could be regarded as a continuous collection of such notes. The *Chronicle* does not survive in Eusebius' original Greek: there is a Latin translation of the second part by Jerome, which makes up for Eusebius' inadequacies as far as Roman history is concerned and brings the story up to his (Jerome's) own day (380), and an Armenian translation of the whole (of a version that went as far as 325). Another work of history Eusebius composed was his *Martyrs of Palestine*, which recorded the progress of the Great Persecution in Caesarea. This is intimately connected with *The History of the Church* and we shall have more to say of it later on. Eusebius compiled various other works of history – a collection of the accounts of the martyrs and his *Life of Pamphilus* – which do not survive; his *Life of Constantine* is also a work of history, though its literary form is not that of a biography but an *encomium*, a celebration of Constantine's virtues and achievements, not a dispassionate account of his life.

Another main group of Eusebius' works is *apologetic*: that is, they stand in the tradition of those works, beginning in the second century with Quadratus' *Apology*, that put forth a defence of Christianity against pagan (and Jewish) objections. (*Apologia* in Greek means 'defence' rather than 'apology' in the modern sense.) These apologists, the most notable of whom was Justin Martyr, defended Christianity against charges that it undermined traditional religion and political loyalty, that it was newfangled and that it was immoral. Their defence was that if there was any truth in traditional religion, it lay not in the myths that provided the justification for the various pagan religious ceremonies but in a lofty philosophical piety, and that the truth glimpsed by the philosophers (especially the Platonists) was grasped more surely by Christianity. Against the charge that Christianity was newfangled, they argued that Christianity was the truth behind Judaism, which had a fair claim to be the most ancient of all religions. Accusations of immorality were misunderstandings, inexcusable in view of the austere moral standards Christians demanded of themselves. Accusations of political disloyalty, even sedition, were met by claims that the prayers of the Christians to the true God were of greater benefit to the stability of the Empire than prayers and sacrifices to false gods who, at best, were no more than deceitful demons. The appeal to philosophy, especially to Platonism, and the claim that Christianity was vindicated by what was best in the philosophers, coupled with the claim that Christianity, through its link with Judaism, was the oldest of all religions, are the parts of this apologetic tradition that most appealed to Eusebius. These themes had been thoroughly worked over in the centuries before Eusebius, especially in Origen's late work *Against Celsus*, and little was left to Eusebius other than massive elaboration based on his own enormous erudition. But this elaboration, which refutes paganism out of its own mouth by citing extensively from the works of the philosophers themselves, is claimed by Eusebius, justly, as a 'way of [my] own'. It has also given us a vast repository of extracts from ancient philosophy. His *Preparation for the Gospel* was valued for its learning, and still is: not a few pagan philosophers would be no more than names to us, had not Eusebius excerpted them for his *Preparation*.[1] It was preceded by his *General Elementary Introduction*, of which only a part survives concerned with the Messianic prophecies of the Old Testament, and followed by his *Proof of the Gospel*, directed against the Jews, in which he explains away the Jewish religion as a temporary concession to human sin which served to prepare the way for the coming of Christ, who restored the ancient, universal religion of the Patriarchs, and goes on to expound the mystery of the Incarnation of the Word of God (about two thirds of the *Proof* survives). His *Theophany* (or 'Divine Manifestation'), which he composed in the last decade of his life, is

1. See Édouard des Places, S. J., *Eusèbe de Césarée, Commentateur: Platonisme et Écriture Sainte* (Théologie Historique, 63; Paris, 1982), esp. chapter 1.

a compendium of the earlier apologetic works and in large part drawn from them (it survives complete only in a Syriac translation). All this apologetic work was not mere erudition: it had direct contemporary relevance. In the first decade of the fourth century, the Church had faced not simply an attempt to exterminate it by means of persecution: that persecution had been backed up by an attempt to ridicule Christianity and call in question its claims (especially in the last stage of the persecution in the East, under the Emperor Maximin). Hierocles, who had been governor of Bithynia, composed a work that compared the life of Jesus with that of the pagan sage and wonder-worker Apollonius of Tyana, and Porphyry, the famous and learned disciple of Plotinus (and something of a man after Eusebius' own heart with his bent for scholarly erudition), composed a massive attack on Christianity in fifteen books, which concerned itself not simply with general points but made much of contradictions in the sacred record of the Christians. Eusebius' *Preparation* is aware of this new angle of attack and attempts to meet it, often enough by crushing it with learning. He also composed separate work against Hierocles (this survives, though Hierocles' work does not), and against Porphyry (both Porphyry's attack and Eusebius' reply are lost).

The rest of Eusebius' works are biblical and doctrinal. He preserved the interest that he had shared with Pamphilus in preparing a reliable text of the Scriptures. When Constantine's new city of Constantinople needed copies of the Bible for use in celebrating the liturgy in its many new churches, the Emperor wrote to Eusebius asking him to provide fifty copies of the Bible, well written and easy to read. Eusebius also wrote commentaries on the Psalms and Isaiah, works on problems posed by the Scriptures – the polygamy of the Patriarchs, the conflicting accounts of the Resurrection in the Gospels – and his 'Gospel Canons', which enabled one to locate and compare parallel passages in the four Gospels. He wrote a work (much of which is lost) on the significance of the Easter festival in relation to the Jewish Passover (it is worth noting, in passing, that Greek uses one word – *pascha* – where we use two – Easter and Passover – and so naturally associates Christian Easter and Jewish Passover, where we tend to separate them) and a work, usually called the *Onomasticon*, which is a gazetteer of biblical sites and is still today the most important source for the topography of the Holy Land. His doctrinal works include his part in the *Defence of Origen*, the last book of which Eusebius wrote himself after the death of Pamphilus, and two late works (*Against Marcellus* and the *Ecclesiastical Theology*) against bishop Marcellus of Ancyra, a supporter of Nicaea who was deposed by an Arian synod in Constantinople in 336 and whom the Arian party (including Eusebius) accused of Sabellianism.

Alongside all this literary work, Eusebius was for some twenty-five years or so bishop of the busy provincial city of Caesarea, and, as bishop of that see, metropolitan bishop of Palestine. We have no idea what kind of a bishop he was, but it seems unlikely that one so attached to Caesarea would have been neglectful of his pastoral charge. His declining to leave Caesarea to become bishop of the much more prestigious see of Antioch *c.* 327 cannot, however, be used as evidence of his affection for Caesarea, as it was clearly the Emperor's wish that he should not accept the see of Antioch. But he stayed at Caesarea until he died and one may presume anyway that he would have been reluctant to leave the library there.

This survey of Eusebius' works has manifested Eusebius the scholar, delighting in his extensive erudition and keen to put this erudition to use: helping the growing numbers of pilgrims to the Holy Land, helping Christians to understand the Scriptures, and indeed have access to reliable texts of the Scriptures, and placing on a sound, scholarly basis the credentials of the religion of the Incarnation. All these concerns were focused in what is without doubt his greatest work: *The History of the Church*.

THE HISTORY OF THE CHURCH

The History of the Church survives in its original Greek in several manuscripts; there is also a translation (often more a paraphrase) into Latin by Rufinus (*c.* 345–410), who added two further books that continued the story up to the death of the Emperor Theodosius (395), and a very early (probably fourth-century) Syriac translation on which was based a very literal old Armenian version that has also survived. No one in ancient times ever attempted to do Eusebius' work over again: the later Greek Church historians (Socrates, Sozomen and others) all pick up the story where Eusebius left off, in a way acknowledging his position as the 'Father of Church History'.

As we have it now, *The History of the Church* is in ten Books. The first Book is introductory in nature, filling in all the background we need to know, both theological and historical, to grasp the significance of Christ as the Incarnation of the Word of God. Books 2–7 give an account of the life of the Church from the Ascension of Christ (A.D. 30) to the outbreak of the Great Persecution (303). Book 8 and Book 9 concern the Great Persecution itself: Book 8, the persecution from the issuing of the edicts by Diocletian to the edict of recantation issued by the Emperor Galerius just before his grisly death in 311; Book 9, the renewal of the persecution a few months later in the East under the Emperor Maximin up to his recantation shortly before his death after his defeat by the Emperor Licinius in 313. Book 9 also includes an account of Constantine's victory over Maxentius at the Milvian Bridge outside Rome in 312. Book 10 celebrates the Church at peace and mainly consists of the great oration or homily Eusebius gave at the dedication of the magnificently rebuilt basilica at Tyre (315/16) and a collection of imperial edicts which show that the Church is no longer just tolerated in the Roman Empire, but the object of imperial favour and patronage on a lavish scale. There then follows a brief account of the fall of Licinius and a few words celebrating the joyful state of the Empire under the Emperor Constantine. Clearly all of this cannot have been written at the same time: the last pages were written after the final defeat of Licinius by Constantine in 324, whereas Book 9 and most of Book 10 envisage a situation where Licinius and Constantine can still be celebrated together as comrades-in-arms, a situation that held from 312 until their first conflict in 316/17. As we shall see presently, some scholars have seen evidence of yet more stages in the composition of *The History of the Church*. Before we look at that question (not merely a tedious question of dates, but one that raises fundamental issues affecting the nature of the work), let us see what kind of a work *The History of the Church* is.

Books 2–7 are composed in a different style from Books 8–10: these last three Books are an impassioned account of the Great Persecution and a celebration (and documentation) of the Great Deliverance – though it several times becomes a list of names, there is plenty of action too. Books 2–7 are quite different: Eusebius hints (at the beginning of Book 1) that it is an expansion of his *Chronicle*, and so, on inspection, it appears to be. The basic structure of the work is the succession of Roman Emperors: all the material is fitted into their successive reigns. Within this division of material the succession of bishops in the four great sees of the pre-Nicene Church – Rome, Alexandria, Antioch and Jerusalem (or Aelia, as it was renamed after the Jewish War of 132–5) – provides a further set of subdivisions. This makes it quite clear what Eusebius has done: the basic framework is provided by the succession lists, collated with one another in the *Chronicle* (Appendix A must be something like the kind of list Eusebius made for himself), and into this framework is fitted all that he has to say.

Such a method of writing history is not, in fact, at all new: in this respect Eusebius is simply following classical precedent. The histories of Thucydides, Polybius, Josephus and others (and also history books in the Bible such as 1 and 2 Samuel and 1 and 2 Kings) are similarly *annalistic*: the narrative proceeds year by year, which makes for all kinds of oddities when the matter under discussion (e.g., foreign policy) cannot be so neatly carved up. So, for instance, if Eusebius has something to say about someone whose career spans several reigns, it is chopped up between the several reigns (e.g., Justin Martyr, who addressed his *Apology* to Antoninus Pius, was martyred under Marcus Aurelius, and is Eusebius' source for information filed under yet other reigns). Equally, if Eusebius is going to say anything at all, it has to be found a slot in the reign of one or other of the Emperors, even if Eusebius has no real clue as to where it ought to go (so, for instance, he dates Pionius' martyrdom a century too early because, having dealt with the martyrdom of Polycarp, he goes on to list the rest of a collection of accounts of martyrs he has to hand).

More important, though, is to notice what kind of material Eusebius inserts into his historical framework. Here he deserts classical precedent and remains essentially a chronicler (or an archivist). Whereas a classical historian told a story, and made up details such as a general's address to his troops on the basis of plausibility (and the historian's view of the character of the individuals involved and the policy they were pursuing), Eusebius hardly ever makes up anything. He quotes and summarizes. In Book 2 and Book 3 it is mainly Josephus, the great Jewish historian, whose account (mainly from the *Jewish War*) Eusebius pillages for the first century; in Book 4 it is Hegesippus, Justin and the *Martyrdom of Polycarp*; in Book 5 the *Martyrs of Lyons and Vienne*, Irenaeus, a dossier on Montanism (the main sources for which are 'Anonymous' and Apollonius), a dossier on the Quartodeciman controversy and a work on heresy in Rome called (though he does not tell us) the *Little Labyrinth*. Book 6 is mostly based on his and Pamphilus' *Defence of Origen* and the rest of Book 6 and Book 7 draw on the letters of Dionysius of Alexandria (this list of sources is by no means complete). Josephus was a historian, the accounts of martyrdom are historical (though in the form of letters from one church to another), but the rest of Eusebius' sources are apologetic works or attacks on heretics; only Dionysius has the curiosity and garrulousness to give us history, or rather reportage, raw material for history. Eusebius was doing something new: no one before him had attempted a history of the Church, and earlier historians had written a very different type of history from that Eusebius attempted, which is, as we have seen, not only annalistic but really the extended notes of a chronologer.[1] Eusebius was not exaggerating when he said that he was the 'first to venture on such a project and to set out on what is indeed a lonely and untrodden path' (I. 1).

It is worth looking at what Eusebius says he had set out to do. He is, he tells us, going to record the 'lines of succession from the holy apostles', the 'many important events recorded in the story of

1. See A. Momigliano's 'Pagan and Christian Historiography in the Fourth Century A.D.' in *The Conflict between Paganism and Christianity in the Fourth Century* (Oxford, 1963), ed. by him, pp. 79–99. esp. 89–91.

the Church', the 'outstanding leaders and heroes ... in the most famous Christian communities', the 'men ... who ... were ambassadors of the divine word', the 'names and dates' of heretics, the destruction of the Jewish race after 'their conspiracy against our Saviour', the persecutions the Church suffered, and finally 'the martyrdoms of later days down to my own time, and at the end of it all the kind and gracious deliverance accorded by our Saviour' (I. 1). If we look at each of these in turn, we shall be able to form some idea of what Eusebius was trying to achieve and the strengths and limitations of his project. (Eusebius mentions yet another theme at III. 3. 3, the history of the canon of Scripture: see under 'canon' in the 'Who's Who'.)

'Lines of succession from the holy apostles': as we have seen, into the basic framework of the succession of the Roman Emperors, Eusebius inserts the lines of succession of the bishops in the principal sees of the Christian Church. These lines of succession had been drawn up earlier, and Eusebius simply makes use of them: Hegesippus had made a succession-list for the Church of Rome, and Irenaeus gives a succession-list for the same Church in his *Against Heresies* (it is Irenaeus' list that Eusebius follows). These lists, as is evident from the way in which Irenaeus produces his list, were used as *guarantees* of the authenticity of the preaching of the Christian faith: they traced a line of succession back to Christ through one (or more) of the apostles (Peter – and sometimes Paul – in the case of Rome) who had appointed the first bishop in the place concerned. Orderly succession from the apostles was regarded as evidence of fidelity to the teaching of the apostles, and therefore of Christ who had appointed them (this idea is first explicitly found in Clement's letter to the Corinthians, *c.* 96: see *I Clement* 42–4): it is not unlike the idea of succession (*diadoche*) in the philosophical schools, seen as guaranteeing fidelity to the teaching of the founder of the school. The Church came to lay great stress on such lines of succession during the struggle against gnosticism in the second century, as the gnostics claimed to authenticate their own secret traditions by producing succession-lists going back usually to one of the more obscure apostles (such as Matthias or Barnabas). Their original significance was not then historical but dogmatic (or apologetic), and even though they function as a historical framework for Eusebius, their value as a guarantee of authenticity is still important to him.

But what of the lists themselves? As far as Jerusalem is concerned, it is clear that the list Eusebius had up to the time of Narcissus (early third century) is no more than that: a list of names, presumably discovered in the library at Jerusalem, founded in the third century by Narcissus' successor, Alexander. Only from the time of Narcissus onwards does Eusebius make any attempt to incorporate it into *The History of the Church*. The list of the bishops of Antioch seems also to have been not much more than a list of names that Eusebius has worked into *The History of the Church* by guesswork (helped by the fact that Ignatius, Theophilus and Serapion were more than just names): he never records the length of an episcopate, as he does in the cases of Rome and Alexandria. For Rome and Alexandria he seems to have had proper data: in the case of Rome several episcopal lists survive that we can check against Eusebius. The way Eusebius uses these lists is revealing. As he works his way through the 'bishops' of Alexandria, he rarely designates any of them 'bishop' until he reaches Demetrius at the end of the second century. It seems very likely that not until then was there anyone who could be regarded as 'the bishop of Alexandria': before Demetrius the succession-list perhaps gave the names of those men who were really the leaders of the congregation in Alexandria that was in communion with the church of Rome and other ancient sees of the Mediterranean world.[1] (Eusebius seems to have taken his episcopal list for Alexandria from Julius Africanus, like Hegesippus an early toiler in the field of Christian origins whom Eusebius probably makes more use of than he cares to admit.) The Roman list poses other problems, for here the list itself (with minor variants of spelling) is pretty well attested. The problem for the first century or so is what it is a list *of*: for evidence that there was a single bishop leading the Roman Church is lacking for that period; indeed what evidence there is suggests a rather different picture. When Clement

---

1. As W. Telfer suggested: see his *The Office of a Bishop* (London, 1962), p. 104.

wrote to the Corinthian Church, he wrote not as bishop in the later sense but as one of the presbyters of the Roman Church entrusted with the task of writing on behalf of the whole Church to the erring Church of Corinth; similarly, Ignatius, writing perhaps a decade later to the Roman Church, does not seem to envisage a 'bishop of Rome', despite his enthusiasm for mon-episcopacy. With the exception of the early 'bishops' of Alexandria (and even here we may be reading more into Eusebius' use of words than he intended), it seems that Eusebius has used the succession-lists to project back into the early Church, right up to apostolic times, the kind of episcopal government of the Church that he was himself familiar with (what is usually called monar-chical episcopacy, or monepiscopacy). The other odd thing about Eusebius' use of the succession-list for Rome is more venial: that for the last half of the third century he has clearly misread it – reading years for months and months for years – so that, overlook-ing the martyrdom of Xystus II, he has him reigning for another ten years, which upsets the chronology of the bishops of Rome for the rest of the century.

The next aim – to list 'the many important events recorded in the life of the Church' – is a bit puzzling, because Eusebius does not tell us much about such important events. Apart from martyr-doms and councils (and even in the case of the latter it is decisions he records, not what happened), hardly any events are recorded at all in Books 2–7. There are seldom any anecdotes (except in the case of Origen, and they are presumably due to Pamphilus' including them in his *Defence of Origen*). It is really quite an uneventful history. The reason for this is not far to seek: Eusebius was a bookish man, and his history is peopled not by men of events, but by those who wrote books. It is much more a survey of Christian literature, with excerpts quoted that struck him as interesting. It is also true to say that there are few events because Eusebius has no idea of the *progress* of the Christian Church, or of the *development* of doctrine: nothing that happens contributes to anything; even the Incarnation only restores the primordial religion of the Patriarchs.

The 'outstanding leaders and heroes . . . in the famous Christian communities', the 'men ... who ... were ambassadors of the divine word': here Eusebius comes into his own, for his history is full of people. Many of these people we would know nothing of, were it not for Eusebius. If nothing else, when reading Eusebius one gets an impression of the whole host of men and women who constitute the Christian Church through the ages. If we inquire more deeply, it seems however that the picture is much more partial than this might suggest. Eusebius compiled *The History of the Church* by working in two great libraries, those at Caesarea and Jerusalem, the former founded by Origen and consolidated by Pamphilus, and the latter founded by Alexander, a great admirer of the theology that had developed in Alexandria and of Origen in particular. Reliance on these two libraries, built up by men with very similar outlooks, slants Eusebius' history. The focus of interest is the Eastern Mediterranean world: from Alexandria up through Palestine to Antioch and Asia Minor. Eusebius knows very little about what went on outside this area. His knowledge of Christianity in Gaul (Irenaeus, and the martyrdoms at Lyons and Vienne with which he begins Book 5) is no real exception. The Christians in Gaul seem to have come from Asia Minor – certainly Irenaeus did – and at any rate had close links with Asia Minor: the letter describing the course of the persecution of the Gallic martyrs was addressed to the Christians in Asia (i.e., the Roman province, Asia Proconsularis) and Phrygia. But he knows very little about Rome and even less about North Africa. Tertullian, Hippolytus, Cyprian, Novatian (whose name he cannot even spell) are scarcely more than names to him. He mentions Sabellius in connexion with the Libyan Christians who found fault with Dionysius of Alexandria's trinitarian theology, but seems unaware that he had been condemned at Rome by Callistus *c.* 220. And even though his focus of interest is the Eastern Mediterranean, he ignores everything other than Greek Christianity. He knows next to nothing about Syriac Christianity (Bardaisan is hardly more than a name), even though he gives a lot of space to the story of the conversion of king Abgar of Edessa, and he tells us very little about Jewish Christianity (i.e., that form of Christianity that continued to express itself in terms of Jewish traditions rather than

Greek philosophy). Part of the reason for his telling us so little about Jewish Christianity is probably that chiliasm (or millenarianism) continued to be attractive to Jewish Christians: chiliasm seems to have upset Eusebius very much indeed. Another limitation in what Eusebius tells us about the Christians he refers to is that although he is particularly interested in literate Christians, and often gives lists of their works, he is not very interested in their *ideas*. Even his account of Origen gives us little notion as to what Origen actually taught, and that is not simply because by Eusebius' time Origen's ideas were exciting more and more anxiety. The main reason for Eusebius' lack of interest in what individual Christians taught seems to be that he thought that if orthodox they must all have taught the same. The only real exception to this is the history of the canon, the formation of the accepted list of Christian Scriptures: here Eusebius does provide valuable material. Christian teachers were witnesses to an unchanging truth, so Eusebius had little interest in the detail of what they had to say. Pagan philosophers and heretics were different : they got it wrong, so there could be some interest in exploring the varieties of error.

This leads us to 'names and dates' of heretics. But though the varieties of error could be recorded (as he records the ideas of the philosophers at great length in his *Preparation for the Gospel*), it is mainly the 'names and dates' that Eusebius is concerned with. It is often very hard to get from the pages of Eusebius any clear idea of the teaching of the heretics. What he tells us about Paul of Samosata, for instance, has more to do with his overbearing and secular behaviour than with his ideas. The only heretics we learn much about are the Montanists, because he chooses to quote so extensively from his sources. Eusebius is more concerned to classify: Carpocrates the first gnostic, Tatian the first docetist, and so on.

The destruction of the Jewish race 'after their conspiracy against our Saviour' is fortunately not a pervasive theme. He regards the first Jewish War (66–73), with the destruction of Jerusalem, as a punishment for the crucifixion of Christ and for the continued persecution of His followers, especially James 'the Lord's brother', and cites Hegesippus and a passage from Josephus (otherwise attested only by Origen) in support. He records that since the second Jewish War (132–5) the 'entire race has been forbidden to set foot anywhere in the neighbourhood of Jerusalem' so that 'not even from a distance might Jews have a view of their ancestral soil'. Eusebius clearly regards it as a just punishment, but he does not dwell on it.

Eusebius distinguishes as themes the persecutions the Church suffered and the 'martyrdoms of our own time', a distinction that corresponds to the persecutions recorded in Books 2–7 and the account of the Great Persecution of his own time in Books 8–9. His account of the persecution of the Church in Books 2–7 has caused a misunderstanding that some still perpetuate. As we have seen, anything recorded has to be allotted a place in the reign of an Emperor: in the case of persecution (with a few exceptions) Eusebius arranges his material to suggest that some Emperors persecuted the Church, while others did not. It is a deliberately created impression. Persecution, as Eusebius knew it, was imperial: it was enforced by imperial edict and the imperial will. In the Great Persecution the West had suffered much less than the East because, even though Diocletian's edicts were of universal force, the Caesar of the West, Constantius, the father of Constantine, had no wish to persecute Christians and only put the edicts into effect in a very limited way (the later edicts were not enforced at all). Hardly surprisingly, Eusebius believed that this was the pattern for all persecutions, and anyway the writings of the apologists contained the idea that only bad Emperors were persecutors. Melito had thought that only wicked Emperors, like Nero and Domitian, had persecuted Christians: good Emperors, like Hadrian and Antoninus Pius had not.[1] Tertullian had thought the same, and the chapter of his *Apology* where he argues this is quoted from by Eusebius no less than four times.[2] Again, Eusebius has projected back on to the early period of the Church the conditions he was familiar with in the early fourth century.

In fact, up to the persecution under the Emperor Decius (250–51) there had been no persecution of Christians ordered by the Emperor on an imperial scale. Nero's persecution of Christians

1. Melito of Sardis, quoted by Eusebius, IV. 26
2. *Defence*, 5: quoted II. 2, 25; III. 20; V. 5.

was confined to Rome; if Domitian singled out Christians for persecution (something not at all certain), it is doubtful if such persecution spread beyond Rome (John's banishment to Patmos is an isolated exception); for the rest, persecution (as Pliny's correspondence with Trajan makes plain) was a matter for the individual governor of a province. Some governors shared the widespread mistrust of Christians and were happy to use them as scapegoats, others (we may presume) did not. The Christians' refusal to acknowledge the ancient gods was felt to be seditious, as it was under the protection of the ancient gods that Rome had expanded and prospered.[1] The same picture emerges from the accounts of the martyrs: it is the governor who conducts the trial and it is the Christians' stubborn refusal to sacrifice to the gods, or even to burn a pinch of incense to them, that leads to their deaths. A number of the accounts of the martyrs survive (occasionally a transcript of the trial, e.g., the *Acts of the Scillitan Martyrs*, or the *Acts of Cyprian's Martyrdom*, more usually a letter from the Church where the persecution had taken place) and Eusebius tells us he had made a collection of them. He quotes extensively from some of them (notably the account of Polycarp's martyrdom and that of the Gallic martyrs) and refers to many more. For the most part he allots them to the reigns of Emperors he considers to have been opposed to the Christian Church, though he recognizes that there was sporadic, local persecution inspired by the mob or by the machinations of the local authorities (III. 33). With Decius the situation changed. Everyone throughout the Empire was required to take part in sacrifice to the ancient gods: the Christian refusal to take part (though very many acquiesced) resulted in martyrdom. That persecution came to an end with Decius' death. A more systematic attempt to weaken and destroy the Church was mounted by the Emperor Valerian: first, in 257, the clergy were arrested and all gathering together for Christian worship forbidden; the following year the clergy and any men of rank who refused to

---

1. On the grounds for the persecution of Christians in the Roman Empire, see the articles by G. E. M. de Ste Croix and A. N. Sherwin-White reprinted from *Past and Present* (1963–4) in *Studies in Ancient Society*, ed. M. I. Finley (London, 1974), pp. 210–62.

renounce Christianity were to be put to death. Eusebius' account of these persecutions is mainly drawn from the correspondence of Dionysius of Alexandria. That persecution came to an end when Valerian was captured on an expedition against Persia and held by the king of Persia. From then on the Church was at peace until the Great Persecution broke out.

Eusebius' accounts of the Great Persecution are quite different, because he lived through that persecution and is recording what he himself experienced. Apart from the account in Books 8–9 of *The History of the Church* there is his account in *Martyrs of Palestine*, which exists in two recensions: a longer recension, which survives now only in Syriac, and a shorter recension which survives in Greek in some manuscripts of *The History of the Church*. The Great Persecution began in 303 when, on 23 February, Diocletian issued an edict ordering the destruction of Christian church-buildings, the handing over of the Scriptures to be burnt, and the deprivation of the rights of Christians of rank; a second edict ordered the imprisonment of the clergy. November of that year saw the beginning of Diocletian's *vicennalia*; in celebration of this he announced an amnesty for the imprisoned clergy (the 'third edict') on condition that they offered sacrifices. According to Eusebius, most clergy were set free, many having been forced to sacrifice. In 304 an edict (the 'fourth edict') was issued ordering a general sacrifice to the gods. In 305 Diocletian and his fellow Augustus, Maximian, abdicated. Persecution continued in the East under the new Augustus of the East, Galerius, and his enthusiastic Caesar, Maximin. In 311 Galerius, struck down with a fatal disease, issued an edict of recantation. The persecution seemed to have come to an end. But later that year Maximin renewed the persecution in his territory (Syria, Palestine, Egypt). With Constantine's victory over Maxentius in 312 general toleration was granted throughout the whole Empire, and with Maximin's defeat and death in 313 the 'tyrant' (as Eusebius calls him) who had so determinedly persecuted the Church was gone.

That sequence of events needs to be kept in mind as we look at Eusebius' accounts of the Great Persecution. The long version of *Martyrs of Palestine* records the persecution in Palestine (mainly at

Caesarea) month by month from 303 to 311 and gives the impression that the whole thing came to an end in May 311. The short recension, though it covers no more ground, refers to Maximin in such a way as to suggest that the later persecution, instigated by Maximin alone, is envisaged (indeed it refers to Maximin in a way that would be seditious were he not safely dead). As it stands, the short recension is without beginning or end. But in the course of it there is a reference back that is explicable only if it is taken as referring to a passage at the beginning of Book 8 of *The History of the Church* (*Martyrs of Palestine* 12, referring back to VIII. 2. 2ff.); the short recension ends just as it would be expected to start quoting the edict of recantation, which is in fact quoted at the end of Book 8. Book 8 and Book 9 seem to belong together in that 8 seems to be aware of events that follow in 9. Further, the 'appendix' to Book 8 (which is preserved in some manuscripts and not in others) is clearly the final section of something, as it gives an account of the fates of the four men who were Emperors when the first edict of persecution was issued in 303. Various solutions to all this have been proposed. It seems plain that the longer version of *Martyrs of Palestine* was written between May and November 311. The short version is either an appendix to Book 8 recording in more detail what happened in Palestine for the period covered by Book 8 (the edict of recantation not being repeated, because it has already been given);[1] or more radically (and more credibly) the short recension, preceded by the present beginning of Book 8 (up to 2. 3) and followed by the edict of recantation and the 'appendix' to Book 8, is in fact the original form of Book 8. This was presumably abandoned and replaced by the present Book 8 because the account of the first stage of the Great Persecution in *Martyrs of Palestine*, an account confined to events in Palestine, seemed parochial and thus out of place in *The History of the Church*.[2]

1. So H. J. Lawlor, *Eusebiana* (Oxford, 1912), pp. 243–91, esp. 285ff., and id. and J. E. L. Oulton, *Eusebius . . . The Ecclesiastical History and the Martyrs of Palestine* (London, 1928), vol. II, p. 9ff.

2. So T. D. Barnes, *Constantine and Eusebius* (Cambridge, Mass., and London, 1981) p. 149ff., based on his article, 'The Editions of Eusebius' *Ecclesiastical History*' in *Greek, Roman and Byzantine Studies* 21 (1980), pp. 191–201.

In bringing *Martyrs of Palestine* into the discussion of Eusebius' treatment of the Great Persecution, we have inevitably raised the question of the successive editions of *The History of the Church*. It would seem that the present Book 8 and Book 9 represent a later stage in Eusebius' account of the Great Persecution, an earlier stage having included the short recension of *Martyrs of Palestine* either as a first draft of Book 8 or as an appendix. Both these attempts must belong to *c.* 314. Book 10 is evidently a later addition to the already existing history (Eusebius says as much: X. 1. 2) and, apart from X. 8–9 which were added still later after the fall of Licinius in 324, consists of material that existed independently of *The History of the Church*: Eusebius' oration at the dedication of the new basilica in Tyre and a dossier of letters illustrating the now favoured (not just tolerated) status of the Church. These were presumably added before the war between Constantine and Licinius of 316/17 (as Licinius is still regarded as Constantine's comrade-in-arms). We therefore have several editions: an early edition (*c.* 314) incorporating the short recension of *Martyrs of Palestine* in some way, another early edition consisting of Book 1–9, an edition (*c.* 316) going up to X. 7 and a final edition, as we have it, *c.* 324 (the Syriac version witnesses to a yet later revision – another edition? – which suppresses the reference to Crispus, Constantine's son, in X. 9, after Crispus had been put to death in 326 by Constantine).

The big question, though, is what was the *first* edition? Eusebius says, in the text of *The History of the Church* as we have it, that he is writing a history of the Church up to the 'martyrdoms of our own time and the kind and gracious deliverance of our Saviour'. That implies that the first edition mentioned above (*c.* 314) *was* the first edition (or, according to Lawlor, an edition consisting of Books 1–8, published in 311), for Eusebius' history envisages the Great Persecution and the deliverance from it as its term. It is possible, however, that the sentence just quoted was added to a later edition and that Eusebius' first edition of *The History of the Church* was written before the Great Persecution, that it was indeed written in the period of peace that the Church knew at the end of the third century. Such a view, that the first edition of *The*

History of the Church, consisting of Books 1–7 only, belongs to the end of the third century (or the very beginning of the fourth), is rapidly becoming the accepted opinion of modern scholarship[1] and has found its weightiest defender in Professor Timothy Barnes.[2] The argument, in general terms (the detailed case cannot be discussed here), is that Books 1–7 are so different from Books 8–10 that they stand by themselves and that they bring the history of the Church up to *c.* 300 (or even earlier if one accepts that the last chapters of Book 7 have been touched up for later editions), which is inconceivable if Eusebius were writing a decade or more later. For instance, the 'lines of succession from the apostles' end in Book 7 at the beginning of the fourth century: they are not continued in Books 8 and 9, where the history of the Church is taken through persecution up to 313. Despite the fashion of recent scholarship, however, there are weighty arguments against the notion that the first edition of *The History of the Church* was written so early.[3] Eusebius seems to make it quite clear that Book 6 is based on the *Defence of Origen*, written by Pamphilus with Eusebius' collaboration when he was in prison in Caesarea between 308 and 310.[4] But a more general point is this: although it is true that Book 7 brings the history of the Church up to 303, this need not be construed as a history of the Church up to the end of the third century; it could equally well be construed as a history of the Church up to the *eve of the outbreak of the Great Persecution*. The Great Persecution (and the miraculous deliverance into what Eusebius was coming to see was a *Christian* Empire) is the goal of his history. History, of course, continues after the Great Persecution, but that is another story, not the story Eusebius has set out to tell us. On such a view, Eusebius' history was only conceived when he

1. See J. Quasten, S. J., *Patrology*, vol. 3 (Utrecht, 1966), p. 315; and more emphatically Frances Young, *From Nicaea to Chalcedon* (London, 1983), p. 4 ('whatever the original date of publication, it seems highly likely that much of the work was conceived and accomplished before persecution broke out . . .').

2. See his article 'The Editions of Eusebius' Ecclesiastical History' in *Greek, Roman and Byzantine Studies* 21 (1980).

3. For a more detailed discussion, see my forthcoming article in *Journal of Theological Studies* (April 1990).

4. See the table for the composition of Book 6 that D. S. Wallace-Hadrill gives in his *Eusebius of Caesarea* (London, 1960), pp. 161–5.

realized that the persecution of his own day was the Great and Final Persecution (and Great, because Final).[1] Indeed it would seem most likely on this view that all the labour that went to make the edition of *The History of the Church* that ends at X. 7 belongs to the years 313–16, when Eusebius was bishop of Caesarea, able to call on the faithful labours of secretaries, copyists and 'research assistants'. *The History of the Church* we have seen, is meticulously *put together*; not a great deal comes from the pen of Eusebius (even the summaries may have been done by his more trusted pupils).

The question about the date of the first edition of *The History of the Church* – whether after the end of the Great Persecution or at the end of the third century when such a persecution was not suspected – is really a question as to the fundamental character of the work. Is it (in the words of Westcott) a work which 'gathers up and expresses ... the experience, the feelings, the hopes of a body which had just accomplished its sovereign success, and was conscious of its inward strength',[2] or (as Professor Barnes puts it) 'contemporary evidence for the standing of the Christian Church in Roman society in the late third century'?[3] The argument threatens to become circular, depending on the importance for the development of the Christian Church attached to the conversion of Constantine. Those who think the Church was prosperous and important by the end of the third century find it quite conceivable that Eusebius could have sat down to compose the history of such an organization, and tend to see *The History of the Church* as part of the evidence; those who think that the Church remained weak without imperial favour find the idea of a history written *c.* 295 inconceivable.

Whatever the truth of that is, the edition of *The History of the Church* that Eusebius published *c.* 316 (up to X. 7) reflects an

1. It may, indeed, not have been all that 'great' in its dimensions: see G. E. M. de Ste Croix. 'Aspects of the "Great" Persecution' in *Harvard Theological Review* 47 (1954), pp. 75–109, though he is probably wrong in regarding *Martyrs of Palestine* as intended to give an exhaustive account of the Great Persecution in Palestine.

2. B. F. Westcott, quoted by J. B. Lightfoot in his article 'Eusebius' in the *Dictionary of Christian Biography*, ed. W. Smith and H. Wace, vol. 2 (1880), p. 323.

3. T. D. Barnes, 'Some Inconsistencies in Eusebius' in *Journal of Theological Studies*, New Series, 35 (1984), p. 471.

understanding of the place of the Church in the Empire that falls a long way short of what Eusebius later came to believe, when he came under the spell of the Emperor Constantine. It ends with a panegyric, not of the Emperor, but – amazingly – of Paulinus, Eusebius' friend, the bishop of Tyre, 'alone after the first and greatest High Priest', who 'having the whole Christ, the Word, the Wisdom, the Light, impressed upon his soul, has built this magnificent shrine for God Most High, resembling in its essence the pattern of the better one as the visible resembles the invisible'. This panegyric on the occasion of the rededication of the basilica at Tyre is one of the rare places in *The History of the Church* where we hear directly the voice of Eusebius. It presents an understanding of Christian worship that was not to last the century: the worship of the Church on earth led by the bishop in his basilica is a copy of the worship of the Church in heaven led by Christ Himself. We worship Christ as God made manifest to us, and through Him worship the Father of all; He directly and immediately worships God Himself. But the perfect worship of God among creatures is found in the soul, which the Son has created in His own image, as He Himself is the image of the Father. The soul was created from the beginning to be a 'holy bride and most sacred temple for Himself and the Father', but she fell away from this state into slavery and sin, whence she has been redeemed by the Word. The Word 'first chose the souls of the supreme emperors' and 'then brought out into the open His own disciples', 'by their means He purged the souls which a little while before were fouled and heaped with rubbish of every sort and the debris of impious decrees'. Eusebius has been so dazzled by recent deliverance that the mystery of the Incarnation itself seems to pale into relative insignificance. It is difficult not to think that it is Eusebius' subordinationism, which sees Christ less as God than as the first of God's ministers, that is responsible for this. It was his subordinationism that put Eusebius amongst those who sided with Arius, and it is this same subordinationism that makes it so easy for him to rank next to Christ, Paulinus on this occasion and later the Emperor Constantine as ministers of the one God.

But there is another reason why Eusebius plays down the newness of Christianity and the newness of the Incarnation.

'Newness' in the hellenistic world meant newfangled, and therefore wrong.[1] From the beginning Christians had defended themselves against the accusation that their religion was a newfangled superstition by arguing that Christianity was 'as old as creation'. This is the burden of the first half of Book I of *The History of the Church*, the other part of the work where Eusebius speaks with his own voice: his own voice as culmination and summing-up of the apologetic tradition. The Incarnation of Christ is not new, the appearances of God (the 'theophanies') to the patriarchs and prophets of Israel – to Jacob who wrestled with Him 'until the breaking of the day' (Gen. xxxii. 24–30), to Moses in the Burning Bush (Exod. iii. 2–6) – were appearances in visible form of the Word of God, who was in the beginning with God and through whom God made the world (I. 2). But, because of the Fall and the increasing sinfulness of mankind, these communications of the Word were grasped only by a few. So God chose a nation, the Hebrews, and gave them a law which prepared a people amongst whom the Word of God could be incarnate and his teaching proclaimed to all. The law of the Hebrews 'became famous and like a fragrant breeze penetrated to every corner of the world ... Savage and cruel brutality changed into mildness, so that profound peace, friendship, and easy intercourse were enjoyed' (I. 2. 23). For Eusebius, the political expression of this state of affairs was the *Pax Romana*, and in the early days of the Roman Empire Christ was born in Bethlehem in Judaea. The peace of the Roman Empire made possible the rapid spread of the Christian faith throughout the (Mediterranean) world. Eusebius returns again to the theme of the alleged novelty or strangeness of Christian teaching by arguing that Christians flourished 'in fact if not in name' amongst the patriarchs before Moses and Abraham and the establishment of Judaism with its Law that defined the sabbath, circumcision and food-laws. So Christ's teaching is 'none other than the first, most ancient, and most primitive of all religions, discovered by Abraham and his followers, God's beloved [or: the friends of God]', it is 'not modern or strange, but ... primitive, unique and true' (I. 4).

1. See Norman Baynes' lecture, 'The Hellenistic Civilization and East Rome', reprinted in *Byzantine Studies and Other Essays* (London, 1955) pp. 1–23.

Christianity is the rediscovery of primordial truth, and *The History of the Church* records the way in which this rediscovery became universal.

The History of the Church is, then, the work of a scholar, but a scholar less interested in ideas than in facts, evidence, information. And people: so it has seemed that the most useful way of providing commentary on *The History of the Church* is by concentrating on the people mentioned by providing a prosopography, a 'Who's Who.' The people Eusebius introduces us to – the people he relies on for his information, the people who fill the pages of *The History of the Church* – are the reference points for almost all the themes included in this history. Whatever hesitations one might have about Eusebius' grasp of the religion of the Incarnation, one cannot deny that he saw that the history of such a religion would be about people.

Note on the Text

The History of the Church survives in a number of Greek manuscripts; the standard critical edition is that prepared by the great German scholar Eduard Schwartz, and published (with an edition of Rufinus' Latin version prepared by Mommsen) in *Die Griechischen Christlichen Schriftsteller*, vol. 9, 3 parts (Leipzig, 1903–9). That text is reprinted, with an English translation by Kirsopp Lake and J. E. L. Oulton, in the *Loeb Classical Library* (2 vols., Cambridge, Mass., and London, 1926–32), which is the most convenient version of the Greek text easily available. Schwartz's text was the basis of G. A. Williamson's translation.

Translator's Note[1]

The translator is faced with many problems; for the Greek of Eusebius is by no means easy. He employs an enormous vocabulary, and some of his words have meanings not met with in classical Greek. These meanings are not always to be found even in the largest lexicons and have to be deduced from the context; and some of the Greek words do not appear in lexicons at all. Other words vary in meaning, and it is not always clear which meaning is intended. Are *martyres* martyrs or witnesses? Are *presbyteroi* presbyters, priests, elders, or old-timers? Is *philosophia* philosophy, science, love of wisdom, profound study, earnest inquiry, or asceticism? And does *logos* mean word, message, book, system, doctrine, or the pre-existent Word? Other words are by their nature ambiguous. Do *theophiles* and *theomises* mean God-loving and God-hating, or God-loved and God-hated? Or do the words denote reciprocity of emotion – mutual attraction and mutual repulsion between God and individual men? These difficulties are due to defects in the Greek language: another difficulty is the fault of Eusebius himself; for he is guilty of quite needless obscurity. He is inordinately fond of long and involved sentences, and he lacks the skill of a Demosthenes to keep them under control. The first sentence of Book I is 166 words long, and we have to plough through 153 of them before we reach the one and only main verb. Sometimes there is no main verb at all, or the sentence is an anacoluthon, beginning in one way and ending in another. The reader may well lose his way in the morass!

In this translation I have endeavoured above all things to make clear what the writer is trying to say. I have broken up the huge sentences into fragments, as anyone must do who professes to be writing the English of today, and I have omitted numbers of the

---

1. From G. A. Williamson's original introduction.

superfluous 'padding' words with which Eusebius fills out his lines. The multitude of quotations from the Bible presented a problem. Should I follow the example of my predecessors, and copy the wording of the Authorized or Revised Version? This would have saved trouble and have made it easy for the reader to recognize the passages quoted. But there were several objections. The difference between the language of 1611 and that of three hundred and fifty years later is very great; the difference between the Greek of Eusebius and that of the Septuagint and the New Testament is comparatively small. Again, while some of his quotations are set out as such, many are worked into his sentences and adapted to his constructions. Thirdly, the wording of the passages as he quotes them often differs from that of the Hebrew and Greek texts on which our standard versions are based, so that an accurate translation would involve the use of synthetic 'old' English. I therefore resolved that the Scriptural quotations must be put into the same kind of English as the rest; in other words, they must be translated afresh. I have however used the customary 'Thou' in prayers, as this usage is still generally followed, and in verse passages I have used conventional 'poetic' language. When Eusebius copies a long passage from a non-Scriptural work, he often indicates omissions by such formulae as 'a little later he adds'; I have substituted a row of dots.

The division of the work into ten books was made by the author: the headings in capitals are mine. A list of contents appears in the manuscripts at the beginning of each book. Some of these lists are so long that no English reader would read them through, or remember them if read. I have thought it better to insert them at appropriate places in the narrative, and to distinguish them by the use of italics. Some that are inordinately long I have shortened, and where they come in too rapid succession I have grouped two or three together, hoping thus to divide each book into manageable sections.

Finally, I have tried to give intelligible titles to the works quoted by Eusebius: I have replaced the *Apology*, *Stromateis*, *Hypotyposes*, and *Hexaemeron* of earlier versions by *Defence*, *Miscellanies*,

Outlines, and *The Six Days*. On the other hand, as genuinely foreign words in an original text should never be translated, I have retained (in italics) all the Latin words transliterated by Eusebius.[1]

1. Such Latin words are explained in Appendix E.

Book 1

Plan of the projected work

1. The chief matters to be dealt with in this work are the following:

a. The lines of succession from the holy apostles, and the periods that have elapsed from our Saviour's time to our own; the many important events recorded in the story of the Church; the outstanding leaders and heroes of that story in the most famous Christian communities; the men of each generation who by preaching or writing were ambassadors of the divine word.

b. The names and dates of those who through a passion for innovation have wandered as far as possible from the truth, proclaiming themselves the founts of Knowledge falsely so called[1] while mercilessly, like savage wolves, making havoc of Christ's flock.[2]

c. The calamities that immediately after their conspiracy against our Saviour overwhelmed the entire Jewish race.

d. The widespread, bitter, and recurrent campaigns launched by unbelievers against the divine message, and the heroism with which when occasion demanded men faced torture and death to maintain the fight in its defence.

e. The martyrdoms of later days down to my own time, and at the end of it all the kind and gracious deliverance accorded by our Saviour.

1. 1 Tim. vi. 20.   2. Acts xx. 29.

Could I do better than start from the beginning of the dispensation of our Saviour and Lord, Jesus the Christ of God?

I trust that kindly disposed readers will pardon the deficiencies of the work, for I confess that my powers are inadequate to do full justice to so ambitious an undertaking. I am the first to venture on such a project and to set out on what is indeed a lonely and untrodden path; but I pray that I may have God to guide me and the power of the Lord to assist me. As for men, I have failed to find any clear footprints of those who have gone this way before me; only faint traces, by which in differing fashions they have left us partial accounts of their own lifetimes. Raising their voices like warning lights far ahead and calling out as from a distant watch-tower perched on some hill, they make clear to me by what path I must walk and guide the course of my book if I am to reach my goal in safety. Thus from the scattered hints dropped by my predecessors I have picked out whatever seems relevant to the task I have undertaken, plucking like flowers in literary pastures the helpful contributions of earlier writers, to be embodied in the continuous narrative I have in mind. If I can save from oblivion the successors, not perhaps of all our Saviour's apostles but at least of the most distinguished, in the most famous and still pre-eminent churches, I shall be content. It is, I think, most necessary that I should devote myself to this project, for as far as I am aware no previous Church historian has been interested in records of this kind; records which those who are eager to learn the lessons of history will, I am confident, find most valuable. It is true that in the *Chronological Tables* that I compiled some years ago I provided a summary of this material; but in this new work I am anxious to deal with it in the fullest detail. As I said before, my book will start with a conception too sublime and overwhelming for man to grasp – the dispensation and divinity of our Saviour Christ. Any man who intends to commit to writing the record of the Church's history is bound to go right back to Christ Himself, whose name we are privileged to share, and to start with the beginning of a dispensation more divine than the world realizes.

The pre-existence and divinity of our Saviour

2. The nature of Christ is twofold; it is like the head of the body in that He is recognized as God, and comparable to the feet in that for our salvation He put on manhood as frail as our own.[1] My account of what follows will therefore be complete if I begin my exposition of His entire story with the basic and essential points of the doctrine. By this means, both the antiquity and the divine character of Christian origins will be demonstrated to those who imagine them to be recent and outlandish, appearing yesterday for the first time.

To explain the origin and worth, the very essence and nature of Christ, no language could be adequate. The Holy Spirit Himself says in prophecy: 'His generation who shall declare?[2] For no one has known the Father, except the Son; nor again has anyone ever known the Son fully, except only the Father who begot Him.[3] As for the Light that existed before the world, the intellectual and essential Wisdom that was before time itself, the living Word that in the beginning was with the Father and was God – who but the Father could clearly conceive of Him?[4] Before anything was created and fashioned, visible or invisible,[5] He was the first and only begotten of God; the commander-in-chief of the spiritual and immortal host of heaven;[6] the angel of mighty counsel;[7] the agent of the ineffable purpose of the Father; the fashioner, with the Father, of all things; the second cause, after the Father, of the universe; the Child of God, true and only-begotten; of all begotten the Lord and God and King, who has received from the Father lordship and dominion, godhead, power, and honour.[8] To His divinity the Scriptures bear mystic witness:

> In the beginning was the Word,
> And the Word was with God,
> And the Word was God.
> All things came into being through Him,
> And apart from Him came into being not one thing.[9]

1. Acts xiv. 15 and Jas v. 17.   2. Is. liii. 8.   3. Matt. xi. 27.
4. John i. 1, 2, 9 and Prov. viii. 23.   5. Col. i. 15–16.   6. Josh. v. 14.
7. Is. ix. 4.   8. Rev. v. 12·13.   9. John i. 1, 3.

This again is the teaching of the great Moses, the earliest prophet of all, when by the Holy Spirit he described the coming into being and marshalling of the whole: the Marshal and Fashioner of the universe gave up to Christ Himself – and to no one, it is plain, but the divine Word, His first-begotten, the making of subordinate beings, and discussed with Him the creation of man:

For God said, 'Let us make man in our image and likeness.' [1]

This saying is confirmed by another of the prophets, who in hymns deifies him thus:

> He spoke, and they were begotten:
> He commanded, and they were created.[2]

The Father and Maker he introduces as giving commands like a supreme ruler by an imperial fiat; the divine Word, who holds the second place to Him – none other than the One whom we proclaim – as subserving His Father's behests.

Ever since man was first created, all who are said to have been distinguished for righteousness and the purity of their religion – the great servant Moses and his companions; before him Abraham, the very first, and his children; and all the righteous men and prophets who have since appeared – recognized Him in visions seen with the pure eyes of the mind, and paid due honour to Him as God's Son. He for His part, showing no slackness in His veneration of the Father, made Himself for all mankind the teacher of knowledge of the Father. Thus the Lord God is stated to have appeared as an ordinary human being to Abraham as he sat by the oak of Mamre. Abraham fell down at once, and though he saw a human being with his eyes he worshipped Him as God, besought Him as Lord, and owned that he knew who He was; for these were his very words:

O Lord, the Judge of all the world, wilt Thou not do justice?[3]

Reason would never allow that the uncreated and immutable substance of Almighty God should be changed into the form of a man, or, alternatively, that by the illusion of any created thing it

1. Gen. i. 26.   2. A conflation of Ps. xxiii. 9 and Ps. cxlviii. 5.
3. Gen. xviii. 1–2, 25.

should deceive the eyes of the beholder, or that Scripture should falsely invent such a tale. Who then could be spoken of as God, and the Lord who is the judge of all the world and does justice, appearing in human shape? As it is not permissible to suggest the First Cause of the universe, there is only one answer – His pre-existent Word. Of Him it is written in the Psalms:

> He sent His Word and healed them,
> And rescued them from their corruptions.[1]

Of Him Moses is unmistakably speaking, as second Lord after the Father, when he says:

> The Lord rained on Sodom and Gomorrah brimstone and fire from the Lord.[2]

To Him, when He later appeared to Jacob in a man's shape, Holy Scripture again refers as God – when He said to Jacob:

> No longer shall your name be called Jacob,
> But Israel shall be your name;
> For you have prevailed with God.

Then too:

> Jacob called the name of that place The Form of God, saying: 'For I saw God face to face, and my life was spared.'[3]

It is clearly not permissible to regard the recorded theophanies as visitations by subordinate angels and ministers of God; for whenever one of these appears to human beings Scripture makes no secret of the fact, but explicitly declares that they are called not God or Lord, but angels, as can easily be proved by any number of instances.

The name which Moses' successor Joshua gave to Him, as Leader of the heavenly angels and archangels and of the celestial powers, and as the Power and Wisdom of the Father, entrusted with the second place in the kingship and rule over all things, was Commander-in-chief of the army of the Lord; yet Joshua like the others saw Him only in human form and shape. Here is the passage:

---

1. Ps. cvii. 20.   2. Gen. xix. 24.   3. Gen. xxxii. 28, 30.

When Joshua was in Jericho, he raised his eyes and saw a man standing facing him, his sword drawn in his hand. Joshua went up to him and said, 'Are you for us or for our opponents?' He replied, 'It is as Commander-in-chief of the army of the Lord that I have now come.' Then Joshua fell face downwards on the ground and asked Him, 'Master, what do you command your servant?' The Commander-in-chief of the Lord replied, 'Take your sandals off your feet: the place where you are standing is a holy place.'[1]

Here, too, you will gather from the actual words that this was the very Person who had instructed Moses; for in his case too the words of Scripture are the same:

When the Lord saw that he was coming near to see, He called out to him from the bush, 'Moses, Moses!' He replied, 'What is it?' The Lord answered, 'Do not come this way: take your sandals off your feet; for the place where you are standing is holy ground.' Then He continued: 'I am the God of your father, the God of Abraham, the God of Isaac, and the God of Jacob.'[2]

That this is in truth a Being, living and subsisting before the world, who assisted the Father and God of the universe in the fashioning of all created things, named the Word of God and Wisdom, the evidence goes beyond the proofs given above: one may hear it from the person of Wisdom herself, who by the mouth of Solomon initiates us most fully into her secret:

I, Wisdom, have made counsel my dwelling,
I have invoked knowledge and thought.
By me kings reign,
And princes decree justice;
By me the great achieve greatness,
And monarchs by me are masters of the earth.

To this she adds:

The Lord created me the beginning of His ways for His works;
Before time began He established me;
In the beginning, before He made the earth,

---

1. Josh. v. 13–15.   2. Ex. iii. 4–6.

> Before the springs of water issued forth,
> Before the mountains were fixed in place,
> And before all hills he begot me.
> When He prepared the heaven, I was at His side;
> And when He made safe the springs under heaven,
> I was with Him, setting them in order.
> I was she in whom He delighted every day,
> And I rejoiced before Him at every time,
> When He rejoiced that He had finished the world.[1]

Such in outline are the proofs that the divine Word pre-existed and showed Himself to some, if not to all.

Why He was not preached long ago, as He is now, to all men and to every nation, what follows will make clear. It was impossible for the teaching of Christ in all its wisdom and virtue to be grasped by the human race in its former state. At the very beginning, after the original life of blessedness, the first man disregarded the divine command and fell into this mortal, transitory state, receiving this earth with its curse in place of the former heavenly delights.

His descendants, who peopled all our world, showed themselves much worse, apart from one or two, plunging into a beastly existence and a life not worth living. City and state, arts and sciences meant nothing to them; laws and statutes, morality and philosophy were not even names; they lived a nomadic life in the desert like wild and savage creatures; nature's gift of reason and the germs of thought and culture in the human soul were destroyed by the immensity of their deliberate wickedness. Unholy practices of every kind had taken complete possession of them, so that at one time they corrupted, at another they murdered each other, at yet another they became cannibals; they dared to join battle with God and to fight those battles of the giants that are everywhere famous; they planned to fortify earth against heaven, and in the madness of a deranged mind prepared for war against the Ruler of all things Himself.

While they followed this reckless course God, from whom

1. Prov. viii. 12–31 (with omissions).

nothing is hidden, visited them with cataclysms and conflagrations
as if they had been a wild forest stretching across the whole world.
With continual famines and pestilences, and again with wars and
with thunderbolts from the sky, He cut them off, making His
punishments more and more drastic as if to check some terrible
and wellnigh fatal sickness of the soul. So at that crisis, when
nearly all mankind had been submerged by a vast surfeit of
wickedness, which like complete intoxication overshadowed and
darkened almost every human soul, the first-begotten and first-
created Wisdom of God, the pre-existent Word Himself in His
measureless love for mankind showed Himself, now by a vision of
angels to His subjects, now in person as God's saving power to one
or two of God's beloved servants of old; but always, always in
human form, since in no other way could He appear to them.
When these in turn had sown the seeds of true religion in numbers
of men, a whole nation, sprung from the ancient Hebrews and
devoted to true religion, arose in the world. On these – a mass of
men still tied and bound by ancient habits – He bestowed,
through the prophet Moses, images and symbols of a mystical
sabbath and of circumcision, and instruction in other spiritual
principles; but without actual, open initiation. Their Law became
famous and like a fragrant breeze penetrated to every corner of the
world. From the Jews the movement spread, and soon the characters of most heathen races began to grow gentler, thanks to the
lawgivers and thinkers in every land. Savage and cruel brutality
changed to mildness, so that profound peace, friendship, and easy
intercourse were enjoyed.

Then at last, when all mankind and every race throughout the
world had already received help and by now were fitted to receive
knowledge of the Father, once again that same Teacher of virtue,
the Father's Minister in all that is good, the divine and heavenly
Word of God, in a human body which in all essentials shared our
own nature, appeared in the early years of the Roman Empire.
What He did and what He suffered accorded with the prophecies,
which foretold that a man who was also God would live in the
world as a worker of miracles and would be revealed to all nations
as a teacher of the worship due to the Father. They foretold also

the miracle of His birth, the new teaching, and the marvels of His works, and furthermore the manner of His death, His resurrection from the dead, and last of all His restoration to heaven by the power of God. His final kingdom was shown by the Holy Spirit to Daniel the prophet, who thus inspired described the vision of God in human terms:

I watched until thrones were placed and an Ancient of Days was seated. His clothing was white like snow, and the hair of his head like pure wool. His throne was a flame of fire, its wheels flaming fire; a river of fire flowed before Him. A thousand thousand ministered to Him, and ten thousand times ten thousand stood before Him. The court of judgement sat, and the books were opened . . . I watched, and lo, with the clouds of heaven came One like a Son of Man, who came quickly to the Ancient of Days and was brought face to face with Him. To Him was given the dominion, the glory, and the kingdom; and all the peoples, tribes, and languages shall serve Him. His authority is an everlasting authority, which shall not pass away, and His kingdom shall not be destroyed.[1]

Such words, clearly, would never be applied to anyone but our Saviour, the Word who was in the beginning with God and was God, called Son of Man because ultimately He became a man. However, I have collected in special pamphlets the *Selections from the Prophets* that concern our Saviour Jesus Christ, and in other works have provided a fuller explanation of the statements about Him; so in the present work I shall add nothing to what has been said.

The names Jesus and Christ known and honoured from the first

3. Both Jesus and Christ were names honoured even by God's beloved prophets of old, as I must now make clear. The extreme sanctity and glory of the name Christ was first proclaimed by Moses himself, who, in obedience to the oracle that said to him, 'See that you make everything according to the pattern shown you in the mount',[2] communicated patterns and symbols of heavenly things, and mystical images. For in describing God's high priest, the most powerful of men, he called him Christ, and

1. Dan. vii. 9–10, 13–14.   2. Ex. xxv. 40 (Heb. viii. 5).

on this high-priestly office, which in his eyes surpassed all pre-eminence among men, he bestows as a mark of honour and glory the name of Christ.[1] It is clear then that he understood the divine import of the word Christ.

Moses again was enabled by the Holy Spirit to foresee quite plainly the title Jesus: it, too, he felt to be worthy of special privilege. Never yet heard by human ears till it was made known to Moses, the title Jesus was bestowed by him for the first and only time on the man who – again as a pattern and symbol – he knew would after his own death succeed to the supreme authority.[2] His successor had not hitherto used the designation Jesus but was known by another name, Hoshea, which his parents had given him;[3] but Moses calls him Jesus, conferring the name on him as a priceless honour, far greater than a kingly crown; for Joshua the son of Nun himself bore the image of our Saviour who alone, after Moses and the completion of the symbolic worship given to men by him, succeeded to the authority over the true and most pure religion.

Moses thus bestows on the two men who in his time surpassed all the people in merit and glory – the high priest and the man chosen to follow him as leader – the name of our Saviour Jesus Christ as a signal honour.

With equal clarity the prophets who came later named Christ in their prophecies, witnessing beforehand alike to the intrigue destined to be levelled against Him by the Jewish people, and to the calling of the Gentiles through Him. At one time Jeremiah says:

The Spirit of our face, Christ the Lord, was caught in their corruptions;
Of whom we said, 'In His shadow we shall live among the Gentiles.'[4]

At another David in his perplexity asks:

---

1. In Lev. iv. 5, 16 and vi. 22 the high priest is described as anointed. It must be remembered that while in English this does not suggest the name Christ, in Greek the two words are the same. Similarly in Hebrew Messiah = anointed.
2. Num. xxvii. 15–20: Jesus in the Greco-Latin transliteration of Joshua.
3. Num. xiii. 16.   4. Lam. iv. 20.

> Why did the Gentiles rage,
> And the peoples imagine vain things?
> The kings of the earth ranged themselves,
> And the rulers gathered themselves together,
> Against the Lord and against His Christ.

Later, speaking in the person of Christ Himself, he continues:

> The Lord said to Me, 'You are my Son;
> I have today begotten you.
> Ask me, and I will give you the Gentiles as your inheritance,
> And as your possession the limits of the world.' [1]

Thus, it was not only those honoured with the high priesthood, anointed with prepared oil for the symbol's sake, who were distinguished among the Hebrews with the name of Christ, but the kings too; for they, at the bidding of God, received the chrism from prophets and were thus made Christs in image, in that they, too, bore in themselves the patterns of the kingly, sovereign authority of the one true Christ, the divine Word who reigns over all. Again, some of the prophets themselves by chrism became Christs in pattern, as the records show, so that they all stand in relation to the true Christ, the divine and heavenly Word who is the sole High Priest of the universe, the sole King of all creation, and of prophets the sole Archprophet of the Father. This is proved by the fact that none of those who of old received the symbolical chrism, whether priest, king, or prophet, ever obtained such power of inspired virtue as our Saviour and Lord, Jesus the only veritable Christ, has revealed.

None of those men, however outstanding in dignity and honour among their own people in the course of so many generations, ever made their being in imagery entitled Christ the justification for calling their subjects Christians. None of them was honoured by his subjects with worship, or held in such affection after his death that anyone was ready to die for the person honoured. No one in those days caused such a stir among all the nations throughout the world, since the power of the symbol could not produce

---

1. Ps. ii, 1–2, 7–8.

in them any effect comparable to that of the truth presented and revealed by our Saviour. He did not receive the symbols and patterns of the high priesthood from anyone; He did not trace his physical descent from the acknowledged priests; He was not promoted by the soldiers' weapons to a kingdom; He did not become a prophet in the same way as those of old; He did not receive from the Jews any rank or pre-eminence whatever. Yet with all these, not indeed in symbols but in very truth, He had been adorned by the Father. He may not have obtained the same honours as those mentioned above, yet He is more entitled than any of them to be called Christ. And being Himself the one true Christ of God He has filled the whole world with Christians – His own truly venerated and holy name. No longer does He communicate to His followers patterns or images but fully revealed virtues and a heavenly life with the very doctrines of truth; and He has received the chrism, not that prepared with physical materials, but the divine chrism with the spirit of God, by sharing in the unbegotten divinity of the Father.

This very point, moreover, is driven home by Isaiah, who, as if from Christ's own lips, cries out:

> The spirit of the Lord is upon me;
> For He anointed me to bring good tidings to the poor.
> He has sent me to proclaim deliverance to captives,
> And new sight to the blind.[1]

And not only Isaiah but David too addresses Him in person:

> Thy throne, O God, is for ever and ever:
> A sceptre of uprightness is the sceptre of Thy Kingdom.
> Thou hast loved righteousness and hated iniquity;
> Therefore God, Thy God, has anointed Thee
> With the oil of gladness beyond Thy fellows.[2]

In the first line the passage calls Him God; in the second it honours Him with a royal sceptre; then next, after divine and royal power, it goes on in the third place to portray Him as having become

1. Is. lxi. 1 (Luke iv. 18).   2. Ps. xlv. 6–7 (Heb. i. 8–9).

Christ, anointed not with oil made of physical substance but with the divine oil of gladness. Furthermore, it signifies the special distinction that makes Him far superior to and quite different from those who in earlier ages had received in imagery a more physical chrism.

Elsewhere, the same writer makes His status clear:

> The Lord said to my Lord, 'Sit at my right hand,
> Till I make Thine enemies the footstool of Thy feet . . .
> From the womb before the daystar I begat Thee.'
> The Lord swore and will not repent:
> 'Thou art a priest for ever
> Of the order of Melchizedek.' [1]

This Melchizedek is introduced in the sacred record as priest of God Most High, though not consecrated with any prepared chrism or even belonging by birthright to the Hebrew priesthood. That is why it is according to his order, not that of the others who received symbols and patterns, that our Saviour has been called Christ and Priest with the backing of an oath. And so the record does not state that He received physical chrism from the Jews, or even that He belonged to the same tribe as the acknowledged priests, but that before the daystar, that is, before the construction of the world, He had His being, and holds His priesthood deathless and ageless to all eternity.

That in His case the chrism was non-physical and divine is clearly and amply proved by the fact that of all who have ever lived till this day He alone is known to all men throughout the entire world as Christ; that He is acknowledged and witnessed to by all men under this title, and is spoken of thus by Greeks and non-Greeks alike; and that to this day He is honoured by His devotees throughout the world as King, revered more than a prophet, and glorified as the true and only High Priest of God, and in addition to all this as the Word of God, pre-existent, having His being before all ages and having received from His Father the right to be worshipped; and that He is adored as God. But the greatest marvel of all is that it is not only with voices and

---

1. Ps. cx. 1, 3–4 (Heb. v–vii *passim*).

the sound of words that we who are dedicated to Him do Him honour, but with all the affection of our soul, so that we care less for life itself than for our testimony to Him.

Nothing novel or strange in the religion preached by Him

4. This must suffice as introduction to my story proper: it was necessary in order to guard against any inclination to think of our Saviour and Lord, Jesus Christ, as novel, because of the date of His sojourn in the flesh. But to prevent anyone from imagining that His teaching either was new and strange, as being put together by a man of recent date no different from his fellows, let us now deal briefly with this point.

When the advent of our Saviour Jesus Christ recently shed its light on all men, it was admittedly a new people – not small or weak or established in some remote corner of the earth, but the most numerous and God-fearing of all peoples, indestructible and invincible in that for all time it receives God's help – that at the mystically appointed time all at once appeared, a people honoured by all with the name of Christ. This so amazed one of the prophets, when with the eye of the Holy Spirit he foresaw what was to be, that he burst out:

> Who ever heard such things?
> And who ever spoke thus?
> Was the earth in travail but one day?
> And was a people born at once? [1]

The same writer also hinted at its future title:

> Those who serve Me shall be called by a new name,
> Which shall be blessed on the earth. [2]

But although we certainly are a youthful people and this undeniably new name of Christians has only lately become known among all nations, nevertheless our life and mode of conduct, together with our religious principles, have not been recently

---

1. Is. lxvi. 8.   2. Is. lxv. 15–16.

invented by us, but from almost the beginnings of man were built on the natural concepts of those whom God loved in the distant past, as I shall proceed to show. The Hebrews are not a youthful people, but are respected by all men for their antiquity and are known to all. Now the spoken and written records of this people embrace men of a very early age, scarce and few in number, but at the same time outstanding in religious devotion, righteousness, and all other virtues. Several of these lived before the flood, others after it — some of Noah's sons and descendants, but especially Abraham, whom the children of the Hebrews boast as their own founder and ancestor. All these, whose righteousness won them commendation, going back from Abraham himself to the first man, might be described as Christians in fact if not in name, without departing far from the truth. For the name means this, that the Christian man, through the knowledge and teaching of Christ, excels in self-discipline and righteousness, in firmness of purpose and manly courage, and in an acknowledged devotion to the one, sole God over all; and for all this they showed no less enthusiasm than do we. They cared nothing for bodily circumcision — nor do we; nor for the keeping of Sabbaths — nor do we; nor for abstentions from certain foods or distinctions between others (all that Moses was the first man ever to hand down, for later generations to carry out, in symbols) — nor do these things matter to Christians now. But it is obvious that they knew God's Christ Himself, since He appeared to Abraham, instructed Isaac, spoke to Israel,[1] and conversed freely with Moses and the prophets who came later, as I have already shown. Hence, you will find that those men, God's beloved, were even honoured with the appellation of Christ, according to the word which says of them:

> Touch not my Christs,
> And among my prophets commit no mischief.[2]

Obviously we must regard the religion proclaimed in recent years to all nations through Christ's teaching as none other than the first, most ancient, and most primitive of all religions, discovered by Abraham and his followers, God's beloved.

1. i.e. Jacob.   2. Ps. cv. 15.

If it is argued that long afterwards Abraham received the ordinance of circumcision, I reply that before this, as we are informed, he had been commended for righteousness through faith, as the sacred record tells us:

Abraham believed God, and it was counted to him for righteousness.[1]

Such he was before his circumcision, and it was then that an oracle was announced to him by God – Christ Himself, the Word of God – who showed Himself to him. This concerned those who in later days were to be justified in the same way as himself. It runs as follows:

In you shall be blessed all the races of the world.[2]

Again:

He shall become a great and mighty nation, and in him shall be blessed all the nations of the world.[3]

That, as we can see, has been fulfilled in us, for it was by faith in Christ the Word of God who appeared to him that he was justified, abandoning the superstition of his fathers and the old error of his ways, acknowledging one God, the God over all, and serving Him with right actions, not with the worship of the Law of Moses, who came later. Such he was when he was told that all the races of the world and all the nations would be blessed in him. And in actions more convincing than words at the present time Christians alone can be seen throughout the world practising religion in the very form in which Abraham practised it.

What then is to prevent us from admitting that we, Christ's followers, share one and the same life and form of religion with those who were dear to God so long ago? Thus the practice of religion as communicated to us by Christ's teaching is shown to be not modern and strange but, in all conscience, primitive, unique, and true. There we will leave the matter.

---

1. Gen. xv. 6 and Rom. iv. 3.   2. Gen. xii. 3.   3. Gen. xviii. 18.

The date of Christ's appearance to men

5. So now, after this necessary introduction to my proposed *History of the Church*, let me begin my journey with the appearance of our Saviour in the flesh, first calling on God, the Father of the Word, and Jesus Christ Himself of whom I am speaking, our Saviour, the heavenly Word of God, to be my helper and co-worker in producing a truthful record.

It was the forty-second year of Augustus's reign, and the twenty-eighth after the subjugation of Egypt and the deaths of Antony and Cleopatra, the last of the Ptolemaic rulers of Egypt, when our Saviour and Lord, Jesus Christ, at the time of the first registration, while Quirinius was governor of Syria,[1] in accordance with the prophecies about Him, was born in Bethlehem, in Judaea.[2] This registration in Quirinius' time is mentioned also by the most famous of Hebrew historians, Flavius Josephus, who gives in addition an account of the Galilean sect which appeared on the scene at the same period, and to which our own Luke refers in the Acts:

After him came the rising of Judas the Galilean at the time of the registration. He persuaded a number of people to revolt under his leadership; but he too perished, and all his followers were dispersed.[3]

This statement is supported by the historian referred to above, in *Antiquities* Book XVIII:

Quirinius, a member of the senate who had filled the minor offices and passed through them all to become consul, and in other ways was a man of great distinction, arrived with a few officials in Syria. He had been sent by Caesar to be supreme judge of the nation and to assess the value of their property ... Judas, a Gaulonite from a city called Gamala, took Zadok, a Pharisee, with him and instigated a revolt. They alleged that the valuation would lead to nothing but complete slavery, and summoned the nation to the defence of their freedom.[4]

And in the *History of the Jewish War*, Book II, he writes this about the same man:

1. Luke ii. 2.   2. Matt. ii. 1, 5–6.   3. Acts v. 7.   4. *Antiquities* XVIII, 1, 4.

In his[1] time a Galilean named Judas tried to stir the natives to revolt, saying that they would be cowards if they submitted to paying taxes to the Romans, and after serving God accepted human masters.[2]

Extinction of the native Jewish dynasty: Herod, the first foreign king

6. At this time Herod became the first foreigner to be king of the Jewish nation, fulfilling the words of Moses:

> There shall not be wanting a ruler from Judah,
> Nor a leader sprung from his loins,
> Until he come for whom it is reserved.[3]

Moses adds that he will be the expectation of the Gentiles. There could be no fulfilment of the prediction as long as they were free to live under rulers of their own race, beginning with Moses himself and continuing to Augustus' reign; in his time the first foreigner, Herod, was entrusted by the Romans with the government of the Jews. Josephus informs us that he was an Idumaean on his father's side and an Arab on his mother's; but according to Africanus – and he was no ordinary historian – the best authorities say that Antipater, Herod's father, was son of a certain Herod of Ascalon, one of the 'temple-slaves' of Apollo. This Antipater was taken prisoner by Idumaean bandits when a small child, and remained in their hands because his father was too poor to put down his ransom. He was brought up in their ways and later befriended by Hyrcanus, the Jewish high priest. His son was the Herod of our Saviour's time.

When a man of such antecedents came to be king of the Jews, at the door already, in accordance with the prophecy, was the expectation of the Gentiles, for with him the succession from Moses of Jewish rulers and governors came to an end. Before their captivity and removal to Babylon they were ruled by kings, Saul and David being the first. Before the kings the government was in the hands of rulers known as judges, who came to the fore after Moses and his successor Joshua. After the return from Babylon they maintained continuously an aristocratic and oligarchic constitu-

---

1. Coponius.   2. *Jewish War*, p. 133.   3. Gen. xlix. 10.

tion, priests being in complete control. This lasted till Pompey, the Roman commander, arrived and besieged Jerusalem with the utmost vigour. He defiled the holy places, going right into the innermost sanctuary of the temple. The man who had continued the succession of his ancestors till that time and was both king and high priest, Aristobulus by name, he dispatched as a prisoner to Rome together with his children. To Hyrcanus, Aristobulus' brother, he transferred the high priesthood, and he made the whole Jewish nation from then on tributary to Rome. As soon as Hyrcanus, the last to whom fell the high-priestly succession, was taken prisoner by the Parthians,[1] Herod, as I have said, was the first foreigner to be entrusted by the Roman senate and the Emperor Augustus with the Jewish nation. It was without question in his time that the advent of Christ occurred; and the expected salvation and calling of the Gentiles followed at once, in accordance with the prophecy.

As soon as the rulers and leaders from Judah – those of Jewish stock – came to an end, not surprisingly the high priesthood, which had passed in regular succession, generation by generation, was plunged into immediate confusion. For this, too, you have a reliable witness in Josephus, who informs us that when entrusted with the kingdom by the Romans Herod no longer appointed high priests of the ancient stock but assigned the office to non-entities, and that a policy similar to Herod's regarding the appointment of priests was adopted by his son Archelaus, and after him by the Romans, when they took over the government of Judaea. The same writer informs us that Herod actually locked up the sacred vestment of the high priest and kept it under his own seal, no longer permitting the high priests to have charge of it. His example was followed by his successor Archelaus, and after him by the Romans.[2]

This evidence I have put forward as proof that in the appearing of our Saviour Jesus Christ another prophecy was fulfilled. It is perfectly clear that in Daniel Scripture specifies the exact number of weeks till the rule of Christ – I have dealt with the subject

---

1. See *Jewish War*, pp. 47, 61.   2. *Antiquities*, various passages.

elsewhere [1] – and prophesies that after the completion of these weeks the anointing of Jews will be brought to an end. [2] There can be no doubt that at the time of the birth of our Saviour Jesus Christ this prophecy was fulfilled. In order to establish the truth of the date it was necessary to make these preliminary points.

The alleged discrepancy in the gospels as to Christ's genealogy

7. The genealogy of Christ has been differently recorded for us in the gospels of Matthew and Luke. Most people see a discrepancy in this, and through ignorance of the truth each believer has been only too eager to dilate at length on these passages. So I feel justified in reproducing an explanation of the difficulty that has come into my hands. This is to be found in a letter which Africanus, to whom I referred a little while back, wrote to Aristides on the harmony of the gospel genealogies. Having first refuted other people's theories as forced and demonstrably false, he sets out the explanation he had himself received. I will quote his actual words:

The names of the families in Israel were reckoned either by nature or by law; by nature, when there was genuine offspring to succeed; by law, when another man fathered a child in the name of a brother who had died childless. For as no clear hope of being raised from the dead had yet been given, they portrayed the promise of the future with a mortal 'raising up', in order that the name of the deceased might be preserved for all time. [3] These genealogies therefore comprise some who succeeded their actual fathers, and some who were the children of one father but were registered as children of another. Thus the memory of both was preserved – of the real and nominal fathers. Thus neither of the gospels is in error, since they take account of both nature and law. For the two families, descended from Solomon and Nathan respectively, were so interlocked by the re-marriage of childless widows and the 'raising up' of offspring, that the same persons could rightly be regarded at different times as the children of different parents – sometimes the reputed fathers, sometimes the real. Thus both accounts are perfectly true, bringing the line down to Joseph in a manner complex perhaps but certainly accurate.

What I am trying to say will become clear if I explain the interrelation

1. *Selections from the Prophets.*   2. Daniel ix. 25–6.   3. Cf. Matt. xxii. 24.

of the families. If we reckon the generations from David through Solomon, we find that the third from the end is Matthan, who begot Jacob, Joseph's father; [1] if we follow Luke and reckon from David's son Nathan, the corresponding third from the end is Melchi, Joseph being the son of Heli, Melchi's son. [2] Joseph then being the subject of our study, I have to explain how each appears in the records as his father, Jacob tracing his descent from Solomon and Heli from Nathan. Before that I must explain how those two, Jacob and Heli, were brothers, and before that how their fathers, Matthan and Melchi, members of different families, are stated to have been Joseph's grandfathers. Well now, Matthan and Melchi, successive husbands of the same wife, fathered half-brothers, for the law allows a woman who has been either divorced or widowed to marry again. The wife in question, whose name is given as Estha, first married Matthan the descendant of Solomon, and bore him Jacob; then on the death of Matthan· the widow married Melchi, whose line went back to Nathan, and who belonged to the same tribe, though not to the same family, and by him had a son Heli. Thus though the families were different, we shall find that Jacob and Heli had the same mother. When Heli died childless, his brother Jacob took his wife and by her became father of Joseph in the third generation. According to nature Joseph was his son – and according to reason, so that Scripture says, 'Jacob begot Joseph'; but according to law he was Heli's son; for Jacob as a good brother 'raised up' offspring to him. It follows that the genealogy in which he finds a place cannot be invalidated, though Matthew the evangelist in his account says, 'Jacob begot Joseph', whereas Luke says, 'Who was, as people imagined' – note this comment – 'the son of Joseph, the son of Heli, the son of Melchi'. It was impossible to express legal descent more explicitly, and never once from beginning to end did he use the word 'begot' with reference to this type of fatherhood, as he traced the line, in the reverse direction, to 'Adam, the son of God'. [3]

This is not dogmatic assertion or mere guesswork: the Saviour's human relations, either in an ostentatious spirit or simply to give information, but in either case telling the truth, have handed down this tradition too. When Idumean bandits swooped on Ascalon, a city in Palestine, along with the other spoil from the temple of Apollo, which was built close to the walls, they carried away captive Antipater, the child of a certain Herod, a temple slave. As the priest was unable to put down the money for his son's ransom, Antipater was brought up in Idumean ways and later befriended by Hyrcanus, the Judaean high priest. Sent to Pompey as

1. Matt. i. 15–16.   2. Luke iii. 23–4, 31.   3. Luke iii. 38.

ambassador for Hyrcanus, he secured from him the freedom of his kingdom – freedom which his brother Aristobulus had filched away. This brought high office to Antipater himself, who was given the title of superintendent of Palestine. When envy of his high office caused him to be treacherously assassinated, he was succeeded by his son Herod, who later was chosen by Antony and Augustus and by decree of the senate to be king of the Jews. His sons were Herod[1] and the other tetrarchs. This information is confirmed by the Greek historians.

But in the archives were still inscribed the Hebrew families and those descended from proselytes, e.g. Achion the Ammonite[2] and Ruth the Moabitess, and the persons of mixed blood who had fled with them from Egypt.[3] So Herod, who had no drop of Israelitish blood in his veins and was stung by the consciousness of his base origin, burnt the registers of their families, thinking that he would appear nobly born if no one else was able by reference to public documents to trace his line back to the patriarchs or proselytes, or to the 'sojourners' of mixed blood.[4] A few careful people had private records of their own, having either remembered the names or recovered them from copies, and took pride in preserving the memory of their aristocratic origin. These included the people mentioned above, known as Desposyni because of their relationship to the Saviour's family. From the Jewish villages of Nazareth and Cochaba they passed through the rest of the country, expounding the genealogy discussed above, quoting from the books of Chronicles as far as they could trace it. This may or may not be the truth of the matter; but in my opinion and that of every fair-minded person no one else could give a clearer exposition, and we must content ourselves with it even if unconfirmed, as we are not in a position to suggest a better or truer one. In any case the gospel record is true.

Africanus concludes his letter as follows:

Matthan, Solomon's descendant, begot Jacob. On Matthan's death Melchi, Nathan's descendant, begot Heli by the same woman. Thus Heli and Jacob had the same mother. When Heli died childless, Jacob 'raised up' offspring to him, begetting Joseph – by nature his own son, by law Heli's. Thus Joseph was the son of both.

In tracing thus the genealogy of Joseph, Africanus has virtually proved that Mary belonged to the same tribe as her husband, in

---

1. Antipas.   2. Judith v. 5 and xiv. 10.   3. Ex. xii. 38.   4. Ex. xii. 19.

view of the fact that under the Mosaic law inter-marriage between different tribes was forbidden, for the rule is that a woman must wed someone from the same town and the same clan, so that the family inheritance may not be moved from tribe to tribe. Let us leave it at that.

Herod's plot against the children, and his terrible end

8. When Christ was born, in accordance with prophecy, at Bethlehem in Judaea at the time already stated, Herod was asked by the magi from the East where they could find the one who was born king of the Jews, for they had seen his star and for that reason had made this long journey in their eagerness to worship as God the child that had been born. Herod was badly shaken by the inquiry, thinking that his throne was in danger. So he consulted the teachers of the Law among the people and asked them where they expected the Christ to be born. When he heard Micah's prophecy foretelling the birth at Bethlehem he issued a single decree ordering the destruction in Bethlehem and all its neighbourhood, of the male infants, of two years and under, in accordance with the time he had found out from the magi, naturally supposing that Jesus would certainly suffer the same fate as those of his own age. However, the plot was forestalled by the removal of the Child to Egypt, as by the appearance of an angel His parents had learnt in time what was to come. The story may be studied in the sacred gospel record.[1]

In this connexion it is worth while to recall the price paid by Herod for his crime against Christ and the other babies. Instantly, without the shortest delay, divine justice overtook him while still alive, giving him a foretaste of what awaited him in the next world. This is not the place to list the ways in which he dimmed the supposed glories of his reign by the successive calamities that befell his house, the revolting murder of wife, children, and all who were bound to him by the closest ties of blood and affection. No tragic drama is as dark as their story, of which Josephus has

1. Matt. ii, 1–16.

given a full account in his *Histories*.[1] How, from the moment of
the plot against our Saviour and the other helpless infants, a
scourge wielded by the hand of God struck Herod and drove him
to death, we should do well to hear from the lips of that historian.
In *Jewish Antiquities* Book XVII he describes his terrible end in
these words:

> Herod's sickness grew steadily worse as God exacted punishment for
> his iniquities. He was consumed by a slow fire which gave no clear
> indication to the touch of the burning heat that added so much to his
> internal miseries. He had an overpowering desire for food, which it was
> impossible to satisfy, ulceration of the intestines with agonizing pains in
> the lower bowel, and a clammy transparent humour covering the feet.
> The abdomen was in the same miserable state, and in the genitals
> mortification set in, breeding worms. Breathing was constricted and only
> possible when sitting upright, and it was most offensive because of the
> heavy stench and feverish respiration. He suffered in every part convulsions
> that were unbearably severe. Those who practised divination and had the
> gift of foretelling such things declared that God was exacting a penalty
> from the king for his continual wickedness.[2]

Such is the story as told by Josephus in the *Antiquities*. In Book
II[3] of the *Histories* he gives a very similar account of Herod's last
days:

> From then on the sickness spread through his entire body, accompanied
> by a variety of painful symptoms. He had a mild fever, an unbearable
> itching all over his body, constant pains in the lower bowel, swellings on
> the feet as in dropsy, inflammation of the abdomen, and mortification of
> the genitals, producing worms; as well as difficulty in breathing, especially
> when lying down, and spasms in all his limbs. The diviners said that his
> diseases were a punishment. But though he was wrestling with so many
> disorders he hung on to life, hoped for recovery, and planned his own
> treatment. He crossed the Jordan and tried the hot baths at Callirrhoe,
> which empty their water into the Dead Sea – water sweet enough to
> drink. The doctors there decided to warm up his whole body with hot oil
> by lowering him into a bathful of it, but he fainted and turned up his eyes

---

1. For the murder of Mariamme, Alexander, and Aristobulus see *Jewish War*,
pp. 86–102.
2. *Antiquities* XVII, vi, 5.   3. Book I in our texts.

as if in a faint. The noise of his attendants beating their breasts brought him back to consciousness; but having no further hope of recovery he ordered the distribution of 50 drachmas a head to the soldiers, and large gratuities to the officers and to his gentlemen.

By the time he arrived at Jericho on the return journey he was melancholy-mad, and in a virtual challenge to death itself he proceeded to devise a monstrous outrage. He brought together the most eminent men of every village in the whole of Judaea and had them locked up in the Hippodrome. Then he sent for his sister Salome and her husband Alexas and said: 'I know the Jews will greet my death with wild rejoicings; but I can be mourned on other people's account and make sure of a magnificent funeral if you will do as I tell you. These men under guard: as soon as I die, kill them all – let loose the soldiers amongst them; then all Judaea and every family will weep for me willy-nilly . . .'

Later he was so tormented by lack of food and a racking cough that his sufferings mastered him and he made an effort to anticipate his appointed end. He took an apple and asked for a knife, it being his habit to cut up apples when he ate them; then looking round to make sure there was no one to stop him he raised his hand to stab himself.

Josephus goes on to relate that just before he died Herod gave orders for the execution of yet a third of his lawful sons[1] in addition to the two already executed, and that his life was instantly broken off, to the accompaniment of agonizing pains.[2] Such was the final end of Herod; he paid a just penalty for the children he had put to death in Bethlehem and its neighbourhood in his attempt against our Saviour.

After this an angel appeared in a dream to Joseph while he was staying in Egypt, and ordered him to leave for Judaea with the Child and His mother, informing him that those who sought the death of the little Child were dead. The evangelist proceeds:

But hearing that Archelaus had succeeded his father Herod as king, he was afraid to go there; and being warned in a dream, he withdrew into the district of Galilee.[3]

---

1. Antipater.   2. *Jewish War*, p. 118.   3. Matt. ii. 19–22.

Pilate's date; high priests at the time of Christ's mission

9. The accession to power of Archelaus after Herod is confirmed by Josephus, who describes how in accordance with the will of Herod his father and the decision of Caesar Augustus he succeeded to the Judaean kingdom; and how after his fall from power ten years later his brothers Philip and the younger Herod,[1] together with Lysanias, continued to rule their tetrarchies.[2]

In *Antiquities* Book XVIII,[3] the same writer informs us that in the twelfth year of Tiberius, who had mounted the imperial throne after the fifty-seven-year reign of Augustus, Judaea was entrusted to Pontius Pilate, and that Pilate remained there ten years, almost till Tiberius's death. This clearly proves the forged character of the *Memoranda* so recently published, blackening our Saviour; at the very start the note of time proves the dishonesty of the forgers. If they are to be believed the crime of the Saviour's Passion must be referred to Tiberius's fourth consulship, i.e. the seventh year of his reign, but at that time it is clear that Pilate was not yet in charge of Judaea, if we may accept the testimony of Josephus, who explicitly declares, in the passage already quoted, that it was in the *twelfth* year of his reign that Tiberius appointed Pilate procurator of Judaea.

10. In their time, when, according to the evangelist, Tiberius Caesar was in the fifteenth year of his reign and Pontius Pilate in the fourth of his governorship, and Herod, Lysanias, and Philip were tetrarchs of the rest of Judaea,[4] our Saviour and Lord, Jesus the Christ of God, beginning His mission at the age of about thirty,[5] came to John's baptism and then and there set to work preaching the gospel. Holy Scripture further tells us that He completed the whole period of His teaching when Annas and Caiaphas were high priest,[6] showing that the years covering

---

1. Antipas.
3. XVIII, ii, 2, and iv, 2.
5. Luke iii. 23.

2. *Jewish War*, pp. 119, 129f., 131, 143.
4. An inaccurate paraphrase of Luke iii. 1.
6. Luke iii. 2.

their ministry include the whole period of His teaching. Since, then, He began His mission in the high priesthood of Annas and continued till the reign of Caiaphas, the period covered does not stretch to four complete years. For, at that time the ordinances of the Law were already obsolescent and the rule was no longer operative under which the duties of God's service were hereditary and lasted for life; the Roman governors bestowed the high priesthood first on one, then on another, and the office was held for not more than a single year. In fact, Josephus records that after Annas there were four successive high priests, Caiaphas being the last. I quote from the book of *Antiquities*:

Valerius Gratus, after depriving Ananus[1] of the priesthood, appointed as high priest Ishmael son of Phabi; but a little later he removed him and nominated as high priest Eleazar, son of the high priest Ananus. When a year had gone by he removed him in turn and transferred the high priesthood to Simon son of Camithus. He too remained in office no more than a year: he was succeeded by Joseph, also known as Caiaphas.[2]

Thus the whole period of our Saviour's teaching is shown to be actually less than four complete years, four high priests in four years, from Annas to the appointment of Caiaphas, having held office for a twelvemonth. Naturally, the gospel narrative named Caiaphas as high priest in the year in which the events of our Saviour's Passion were enacted; it also shows that the period of Christ's teaching harmonizes with the foregoing line of inquiry.

Not very long after the start of His preaching our Saviour and Lord called the twelve apostles, to whom alone of all His disciples He gave, as a special privilege, the name of apostles.[3] Furthermore, He appointed seventy others; these, too, He sent out two and two ahead of Him to every town or place to which He Himself intended to come.[4]

1. Annas.   2. *Antiquities* XVIII, ii, 2.   3. Matt. xi and Luke vi. 13.
4. Luke x. 1.

Evidence regarding John the Baptist and Christ

11. Not long afterwards John the Baptist was beheaded by the younger Herod, as we learn from the inspired gospel narrative.[1] Confirmation comes from Josephus, who mentions Herodias by name and tells how though she was his brother's wife Herod married her, discarding his existing lawful wife – daughter of King Aretas of Petrea – and separating Herodias from her husband, who was still alive. For her sake, too, he put John to death and was involved in war with Aretas, whose daughter he had slighted. The war ended, as Josephus records, with a pitched battle in which Herod's army was totally destroyed, the direct result of his outrageous treatment of John. The same writer acknowledges that John was a man of unimpeachable virtue, and a baptist, confirming the description of him contained in the gospel narrative. He also records the fact that Herod was deprived of his throne on account of the same woman, with whom he was driven into exile and condemned to live in Vienne, a city in Gaul.[2] The story will be found in *Antiquities* Book XVIII, from which I quote verbatim what he has to say about John:

Some of the Jews believed that Herod's army had been destroyed by God, as a richly deserved punishment for his treatment of John who was called the Baptist. For Herod killed him, a good man who urged the Jews to train themselves in virtue, to be just to each other and pious towards God, and to come together for baptism: on one condition only would their baptism be acceptable to Him – if it was undergone not to escape the penalty of sins but to purify the body, since the soul had been already purged by righteousness. When crowds assembled, very excited on hearing his words, Herod was afraid that his extraordinary hold over the people would lead to some revolt, as they seemed prepared to do anything at his suggestion. So he thought it much better to forestall any revolutionary movement prompted by John by putting him out of the way, rather than wait for an outbreak to occur and reproach himself when it was too late. Because of Herod's suspicion John was sent in chains to Machaerus, the fortress mentioned above, and there executed.[3]

1. Mark vi. 14–29.
2. According to *Antiquities* XVIII, vii, 2, Lyons; according to *Jewish War*, p. 139, Spain.
3. *Antiquities* XVIII, v, 2.

After giving this account of John, in the same part of his work he goes on to speak as follows of our Saviour:

At this time appeared Jesus, a very gifted man – if indeed it is right to call him a man; for he was a worker of miracles, a teacher of such men as listened with pleasure to the truth, and he won over many of the Jews and many of Gentile origin as well. This was the Christ; and when at the instigation of our leading men he had been condemned to the cross by Pilate, those who had loved him at the first did not cease to do so; for on the third day he appeared to them alive again, the inspired prophets having foretold this and countless other wonderful things about him. Even now the group of people called Christians after him has not died out.[1]

When a historian sprung from the Hebrews themselves has furnished in his own writing an almost contemporary record of John the Baptist and our Saviour too, what excuse is there left for not condemning the shameless dishonesty of those who forged the *Memoranda* blackening them both? And there we will leave the matter.

Our Saviour's disciples

12. The names of our Saviour's apostles are in the gospels for all to read: of the seventy disciples no list has ever been found. It is stated that one of them was Barnabas, who is mentioned several times in the Acts of the Apostles, and notably by Paul in writing to the Galatians.[2] Another is said to have been Sosthenes, who wrote with Paul to the Corinthians.[3] Then there is Clement's story (*Outlines* Book V) in which he says that Cephas – of whom Paul writes: 'When Cephas came to Antioch I withstood him to his face'[4] – was one of the seventy disciples, who happened to have the same name as Peter the Apostle. There is evidence also that Matthias, who took Judas' place in the list of apostles, and the

1. *Antiquities* XVIII, ii, 3.   2. Gal. ii. 1, 9, 13.
3. I Cor. i. 1.   4. Gal. ii. 11.

other man honoured like him in the drawing of lots,[1] had both been called to be among the seventy. Thaddaeus, again, is said to have been one of them; about him a story has come to my notice which I shall very shortly recount.

In addition to the Seventy there were other disciples of the Saviour, as you would find if you considered the matter and accepted the testimony of Paul, who states that after His resurrection from the dead He was seen first by Cephas, then by the Twelve, and after them by more than five hundred brethren at once, of whom some, he says, have fallen asleep, but most remain alive at the time of writing. Next, he says, He was seen by James – one of the reputed brothers of the Lord; then, as if in addition to these there had been, on the pattern of the Twelve, a large number of apostles such as Paul himself, he adds: 'Later He was seen by all the apostles.'

A story about the Prince of Edessa

13. The story about Thaddaeus is as follows: Because of His power to work miracles the divinity of our Lord and Saviour Jesus Christ became in every land the subject of excited talk and attracted a vast number of people in foreign lands very remote from Judaea, who came in the hope of being cured of diseases and disorders of every kind. Thus it happened that when King Abgar, the brilliantly successful monarch of the peoples of Mesopotamia, who was dying from a terrible physical disorder which no human power could heal, heard continual mention of the name of Jesus and unanimous tribute to His miracles, he sent a humble request to Him by a letter-carrier, begging for relief from his disease. Jesus did not immediately accede to his request, but honoured him with a personal letter, promising to send one of His disciples to cure his disease, and at the same time to bring salvation to him and all his kin. In a very short time the promise was fulfilled. After His resurrection and ascent into heaven, Thomas, one of the twelve apostles, was moved by inspiration to send Thaddaeus, himself in the list of Christ's seventy disciples, to Edessa as preacher and

1. Joseph Barsabbas.

evangelist of the teaching about Christ. Through him every word of our Saviour's promise was fulfilled.

Written evidence of these things is available, taken from the Record Office at Edessa, at that time the royal capital. In the public documents there, embracing early history and also the events of Abgar's time, this record is found preserved from then till now; and the most satisfactory course is to listen to the actual letters, which I have extracted from the archives and translated word for word from the Syriac as follows:

COPY OF A LETTER WRITTEN BY ABGAR THE TOPARCH TO
JESUS AND SENT TO HIM AT JERUSALEM BY
THE COURIER ANANIAS

Abgar Uchama the Toparch to Jesus, who has appeared as a gracious saviour in the region of Jerusalem – greeting.

I have heard about you and about the cures you perform without drugs or herbs. If report is true, you make the blind see again and the lame walk about; you cleanse lepers, expel unclean spirits and demons, cure those suffering from chronic and painful diseases, and raise the dead.[1] When I heard all this about you, I concluded that one of two things must be true – either you are God and came down from heaven to do these things, or you are God's Son doing them. Accordingly I am writing to beg you to come to me, whatever the inconvenience, and cure the disorder from which I suffer. I may add that I understand the Jews are treating you with contempt and desire to injure you: my city is very small, but highly esteemed, adequate for both of us.

[He wrote this letter when the heavenly light had shone on him only a little while. It is desirable also to hear the letter which Jesus sent him by the same letter-carrier. It is only a few lines long, but very impressive. Here it is.[2]]

JESUS'S REPLY TO THE TOPARCH ABGAR BY THE
COURIER ANANIAS

Happy are you who believed in me without having seen me![3] For it is

1. Similar to, but not identical with, the list in Matt. xi. 5 and Luke vii. 2.
2. The bracketed passages are wanting in some MSS.   3. See John xx. 29.

written of me that those who have seen me will not believe in me, and that those who have not seen will believe and live. As to your request that I should come to you, I must complete all that I was sent to do here, and on completing it must at once be taken up to the One who sent me. When I have been taken up I will send you one of my disciples to cure your disorder and bring life to you and those with you.

To these letters is subjoined the following in Syriac:

After Jesus was taken up, Judas, also known as Thomas, sent to him as an apostle Thaddaeus, one of the Seventy, who came and stayed with Tobias, son of Tobias. When his arrival was announced [and he had been made conspicuous by the wonders he performed], Abgar was told: 'An apostle has come here from Jesus, as He promised you in His letter.' Then Thaddaeus began in the power of God to cure every disease and weakness, to the astonishment of everyone. When Abgar heard of the magnificent and astonishing things that he was doing and especially his cures, he began to suspect that this was the one to whom Jesus referred when He wrote in His letter: 'When I have been taken up I will send you one of my disciples who will cure your disorder.' So summoning Tobias, with whom Thadaeus was staying, he said: 'I understand that a man with unusual powers has arrived and is staying in your house [and is working many cures in the name of Jesus.' Tobias answered: 'Yes, sir. A man from foreign parts has arrived and is living with me, and is performing many wonders.' Abgar replied:] 'Bring him to me.'

So Tobias went to Thaddaeus and said to him: 'The Toparch Abgar has summoned me and told me to bring you to him so that you can cure him.' Thaddaeus answered: 'I will present myself, since the power of God has sent me to him.' The next day Tobias got up early and escorted Thaddaeus to Abgar. As he presented himself, with the king's grandees standing there, at the moment of his entry a wonderful vision appeared to Abgar on the face of Thaddaeus. On seeing it Abgar bowed low before the apostle, and astonishment seized all the bystanders; for they had not seen the vision, which appeared to Abgar alone. He questioned Thaddaeus.

'Are you really a disciple of Jesus the Son of God, who said to me, "I will send you one of my disciples who will cure you and give you life"?'

'You wholeheartedly believed in the One who sent me, and for that reason I was sent to you. And again, if you believe in Him, in proportion to your belief shall the prayers of your heart be granted.'

'I believed in Him so strongly that I wanted to take an army and destroy the Jews who crucified Him, if I had not been prevented by the imperial power of Rome from doing so.'

'Our Lord has fulfilled the will of His Father: after fulfilling it He was taken up to the Father.'

'I too have believed in Him and in His Father.'

'For that reason I lay my hand on you in His name.'

When he did this, Abgar was instantly cured of the disease and disorder from which he suffered. It surprised Abgar that the very thing he had heard about Jesus had actually happened to him through His disciple Thaddaeus, who had cured him without drugs or herbs – and not only him but also Abdus son of Abdus, who had gout. He too came, and falling at his feet found his prayer answered through the hands of Thaddaeus, and was cured. Many other fellow-citizens of theirs Thaddaeus restored to health, performing many wonders and preaching the word of God.

After this Abgar said: 'It is by the power of God that you, Thaddaeus, do these things; and we ourselves were amazed. But I have a further request to make: explain to me about the coming of Jesus and how it happened, and about His power – by what power did He do the things I have heard about?'

Thaddaeus replied: 'For the time being I shall say nothing; but as I was sent to preach the word, be good enough to assemble all your citizens tomorrow, and I will preach to them and sow in them the word of life – about the coming of Jesus and how it happened; about His mission and the purpose for which His Father sent Him; about His power and His deeds, and the mysteries He spoke in the world, and the power by which He did these things; about His new preaching; about His lowliness and humility, and how He humbled Himself and put aside and made light of His divinity, was crucified and descended into Hades, and rent asunder the partition which had never been rent since time began, and raised the dead; how He descended alone, but ascended with a great multitude to His Father [; and how He is seated on the right hand of God the Father with glory in the heavens; and how He will come again with power to judge living and dead].'

So Abgar instructed his citizens to assemble at daybreak and hear the preaching of Thaddaeus. After that he ordered gold and silver to be given to him. But Thaddaeus refused them and asked, 'If we have left our own property behind, how can we accept other people's?'

All this happened in the year 340.[1]

Here we may leave for the present this valuable document, literally translated from Syriac.

1. of the Seleucid era – apparently A.D. 30, the probable year of the Ascension.

Book 2

(Compiled by me from the works of Clement, Tertullian, Josephus, and Philo)

TIBERIUS TO NERO: THE WORK OF THE APOSTLES FROM THE CHOICE OF MATTHIAS TO THE DEATHS OF PAUL AND PETER

Those facts about the story of the Church that needed to be explained by way of preface – the divinity of the saving Word, the early history of our teaching, the antiquity of the Christian way of life in accordance with the gospel, and especially the details of Christ's recent advent, the events before His Passion, and the choice of the apostles – I discussed in the previous book, outlining the arguments. Let us now in the present book inquire into the events following His Ascension, drawing on Holy Writ for some, and deriving others from outside sources which I shall name as occasion demands.

How the apostles lived after the Ascension

1. The first, then, to be chosen by lot for the apostleship in place of the traitor Judas was Matthias,[1] who, as has been mentioned, had been one of the Lord's disciples. By prayer and the laying-on of the apostles' hands there were appointed to the diaconate for the service of the community men of proved worth to the number of seven.[2] These were headed by Stephen, who was the first after the Lord – almost as soon as he was ordained, as if this was the real purpose of his advancement – to be put to death, stoned by the Lord's murderers.[3] Thus he was the first to win the crown called by the same name as he,[4] and reserved for Christ's worthily victorious martyrs.

Then there was James, who was known as the brother of the

---

1. Acts i. 15–26.   2. Acts vi. 1–6.   3. Acts vii. 59.
4. In Greek 'Stephen' and 'crown' are identical.

Lord; for he, too, was called Joseph's son, and Joseph Christ's father, though in fact the Virgin was his betrothed, and before they came together she was found to be with child by the Holy Ghost, as the inspired gospel narrative tells us.[1] This James, whom the early Christians surnamed the Righteous because of his outstanding virtue, was the first, as the records tell us, to be elected to the episcopal throne of the Jerusalem church. Clement, in *Outlines* Book VI, puts it thus:

Peter, James, and John, after the Ascension of the Saviour, did not claim pre-eminence because the Saviour had specially honoured them, but chose James the Righteous as Bishop of Jerusalem.

In Book VIII of the same work the writer makes this further statement about him:

James the Righteous, John, and Peter were entrusted by the Lord after his resurrection with the higher knowledge. They imparted it to the other apostles, and the other apostles to the Seventy, one of whom was Barnabas. There were two Jameses, one the Righteous, who was thrown down from the parapet and beaten to death with a fuller's club, the other the James who was beheaded.[2]

James the Righteous is also mentioned by Paul when he writes:

Of the other apostles I saw no one except James the Lord's brother.[3]

It was at this time that our Saviour's promise to the king of the Osrhoenes was receiving its fulfilment. Thomas was moved by inspiration to send Thaddaeus to Edessa as preacher and evangelist of the teaching about Christ, as I showed a little way back from the document found there. When he arrived in the country Thaddaeus restored Abgar to health by the word of Christ, and amazed all the inhabitants by his wonderful miracles. By his actions he exerted such an influence on them that he led them to reverence the power of Christ, and made disciples of the saving doctrine. From that day to this the whole city of Edessa has been devoted to the name of Christ, providing most convincing proof of our Saviour's goodness to them also.

1. Matt. i. 18.   2. Acts xii. 2.   3. Gal. i. 19.

After this excursion into early history let us return once more to the inspired record.

Stephen's martyrdom was followed by the first and greatest persecution by the Jews themselves of the Jerusalem church. All the disciples except the Twelve alone were dispersed about Judaea and Samaria.[1] Some, as the inspired record says, travelled as far as Phoenicia, Cyprus, and Antioch; but they could not yet venture to share the message of the Faith with Gentiles, and proclaimed it to Jews alone.[2] At that time also Paul was still raging against the Church, entering the houses of the faithful, dragging off men and women, and handing them over for imprisonment.[3] But Philip, one of the men already ordained with Stephen to the diaconate, was among the dispersed. He went down into Samaria, and filled with divine power was the first to preach the word there. So great was the divine grace working with him that even Simon the Magus with very many others was won over by his words. Such a name had Simon obtained at that time by the sorceries with which he got his dupes into his power that he was believed to be the Great Power of God, but now even he was struck dumb by the miracles that Philip performed by divine power, and slipped in: he actually received baptism, in his hypocritical pretence of belief in Christ. It is an astonishing fact that this is still the practice of those who to the present day belong to his disgusting sect. Following in their progenitor's footsteps they slip into the Church like a pestilential and scabby disease, and do the utmost damage to all whom they succeed in smearing with the horrible, deadly poison concealed on them. By now, however, most of these have been expelled – just as Simon himself, when his real character had been exposed by Peter, paid the appropriate penalty.[4]

While every day the saving message spread farther afield, some providence brought from Ethiopia, a country traditionally ruled by a woman, one of the queen's principal officers. The first Gentile to receive from Philip by revelation the mysteries of the divine word, and the first-fruits of the faithful throughout the world, he is believed to have been the first to go back to his native

1. Acts viii. 1.   2. Acts xi. 19.   3. Acts viii.
4. Summarized from Acts viii. 5–23.

land and preach the gospel of the knowledge of the God of the universe and the life-giving sojourn of our Saviour among men. Through him came the actual fulfilment of the prophecy:

Ethiopia shall stretch out her hand to God.[1]

The next stage began when Paul, the chosen vessel – neither from men nor through men, but through revelation of Jesus Christ Himself and God the Father who raised Him from the dead – was appointed an apostle, receiving his call through a vision and the heavenly voice that accompanied the revelation.[2]

Tiberius's reaction on learning Christ's story, which soon sped to every part of the world

2. Our Saviour's marvellous resurrection and ascension into heaven were by now everywhere famous, and it had long been customary for provincial governors to report to the holder of the imperial office any change in the local situation, so that he might be aware of all that was going on. The story of the resurrection from the dead of our Saviour Jesus, already the subject of general discussion all over Palestine, was accordingly communicated by Pilate to the Emperor Tiberius. For Pilate knew all about Christ's supernatural deeds, and especially how after death He had risen from the dead and was now generally believed to be a god. It is said that Tiberius referred the report to the senate, which rejected it. The apparent reason was that they had not gone into the matter before, for the old law still held good that no one could be regarded by the Romans as a god unless by vote and decree of the senate; the real reason was that no human decision or commendation was required for the saving teaching of the divine message. In this way the Roman council rejected the report sent to it about our Saviour, but Tiberius made no change in his attitude and formed no evil designs against the teaching of Christ.

These facts were noted by Tertullian, an expert in Roman law and famous on other grounds – in fact one of the most brilliant

1. Ps. lxviii. 31.   2. Acts ix. 3–4 and Gal. i. 1.

men in Rome. In his *Defence of the Christians*, written in Latin and translated into Greek, he has this to say:

To go back to the origin of such laws, there was an old decree that no one should be consecrated a god by an emperor till he had been approved by the senate. Marcus Aemilius followed this procedure in the case of a false god, Alburnus. This reinforces my argument that among you godhead is conferred by human approval. If a god does not satisfy man, he does not become a god; so according to this it is for man to show favour to God. Tiberius then, in whose time the name of Christian came into the world, when a report of this doctrine reached him from Palestine where it originated, communicated it to the senate, making it clear to them that he favoured the doctrine. The senate however, because they had not examined the doctrine for themselves, rejected it; but Tiberius stuck to his own view, and threatened to execute any who accused the Christians.[1]

Heavenly providence had purposefully put this in the emperor's mind, in order that the gospel message should get off to a good start and speed to every part of the world.

3. Thus with the powerful cooperation of Heaven the whole world was suddenly lit by the sunshine of the saving word. At once, in accordance with the Holy Scriptures, the voice of its inspired evangelists and apostles went forth into all the earth, and their words to the ends of the world.[2] In every town and village, like a well-filled threshing-floor, churches shot up bursting with eager members. Men who through the error they had inherited from generations of ancestors were in the grip of the old spiritual sickness of idol-worship, by the power of Christ and through the teaching of His followers and the miracles they wrought were freed, as it were, from cruel masters and found release from galling fetters. They turned their backs on devilish polytheism in all its forms, and acknowledged that there was one God only, the Fashioner of all things. Him they honoured with the ordinances of true religion through that divine, reasonable worship of which our Saviour sowed the seed in the life of men.

1. *Defence*, 5.   2. Ps. xix. 4.

The divine grace was now being poured on the other nations too. First, at Palestinian Caesarea Cornelius with his entire house-hold, through divine revelation and the agency of Peter, embraced the Christian faith.[1] He was followed by many other Gentiles at Antioch, who had heard the preaching of those dispersed by the persecution of Stephen's time. The Antioch church was now flourishing and growing rapidly, and a large number of the prophets from Jerusalem were there, accompanied by Barnabas and Paul and another group of brethren as well. It was at that time and in that city that the name of Christian first appeared, as if from a copious and life-giving fountain. Agabus again, one of the prophets staying with them, foretold the coming famine, and Paul and Barnabas were sent to do everything possible for the relief of the brethren.[2]

Agrippa appointed king and Herod banished: sufferings of the
Jews: suicide of Pilate

4. After a reign of about twenty-two years Tiberius died, and the principate passed to Gaius,[3] who at once had Agrippa crowned ruler of the Jews. He made him king of the tetrarchies of Philip and Lysanias, to which a little later he added the tetrarchy of Herod, having sentenced that monarch – the Herod of our Saviour's Passion – to banishment for life, along with his wife Herodias, because of a long list of offences. The details will be found in Josephus.[4]

In Gaius' reign Philo became widely known as one of the greatest scholars, not only among our own people but also among those brought up as pagans. By descent a Hebrew, he could hold his own with any of the eminent occupants of official positions in Alexandria. The constant and conscientious labour that he bestowed on theological and traditional studies is plain for all to see, while of his proficiency in the philosophical and liberal thought of the pagan world there is no need to speak, since it is

1. Acts x.   2. Acts xi. 19–30.   3. Caligula.   4. *Jewish War*, pp. 139–40.

on record that in his enthusiasm for the systems of Plato and
Pythagoras he surpassed all his contemporaries.

5. What happened to the Jews in Gaius' reign Philo has related in
five books. In these he describes the emperor's insanity and how
he proclaimed himself a god and over and over again abused his
position; the sufferings of the Jews in his time; the mission to
Rome that Philo undertook on behalf of his compatriots in
Alexandria; his appearance before Gaius, when his defence of their
ancestral laws met with nothing but derisive laughter and well
nigh cost him his life.

These facts are mentioned also by Josephus, who in *Antiquities*
Book XVIII writes as follows:

> When a clash took place in Alexandria between the Jewish colony and
> the Greeks, three men were chosen by each faction to represent them
> before Gaius. One of the Alexandrian representatives was Apion, who
> brought many damaging accusations against the Jews, alleging in particular
> that they neglected the honours due to Caesar – all the subjects of the
> Roman government raised altars and temples to Gaius, and in every other
> respect accepted him as they did the gods: the Jews alone thought it
> improper to honour him with statues and swear by his name. When
> Apion had brought many serious charges, by which he hoped with good
> reason that Gaius would be roused, Philo, the leading Jewish repre-
> sentative, rose to reply. A man highly esteemed on every ground, brother
> of Alexander the alabarch, and a skilled philosopher, he was quite capable
> of rebutting the charges; but he was cut short by Gaius, who ordered him
> to clear out, being so infuriated that he was obviously on the point of
> taking drastic action against them. Out went Philo, grossly insulted, and
> told his Jewish colleagues they need have no fear: Gaius might be furious
> with them, but in reality he was already taking the field against God.[1]

So much we learn from Josephus. Philo himself, in his historical
work *The Mission*, gives us a detailed and precise account of his
actions at that time. I shall omit the greater part, quoting only
those points that will make abundantly clear to my readers the
calamities which befell the Jews so promptly and after so short an
interval, in consequence of their crimes against Christ. In the first
place he relates that in Tiberius's reign, at Rome, Sejanus, then

1. *Antiquities* XVIII, viii, 1.

most influential at the emperor's court, took energetic steps to exterminate the entire race. Meanwhile, in Judaea, Pilate, in whose period of office the crime against our Saviour was committed, made an attempt on the temple (then still standing) at Jerusalem in defiance of Jewish privileges, goading the people to absolute frenzy.

6. After the death of Tiberius, he continues, Gaius ascended the throne, and among the many victims of his numerous outrages the whole Jewish race suffered to a peculiar and extreme degree. This we may learn in brief from his own words, which I reproduce exactly as written:

> So incalculable was the behaviour of Gaius towards everyone, especially the Jewish race. He hated them so bitterly that in city after city, beginning with Alexandria, he seized the synagogues and filled them with images and statues of himself – for as he gave permission for them to be erected, it was really he who put them there – and in the Holy City he tried to change the sanctuary, which was still untouched and regarded as inviolable, and transform it into a temple of his own, to be called the Temple of Jupiter the Glorious, the Younger Gaius.[1]

Countless other atrocities that beggar description, inflicted on the Jews at Alexandria in the same reign, are related by Philo in a second short work, entitled *The Virtues*. His statements are confirmed by Josephus, who similarly points out that the calamities which overtook the whole nation began with the time of Pilate and the crimes against the Saviour. Listen to what he has to say in *The Jewish War* Book II. Here are his actual words:

> As procurator of Judaea Tiberius sent Pilate, who during the night, secretly and under cover, conveyed to Jerusalem the images of Caesar known as *signa*. When day dawned this put the Jews into a frenzy; for those who were near were amazed at the sight, which meant that their laws had been trampled on – they do not permit any portrait-image to be set up in the city.[2]

If you compare this with the gospel account, you will see that it was not long before they paid the penalty for the cry they uttered

---

1. The elder Gaius being Julius Caesar.   2. *Jewish War*, p. 138.

before Pilate himself, when they shouted that they had no other king than Caesar alone.[1] Josephus goes on to relate a second calamity that overtook them soon after:

> After this he stirred up further trouble by expending the sacred treasure known as Corban[2] on an aqueduct thirty-five miles long. This roused the populace to fury, and when Pilate visited Jerusalem they surrounded the tribunal and shouted him down. But he had foreseen this disturbance, and had made the soldiers mix with the mob, wearing civilian clothing over their armour, and with orders not to draw their swords but to use clubs on the obstreperous. He now gave the signal from the tribunal and the Jews were cudgelled, so that many died from the blows, and many as they fled were trampled to death by their friends. The fate of those who perished horrified the crowd into silence.[3]

Besides this, the same writer shows that in Jerusalem itself a great many other revolts broke out, making it clear that from then on the city and all Judaea were in the grip of faction, war, and an endless succession of criminal plots, until the final hour overtook them – the siege under Vespasian. Such was the penalty laid upon the Jews by divine justice for their crimes against Christ.

7. It is worthy of note that, as the records show, in the reign of Gaius, whose times I am describing, Pilate himself, the governor of our Saviour's day, was involved in such calamities that he was forced to become his own executioner and to punish himself with his own hand: divine justice, it seems, was not slow to overtake him. The facts are recorded by those Greeks who have chronicled the Olympiads[4] together with the events occurring in each.

The famine in Claudius' time: martyrdom of James: punishment of Agrippa

8. The reign of Gaius had not yet lasted four years when he was succeeded as emperor by Claudius. In his time famine descended on the whole world, a fact which writers whose point of view is

1. John xix. 15, reworded.
2. See Mark vii. 11, where 'Corban' is retained in English Bibles, and Matt xxvii. 6, where it is translated 'treasury' or 'temple fund'.
3. *Jewish War*, p. 139.   4. Four-year periods, the basis of Greek chronology.

very different from ours have recorded in their histories.[1] Thus, the prediction of Agabus in the Acts of the Apostles about the famine that was to occur all over the world received its fulfilment. The famine in Claudius' time is indicated in the Acts by Luke, who relates how by Paul and Barnabas the Christians in Antioch, each according to his means, sent help to those in Judaea.[2] He continues:

9. At that time [obviously that of Claudius] King Herod made a determined attack on certain members of the Church, killing James the brother of John with the sword.

Referring to this James, Clement in *Outlines* Book VII tells an interesting story, on the strength of an authentic tradition. It appears that the man who brought him into court was so moved when he saw him testify that he confessed that he, too, was a Christian:

So they were both taken away together, and on the way he asked James to forgive him. James thought for a moment; then he said,'I wish you peace', and kissed him. So both were beheaded at the same time.

Then as we read in the sacred record, Herod, seeing that his action in putting James to death had given satisfaction to the Jews, laid hands on Peter as well, clapped him in prison, and was on the very point of perpetrating his murder too, but for divine intervention: in the night an angel stood by him, and he was miraculously released from his fetters and set free for the ministry of preaching. It was in this way that Peter's life was ordained by heaven.[3]

10. The king's attempt on the apostles brought swift retribution: the avenging minister of divine justice overtook him at once, immediately after his action against the apostles, as the narrative of the Acts records. He had set out for Caesarea, and there on an important feast day, adorned with magnificent royal robes, he mounted on a dais, and standing in front of his throne delivered a harangue which the entire audience received with thunderous

1. Tacitus and Dio Cassius.   2. Acts xi. 28–9.
3. Condensed from Acts xii. 3–10.

applause, as the utterance of a god, not a man; and the inspired record tells us that instantly he was struck by an angel of the Lord, was eaten by worms, and expired.[1] It is remarkable how in the case of this miracle also the sacred record is borne out by the account in Josephus, who clearly testifies to the truth in *Antiquities* Book XIX, where he tells us the amazing story in these words:

He had reached the end of his third year as king of all Judaea; and he came to the city of Caesarea, formerly known as Strato's Tower. There he was celebrating public games in Caesar's honour, knowing that this was a festival for his safety. It was attended by a great number of provincial officials and other leading men. On the second day of the games he put on a robe made entirely of silver, remarkable in texture, and at daybreak entered the theatre. There the silver was lit up by the first glint of the sun's rays, and shone dazzlingly, glittering in such a way that those who gazed at it trembled with fear. At once his flatterers shouted aloud from every side – little good did it do him – and hailed him as a god, adding: 'Be gracious! Hitherto we have reverenced you as a man; henceforth we acknowledge you as of more than mortal nature.' The king did not rebuke these people or repudiate their blasphemous flattery.

A moment later he looked up, and sitting over his head he saw an angel. This, as he at once realized, was the bringer of evil, as he had once been of good. He felt a pang in his breast, and all at once a violent pain gripped his belly, agonizing from the start. So looking hard at his friends, he murmured: 'I, your god, am now commanded to depart this life, for fate has instantly disproved the lies you have just told about me. You called me immortal, and now I am being taken away to die. I must bow to destiny, as God has willed it. Anyway my life has not been a poor one, but has reached the length that people envy.'

As he said this, the severity of his pain got the better of him; so no time was lost in carrying him into the palace, and soon the news reached all ears that he was bound to die in a matter of hours. By ancestral custom the crowd at once sat down, women and children as well, on sackcloth, and began to supplicate God for the king, and wailing and lamentation resounded everywhere. Lying in a top-floor room and looking down at them as they fell on their faces, the king could not restrain his own tears. For five days without intermission he was tortured by the pain in his belly; then he passed away in the fifty-fourth year of his life and the seventh of his reign. He had reigned four years in the time of Gaius

1. Compressed from Acts xii. 19–23.

Caesar, ruling Philip's tetrarchy for three years, and in the fourth receiving Herod's too, and three more while Claudius Caesar was emperor.[1]

On these and other matters Josephus confirms the truth of Holy Scripture in a way that surprises me. If regarding the king's name some consider that there is a discrepancy, the answer is that the date and the facts prove that he is the same: either the name has been changed by a copyist's error, or else, like many others, the same man had two names.

Theudas the impostor: Queen Helen of Adiabene

11. In the Acts, again, Luke introduces Gamaliel as saying at the examination of the apostles that at the time referred to Theudas rose in revolt, claiming to be somebody, and that he was killed and his entire following dispersed.[2] Well now, let us compare this with what Josephus writes about him. Here is his account, quoted verbatim from the work just referred to:

When Fadus was procurator of Judaea, an impostor called Theudas persuaded a vast crowd to take their belongings and follow him to the River Jordan; for he claimed to be a prophet, and promised to divide the river by his command and provide them with an easy crossing. A great many people were deceived by this talk. Fadus however did not allow them to enjoy their folly, but sent a troop of cavalry against them. These attacked them without warning, killed many, and took many alive, capturing Theudas himself, whose head they cut off and conveyed to Jerusalem.

Immediately after this he mentions the famine that took place in Claudius' time:

12. It was just after this that the great famine took place in Judaea, in which Queen Helen at great expense bought corn from Egypt and distributed it among those in want.

You will find that this too agrees with the account in the Acts of the Apostles, which tells how the disciples at Antioch, each in proportion to his means, resolved to send relief to those living in

1. *Antiquities* XIX, viii, 2.   2. Compressed from Acts v. 34–6.

Judaea. This they did, sending to the presbyters by Barnabas and Paul.[1] To this day splendid monuments of the Helen referred to by the historian are pointed out in the suburbs of what is now called Aelia. She was said to have been Queen of Adiabene.

Simon the Magus and Peter at Rome

13. As faith in our Saviour and Lord Jesus Christ was now spreading in all directions, the enemy of man's salvation, in a wily attempt to capture the imperial city in time, brought there Simon who was mentioned earlier, and by lending his own weight to the man's artful impostures took possession of many people in Rome and led them astray. This we learn from Justin, an ornament of our Faith soon after the apostles' time. I shall state the essential facts about him in due course. In his first *Defence* of our doctrines to Antoninus he writes:

After the Lord was taken up into heaven the demons put forward a number of men who claimed to be gods. These not only escaped being persecuted by you, but were actually the objects of worship – for example Simon, a Samaritan from a village called Gittho, who in Claudius Caesar's time, thanks to the art of the demons who possessed him, worked wonders of magic, and in your imperial city of Rome was regarded as a god, and like a god was honoured by you with a statue in the River Tiber between the two bridges. It bears this inscription in Latin, SIMONI DEO SANCTO.[2] Almost all Samaritans, and a few from other nations too, acknowledge him as their principal god, and worship him. And a woman named Helen, who travelled around with him at that time and had previously lived in a brothel, they call the First Emanation from him.[3]

This is Justin's version, and it is supported by Irenaeus, who in Book I of his *Against Heresies* gives a brief account of the man and his unholy, sordid teaching. To reproduce the latter in the present work would be superfluous: those who wish can learn all about the origins and lives of the heresiarchs who followed him, the bases of their false doctrines and the practices they introduced, for they are most carefully described in the work of Irenaeus mentioned above.

1. Acts xi, 29–30.   2. i.e. 'to Simon the Holy God'.   3. *Defence* 1. 26.

Simon, we are given to understand, was the prime author of every heresy. From his time to our own those who follow his lead, while pretending to accept that sober Christian philosophy which through purity of life won universal fame, are as devoted as ever to the idolatrous superstition from which they seemed to have escaped: they prostrate themselves before pictures and images of Simon himself and his companion, the Helen already mentioned, and give themselves to worshipping them with incense, sacrifices, and libations. Their more secret rites, which they claim will so amaze a man when he first hears them that, in their official jargon, he will be wonderstruck, are indeed something to wonder at, brimfull of frenzy and lunacy, and of such a kind that not only can they not be put down in writing; they involve such appalling degradation, such unspeakable conduct, that no decent man would let a mention of them pass his lips. For whatever could be imagined more disgusting than the foulest crime known has been outstripped by the utterly revolting heresy of these men, who make sport of wretched women, burdened indeed with vices of every kind.[1]

14. Of such vices was Simon the father and contriver, raised up at that time by the evil power which hates all that is good and plots against the salvation of mankind, to be a great opponent of great men, our Saviour's inspired apostles. Nevertheless, divine and celestial grace worked with its ministers, by their advent and presence speedily extinguishing the flames of the Evil One before they could spread, and through them humbling and pulling down every lofty barrier raised against the knowledge of God.[2] Consequently, neither Simon nor any of his contemporaries managed to form an organized body in those apostolic days, for every attempt was defeated and overpowered by the light of the truth and by the divine Word Himself who had so recently shone from God on men, active in the world and immanent in His own apostles.

The impostor of whom we have been speaking, as though his mind's eye had been struck by a divine miraculous flash of light

1. A reminiscence of 2 Tim. iii. 6.   2. 2 Cor. x. 5.

when earlier, in Judaea, his mischievous practices had been exposed by the apostle Peter,[1] promptly undertook a very long journey overseas from east to west, and fled precipitately, thinking that only so could he live according to his inclinations. He arrived in Rome, where he was greatly helped by the power that awaited its opportunity there, and in a short time his efforts met with such success that the citizens actually set up a statue of him and honoured him as a god. However, this success of his was short-lived. Close on his heels, in the same reign of Claudius, the all-gracious and kindly providence of the universe brought to Rome to deal with this terrible threat to the world, the strong and great apostle, chosen for his merits to be spokesman for all the others, Peter himself. Clad in the divine armour,[2] like a noble captain of God, he brought the precious merchandise of the spiritual light from the East to those in the West, preaching the good news of light itself and the soul-saving word, the proclamation of the Kingdom of Heaven.   15. Thus, when the divine word had made its home among them, Simon's power was extinguished and destroyed at once with the man himself.

So brightly shone the light of true religion on the minds of Peter's hearers that, not satisfied with a single hearing or with the oral teaching of the divine message, they resorted to appeals of every kind to induce Mark (whose gospel we have), as he was a follower of Peter, to leave them in writing a summary of the instruction they had received by word of mouth, nor did they let him go till they had persuaded him, and thus became responsible for the writing of what is known as the Gospel according to Mark. It is said that, on learning by revelation of the spirit what had happened, the apostle was delighted at their enthusiasm and authorized the reading of the book in the churches. Clement quotes the story in *Outlines* Book VI, and his statement is confirmed by Bishop Papias of Hierapolis, who also points out that Mark is mentioned by Peter in his first epistle, which he is said to have composed in Rome itself, as he himself indicates when he speaks of the city figuratively as Babylon:

---

1. Acts viii. 18–23.   2. A loose reference to Eph. vi. 11.

The church in Babylon, chosen like yourselves, sends you greeting, and so does my son Mark.[1]

16. Mark is said to have been the first man to set out for Egypt and preach there the gospel which he had himself written down, and the first to establish churches in Alexandria itself. So large was the body of believers, men and women alike, built up there at the first attempt, with an extremely severe rule of life, that Philo decided that he must record in writing their activities, gatherings, meals, and everything else about their way of living.

Philo's account of the Egyptian ascetics

17. It is also recorded that under Claudius Philo came to Rome to have conversations with Peter, then preaching to the people there. This would not be improbable, as the short work to which I am referring, and which he produced at a considerably later date, clearly contains the rules of the Church still observed in our own day. And again, when he describes the life of our ascetics with the greatest precision, it is plain enough that he not only knew but welcomed with whole-hearted approval the apostolic men of his day, who it seems were of Hebrew stock and therefore, in the Jewish manner, still retained most of their ancient customs. In the work that he entitled *The Contemplative Life, or The Suppliants*, he first assures us that he will add nothing that goes beyond the truth, nothing of his own invention, to the account he is about to give. Then he says that they are called *Therapeutae* and their womenfolk *Therapeutrides*, and goes on to explain this title. It was conferred either because like doctors they rid the souls of those who come to them from moral sickness and so cure and heal[2] them, or in view of their pure and sincere service[3] and worship of God. Whether he invented this designation and applied it to them, fitting a suitable name to their mode of life, or whether they were actually called this from the very start, because the title Christian was not yet in general use, need not be discussed now.

1. 1 Peter v. 13.   2. Greek *therapeuo*.   3. Greek *therapeia*.

This much is certain. He lays special emphasis on their renunciation of property, saying that when they embark on the philosophic life they hand over their possessions to their relations, then, having renounced all worldly interests, they go outside the walls and make their homes on lonely farms and plantations well aware that association with men of different ideas is unprofitable and harmful. That, apparently, was the practice of the Christians of that time, who with eager and ardent faith disciplined themselves to emulate the prophetic way of life. Similarly, in the canonical Acts of the Apostles it is stated that all the disciples of the apostles sold their possessions and belongings and shared them out among the others in accordance with individual needs, so that no one was in want among them; all who were owners of land or houses, Scripture tells us, sold them and brought the price they fetched and laid it at the apostles' feet, so that it was distributed to everyone in accordance with individual needs.[1] Having testified to practices very similar to these, Philo goes on:

The community is to be found in many parts of the world, for it was right that what is perfectly good should be shared by both Greek and foreign lands. It is very strong in Egypt in each of the *nomes*, and especially in the Alexandrian area. The best men in each region set out as colonists for a highly suitable spot, regarding it as the homeland of the *Therapeutae*. It is situated above Lake Mareotis[2] on a low hill, very convenient in view of its security and the mildness of the climate.

Next, after describing the character of their dwellings, he has this to say about the churches in the area:

In every house there is a holy chamber called a sanctuary or 'monastery', where they celebrate in seclusion[3] the mysteries of the sanctified life, bringing in nothing – drink, food, or anything else required for bodily needs – but laws and inspired oracles spoken by prophets, hymns, and everything else by which knowledge and true religion are increased and perfected ... The whole period from dawn to dusk is given up to spiritual discipline.[4] They read the sacred scriptures, and study their

---

1. Loosely quoted from Acts iv. 34–5.
2. Lake Mariut, adjoining Alexandria on the south.
3. 'Monastery' means a place of seclusion.
4. The word from which 'ascetic' is derived.

ancestral wisdom philosophically, allegorizing it, since they regard the literal sense as symbolic of a hidden reality revealed in figures. They possess also short works by early writers, the founders of their sect, who left many specimens of the allegorical method, which they take as their models, following the system on which their predecessors worked.

It seems likely that Philo wrote this after listening to their exposition of the Holy Scriptures, and it is very probable that what he calls short works by their early writers were the gospels, the apostolic writings, and in all probability passages interpreting the old prophets, such as are contained in the Epistle to the Hebrews and several others of Paul's epistles. He then goes on to write this about their composing new psalms:

Thus they not only practise contemplation but also compose songs and hymns to God in all kinds of metres and melodies, setting them, as might be expected, to solemn measures.

A great many other points relevant to our subject are discussed in the same book, but it seemed necessary to pick out those in which the characteristics of Church life are displayed. If anyone does not agree that what has been described is peculiar to the gospel way of life but thinks it applicable to other people too, he will surely be convinced by Philo's next paragraph, in which, if he is reasonable, he will find the evidence on this point beyond dispute:

Having first laid down self-control as a foundation for the soul, they build the other virtues on it. None of them would take food or drink before sundown, as they hold that philosophy deserves daylight but darkness is good enough for bodily needs. So to the one they assign the day, to the others a small part of the night. Some think of food only once in three days – those in whom a greater passion for knowledge is rooted; others so delight and luxuriate as they feast on the wisdom that richly and ungrudgingly supplies their doctrines that they hold out even for twice that time, and scarcely taste necessary food once in six days, having accustomed themselves to this.

These statements of Philo seem to me to refer plainly and

unquestionably to members of our Church. But, if after this someone insists on denying it, he will surely abandon his scepticism and be convinced by still clearer evidences which cannot be found anywhere but in the religious practices of Christians who follow the gospel. For Philo states that among the people in question there are women also, most of them elderly spinsters

who have remained single, not of necessity, like some priestesses of pagan cults, but of their own free will, through their passionate craving for wisdom, with which they were so eager to live that they scorned bodily pleasures, and set their hearts not on mortal children but on immortal, which only the soul that loves God can bring into the world.

A little farther on he adds this, in his vivid way:

Their explanations of the sacred scriptures are expressed figuratively in allegories. For the whole Law seems to them to resemble a living being, which for body has the literal precepts, for soul the meaning that is hidden in the words out of sight. This community was the first to make such meaning the object of special investigation, the words providing a mirror in which thoughts of extraordinary beauty are revealed.

Need I add to this an account of their meetings, or of the segregation of men and women living in the same place, or of the regular spiritual discipline still practised among us, especially during the commemoration of our Saviour's Passion, when it is our habit to abstain from food, spend whole nights in prayer, and devote ourselves to the word of God? All this is described, in precise accordance with the practice observed by us and us alone to this day, in Philo's own writings. He describes the all-night vigils of the great festival, the spiritual discipline in which they are spent, the hymns that we always recite, and how while one man sings in regular rhythm the others listen silently and join in singing the refrains of the hymns; how on the appointed days they lie on straw mattresses on the ground and – as he expressly writes – absolutely refuse to touch wine or any flesh food, drinking nothing but water and seasoning their bread with salt and hyssop. He further writes about the comparative status of those entrusted with the ministries of the Church, from the diaconate to the highest and most important office, the episcopate. Anyone who is anxious to gain precise knowledge of these things can learn them from Philo's account: anyone can see that when he wrote it he had in mind the first preachers of the gospel teaching and the customs handed down by the apostles from the beginning.

Philo's extant works

18. A copious writer and a thinker of wide range, studying Holy Writ from a lofty and elevated viewpoint, Philo expounded the sacred books from many different angles. At one stage he carried out his detailed examination of Genesis in systematic order, in the books which he entitled *Allegories of the Sacred Laws*. At another he carefully arranged under chapter headings the difficulties in the Scriptures, stating them and offering his solutions in the books to which he gave the titles of *Questions and Answers in Genesis* and *Questions and Answers in Exodus*. In addition to these, there are authoritative works by him on special problems, e.g. two on *Farming*, two on *Drunkenness*, and others with various appropriate titles such as *What the Sober Mind Desires and Detests*; *The Confounding of Tongues*; *Flight and Discovery*; *Study Groups*; *Who Inherits the Treasures of God?* or *The Division into Equivalents and Opposites*; and again, *The Three Cardinal Virtues Propounded by Moses*. In addition to these, there is his *New Names and Why They were Given*, in which he states that he also composed *Covenants* Books I and II. There are also works of his on *Emigration*; *Life of a Wise Man Perfected in Righteousness, or Unwritten Laws*; *Giants, or The Immutability of the Godhead*; and *The Mosaic Conviction that Dreams are Sent from God*, Books I–V.

These are the books that have come into my hands dealing with Genesis. On Exodus I am acquainted with *Questions and Answers* Books I–V; *The Tabernacle*; *The Ten Commandments*; *Laws Classified under the Appropriate Headings of the Decalogue* Books I–IV; *Sacrificial Animals and Varieties of Sacrifice*; and *How the Law Rewards Virtue and Punishes and Denounces Vice*. His extant writings also include single volumes, e.g. *The Statesman*; the essay on *Providence*; and another work, *The Jews*; also *Alexander, or Rational Behaviour in Irrational Animals*. Nor must we forget *Every Bad Man is a Slave*, followed by *Every Good Man is Free*. Then came *The Contemplative Life, or Suppliants*, from which I have quoted passages describing life in the apostolic community. *Interpretations of Hebrew Names in the Law and the Prophets* is also said to be his work.

In Gaius' time he came to Rome and wrote an account of that monarch's revolting conduct, with characteristic irony entitling it *Virtue*. It is stated that when Claudius came to the throne Philo read this work from end to end at a full meeting of the Roman senate, and that his writings were so greatly admired that they were honoured with a place in libraries.

At this time, while Paul was completing his journey from Jerusalem by a roundabout route as far as Illyricum,[1] Claudius expelled the Jews from Rome, and Aquila and Priscilla with the other Jews left Rome and sailed to Asia Minor, where they stayed with Paul the Apostle, who was busy strengthening the foundations of the churches, foundations laid by himself not long before. Our source of information is the inspired narrative of the Acts.[2]

Disaster in Jerusalem at the Passover, and events there in Nero's reign

19. While Claudius was still on the throne, during the Passover Feast so riotous a tumult broke out in Jerusalem that of those Jews alone who were forcibly crushed together round the temple exits 30,000 trampled each other to death.[3] Thus the Feast ended in distress to the whole nation and bereavement to every household. Josephus goes on to say that Claudius made Agrippa the son of Agrippa king of the Jews, and sent Felix as procurator of the whole country, including Samaria, Galilee, and the district known as Peraea in addition. He himself, having ruled the empire for thirteen years and eight months, died, leaving his throne to Nero.[4]

20. In Nero's reign, when Felix was procurator of Judaea, Josephus

1. Rom. xv. 9; see also Acts xx. 2.
2. See Acts xviii. 2, 18–19, 23; xix. 1–7.
3. Loosely quoted from *Jewish War*, p. 144.
4. Loosely quoted from *Jewish War*, p. 146.

relates the quarrel between the priests, writing as follows in *Antiquities* Book XX:

A quarrel broke out between the chief priests on the one side and the priests and leaders of the Jerusalem populace on the other. Each of them recruited a band of the most reckless revolutionaries and put himself at their head, and when collisions occurred they greeted each other with abuse and stone-throwing. There was not a single person to reprimand them; the scandal went on with impunity, as though in a city without a government. Such impudence and audacity possessed the chief priests that they actually sent slaves to the threshing-floors to seize the tithes that were the priests' by right, so that destitute priests could be seen perishing of want. So completely was justice obliterated by the violence of the warring parties.[1]

Josephus also records that at the same period a type of bandits sprang up in Jerusalem. These, he says, in broad daylight and in the middle of the city murdered those who met them. Their favourite trick was to mingle with festival crowds, concealing under their garments small daggers with which they stabbed their opponents. When their victims fell the assassins melted into the indignant crowd, and through their plausibility entirely defied detection. First to have his throat cut by them was Jonathan the high priest, and after him many were murdered every day. More terrible than the crimes themselves was the fear they aroused, every man, as in war, hourly expecting death.[2]

21. A little later he goes on:

A greater blow than this was inflicted on the Jews by the Egyptian false prophet. Arriving in the country this man, a fraud who posed as a seer, collected about 30,000 dupes, led them round by the wild country to the Mount of Olives, and from there was ready to force an entry into Jerusalem, overwhelm the Roman garrison, and seize supreme power, with his fellow-raiders as bodyguard. But Felix anticipated his attempt by meeting him with the Roman heavy infantry, the whole population rallying to the defence, so that when the clash occurred the Egyptian fled with a handful of men and most of his followers were killed or captured.[3]

1. *Antiquities* XX, viii, 8.   2. *Jewish War*, p. 147.   3. *Jewish War*, p. 147.

This passage comes from Book II of the *Histories*. It is worth while to note what is stated about the Egyptian there and in the Acts of the Apostles, where in the time of Felix the military tribune at Jerusalem said to Paul, when the Jewish mob was rioting against him: 'Then you're not the Egyptian who a little while back started a revolt and led the 4,000 *sicarii* out in the wilds?' [1]

Paul sent as a prisoner to Rome and there acquitted

22. As successor to Felix, Nero sent Festus. It was in his time that Paul was put on trial, and then conveyed in fetters to Rome. [2] With him went Aristarchus, to whom somewhere in the epistles he naturally refers as a fellow-prisoner. [3] And Luke, who committed to writing the Acts of the Apostles, ended his story at this point, after informing us that Paul spent two complete years at Rome under no restraint and preached the word of God without hindrance. There is evidence that, having then been brought to trial, the apostle again set out on the ministry of preaching, and having appeared a second time in the same city found fulfilment in his martyrdom. In the course of this imprisonment he composed the second Epistle to Timothy, referring both to his earlier trial and to his impending fulfilment. Listen to his testimony on this point:

At my first trial nobody supported me: they all left me to my fate – may God forgive them! But the Lord stood by me and gave me strength, that through me the message might be fully proclaimed in the hearing of the whole pagan world. Thus I was rescued out of the lion's mouth. [4]

This passage proves beyond question that on the first occasion, in order that the message proclaimed through him might be fully preached, he was rescued out of the lion's mouth, the reference being apparently to Nero, because of his bestial cruelty. He does not go on to add anything like 'he *will* rescue me out of the lion's mouth', for he saw by the Spirit that his death was imminent. And so after the words 'and I was rescued out of the lion's mouth' he

1. Acts xxi. 38.   2. See Acts xxiv. 27 to xxv. 27.   3. Col. iv. 10.
4. 2 Tim. iv. 18.

goes on to say 'The Lord will rescue me from every evil attempt and keep me safe for His heavenly kingdom',[1] indicating his forthcoming martyrdom. This he foretells more clearly still in the same letter, when he says: 'For I am already being offered as a sacrifice, and the time for my departure has come.'[2] In this second Epistle to Timothy he remarks that only Luke is with him as he writes, and at his first trial not even he: presumably that is why Luke concluded the Acts of the Apostles at that point, having traced the course of events throughout the time he was with Paul. I have said this to show that it was not during the stay in Rome described by Luke that Paul's martyrdom was accomplished. The probability is that since at first Nero's disposition was milder, it was easier for Paul's defence of the Faith to be received, but that when he had gone on to commit abominable crimes, above all else he launched his attack on the apostles.

The martyrdom of James 'the Lord's brother'

23. When Paul appealed to Caesar and was sent to Rome by Festus, the Jews were disappointed of the hope in which they had devised their plot against him and turned their attention to James the Lord's brother, who had been elected by the apostles to the episcopal throne at Jerusalem. This is the crime that they committed against him. They brought him into their midst and in the presence of the whole populace demanded a denial of his belief in Christ. But when, contrary to all expectation, he spoke as he liked and showed undreamt-of fearlessness in the face of the enormous throng, declaring that our Saviour and Lord, Jesus, was the Son of God, they could not endure his testimony any longer, since he was universally regarded as the most righteous of men because of the heights of philosophy and religion which he scaled in his life. So they killed him, seizing the opportunity for getting their own way provided by the absence of a government, for at that very time Festus had died in Judaea, leaving the province without governor or procurator. How James died has already been shown by the words quoted from Clement, who tells us that he was

1. 2 Tim. iv. 16–17.   2. 2 Tim. iv. 6.

thrown from the parapet and clubbed to death. But the most
detailed account of him is given by Hegesippus, who belonged
to the first generation after the apostles. In his fifth book he
writes:

Control of the Church passed to the apostles, together with the Lord's
brother James, whom everyone from the Lord's time till our own has
called the Righteous, for there were many Jameses, but this one was holy
from his birth; he drank no wine or intoxicating liquor and ate no animal
food; no razor came near his head;[1] he did not smear himself with oil,
and took no baths. He alone was permitted to enter the Holy Place, for
his garments were not of wool but of linen. He used to enter the
Sanctuary alone, and was often found on his knees beseeching forgiveness
for the people, so that his knees grew hard like a camel's from his
continually bending them in worship of God and beseeching forgiveness
for the people. Because of his unsurpassable righteousness he was called
the Righteous and *Oblias*[2] – in our own language 'Bulwark of the
People, and Righteousness' – fulfilling the declarations of the prophets
regarding him.[3]

Representatives of the seven popular sects already described by me
asked him what was meant by 'the door of Jesus', and he replied that
Jesus was the Saviour.[4] Some of them came to believe that Jesus was
the Christ: the sects mentioned above did not believe either in a resurrection or in One who is coming to give every man what his deeds
deserve,[5] but those who did come to believe did so because of James.
Since therefore many even of the ruling class believed,[6] there was an
uproar among the Jews and Scribes and Pharisees, who said there was a
danger that the entire people would expect Jesus as the Christ. So they
collected and said to James: 'Be good enough to restrain the people,
for they have gone astray after Jesus in the belief that he is the Christ.
Be good enough to make the facts about Jesus clear to all who come
for the Passover Day. We all accept what you say: we can vouch for
it, and so can all the people, that you are a righteous man and take no
one at his face value. So make it clear to the crowd that they must not
go astray as regards Jesus: the whole people and all of us accept what
you say. So take your stand on the Temple parapet, so that from that
height you may be easily seen, and your words audible to the whole

1. See Num. iv. 1–5, where the Nazirite rules are laid down; see also Luke i. 15.
2. A Hebrew or Aramaic word, as yet unexplained.
3. Reference unknown.   4. John x. 9.   5. Rev. xxii. 12.   6. John xii. 42.

people. For because of the Passover all the tribes have forgathered, and the Gentiles too.'

So the Scribes and Pharisees made James stand on the Sanctuary parapet and shouted to him: 'Righteous one, whose word we are all obliged to accept, the people are going astray after Jesus who was crucified; so tell us what is meant by "the door of Jesus".' He replied as loudly as he could: 'Why do you question me about the Son of Man? I tell you, He is sitting in heaven at the right hand of the Great Power, and He will come on the clouds of heaven.'[1] Many were convinced, and gloried in James's testimony, crying: 'Hosanna to the Son of David!' Then again the Scribes and Pharisees said to each other: 'We made a bad mistake in affording such testimony to Jesus. We had better go up and throw him down, so that they will be frightened and not believe him.' 'Ho, ho!' they called out, 'even the Righteous one has gone astray!' – fulfilling the prophecy of Isaiah:

> Let us remove the Righteous one, for he is unprofitable to us.
> Therefore they shall eat the fruit of their works,[2]

So they went up and threw down the Righteous one. Then they said to each other 'Let us stone James the Righteous', and began to stone him, as in spite of his fall he was still alive. But he turned and knelt, uttering the words: 'I beseech Thee, Lord God and Father, forgive them; they do not know what they are doing.'[3] While they pelted him with stones, one of the descendants of Rechab the son of Rachabim – the priestly family to which Jeremiah the Prophet bore witness,[4] called out: 'Stop! what are you doing? the Righteous one is praying for you.' Then one of them, a fuller, took the club which he used to beat out the clothes, and brought it down on the head of the Righteous one. Such was his martyrdom. He was buried on the spot, by the Sanctuary, and his headstone is still there by the Sanctuary. He has proved a true witness to Jews and Gentiles alike that Jesus is the Christ.

Immediately after this Vespasian began to besiege them.

This is the full account which, in agreement with Clement, is given by Hegesippus. So remarkable a person must James have been, so universally esteemed for righteousness, that even the more intelligent Jews felt that this was why his martyrdom was

---

1. Matt. xxvi. 64; Acts vii. 56.   2. Is. iii. 10 (LXX).   3. Luke xxiii. 34.
4. Jer. xxxv.

immediately followed by the siege of Jerusalem, which happened to them for no other reason than the wicked crime of which he had been the victim. And indeed Josephus did not hesitate to write this down in so many words:

> These things happened to the Jews in requital for James the Righteous, who was a brother of Jesus known as Christ, for though he was the most righteous of men, the Jews put him to death.

Josephus has also recounted his death in *Antiquities* Book XX:

> Caesar sent Albinus to Judaea as procurator, when he was informed of the death of Festus. But the younger Ananus, who as I said had received the high priesthood, was headstrong in character and audacious in the extreme. He belonged to the sect of the Sadducees, who in judging offenders are cruel beyond any of the Jews, as I have already made clear. Being a man of this kind, Ananus thought that he had a convenient opportunity, as Festus was dead and Albinus still on the way. So he assembled a council of judges and brought before it James, the brother of Jesus, known as Christ, and several others, on a charge of breaking the law, and handed them over to be stoned. But those who were considered the most fair-minded people in the City, and strict in their observance of the Law, were most indignant at this, and sent secretly to the king imploring him to write to Ananus to stop behaving in this way: his conduct had been wrong from the first. Some of them, too, waylaid Albinus on the road from Alexandria, and explained that it was illegal for Ananus to assemble a council without his authority. Convinced by their arguments, Albinus wrote an angry letter to Ananus, threatening to punish him; in consequence King Agrippa deprived him of the high priesthood, which he had held for three months only, and appointed Jeshua son of Dammaeus.[1]

Such is the story of James, to whom is attributed the first of the 'general' epistles. Admittedly its authenticity is doubted, since few early writers refer to it, any more than to 'Jude's', which is also one of the seven called general. But the fact remains that these two, like the others, have been regularly used in very many churches.

1. *Antiquities* XX, ix. 1.

Annianus bishop of Alexandria

24. In the eighth year of Nero's reign Annianus was the first after Mark the evangelist to take charge of the see of Alexandria.

The Neronian persecution, in which Paul and Peter died

25. When Nero's power was now firmly established he gave himself up to unholy practices and took up arms against the God of the universe. To describe the monster of depravity that he became lies outside the scope of the present work. Many writers have recorded the facts about him in minute detail, enabling anyone who wishes to get a complete picture of his perverse and extraordinary madness, which led him to the senseless destruction of innumerable lives, and drove him in the end to such a lust for blood that he did not spare even his nearest and dearest but employed a variety of methods to do away with mother, brothers, and wife alike, to say nothing of countless other members of his family, as if they were personal and public enemies. All this left one crime still to be added to his account – he was the first of the emperors to be the declared enemy of the worship of Almighty God. To this the Roman Tertullian refers in the following terms:

Study your records: there you will find that Nero was the first to persecute this teaching when, after subjugating the entire East, in Rome especially he treated everyone with savagery. That such a man was author of our chastisement fills us with pride. For anyone who knows him can understand that anything not supremely good would never have been condemned by Nero.[1]

So it came about that this man, the first to be heralded as a conspicuous fighter against God, was led on to murder the apostles. It is recorded that in his reign Paul was beheaded in Rome itself, and that Peter likewise was crucified, and the record is confirmed by the fact that the cemeteries there are still called by the names of Peter and Paul, and equally so by a churchman named Gaius, who was living while Zephyrinus was Bishop of Rome. In his published

1. *Defence*, 5.

Dialogue with Proclus, the leader of the Phrygian heretics, Gaius has this to say about the places where the mortal remains of the two apostles have been reverently laid:

I can point out the monuments of the victorious apostles. If you will go as far as the Vatican or the Ostian Way, you will find the monuments of those who founded this church.

That they were both martyred at the same time Bishop Dionysius of Corinth informs us in a letter written to the Romans:

In this way by your impressive admonition you have bound together all that has grown from the seed which Peter and Paul sowed in Romans and Corinthians alike. For both of them sowed in our Corinth[1] and taught us jointly: in Italy too they taught jointly in the same city, and were martyred at the same time.

These evidences make the truth of my account still more certain.

Beginning of the last Jewish war against Rome

26. In the course of his very long account of the catastrophe that overwhelmed the entire Jewish nation Josephus expressly states that, in addition to very many others, innumerable Jews in high positions were flogged with scourges and crucified in Jerusalem itself by Florus,[2] and that he was procurator of Judaea at the time when the beginning of the war blazed up in the twelfth year of Nero's reign.[3] Then he says that throughout Palestine the revolt of the Jews was followed by hopeless confusion, and that on every side the members of the nation were mercilessly destroyed, as if they were enemies, by the inhabitants of the various cities:

The cities could be seen full of unburied corpses, the dead bodies of the aged flung down alongside those of infants, women without a rag to conceal their nakedness, and the whole province full of indescribable

1. I Cor. i. 12.
2. *Jewish War*, p. 152.
3. *Jewish War*, p. 150.

horrors. Even worse than the atrocities continually committed were the threats of terrors to come.[1]

Such is the account of Josephus, and such was the plight of the Jews.

1. *Jewish War*, p. 169.

Book 3

VESPASIAN TO TRAJAN: THE DISTRIBUTION AND
WRITINGS OF THE APOSTLES AND THEIR
SUCCESSORS: ENEMIES WITHIN THE
CHURCH: PERSECUTIONS

*Countries evangelized by the apostles: the first Bishop of Rome:
apostolic epistles: the apostles' first successors*

1. Such then was the plight of the Jews. Meanwhile the holy
apostles and disciples of our Saviour were scattered over the whole
world. Thomas, tradition tells us, was chosen for Parthia, Andrew
for Scythia, John for Asia, where he remained till his death at
Ephesus. Peter seems to have preached in Pontus, Galatia and
Bithynia, Cappadocia and Asia, to the Jews of the Dispersion.[1]
Finally, he came to Rome where he was crucified, head down-
wards at his own request. What need be said of Paul, who from
Jerusalem as far as Illyricum preached in all its fullness the gospel of
Christ,[2] and later was martyred in Rome under Nero? This is
exactly what Origen tells us in Volume III of his *Commentary on
Genesis*.

2. After the martyrdom of Paul and Peter the first man to be
appointed Bishop of Rome was Linus. He is mentioned by Paul
when writing to Timothy from Rome, in the salutation at the end
of epistle.[3]

3. Of Peter one epistle, known as his first, is accepted, and this the
early fathers quoted freely, as undoubtedly genuine, in their own
writings. But the second Petrine epistle we have been taught to
regard as uncanonical; many, however, have thought it valuable
and have honoured it with a place among the other Scriptures. On

1. Cf. 1 Peter i. 1.   2. Romans xv. 19.   3. 2 Tim. iv. 21.

the other hand, in the case of the 'Acta' attributed to him, the 'Gospel' that bears his name, the 'Preaching' called his, and the so-called 'Revelation', we have no reason at all to include these among the traditional Catholic Scriptures, for neither in early days nor in our own has any Church writer made use of their testimony. In the course of my narrative I shall take care to indicate in each period which of the Church writers of the time used the various disputed books; their comments on the canonical and recognized Scriptures; and their remarks about the other sort.

These then are the works attributed to Peter, of which I have recognized only one epistle as authentic and accepted by the early fathers. Paul on the other hand was obviously and unmistakably the author of the fourteen epistles, but we must not shut our eyes to the fact that some authorities have rejected the Epistle to the Hebrews, pointing out that the Roman Church denies that it is the work of Paul: what our predecessors have said about it I will quote at the proper time. As for the 'Acts' attributed to him, no one has ever suggested to me that they are genuine.

As the same apostle, in the salutations that conclude the Epistle to the Romans, has referred among others to Hermas, the reputed author of the 'Shepherd', it is to be noted that this, too, has been rejected by some authorities and therefore cannot be placed among the accepted books. Others, however, have judged it indispensable, especially to those in need of elementary instruction. Hence we know that it has been used before now in public worship, and some of the earliest writers made use of it, as I have discovered.

4. That by his preaching to the Gentiles Paul had laid the foundations of the churches from Jerusalem by a roundabout route as far as Illyricum is obvious from his own words and from Luke's account in the Acts. Similarly, from Peter's language we can gather the names of the provinces in which he preached the gospel of Christ to the circumcised, proclaiming the message of the New Covenant. It is clearly stated in the epistle which, as I said, is accepted as his, in which he writes to the Hebrews of the Dispersion in Pontus and Galatia, Cappadocia, Asia, and Bithynia. But how

many of them and which ones became genuine enthusiasts, and were judged fit to shepherd the churches founded by the apostles, is not easy to determine, except for those who names can be extracted from the statements of Paul. For he had innumerable fellow-workers or – as he himself called them – fellow-soldiers.[1] Most of these he has honoured with an imperishable memory, paying them constant tribute in his own letters. Again Luke in the Acts, in listing Paul's disciples, mentions them by name. We may instance Timothy, stated to have been the first bishop appointed to the see of Ephesus, as was Titus to the churches of Crete.

Luke, by birth an Antiochene and by profession a physician, was for long periods a companion of Paul and was closely associated with the other apostles as well. So he has left us examples of the art of healing souls which he learnt from them in two divinely inspired books, the Gospel and the Acts of the Apostles. The former, he declares, he wrote in accordance with the information he received from those who from the first had been eye-witnesses and ministers of the word, information which, he adds, he had followed in its entirety from the first.[2] The latter he composed not this time from hearsay but from the evidence of his own eyes. It is actually suggested that Paul was in the habit of referring to Luke's gospel whenever he said, as if writing of some Gospel of his own: 'According to my gospel.'[3]

Of his other followers, Paul informs us that Crescens had set out for Gaul.[4] Linus, who is mentioned in the Second Epistle to Timothy as being with Paul in Rome, as stated above was the first after Peter to be appointed Bishop of Rome. Clement again, who became the third Bishop of Rome, was, as the Apostle himself testifies, Paul's fellow-worker and fellow-combatant.[5] Besides these there was the Areopagite, Dionysius by name, who was, as Luke related in the Acts, the first convert after Paul's address to the Athenians in the Areopagus.[6] He became the first Bishop of Athens, a fact recorded by a very early writer, another Dionysius, pastor of the see of Corinth. As we go on our way I shall take the

1. Phil. ii. 25, Philem. 2.   2. Luke i. 2–3.   3. Rom. ii. 16, xvi. 25; 2 Tim. ii. 8.
4. 2 Tim. iv. 10.   5. Phil. iv. 3.   6. Acts xvii. 34.

opportunity to set out the details of the chronological sequence from the apostles. For the moment I had better proceed to the next stage in the story.

The final siege of the Jews after Christ: the crushing weight of famine

5. When Nero had been master of the empire for thirteen years, the business of Galba and Otho occupied a year and a half; and then Vespasian, after his dazzling success in the campaigns against the Jews, was proclaimed emperor while still in Judaea, after being hailed as *Imperator* by the armies there. He at once set out for Rome, entrusting the war against the Jews to his son Titus.

After the Ascension of our Saviour, the Jews had followed up their crime against Him by devising plot after plot against His disciples. First they stoned Stephen to death; then James the son of Zebedee and brother of John was beheaded; and finally James, the first after our Saviour's Ascension to be raised to the bishop's throne there, lost his life in the way described, while the remaining apostles, in constant danger from murderous plots, were driven out of Judaea. But to teach their message they travelled into every land in the power of Christ, who had said to them: 'Go and make disciples of all the nations in my name.'[1] Furthermore, the members of the Jersusalem church, by means of an oracle given by revelation to acceptable persons there, were ordered to leave the City before the war began and settle in a town in Peraea called Pella. To Pella those who believed in Christ migrated from Jerusalem; and as if holy men had utterly abandoned the royal metropolis of the Jews and the entire Jewish land, the judgement of God at last overtook them for their abominable crimes against Christ and His apostles, completely blotting out that wicked generation from among men.

The calamities which at that time overwhelmed the whole nation in every part of the world; the process by which the inhabitants of Judaea were driven to the limits of disaster; the thousands and thousands of men of every age who together with

1. Matt. xxviii. 19.

women and children perished by the sword, by starvation, and by countless other forms of death; the number of Jewish cities besieged and the horrors they endured – especially the terrible and worse than terrible sights that met the eyes of those who sought refuge in Jerusalem itself as an impregnable fortress; the character of the whole war and the detailed events at all its stages; the last scene of all when the Abomination of Desolation announced by the prophets was set up in the very Temple of God, once world-renowned, when it underwent utter destruction and final dissolution by fire – all this anyone who wishes can gather in precise detail from the pages of Josephus' history.[1] I must draw particular attention to his statement that the people who flocked together from all Judaea at the time of the Passover Feast and – to use his own words – were shut up in Jerusalem as if in a prison, totalled nearly three million.[2] It was indeed proper that in the very week in which they had brought the Saviour and Benefactor of mankind, God's Christ, to His Passion, they should be shut up as if in a prison and suffer the destruction that came upon them by the judgement of God.

Passing over the details of the successive disasters that befell them from the sword and in other ways, I think it necessary to mention only the miseries they suffered from starvation, so that readers of this book may have some knowledge at least of how their crime against the Christ of God a very little time later brought on them God's vengeance.

6. Come then, pick up once more Book V of Josephus' *Histories*, and go through the tragic story of what then happened.

For the wealthy it was just as dangerous to stay in the city as to leave it, for on the pretext that he was a deserter many a man was killed for the sake of his money. As the famine grew worse, the frenzy of the partisans increased with it, and every day these two terrors strengthened their grip. For as nowhere was there corn to be seen, men broke into the houses and ransacked them. If they found some, they maltreated the occupants for

---

1. *Jewish War*, pp. 355–60.   2. *Jewish War*, p. 371f.

saying there was none; if they did not, they suspected them of having hidden it more carefully, and tortured them. Proof that they had or had not food was provided by the appearance of the unhappy wretches. If they still had flesh on their bones, they were deemed to have plenty of stores; if they were already reduced to skeletons they were passed over, for it seemed pointless to dispatch those who were certain to die of starvation before long. Many secretly exchanged their possessions for a measure of corn – wheat if they happened to be rich, barley if they were poor. Then they shut themselves up in the darkest corners of their houses, where some through extreme hunger ate their grain as it was, and others made bread, necessity and fear being the only guides. Nowhere was a table laid – they snatched the food from the fire while still uncooked, and ate like wolves.

The sight of such misery would have brought tears to the eyes, for while the strong had more than enough, the weak were in desperate straits. All human feelings, alas, yield to hunger, of which decency is always the first victim; for when hunger reigns, restraint is abandoned. Thus it was that wives robbed their husbands, children their fathers, and – most horrible of all – mothers their babes, snatching the food out of their very mouths; and when their dearest ones were dying in their arms, they did not hesitate to deprive them of the morsels that might have kept them alive. This way of satisfying their hunger did not go unnoticed: everywhere the partisans were ready to swoop even on such pickings. Wherever they saw a locked door, they concluded that those within were having a meal, and instantly bursting the door open, they rushed in and hardly stopped short of squeezing their throats to force out the morsels of food. They beat old men who held on to their crusts, and tore the hair of women who hid what was in their hands. They showed no pity for grey hairs or helpless babyhood, but picked up the children as they clung to their precious scraps and dashed them on the floor. If anyone anticipated their entry by gulping down what they hoped to seize, they felt themselves defrauded and retaliated with worse savagery still.

Terrible were the methods of torture they devised in their quest for food. They stuffed bitter vetch up the genital passages of their victims, and drove sharp stakes into their seats. Torments horrible even to think about they inflicted on people, to make them admit possession of one loaf or reveal the hiding-place of a single handful of barley. It was not that the tormentors were hungry – their actions would have been less barbarous had they sprung from necessity – but rather they were keeping their passions exercised, and laying in stores for use in the coming days. Again, when men had crawled out in the night as far as the Roman guardposts to collect wild plants and herbs, just when they thought they had got safely away from the enemy lines these marauders met them and snatched their treasures from them. Piteous entreaties and appeals to the awful Name of God could not secure the return of even a fraction of what they had collected at such risk: they were lucky to be only robbed, and not killed as well . . .

The Jews, unable now to leave the city, were deprived of all hope of survival. The famine became more intense, and devoured whole houses and families. The roofs were covered with women and infants too weak to stand, the streets full of old men already dead. Young men and boys, swollen with hunger, haunted the squares like ghosts and fell wherever faintness overcame them. To bury their kinsfolk was beyond the strength of the sick, and those who were fit shirked the task because of the number of the dead and uncertainty about their own fate; for many while burying others fell dead themselves, and many set out for their graves before their hour struck. In their misery no weeping or lamentation was heard; hunger stifled emotion; with dry eyes those who were slow to die watched those whose end came sooner. Deep silence enfolded the city, and a darkness burdened with death. Worse still were the bandits, who broke like tomb-robbers into the houses of the dead and stripped the bodies, snatching off their wrappings, then came out laughing. They tried the points of their swords on the corpses, and even transfixed some of those who lay helpless but still alive, to test the steel. But if any begged for a sword-thrust to end their sufferings, they contemptuously left them to die of hunger. Everyone as he breathed his last fixed his eyes on the Temple, turning his back on the partisans he was leaving alive. The latter at first ordered the dead to be buried at public expense, as they could not bear the stench; later, when this proved impossible, they threw them from the walls into the valleys. When in the course of his rounds Titus saw them choked with dead, and a putrid stream trickling from under the decomposing bodies, he groaned, and uplifting his hands called God to witness that this was not his doing . . .

I cannot refrain from saying what my feelings dictate. I think that if the Romans had delayed their attack on these sacrilegious ruffians, either the ground would have opened and swallowed up the city, or a flood would have overwhelmed it, or lightning would have destroyed it like Sodom. For it produced a generation far more godless than those who perished thus, a generation whose mad folly involved the nation in ruin.[1]

1. *Jewish War*, pp. 323–4, 331, 335.

In Book VI he writes:

In the city famine raged, its victims dropping dead in countless numbers, and the horrors were unspeakable. In every home, if the shadow of something to eat was anywhere detected, war broke out and the best of friends came to grips with each other, snatching away the wretchedest means of support. Not even the dying were believed to be in want; at their last gasp they were searched by the bandits, in case some of them had food inside their clothes and were feigning death. Open-mouthed with hunger like mad dogs, the desperadoes stumbled and staggered along, hammering at the doors like drunken men, and in their helpless state breaking into the same houses two or three times in a single hour. Necessity made them put their teeth in everything; things not even the filthiest of dumb animals would look at, they picked up and brought themselves to swallow. In the end they actually devoured belts and shoes, and stripped off the leather from their shields and chewed it. Some tried to live on scraps of old hay, for there were people who collected the stalks and sold a tiny bunch for four Attic drachmas!

But why should I speak of the inanimate things that hunger made them shameless enough to eat? I am now going to relate a deed for which there is no parallel in the annals of Greece or any other country, a deed horrible to speak of and incredible to hear. For myself I am so anxious that future ages should not suspect me of grotesque inventions that I would gladly have passed over this calamity in silence, had there not been countless witnesses of my own generation to bear me out; and besides, my country would have little reason to thank me if I drew a veil over the miseries that were so real to her.

There was a woman, Mary the daughter of Eleazar, who lived east of Jordan in the village of Bathezor ('House of Hyssop'). She was of good family and very rich, and had fled with the rest of the population to Jerusalem, where she shared in the horrors of the siege. Most of the property that she had packed up and moved from Peraea into the city had been plundered by the party chiefs; the remnants of her treasures, and any food she had managed to obtain, were being carried off in daily raids by their henchmen. The wretched woman was filled with uncontrollable fury, and let loose a stream of abuse and curses that enraged the looters against her. When neither resentment nor pity caused anyone to kill her, and she grew tired of finding food for others – and whichever way she turned it was almost impossible to find – and while hunger was eating her heart out and rage was consuming her still faster, she yielded to the suggestions of fury and necessity, and in defiance of all natural feeling laid hands on her own child, a babe at the breast. 'Poor little mite!' she cried. 'In war, famine, and civil strife, why do I keep you alive? With the Romans there is only slavery, even if we are alive when they come; but famine is forestalling slavery, and the partisans are crueller than either. Come, you must be food for me, to the partisans an avenging spirit, and to the world a tale, the only thing left to fill up the measure of Jewish misery.' As she spoke she killed her son, then roasted him and ate one half, concealing and saving up the rest.

At once the partisans appeared, and sniffing the unholy smell, threatened that if she did not produce what she had prepared they would kill her on the spot. She replied that she had kept a fine helping for them, and uncovered what was left of her child. They, overcome with instant horror and amazement, could not take their eyes off the sight. But she went on: 'This child is my own, and the deed is mine too. Help yourselves: I have had my share. Don't be softer than a woman or more tender-hearted than a mother! But if you are squeamish, and don't approve of my sacrifice – well, I have eaten half, so you may as well leave me the rest.' That was the last straw, and they went away quivering. They had never before shrunk from anything, and did not much like giving up even this food to the mother. From that moment the entire city could think of nothing else but this abomination; everyone saw the tragedy before his own eyes, and shuddered as if the crime was his. The one desire of the starving was for death: how they envied those who had gone before seeing or hearing of these appalling horrors! [1]

Christ's predictions: warnings before the war

7. Such was the reward of the Jews' iniquitous and wicked treat-ment of God's Christ. It is worth while to set alongside it our Saviour's absolutely true prediction, in which He reveals those very things in this prophecy:

Alas for those who have a child unborn or at the breast in those days! Pray that your flight may not take place in winter or on a sabbath. For then there will be great distress, such as there has never been from the beginning of the world till now, and will never be again. [2]

1. *Jewish War*, pp. 352–4.   2. Matt. xxiv. 19–21.

In computing the whole number of those who lost their lives, the historian says that famine and the sword destroyed 1,100,000 persons; that those who had taken part in sedition and terrorism informed against each other after the capture of the city and were put to death; that the tallest and handsomest of the youngsters were kept for the triumphal procession; that of the rest, those over seventeen were put in irons and sent to hard labour in Egypt, and still more were distributed among the provinces to perish in the theatres by sword or by wild beasts, while those under seventeen were carried off captive and sold, the number of these alone reaching 90,000.[1]

These things happened in the second year of Vespasian's reign, in exact accordance with the prophetic predictions of our Lord and Saviour Jesus Christ, who by divine power had foreseen them as though already present, and wept and mourned over them, as we learn from the holy evangelists, who have set down His very words. On one occasion He said, as if to Jerusalem herself:

If only you, even you, had known today the way to your peace! But now it has been hidden from your sight. For a time will come upon you when your enemies will throw up an earthwork round you and encircle you and hem you in on every side, and bring to the ground both you and your children.[2]

On another occasion, with the people in mind, He said:

For there will be great distress in the land, and indignation against this people: they will fall at the point of the sword, and they will be carried into captivity in every heathen land; and Jerusalem will be trampled on by heathen, till the day of the heathen is over.[3]

And again:

When you see Jersualem encircled by armies, then you may be sure that her desolation has drawn near.[4]

Anyone who compared our Saviour's words with the rest of the

---

1. *Jewish War*, p. 371f.   2. Luke xix. 42–4.   3. Luke xxi. 23–4.
4. Luke xxi. 20.

historian's account of the whole war could not fail to be astonished, and to acknowledge as divine and utterly marvellous the foreknowledge revealed by our Saviour's prediction.

After the Saviour's Passion, and the cries with which the Jewish mob clamoured for the reprieve of the bandit and murderer and begged that the Author of Life should be removed from them,[1] disaster befell the entire nation. There is no need to add anything to the historical records. But it would be right to mention, too, certain facts which bring home the beneficence of all-gracious Providence, which for forty years after their crime against Christ delayed their destruction. All that time most of the apostles and disciples, including James himself, the first Bishop of Jerusalem, known as the Lord's brother, were still alive, and by remaining in the city furnished the place with an impregnable bulwark. For the overruling power of God was still patient, in the hope that at last they might repent of their misdeeds and obtain pardon and salvation; and besides this wonderful patience, it granted miraculous warnings from God of what would happen to them if they did not repent. These occurrences were thought worthy of mention by the historian whom I have been quoting, and I cannot do better than make them available to readers of this work.

8. Turn then to Book VI of the *Histories*, and read what he says:

The unhappy people were beguiled at that stage by cheats and false messengers of God, while the unmistakable portents that foreshadowed the coming desolation they treated with indifference and incredulity, disregarding God's warnings as if they were moonstruck, blind, and senseless. First a star stood over the city, very like a broadsword, and a comet that remained a whole year. Then before the revolt and the movement to war, while the people were assembling for the Feast of Unleavened Bread, on the 8th of Xanthicus at three in the morning so bright a light shone round the Altar and the Sanctuary that it might have been midday. This lasted half an hour. The inexperienced took it for a good omen, but the sacred scribes at once gave the true interpretation, before the events. During the same feast a cow brought by the high priest to be sacrificed gave birth to a lamb in the middle of the Temple courts,

---

1. Acts iii. 14–17.

while at midnight it was observed that the east gate of the inner Sanctuary had opened of its own accord – a gate made of bronze, and so solid that every evening twenty strong men were required to shut it, fastened with iron-bound bars and secured by bolts which went down a long way.

A few days after the Feast, on the 21st of Artemisius, a supernatural apparition was seen, too amazing to be believed. What I have to relate would have been dismissed as an invention had it not been vouched for by eyewitnesses and followed by disasters that bore out the signs. Before sunset there were seen in the sky over the whole country chariots and regiments in arms speeding through the clouds and encircling the towns. Again, at the Feast of Pentecost, when the priests had gone into the Temple at night to perform the usual ceremonies, they declared that they were aware, first of a violent movement and a loud crash, then of a concerted cry: 'Let us go hence!'

An incident more alarming still had occurred four years before the war, at a time of exceptional peace and prosperity for the city. One Jesus son of Ananias, a very ordinary yokel, came to the feast at which every Jew is expected to set up a tabernacle for God. As he stood in the Temple he suddenly began to shout: 'A voice from the east, a voice from the west, a voice from the four winds, a voice against Jerusalem and the Sanctuary, a voice against bridegrooms and brides, a voice against the whole people!' Day and night he uttered the cry as he went through the streets. Some of the more prominent citizens, very annoyed at these ominous words, laid hold of the fellow and beat him savagely. Without saying a word in his own defence or for the private information of his persecutors, he persisted in shouting the same warning as before. The Jewish authorities, rightly concluding that some supernatural force was responsible for the man's behaviour, took him before the Roman procurator. There, though scourged till his flesh hung in ribbons, he neither begged for mercy nor shed a tear, but lowering his voice to the most mournful of tones answered every blow with: 'Woe to Jerusalem!' [1]

A still more astonishing story follows a paragraph later, where it is stated that an oracle was found in their sacred writings to the effect that at that time a man from their country would become monarch of the whole world: this oracle the historian himself believed to have been fulfilled in Vespasian.[2] But Vespasian did not reign over the entire world, but only the part under Roman

---

1. *Jewish War*, pp. 360–62.   2. *Jewish War*, p. 362f.

rule: it would be more justly applied to Christ, to whom the Father had said,

> Ask of me, and I will give you the heathen world for your inheritance,
> And for your possession the ends of the earth.[1]

At that very time it was true of His apostles that

> Their speech went out to the whole earth,
> And their words to the ends of the world.[2]

Josephus and the writings that he left: his allusions to the sacred books

9. Besides all this it is well that the origin and ancestry of Josephus himself, who has provided so much material for this present history, should be generally known. He furnishes this information himself:

I, Josephus, son of Matthias, am a priest from Jerusalem; in the early stages I myself fought against the Romans, and of the later events I was an unwilling witness.[3]

Of the Jews at that time he was the most famous, not only among his fellow-countrymen but among the Romans too, so that he was honoured with the erection of a statue in the city of Rome, and the labours of his pen found a place in the Library. He has set out the whole of *Ancient Jewish History*[4] in twenty books, and the story of the Roman war of his own day in seven.[5] The latter work he committed not only to Greek but also to his native language, as he himself testifies[6] – and in view of his general truthfulness, we may accept this. Two other worth-while books of his are extant, entitled *The Antiquity of the Jews*,[7] his reply to Apion the grammarian, who had recently published an attack on the Jews, and to others who had made similar attempts to misrepresent the ancestral customs of the Jewish people. In the first of

---

1. Ps. ii. 8.   2. Ps. xix. 4.   3. *Jewish War*, p. 27.
4. The author's own title; we have unfortunately adopted the Latin substitute *Antiquities*.
5. The author's own title is *The Jewish War*.   6. *Jewish War*, p. 27.
7. Needlessly renamed in Latin *Against Apion*.

these he gives the number of the canonical scriptures forming the Old Testament, as it is called, showing which of them are undisputed among the Hebrews as being backed by ancient tradition:

10. We do not have vast numbers of books, discordant and conflicting, but only twenty-two, containing the record of all time and with reason believed to be divine. Of these five are books of Moses, containing the Laws and the tradition of the origin of mankind up to his death. This period covers nearly 3,000 years. From Moses' death to that of Artaxerxes, who followed Xerxes as King of Persia, the prophets after Moses recorded the events of their own time in thirteen books. The remaining four contain hymns to God and precepts for human conduct. From Artaxerxes to the present day the whole story has been written down, but does not command the same belief as the earlier narrative because there was not an unbroken succession of prophets. It is evident from our actions what is our attitude to our own scriptures; for though so many centuries have gone by, no one has presumed to add, to take away, or alter anything in them, but it is innate in every Jew from the day of his birth to regard them as the ordinances of God, to abide in them, and if need to be die for them gladly.[1]

This quotation from the historian is of obvious value. He produced yet another work of considerable merit, *The Supremacy of Reason*, entitled *Maccabees* by some, because it deals with the struggles of those Hebrews who, as related in the books bearing the same name *Maccabees*, fought so manfully for the worship of Almighty God. And at the end of Book XX of *Antiquities* he announces that he has decided to write a work in four books on the traditional beliefs of the Jews about God and His nature, and about the reasons why the Laws permit certain things and forbid others.[2] Other books, already published, are also referred to in his surviving works.

Finally, it would be appropriate to reproduce the words attached to the end of *Antiquities* and so confirm the testimony of the passages I have borrowed from him. In impugning the historical accuracy of Justus of Tiberias, who had attempted to record the

1. *Against Apion* I, 8.   2. *Antiquities*, last sentence.

events of the same period as himself, after bringing many other charges against him he adds the following:

I had no such apprehensions as yourself with regard to what I myself had written: I submitted the work to the emperors themselves.[1] when the events had hardly passed out of sight. For, conscious that I had observed absolute truthfulness in my account, I expected to receive testimony to my accuracy, and was not disappointed. I also submitted my history to many others, some of whom had actually seen service in the war, including King Agrippa[2] and several of his relations. For the Emperor Titus was so anxious that from my work alone should men derive their knowledge of the events, that he wrote with his own hand an order for its publication, while King Agrippa wrote sixty-two letters testifying to the truthfulness of my account.[3]

Two of these letters he quotes. And there we may leave Josephus and go on to the next stage.

11. After the martyrdom of James and the capture of Jerusalem which instantly followed, there is a firm tradition that those of the apostles and disciples of the Lord who were still alive assembled from all parts together with those who, humanly speaking, were kinsmen of the Lord – for most of them were still living. Then they all discussed together whom they should choose as a fit person to succeed James, and voted unanimously that Symeon, son of the Clopas mentioned in the gospel narrative,[4] was a fit person to occupy the throne of the Jerusalem see. He was, so it is said, a cousin of the Saviour, for Hegesippus tells us that Clopas was Joseph's brother.

12. Hegesippus also records that after the capture of Jerusalem Vespasian issued an order that, to ensure that no member of the royal house should be left among the Jews, all descendants of David should be ferreted out; and that this resulted in a further widespread persecution of the Jews.

13. When Vespasian had reigned for ten years he was succeeded as

---

1. Vespasian and Titus, on whom in *The Jewish War* he had lavished compliments.
2. Herod Agrippa II.   3. *Life of Josephus*, 65.
4. John xix. 25; perhaps Luke xxiv. 18.

emperor by his son Titus. In the second year of Titus' reign Linus, Bishop of Rome, after holding his office for twelve years yielded it to Anencletus.

Titus was succeeded by his brother Domitian after reigning for two years and as many months.

14. In the fourth year of Domitian the first Bishop of Alexandria, Annianus, after completing twenty-two years, passed away, and was succeeded by the second, Avilus.

15. In the twelfth year of the same principate Anencletus, after twelve years as Bishop of Rome, was succeeded by Clement, who is described by the Apostle in his Epistle to the Philippians as a fellow-worker:

With Clement and the rest of my fellow-workers, whose names are in the book of life.[1]

16. Clement has left us one recognized epistle, long and wonderful, which he composed in the name of the church at Rome and sent to the church at Corinth, where dissension had recently occurred. I have evidence that in many churches this epistle was read aloud to the assembled worshippers in early days, as it is in our own. That it was in Clement's time that the dissension at Corinth broke out is plain from the testimony of Hegesippus.

Domitian's persecution: John the apostle and our Saviour's relatives

17. Many were the victims of Domitian's appalling cruelty. At Rome great numbers of men distinguished by birth and attainments were for no reason at all banished from the country and their property confiscated. Finally, he showed himself the successor of Nero in enmity and hostility to God. He was, in fact, the second to organize persecution against us, though his father Vespasian had had no mischievous designs against us.

18. There is ample evidence that at that time the apostle and

1. Phil. iv. 3.

evangelist John was still alive, and because of his testimony to the word of God was sentenced to confinement on the island of Patmos. Writing about the number of the name given to antichrist in what is called the Revelation of John,[1] Irenaeus has this to say about John in Book V of his *Against Heresies*:

Had there been any need for his name to be openly announced at the present time, it would have been stated by the one who saw the actual revelation. For it was seen not a long time back, but almost in my own lifetime, at the end of Domitian's reign.[2]

Indeed, so brightly shone at that time the teaching of our faith that even historians who accepted none of our beliefs unhesitatingly recorded in their pages both the persecution and the martyrdoms to which it led. They also indicated the precise date, noting that in the fifteenth year of Domitian Flavia Domitilla, who was a niece of Flavius Clemens, one of the consuls at Rome that year, was with many others, because of the testimony to Christ, taken to the island of Pontia as a punishment.

19. The same emperor ordered the execution of all who were of David's line, and there is an old and firm tradition that a group of heretics accused the descendants of Jude – the brother, humanly speaking, of the Saviour – on the ground that they were of David's line and related to Christ Himself. This is stated by Hegesippus in so many words:

20. And there still survived of the Lord's family the grandsons of Jude, who was said to be His brother, humanly speaking. These were informed against as being of David's line, and brought by the *evocatus* before Domitian Caesar, who was as afraid of the advent of Christ as Herod had been.[3] Domitian asked them whether they were descended from David, and they admitted it. Then he asked them what property they owned and what funds they had at their disposal. They replied that they had only 9,000 denarii between them, half belonging to each; this, they said, was not available in cash, but was the estimated value of only thirty-nine *plethra* of land, from which they raised the money to pay their taxes and the wherewithal to support themselves by their own toil.

1. Rev. xiii. 18.   2. Irenaeus, *Against Heresies*, V. 30. 3.   3. Matt 11. 3–4.

Then, the writer continues, they showed him their hands, putting forward as proof of their toil the hardness of their bodies and the calluses impressed on their hands by incessant labour. When asked about Christ and His Kingdom – what it was like, and where and when it would appear – they explained that it was not of this world or anywhere on earth but angelic and in heaven, and would be established at the end of the world, when He would come in glory to judge the quick and the dead and give every man payment according to his conduct. On hearing this, Domitian found no fault with them, but depising them as beneath his notice let them go free and issued orders terminating the persecution of the Church. On their release they became leaders of the churches, both because they had borne testimony and because they were of the Lord's family; and thanks to the establishment of peace they lived on into Trajan's time.

So much we learn from Hegesippus. Tertullian, again, has this to say about Domitian:

A similar attempt had once been made by Domitian, who almost equalled Nero in cruelty; but – I suppose because he had some common sense – he very soon stopped, even recalling those he had banished.[1]

After fifteen years of Domitian's rule Nerva succeeded to the throne. By vote of the Roman senate Domitian's honours were removed, and those unjustly banished returned to their homes and had their property restored to them. This is noted by the chroniclers of the period. At that time too the apostle John, after his exile on the island, resumed residence at Ephesus, as early Christain tradition records.

Bishops of Alexandria and Antioch

21. When Nerva had reigned a little more than a year he was succeeded by Trajan. It was in his first year that Avilius, after heading the church of Alexandria for thirteen years, was succeeded by Cerdo: he was the third of the see, Annianus having been the first. At that time Clement was still head of the Roman community,

1. *Defence*, 5.

occupying in the same way the third place among the bishops who followed Paul and Peter. Linus was the first and Anencletus the second.

22. At Antioch, where Evodius had been the first bishop, Ignatius was becoming famous at this time; his contemporary Symeon was similarly the next after our Saviour's brother to be in charge of the church at Jerusalem.

A story about John the apostle

23. In Asia, moreover, there still remained alive the one whom Jesus loved, apostle and evangelist alike, John, who had directed the churches there since his return from exile on the island, following Domitian's death. That he survived so long is proved by the evidence of two witnesses who could hardly be doubted, ambassadors as they were of the orthodoxy of the Church – Irenaeus and Clement of Alexandria. In Book II of his *Against Heresies*, Irenaeus writes:

> All the clergy who in Asia came in contact with John, the Lord's disciple, testify that John taught the truth to them; for he remained with them till Trajan's time.[1]

In Book III of the same work he says the same thing:

> The church at Ephesus was founded by Paul, and John remained there till Trajan's time; so she is a true witness of what the apostles taught.[2]

Clement, in addition to indicating the date, adds a story that should be familiar to all who like to hear what is noble and helpful. It will be found in the short work entitled *The Rich Man Who Finds Salvation*. Turn up the passage, and read what he writes:

> Listen to a tale that is not just a tale but a true account of John the apostle, handed down and carefully remembered. When the tyrant was dead, and John had moved from the island of Patmos to Ephesus, he used

---

1. *Against Heresies*, II. 33. 2.   2. Ibid., III. 3. 4.

to go when asked to the neighbouring districts of the Gentile peoples, sometimes to appoint bishops, sometimes to organize whole churches, sometimes to ordain one person of those pointed out by the Spirit. So it happened that he arrived at a city not far off, named by some,[1] and after settling the various problems of the brethren, he finally looked at the bishop already appointed, and indicating a youngster he had noticed, of excellent physique, attractive appearance, and ardent spirit, he said: 'I leave this young man in your keeping, with all earnestness, in the presence of the Church and Christ as my witness.' When the bishop accepted him and promised everything, John addressed the same appeal and adjuration to him a second time.

He then returned to Ephesus, and the cleric took home the youngster entrusted to his care, brought him up, kept him in his company, looked after him, and finally gave him the grace of baptism. After this he relaxed his constant care and watchfulness, having put upon him the seal of the Lord as the perfect protection. But the youngster snatched at liberty too soon, and was led sadly astray by others of his own age who were idle, dissolute, and evil-livers. First they led him on by expensive entertainments; then they took him with them when they went out at night to commit robbery; then they urged him to take part in even greater crimes. Little by little he fell into their ways; and like a hard-mouthed powerful horse he dashed off the straight road, and taking the bit between his teeth rushed down the precipice the more violently because of his immense vitality. Completely renouncing God's salvation, he was no longer content with petty offences, but, as his life was already in ruins, he decided to commit a major crime and suffer the same fate as the others. He took these same young renegades and formed them into a gang of bandits of which his was the master mind, surpassing them all in violence, cruelty, and bloodthirstiness.

Time went by, and some necessity having arisen, John was asked to pay another visit. When he had dealt with the business for which he had come, he said: 'Come now, bishop, pay me back the deposit which Christ and I left in your keeping, in the presence of the Church over which you preside as my witness.' At first the bishop was taken aback, thinking that he was being dunned for money he had never received. He could neither comply with a demand for what he did not possess, nor refuse to comply with John's request. But when John said 'It is the young man I am asking for, and the soul of our brother', the old man sighed deeply and shed a tear.

1. Smyrna.

'He is dead.'

'How did he die?'

'He is dead to God: he turned out wicked and profligate, in short, a bandit; and now, instead of the Church, he has taken to the mountain with an armed gang of men like himself.'

The apostle rent his garment, groaned aloud, and beat his head. 'A fine guardian,' he cried, 'I left of our brother's soul! However, let me have a horse immediately, and someone to show me the way.' He galloped off from the church, then and there, just as he was. When he arrived at the place, and was seized by the bandits' sentry-group, he made no attempt to escape and asked no mercy, but shouted: 'This is what I have come for:[1] take me to your leader.' For the time being the young man waited, armed as he was; but as John approached he recognized him, and filled with shame, turned to flee. But John ran after him as hard as he could, forgetting his years and calling out: 'Why do you run away from me, child – from your own father, unarmed and very old? Be sorry for me, child, not afraid of me. You still have hopes of life. I will account to Christ for you. If need be, I will gladly suffer your death, as the Lord suffered death for us; to save you I will give my own life. Stop! believe! Christ sent me.'

When he heard this, the young man stopped and stood with his eyes on the ground; then he threw down his weapons; then he trembled and began to weep bitterly. When the old man came up he flung his arms round him, pleading for himself with groans as best he could, and baptized a second time with his tears, but keeping his right hand out of sight. But John solemnly pledged his word that he had found pardon for him from the Saviour: he prayed, knelt down, and kissed that very hand as being cleansed by his repentance. Then he brought him back to the church, interceded for him with many prayers, shared with him the ordeal of continuous fasting, brought his mind under control by all the enchanting power of words, and did not leave him, we are told, till he had restored him to the Church, giving a perfect example of true repentance and a perfect proof of regeneration, the trophy of a visible resurrection.[2]

This story from Clement I have included both for its historical interest and for the benefit of future readers.

1. A reminiscence of John xviii. 37.   2. *The Rich Man who finds Salvation*, 42. 1–15.

The order of the gospels

24. Now let me indicate the unquestioned writings of this apostle. Obviously his gospel, recognized as it is by all the churches in the world, must first be acknowledged. That the early fathers had good reason to assign it the fourth place after the other three can easily be seen. Those inspired and wonderful men, Christ's apostles, had completely purified their lives and cultivated every spiritual virtue, but their speech was that of every day. The divine wonder-working power bestowed on them by the Saviour filled them with confidence; and having neither the ability nor the desire to present the teachings of the Master with rhetorical subtlety or literary skill, they relied only on demonstrating the divine Spirit working with them, and on the miraculous power of Christ fully operative in them.[1] Thus they proclaimed the knowledge of the Kingdom of Heaven through the whole world, giving very little thought to the business of writing books. The reason for this practice was the ever-present help of a greater, superhuman ministry. We may instance Paul, who, though he surpassed all others in the marshalling of his arguments and in the abundance of his ideas, committed to writing nothing but his very short epistles; and yet he had countless unutterable things to say, for he had reached the vision of the third heaven, he had been caught up to the divine paradise itself, and had been privileged to hear there unspeakable words.[2]

Similar experiences were enjoyed by the rest of our Saviour's pupils — the twelve apostles, the seventy disciples, and countless others besides. Yet of them all Matthew and John alone have left us memoirs of the Lord's doings, and there is a firm tradition that they took to writing of necessity. Matthew had begun by preaching to Hebrews; and when he made up his mind to go to others too, he committed his own gospel to writing in his native tongue, so that for those with whom he was no longer present the gap left by his departure was filled by what he wrote. And when Mark and Luke had now published their gospels, John, we are told, who

1. See 1 Cor. ii. 4.   2. See 2 Cor. xii. 2–4.

hitherto had relied entirely on the spoken word, finally took to writing for the following reason. The three gospels already written were in general circulation and copies had come into John's hands. He welcomed them, we are told, and confirmed their accuracy, but remarked that the narrative only lacked the story of what Christ had done first of all at the beginning of His mission.

This tradition is undoubtedly true. Anyone can see that the three evangelists have recorded the doings of the Saviour for only one year, following the consignment of John the Baptist to prison, and that they indicated this very fact at the beginning of their narrative. After the forty days' fast and the temptation that followed Matthew shows clearly the period covered by his narrative when he says: 'Hearing that John had been arrested, He withdrew from Judaea into Galilee.'[1] In the same way, Mark says: 'After the arrest of John, Jesus went into Galilee.[2] Luke too, before beginning the acts of Jesus, makes a similar observation, saying that Herod added one more to his other crimes by shutting up John in gaol.[3]

We are told, then, that for this reason the apostle John was urged to record in his gospel the period which the earlier evangelists had passed over in silence and the things done during that period by the Saviour, i.e. all that happened before the Baptist's imprisonment; that this is indicated, first by his words 'Thus did Jesus begin His miracles',[4] and later by his mentioning the Baptist, in the middle of his account of Jesus's doings, as then still baptizing at Aenon near Salim; and that he makes this plainer when he adds 'for John had not yet been thrown into gaol'.[5]

Thus John in his gospel narrative records what Christ did when the Baptist had not yet been thrown into gaol, while the other three evangelists describe what happened after the Baptist's consignment to prison. Once this is grasped, there no longer appears to be a discrepancy between the gospels, because John's deals with the early stages of Christ's career and the others cover the last period of His story; and it seems natural that as the genealogy of our

---

1. Matt. iv. 12.   2. Mark i. 14.   3. Luke iii. 19–20.
4. John ii. 11.   5. John iii. 23–4.

Saviour as a man had already been set out by Matthew and Luke, John should pass it over in silence and begin with the proclamation of His divinity since the Holy Spirit had reserved this for him, as the greatest of the four.

This is all that I propose to say about the composition of John's gospel: the origin of Mark's has already been explained. Luke's work begins with a preface in which the author himself explains the reason for its composition. Many others had somewhat hastily undertaken to compile an account of things of which he himself was fully assured; [1] so, feeling it his duty to free us from doubts as to our attitude to the others, he furnished in his own gospel an authentic account of the events of which, thanks to his association and intercourse with Paul and his conversations with the other apostles, he had learnt the undoubted truth. [2] This is how I see the matter: at a more appropriate moment I shall endeavour to show, by quoting early writers, what others have said about it.

Of John's writings, besides the gospel, the first of the epistles had been accepted as unquestionably his by scholars both of the present and of a much earlier period: the other two are disputed. As to the Revelation, the views of most people to this day are evenly divided. At the appropriate moment, the evidence of early writers shall clear up this matter too.

Writings accepted as sacred, and those not accepted

25. It will be well, at this point, to classify the New Testament writings already referred to. We must, of course, put first the holy quartet of the gospels, followed by the Acts of the Apostles. The next place in the list goes to Paul's epistles, and after them we must recognize the epistle called 1 John; likewise 1 Peter. To these may be added, if it is thought proper, the Revelation of John, the arguments about which I shall set out when the time comes. These are classed as Recognized Books. Those that are disputed, yet familiar to most, include the epistles known as James, Jude, and 2

---

1. Luke i. 1.   2. Luke i. 3–4.

Peter, and those called 2 and 3 John, the work either of the evangelist or of someone else with the same name.

   Among Spurious Books must be placed the 'Acts' of Paul, the 'Shepherd', and the 'Revelation of Peter'; also the alleged 'Epistle of Barnabas', and the 'Teachings of the Apostles', together with the Revelation of John, if this seems the right place for it: as I said before, some reject it, others include it among the Recognized Books. Moreover, some have found a place in the list for the 'Gospel of Hebrews', a book which has a special appeal for those Hebrews who have accepted Christ. These would all be classed with the Disputed Books, but I have been obliged to list the latter separately, distinguishing those writings which according to the tradition of the Church are true, genuine, and recognized, from those in a different category, not canonical but disputed, yet familiar to most churchmen; for we must not confuse these with the writings published by heretics under the name of the apostles, as containing either Gospels of Peter, Thomas, Matthias, and several others besides these, or Acts of Andrew, John, and other apostles. To none of these has any churchman of any generation ever seen fit to refer in his writings. Again, nothing could be farther from apostolic usage than the type of phraseology employed, while the ideas and implications of their contents are so irreconcilable with true orthodoxy that they stand revealed as the forgeries of heretics. It follows that so far from being classed even among Spurious Books, they must be thrown out as impious and beyond the pale.

Menander the impostor

26. Let us now return to the course of our story. Simon the Magus was succeeded by Menander, a second tool of the devil's ingenuity as bad as his predecessor, as he showed by his conduct. He too was a Samaritan, and having risen to the same heights of imposture as his master, he poured out a stream of still more marvellous tales. He actually claimed to be the saviour sent down from somewhere aloft to save mankind from invisible aeons, and taught that there was no way by which a man could get the better even of the

angels who made the world, unless he had first been taken through the magical skills transmitted by himself and the baptism which he bestowed: those who were admitted to this baptism would share in everlasting immortality in this present world, no longer subject to death but destined to continue here for ever, ageless and immortal. All this is clearly stated in the writings of Irenaeus. Justin, too, follows up his comments on Simon with an account of his successor:

> Another Samaritan, called Menander, from the village of Caparattaea, became a disciple of Simon and like him was driven mad by the demons. It is known that he arrived in Antioch and deluded many by magical trickery. He even persuaded his followers that they would not die: and there are still some who on the strength of his assertion maintain this belief.[1]

It was certainly characteristic of the devil's ingenuity to make use of such impostors, who usurped the name of Christian, in his determination to misrepresent in the interests of magic the great mystery of religion,[2] and to make a mockery of the Church's teaching on the immortality of the soul and the resurrection of the dead. But those who have entitled these men 'saviours' have fallen from the true hope.

The Ebionite sect: the heresies of Cerinthus and Nicolaus

27. There were others whom the evil demon, unable to shake their devotion to the Christ of God, caught in a different trap and made his own. Ebionites they were appropriately named by the first Christians, in view of the poor and mean opinions they held about Christ. They regarded Him as plain and ordinary, a man esteemed as righteous through growth[3] of character and nothing more, the child of a normal union between a man and Mary; and they held that they must observe every detail of the Law – by faith in Christ alone, and a life built upon that faith, they would never win salvation.

---

1. Justin Martyr, *Defence*, 1.26.   2. 1 Tim. iii. 16.   3. Cf. Luke ii. 52.

A second group went by the same name, but escaped the outrageous absurdity of the first. They did not deny that the Lord
was born of a virgin and the Holy Spirit, but nevertheless shared
their refusal to acknowledge His pre-existence as God the Word
and Wisdom. Thus the impious doctrine of the others was their
undoing also, especially as they placed equal emphasis on the
outward observance of the Law. They held that the epistles of the
Apostle ought to be rejected altogether, calling him a renegade
from the Law; and using only the 'Gospel of the Hebrews', they
treated the rest with scant respect. Like the others, they observed
the Sabbath and the whole Jewish system; yet on the Lord's Day
they celebrated rites similar to our own in memory of the Saviour's
resurrection. It is then because of such practices that they have
been dubbed with their present name: the name of Ebionites hints
at the poverty of their intelligence, for this is the way in which a
poor man is referred to by the Hebrews.

28. At the time under discussion, tradition tells us, another heretical
sect was founded by Cerinthus. Gaius, whose words I quoted
earlier, in the *Dialogue* attributed to him writes this about him:

> Then there is Cerinthus, who by revelations purporting to have been
> written by a great apostle presents us with tales of wonder falsely alleged
> to have been shown to him by angels. He declares that after the Resurrec-
> tion the Kingdom of Christ will be on earth, and that carnal humanity
> will dwell in Jerusalem, once more enslaved to lusts and pleasures.[1] And
> in his enmity towards the Scriptures of God, and his anxiety to lead men
> astray, he foretells a period of a thousand years given up to wedding fes-
> tivities.

Dionysius again, who held the bishopric of the Alexandrian see
in my own time, in Book II of his *Promises* makes certain statements
about the Revelation of John on the basis of very ancient tradition.
He then refers to Cerinthus in the following terms.

> Cerinthus: the founder of a sect called Cerinthian after him, who
> wished to attach a name commanding respect to his own creation. This,
> they say, was the doctrine he taught – that Christ's Kingdom would be

---

1. Titus iii. 3.

on earth: and the things he lusted after himself, being the slave of his body and sensual through and through, filled the heaven of his dreams – unlimited indulgence in gluttony and lechery at banquets, drinking-bouts, and wedding-feasts, or (to call these by what he thought more respectable names) festivals, sacrifices, and the immolation of victims.

That is how Dionysius put it. Irenaeus in Book I of his *Against Heresies* set out some of his more revolting errors, and in Book III has placed on record a memorable story. He states on the authority of Polycarp that one day John the apostle went into a bath-house to take a bath, but when he found that Cerinthus was inside he leapt from the spot and ran for the door, as he could not endure to be under the same roof. He urged his companions to do the same, calling out: 'Let us get out of here, for fear the place falls in, now that Cerinthus, the enemy of the truth, is inside.'

29. In their day, too, the very short-lived sect of the Nicolaitans came into existence. It is mentioned in the Revelation of John.[1] These sectaries laid claim to Nicolaus, who like Stephen was one of the deacons appointed by the apostles to assist those in want.[2] Clement of Alexandria in Book III of his *Miscellanies* gives this account of him:

This man, we are told, had an attractive young wife. After the Saviour's Ascension the apostles accused him of jealousy, so he brought his wife forward and said that anyone who wished might have her. This action, we are told, followed from the injunction 'the flesh must be treated with contempt'; and by following example and precept crudely and unquestioningly the members of the sect do in fact practise utter promiscuity. But my own information is that Nicolaus had no relations with any woman but his wife; and that, of his children, his daughters remained unmarried till the end of their days and his son's chastity was never in doubt. Such being the case, his bringing the wife whom he loved so jealously into the midst of the apostles was the renunciation of desire, and it was mastery of the pleasures so eagerly sought that taught him the rule 'treat the flesh with contempt'. For in obedience to the Saviour's command, I imagine, he had no wish to serve two masters, Pleasure and Lord. It is believed that Matthias also taught this, that we must fight

1. Rev. ii. 16.   2. Acts vi. 5.

against the flesh and treat it with contempt, never yielding to it for pleasure's sake, but must nourish the soul through faith and knowledge.[1]

So much for those who during that period endeavoured to twist the truth, only to be extinguished completely, in less time than it takes to tell.

Apostles who were married men

30. Clement, whose words we have just been reading, goes on from the passage I have quoted to rebut those who deprecated marriage, by listing the apostles known to have been married men. He says:

Or will they condemn even the apostles? For Peter and Philip had families, and Philip gave his daughters in marriage, while Paul himself does not hesitate in one of his epistles to address his yoke-fellow,[2] whom he did not take round with him[3] for fear of hindering his ministry.[4]

While I am on the subject, I may as well quote another of Clement's interesting stories, to be found in Book VII of his *Miscellanies*:

We are told that when blessed Peter saw his wife led away to death he was glad that her call had come and that she was returning home, and spoke to her in the most encouraging and comforting tones, addressing her by name: 'My dear, remember the Lord.' Such was the marriage of the blessed, and their consummate feeling towards their dearest.[5]

These quotations, relevant as they are to this section of my work, must suffice for the moment.

The deaths of John and Philip

31. When and how Paul and Peter died, and where after their departure from this life their mortal remains were laid, I have

1. *Miscellanies*, III. 4. 25f.
2. Phil. iv. 3; though 'yoke-fellow' (*syzygos*) would naturally mean 'wife', it could mean 'comrade'.
3. Cf. 1 Cor. ix. 5.   4. *Miscellanies*, III. 6. 52f.   5. *Miscellanies*, VII. 11. 63f.

already explained. The date of John's death has also been roughly fixed: the place where his mortal remains lie can be gathered from a letter of Polycrates, Bishop of Ephesus, to Victor, Bishop of Rome. In it he refers not only to John but to Philip the apostle and Philip's daughters as well:

In Asia great luminaries sleep who shall rise again on the last day, the day of the Lord's advent, when He is coming with glory from heaven and shall search out all His saints – such as Philip, one of the twelve apostles, who sleeps in Hierapolis with two of his daughters, who remained unmarried to the end of their days, while his other daughter lived in the Holy Spirit and rests in Ephesus. Again there is John, who leant back on the Lord's breast, and who became a priest wearing the mitre, a martyr and a teacher; he too sleeps in Ephesus.

So much Polycrates tells us about their deaths. And in the *Dialogue* of Gaius of whom I spoke a little while ago, Proclus, with whom he was disputing, speaks thus about the deaths of Philip and his daughters, in agreement with the foregoing account:

After him there were four prophetesses at Hierapolis in Asia, daughters of Philip. Their grave is there, as is their father's.

That is Gaius' account. Luke in the Acts of the Apostles refers to Philip's daughters as then living with their father at Caesarea in Judaea and endowed with the prophetic gift. His words are:

We arrived at Caesarea, where we went to the house of Philip the Evangelist, one of the Seven, and stayed with him. He had four unmarried daughters who were prophetesses.[1]

In these pages I have set down all the facts that have come to my knowledge regarding the apostles and the apostolic period; the sacred writings they have left us; the books which though disputed are nevertheless constantly used in very many churches; those that are unmistakably spurious and foreign to apostolic orthodoxy. Let us now go on to the story of what followed.

---

1. Acts xxi. 8–9.

The martyrdom of Symeon, Bishop of Jerusalem

32. After Nero and Domitian, under the emperor whose times I am now describing, there is a firm tradition that persecution broke out against us sporadically in one city at a time as a result of popular risings. In the course of it Symeon, son of Clopas, the second to be appointed Bishop of Jerusalem, as already stated, is known to have ended his life by martyrdom. The authority for this statement is the writer to whose history I have appealed several times already, Hegesippus. When writing of certain heretics he goes on to explain how at this time they brought an accusation against Symeon, and how after being subjected for days on end to a variety of tortures for being a Christian, to the utter amazement of the judge and his assessors, he won the prize of an end like that suffered by the Lord. But we cannot do better than listen to the writer's own version of the story:

Some of these [heretics] charged Simon son of Clopas with being a descendant of David and a Christian; as a result he suffered martyrdom at the age of 120, when Trajan was emperor and Atticus consular governor.

The same writer tells us that in the sequel, when members of the royal house of Judah were being hunted, Symeon's accusers were arrested too, on the ground that they belonged to it. And it would be reasonable to suggest that Symeon was an eyewitness and earwitness of the Lord, having regard to the length of his life and the reference in the gospel narrative to Mary, wife of the Clopas whose son he was, as explained in an earlier section.

The same historian tells us that other descendants of one of the 'brothers' of the Saviour named Jude lived on into the same reign, after bravely declaring their faith in Christ, as already recorded, before Domitian himself. He writes:

Consequently they came and presided over every church, as being martyrs and members of the Lord's family, and since profound peace came to every church they survived till the reign of Trajan Caesar – till the son of the Lord's uncle, the aforesaid Simon son of Clopas, was similarly informed against by the heretical sects and brought up on the same charge before Atticus, the provincial governor. Tortured for days on end, he bore a martyr's witness, so that all, including the governor, were astounded that at the age of 120 he could endure it; and he was ordered to be crucified.

In describing the situation at that time Hegesippus goes on to say that until then the Church had remained a virgin, pure and uncorrupted, since those who were trying to corrupt the wholesome standard of the saving message, if such there were, lurked somewhere under cover of darkness. But when the sacred band of the apostles had in various ways reached the end of their life, and the generation of those privileged to listen with their own ears to the divine wisdom had passed on, then godless error began to take shape, through the deceit of false teachers, who now that none of the apostles was left threw off the mask and attempted to counter the preaching of the truth by preaching the knowledge falsely so called.

Christian-hunting stopped by Trajan

33. So great was the intensification of the persecution directed against us in many parts of the world at that time, that Pliny the Younger, one of the most distinguished governors, was alarmed by the number of martyrs and sent a report to the emperor about the number of those who were being put to death for the faith. In the same dispatch he informed him that he understood they did nothing improper or illegal: all they did was to rise at dawn and hymn Christ as a god, to repudiate adultery, murder, and similar disgraceful crimes, and in every way to conform to the law. Trajan's response was to issue a decree that members of the Christian community were not to be hunted, but if met with were to be punished. This meant that though to some extent the terrifyingly imminent threat of persecution was stifled, yet for those who wanted to injure us there were just as many pretexts left. Sometimes it was the common people, sometimes the local authorities, who devised plots against us, so that even without open persecution sporadic attacks blazed up in one province or another, and many of the faithful endured the ordeal of martyrdom in various forms.

I have taken this story from a book referred to above, Tertullian's Latin *Defence*. The translation is as follows:

> And yet we have found that even hunting us is forbidden. For Pliny the Younger, as governor of a province, after condemning several Christians and depriving them of their status, was at a loss because of their numbers; and not knowing what to do in the future, he sent a report to the Emperor Trajan to the effect that except for their refusal to worship idols he had detected nothing improper in their behaviour. He also informed him that the Christians got up at dawn and hymned Christ as a god, and in order to uphold their principles were forbidden to commit murder, adultery, fraud, theft, and the like. In response. Trajan sent a rescript ordering that members of the Christian community were not to be hunted, but if met with were to be punished.[1]

Bishops of Rome and Jerusalem

34. In the bishopric of Rome, in the third year of Trajan's reign, Clement departed this life, yielding his office to Evarestus. He had been in charge of the teaching of the divine message for nine years in all.

35. When Symeon had found fulfilment in the manner described, his successor on the throne of the Jerusalem bishopric was a Jew named Justus, one of the vast number of the circumcision who by then believed in Christ.

Ignatius and his epistles

36. Pre-eminent at that time in Asia was a companion of the apostles, Polycarp, on whom the eyewitnesses and ministers[2] of the Lord had conferred the episcopate of the church at Smyrna. Famous contemporaries of his were Papias, bishop of the see of Hierapolis, and one who to this day is universally remembered – Ignatius, the second to be appointed to the bishopric of Antioch in succession to Peter.

1. *Defence*, 2.   2. Luke i. 2.

There is evidence that Ignatius was sent from Syria to Rome and became food for wild animals because of his testimony to Christ. He made the journey through Asia under the strictest military guard, encouraging the Christian community, by homilies and exhortations, in every city where he stayed. In particular he warned them to guard most carefully against the heresies which were then first becoming prevalent, and exhorted them to hold fast to the apostolic tradition, which, as he was now on his way to martyrdom, he thought it necessary for safety's sake to set down clearly in writing. Thus, when he arrived at Smyrna where Polycarp was, he wrote one epistle to the church at Ephesus referring to their pastor Onesimus, another to the church at Magnesia on the Maeander, where he refers to Bishop Damas, and a third to the church at Tralles, which, as he states, was then under the rule of Polybius. In addition he wrote to the church at Rome; in his letter he implores them not to beg him off from his martyrdom and so rob him of his longed-for hope.

In support of these statements it will be well to quote some very short passages from these letters:

All the way from Syria to Rome I am fighting with wild animals on land and sea, by night and day, fettered to ten leopards – a squad of soldiers – whom kindness makes even worse. Their disgraceful conduct makes me still more a disciple, but that does not justify me.[1] May it be for my good that the wild animals are ready for me: I pray that I may find them prompt. I shall coax them to devour me promptly, unlike some whom they have been afraid to touch; if they are unwilling and refuse, I will compel them to do it. Pardon me: I know what is best for me, and now I am beginning to be a disciple. May nothing seen or unseen grudge my attaining to Jesus Christ! Let fire and cross, encounters with wild animals, tearing apart of bones, hacking of limbs, crushing of the whole body, tortures of the devil come upon me, if only I may attain to Jesus Christ![2]

These letters he wrote from Smyrna to the churches named. At a further stage of his journey he communicated in writing from Troas with the Christians at Philadelphia and the church at

1. 1 Cor. iv. 4.   2. Ignatius, *Romans*, 5.

Smyrna, along with a personal letter to the head of that church,
Polycarp. He was well aware that Polycarp was an apostolic man,
so like a true and kind shepherd he commended to him the flock
at Antioch, asking him to take great care of it. In his letter to
Smyrna he quotes a saying from an unknown source to support
what he is saying about Christ:

I know and am convinced that even after the Resurrection He was in
the flesh. When He came to Peter and his companions He said to them:
'Take hold, handle me, and see that I am not a bodiless phantom.' And
they at once touched Him and were convinced.[1]

His martyrdom was well known to Irenaeus, who draws on his
epistles:

As one of our people said, when because of his witness he was
condemned to the beasts: 'I am God's wheat, ground by the teeth of
beasts, that I may be found pure bread.'[2]

Polycarp also alludes to these same epistles in the letter to the
Philippians that bears his name:

I urge you all to be obedient and to practise the unfailing endurance
that you saw before your eyes, not only in blessed Ignatius, Rufus, and
Zosimus, but in others from your own number, and in Paul himself and
the rest of the apostles: satisfied that all these did not run in vain[3] but in
faith and righteousness, and that they are in the place that is their due, by
the side of the Lord whose sufferings they shared. For they did not love
this present world[4] but the One who died on our behalf and for our sakes
was raised by God . . . You wrote to me as did Ignatius, requesting that if
anyone was going to Syria he should take your letters with him. I will
do so, if I find a convenient opportunity, either personally or by sending
an agent on our joint behalf. The epistles which Ignatius sent us, and any
others I have by me, I am sending you as requested: they are enclosed
with this letter. You will find them most helpful, for they contain faith,
endurance, and all the edification that concerns our Lord.[5]

1. Ignatius, *Smyrnaeans*, 3.
2. Irenaeus, *Against Heresies*, V. 28. 3 quoting Ignatius, *Romans*, 4.
3. Phil. ii. 26.   4. 2 Tim. iv. 10.   5. Polycarp, *Philippians*, 10, 13.

There we must leave Ignatius. As Bishop of Antioch he was succeeded by Hero.

Evangelists still eminent at that time

37. Among the shining lights of the period was Quadratus, who according to the written evidence was, like Philip's daughters, eminent from a prophetic gift. Besides them many others were well known at the time, belonging to the first stage in the apostolic succession. These earnest disciples of great men built on the foundations of the churches everywhere laid by the apostles,[1] spreading the message still further and sowing the saving seed of the Kingdom of Heaven far and wide through the entire world. Very many of the disciples of the time, their hearts smitten by the word of God with an ardent passion for true philosophy, first fulfilled the Saviour's command by distributing their possessions among the needy; then, leaving their homes behind, they carried out the work of evangelists,[2] ambitious to preach to those who had never yet heard the message of the faith[3] and to give them the inspired gospels in writing. Staying only to lay the foundations of the faith in one foreign place or another, appoint others as pastors, and entrust to them the tending of those newly brought in, they set off again for other lands and peoples with the grace and cooperation of God, for even at that late date many miraculous powers of the divine Spirit worked through them, so that at the first hearing whole crowds in a body embraced with a wholehearted eagerness the worship of the universal Creator.

Clement's Epistle: works mistakenly attributed to him

As it is impossible for me to enumerate by name all who in the first succession from the apostles became pastors or evangelists in the churches of all the known world, I have naturally included in my account the individual stories only of those whose transmission of the apostolic teaching can still be studied in their writings. 38. Obvi-

---

1. 1 Cor. iii. 10.   2. 1 Tim. iv. 5.   3. A reminiscence of Rom. xv. 20–21.

ous instances are Ignatius, in the epistles already listed, and Clement in the one universally recognized, which he indited in the name of the church at Rome to that at Corinth. In this he echoes many thoughts from the Epistle to the Hebrews, and indeed makes many verbal quotations from it, proving beyond a doubt that the document was not of recent origin, and making it seem quite natural to include it with the rest in the list of the Apostle's writings. Paul had communicated with the Hebrews by writing to them in their native tongue; and some say that the evangelist Luke, others that this same Clement translated the original text. The second suggestion is the more convincing, in view of the similarity of phraseology shown throughout by the Epistle of Clement and the Epistle to the Hebrews, and of the absence of any great difference between the two works in the underlying thought.

It must not be overlooked that there is a second epistle said to be from Clement's pen, but I have no reason to suppose that it was well known like the first one, since I am not aware that the early fathers made any use of it. A year or two ago other long and wordy treatises were put forward as Clement's work. They contain alleged dialogues with Peter and Apion, but there is no mention whatever of them by early writers, nor do they preserve in its purity the stamp of apostolic orthodoxy.

The writings of Papias

39. I have now made it clear what is the acknowledged work of Clement, and have discussed the works of Ignatius and Polycarp. Papias has left us five volumes entitled *The Sayings of the Lord Explained*. These are mentioned by Irenaeus as the only works from his pen:

> To these things Papias, who had listened to John and was later a companion of Polycarp, and who lived at a very early date, bears written testimony in the fourth of his books; he composed five.[1]

That is what Irenaeus says; but Papias himself in the preface to his work makes it clear that he was never a hearer or eyewitness of

---

1. *Against Heresies*, V. 33. 4.

the holy apostles, and tells us that he learnt the essentials of the
Faith from their former pupils:

> I shall not hesitate to furnish you, along with the interpretations, with
> all that in days gone by I carefully learnt from the presbyters and have
> carefully recalled, for I can guarantee its truth. Unlike most people, I felt
> at home not with those who had a great deal to say, but with those who
> taught the truth; not with those who appeal to commandments from
> other sources but with those who appeal to the commandments given by
> the Lord to faith and coming to us from truth itself. And whenever
> anyone came who had been a follower of the presbyters, I inquired into
> the words of the presbyters, what Andrew or Peter had said, or Philip or
> Thomas or James or John or Matthew, or any other disciple of the Lord,
> and what Aristion and the presbyter John, disciples of the Lord, were still
> saying. For I did not imagine that things out of books would help me as
> much as the utterances of a living and abiding voice.[1]

Here it should be observed that he twice includes the name of
John. The first John he puts in the same list as Peter, James,
Matthew, and the rest of the apostles, obviously with the evangelist
in mind; the second, with a changed form of expression, he places
in a second group outside the number of the apostles, giving
precedence to Aristion and clearly calling John a presbyter. He
thus confirms the truth of the story that two men in Asia had the
same name, and that there were two tombs in Ephesus, each of
which is still called John's. This is highly significant, for it is likely
that the second – if we cannot accept the first – saw the Revelation
that bears the name of John. Papias, whom we are now discussing,
owns that he learnt the words of the apostles from their former
followers, but says that he listened to Aristion and the presbyter
John with his own ears. Certainly he often mentions them by
name, and reproduces their teachings in his writings.

I hope that these suggestions are of some value. Now we must
go on, from the remarks of Papias already quoted, to other
passages in which he tells us of certain miraculous events and other
matters, on the basis, it would seem, of direct information. It has
already been mentioned that Philip the Apostle resided at Hier-

---

1. A reminiscence of 1 Peter i. 23.

apolis with his daughters: it must now be pointed out that their contemporary Papias tells how he heard a wonderful story from the lips of Philip's daughters. He describes the resurrection of a dead person[1] in his own lifetime, and a further miracle that happened to Justus, surnamed Barsabas, who swallowed a danger-ous poison and by the grace of the Lord was none the worse. After the Saviour's ascension, this Justus was put forward with Matthias by the holy apostles, who prayed over them before drawing lots for someone to fill up their number in place of the traitor Judas. This incident is described in the Acts:

And they put forward two men, Joseph called Barsabas and surnamed Justus, and Matthias. Then they prayed and said . . .[2]

Papias reproduces other stories communicated to him by word of mouth, together with some otherwise unknown parables and teachings of the Saviour, and other things of a more allegorical character. He says that after the resurrection of the dead there will be a period of a thousand years, when Christ's kingdom will be set up on this earth in material form. I suppose he got these notions by misinterpreting the apostolic accounts and failing to grasp what they had said in mystic and symbolic language. For he seems to have been a man of very small intelligence, to judge from his books. But it is partly due to him that the great majority of churchmen after him took the same view, relying on his early date; e.g. Irenaeus and several others, who clearly held the same opinion.

In his own book Papias gives us accounts of the Lord's sayings obtained from Aristion or learnt direct from the presbyter John. Having brought these to the attention of scholars, I must now follow up the statements already quoted from him with a piece of information which he sets out regarding Mark, the writer of the gospel:

This, too, the presbyter used to say. 'Mark, who had been Peter's interpreter, wrote down carefully, but not in order, all that he remem-bered of the Lord's sayings and doings. For he had not heard the

---

1. Named by Papias as the wife of Manaen.   2. Acts i. 23.

Lord or been one of His followers, but later, as I said, one of Peter's. Peter used to adapt his teachings to the occasion, without making a systematic arrangement of the Lord's sayings, so that Mark was quite justified in writing down some things just as he remembered them. For he had one purpose only – to leave out nothing that he had heard, and to make no misstatement about it.'

Such is Papias' account of Mark. Of Matthew he has this to say:

Matthew compiled the *Sayings* in the Aramaic language, and everyone translated them as well as he could.

Papias also makes use of evidence drawn from 1 John and 1 Peter, and reproduces a story about a woman falsely accused before the Lord of many sins. This is to be found in the Gospel of the Hebrews.

This is all that it is necessary to add to the passages I have quoted.

Book 4

TRAJAN TO MARCUS AURELIUS: THE SUCCESSION
OF BISHOPS: THEIR WRITINGS AND MARTYRDOMS

Bishops of Rome and Alexandria in Trajan's reign: the Jewish tragedy

1. About the twelfth year of Trajan's reign the Bishop of Alexandria mentioned a few pages back departed this life, and Primus, the fourth from the apostles, was chosen to hold office there. Meanwhile at Rome, when Evarestus had completed his eighth year, Alexander took up the bishopric as fifth successor to Peter and Paul.

2. While our Saviour's teaching and His Church were flourishing and progressing further every day, the Jewish tragedy was moving through a series of disasters towards its climax. When the emperor was about to enter his eighteenth year another rebellion broke out and destroyed vast numbers of Jews. In Alexandria and the rest of Egypt, and in Cyrene as well, as if inflamed by some terrible spirit of revolt they rushed into a faction fight against their Greek fellow-citizens, raised the temperature to fever heat, and in the following summer started a full-scale war, Lupus being at that time governor of all Egypt. From the first encounter they emerged victorious. But the Greeks fled to Alexandria, where they killed or captured the Jews in the city. But though deprived of their aid, the Jews of Cyrene went on plundering the territory of Egypt and ravaging the various districts, led by Lucuas. Against them the emperor sent Marcius Turbo with land and sea forces, including a contingent of cavalry. He pursued the war against them relentlessly in a long series of battles, destroying many thousands of Jews, not only those from Cyrene but others who had come from Egypt to assist Lucuas their king.

The emperor, suspecting that the Jews in Mesopotamia also

would attack the people there, instructed Lusius Quietus to clear them out of the province. Lusius deployed his forces and slaughtered great numbers of the people there – a success for which the emperor appointed him governor of Judaea. These events were recorded in similar terms by the Greek authors who wrote histories of the same period.[1]

Hadrian's reign: defenders of the Faith, and Bishops of Rome and Alexandria

3. When Trajan had ruled for six months short of twenty years Aelius Hadrianus succeeded to the throne. To him Quadratus addressed and sent a pamphlet which he had composed in defence of our religion, because unscrupulous persons were trying to get our people into trouble. Many of the brethren still possess copies of this little work; indeed, I have one myself. In it can be found shining proofs of the author's intellectual grasp and apostolic correctness. He reveals his very early date by the wording of his composition.

Our Saviour's works were always there to see, for they were true – the people who had been cured and those raised from the dead, who had not merely been seen at the moment when they were cured or raised, but were *always* there to see, not only when the Saviour was among us, but for a long time after His departure; in fact some of them survived right up to my own time.

Aristides again, a loyal and devoted Christian, has like Quadratus left us a *Defence of the Faith* addressed to Hadrian. Many people still preserve copies of his work also.

4. In the third year of the same reign Alexander Bishop of Rome died, after completing the tenth year of his ministry: Xystus was his successor. In the diocese of Alexandria at about the same time Primus passed away in the twelfth year of his rule and was succeeded by Justus.

1. e.g. Appian and Dio Cassius.

Bishops of Jerusalem up to Hadrian's time

5. Of the dates of the bishops at Jerusalem I have failed to find any written evidence – it is known that they were very short lived – but I have received documentary proof of this, that up to Hadrian's siege of the Jews there had been a series of fifteen bishops there. All are said to have been Hebrews in origin, who had received the knowledge of Christ with all sincerity, with the result that those in a position to decide such matters judged them worthy of the episcopal office. For at that time their church consisted of Hebrew believers who had continued from apostolic times down to the later siege in which the Jews, after revolting a second time from the Romans, were overwhelmed in a full-scale war.

As that meant the end of bishops of the Circumcision, this is the right moment to list their names from the first. The first, then, was James 'the Lord's brother'. Second came Symeon, third Justus, fourth Zacchaeus, fifth Tobias, sixth Benjamin, seventh John, eighth Matthias, ninth Philip, tenth Seneca, eleventh Justus, twelfth Levi, thirteenth Ephres, fourteenth Joseph, fifteenth and last Judas. That was the number of bishops in the city of Jerusalem from apostolic times to the date mentioned, all of them of the Circumcision.

In Hadrian's twelfth year, Xystus, Bishop of Rome for a decade, was succeeded by the seventh from the apostles, Telesphorus. A year and some months later the see of Alexandria came under the rule of Eumenes, the sixth to be appointed, his predecessor having been in office eleven years.

The final siege of the Jews

6. When the Jewish revolt again grew to formidable dimensions, Rufus governor of Judaea, on receiving military reinforcements from the emperor, took merciless advantage of their crazy folly and marched against them, destroying at one stroke unlimited numbers of men, women, and children alike, and – as the laws of war permitted – confiscating all their lands. The Jews at that time were under the command of a man called Bar Cochba, which

means a star – a bloodthirsty bandit who on the strength of his name, as if he had slaves to deal with, paraded himself as a luminary come down from heaven to shine upon their misery.

The climax of the war came in Hadrian's eighteenth year, in Betthera, an almost impregnable little town not very far from Jerusalem. The blockade from without lasted so long that hunger and thirst brought the revolutionaries to complete destruction, and the instigator of their crazy folly paid the penalty he deserved. From that time on, the entire race has been forbidden to set foot anywhere in the neighbourhood of Jerusalem, under the terms and ordinances of a law of Hadrian which ensured that not even from a distance might Jews have a view of their ancestral soil. Aristo of Pella tells the whole story. When in this way the city was closed to the Jewish race and suffered the total destruction of its former inhabitants, it was colonized by an alien race, and the Roman city which subsequently arose changed its name, so that now, in honour of the emperor then reigning, Aelius Hadrianus, it is known as Aelia. Furthermore, as the church in the city was now composed of Gentiles, the first after the bishops of the Circumcision to be put in charge of the Christians there was Mark.

Leaders at that time of Knowledge falsely so called

7. Like dazzling lights the churches were now shining all over the world, and to the limits of the human race faith in our Saviour and Lord Jesus Christ was at its peak, when the demon who hates the good, sworn enemy of truth and inveterate foe of man's salvation, turned all his weapons against the Church. In earlier days he had attacked her with persecutions from without; but now that he was debarred from this, he resorted to unscrupulous impostors as instruments of spiritual corruption and ministers of destruction, and employed new tactics, contriving by every possible means that impostors and cheats, by cloaking themselves with the same name as our religion, should at one and the same time bring to the abyss of destruction every believer they could entrap, and by their own actions and endeavours turn those ignorant of the Faith away from the path that leads to the message of salvation.

Thus it was that from Menander – who was mentioned above as successor to Simon – proceeded a power with the two mouths and twin heads of a snake, which set up the originators of two heresies, Saturninus, an Antiochene by birth, and Basilides of Alexandria, who – one in Syria and one in Egypt – established schools of detestable heresies. For the most part Saturninus taught the same false doctrines as Menander, as Irenaeus makes clear; but Basilides, under the pretence of deeper mysteries, extended his fantasies into the infinite, inventing monstrous fictions to support his impious heresy. Consequently, while a great number of church-men were busy at the time fighting for the truth and eloquently championing the beliefs of the apostles and the Church, some also set down on paper for the benefit of later generations the means of defence against these very heresies.

I have in my hands, from the pen of a very well-known writer of the day, Agrippa Castor, a most effective refutation of Basilides, which unmasks the man's clever imposture. In laying bare his mysteries he says that Basilides compiled twenty-four books on the gospel and that he named as his prophets Barcabbas and Barcoph, inventing for himself several others, creatures of his imagination, and calling them by barbarous names to amaze those who gape at such things. He taught that there was no objection to eating meat offered to idols, or to cheerfully forswearing the Faith in times of persecution. Like Pythagoras he enjoined on his neophytes a five-year silence. Other facts of the same sort about Basilides are catalogued by Agrippa, who thus admirably exposed the erroneous character of this heresy.

Irenaeus also writes that contemporary with these was Car-pocrates, father of another heresy known as that of the Gnostics. These claimed to transmit Simon's magic arts, not secretly like Basilides but quite openly, as if this was something marvellous, preening themselves as it were on the spells which they cast by sorcery, on dream-bringing familiar spirits, and on other goings-on of the same sort. In keeping with this they teach that all the vilest things must be done by those who intend to go through with their initiation into these 'mysteries' or rather abominations; for in no other way can they escape the 'cosmic rulers' than by rendering to them all the due performance of unspeakable rites.

Thus it came about that with the help of these ministers the demon that delights in evil enslaved their pitiable dupes and brought them to ruin, furnishing the unbelieving heathen with ample grounds for speaking ill of the divine message, since the talk to which they gave rise circulated widely and involved the whole Christian people in calumny. This was the main reason why that wicked and outrageous suspicion regarding us was current among the unbelievers of that time – the suspicion that we practised unlawful intercourse with mothers and sisters and took part in unhallowed feasts.

But this propaganda brought Carpocrates no lasting success, for Truth asserted herself, and with the march of time shone with increasing light. For by her activity the machinations of her foes were promptly shown up and extinguished, though one after another new heresies were invented, the earlier ones constantly passing away and disappearing, in different ways at different times, into forms of every shape and character. But the splendour of the Catholic and only true Church, always remaining the same and unchanged, grew steadily in greatness and strength, shedding on every race of Greeks and non-Greeks alike the majestic, spotless, free, sober, pure light of her inspired citizenship and philosophy. Thus the passage of time extinguished the calumnies against the whole of our doctrine, and our teaching remained alone, everywhere victorious and acknowledged as supreme in dignity and sobriety, in divine and philosophic doctrines, so that no one today could dare to subject our Faith to vile abuse or to any such misrepresentation as in the past those who conspired against us were in the habit of using.

Church writers

However, at the time of which I am speaking Truth again put forward many to do battle for her, and they, not only with spoken arguments but also with written demonstrations, took the field against the godless heresies. Among these Hegesippus was prominent. 8. I have already quoted him on numerous occasions, using information gained from him to establish facts about the apostolic age. In five short books, written in the simplest style, he gave an authentic account of the apostolic preaching. His *floruit* is indicated by his remarks on those who first set up idols:

> In their honour they erected cenotaphs and temples, as they still do. One of these was Antinous, a slave of Hadrian Caesar's, in memory of whom the Antinoian Games are held. He was my own contemporary. Hadrian even built a city called after him, and appointed prophets.

In his time also Justin, a genuine lover of the true philosophy, was still busy studying Greek learning. He too indicates this date, when in his *Defence* to Antoninus he writes:

> I think it not out of place at this point to mention Antinous who died so recently. Everyone was frightened into worshipping him as a god, though everyone knew who he was and where he came from.[1]

Again, speaking of the war which had just been fought against the Jews, Justin remarks:

> In the recent Jewish war, Bar Cochba, leader of the Jewish insurrection, ordered the Christians alone to be sentenced to terrible punishments if they did not deny Jesus Christ and blaspheme Him.[2]

In the same volume he also shows that his change from Greek philosophy to true religion was not made hastily but after mature reflection:

> I myself found satisfaction in Plato's teaching, and used to hear the Christians abused, but when I found them fearless in the face of death and all that men think terrible, it dawned on me that they could not possibly be living in wickedness and self-indulgence. For how could a self-indulgent or licentious person who took pleasure in devouring human flesh greet death with a smile, as if he wanted to be deprived of the things he loved most? Would he not rather strive by all means to prolong his present existence indefinitely, and keep out of sight of the secular authorities, rather than give himself up to certain death?[3]

Justin also notes that when Hadrian received from His Excellency the Governor Serennius Granianus an appeal on behalf of the

1. *Defence*, I. 29.   2. Ibid., I. 31.   3. Ibid., II. 12.

Christians, maintaining that it was not right when no charge had been brought to gratify popular clamour by putting them to death without a trial, he sent a rescript to Minucius Fundanus, proconsul of Asia, forbidding him to try anyone unless properly charged and prosecuted in a reasonable manner. He appends a copy of the letter, retaining the original Latin and prefacing it with the following:

Though on the strength of a letter from the great and glorious Caesar Hadrian, your father, I might have petitioned you to carry out my request and order the trials to be held, I am basing this request not on the command of Hadrian but on my awareness that in my address I am requesting what is just. However I am appending a facsimile of Hadrian's letter, that you may know that on this point also I am speaking the truth. Here it is.[1]

To this the writer appends the actual Latin rescript: I have rendered it into Greek as well as I can.

Hadrian's letter forbidding persecution without trial

9. To Minucius Fundanus. I have received a letter written to me by His Excellency Serennius Granianus, your predecessor. It is not my intention to leave the matter uninvestigated, for fear of causing the men embarrassment and abetting the informers in their mischief-making. If then the provincials can so clearly establish their case against the Christians that they can sustain it in a court of law, let them resort to this procedure only, and not rely on petitions or mere clamour. Much the most satisfactory course, if anyone should wish to prosecute, is for you to decide the matter. So if someone prosecutes them and proves them guilty of any illegality, you must pronounce sentence according to the seriousness of the offence. But if anyone starts such proceedings in the hope of financial reward, then for goodness sake arrest him for his shabby trick, and see that he gets his deserts.[2]

Such were the terms of Hadrian's rescript.

Bishops of Rome and Alexandria in Antoninus' reign: the heresiarchs

10. When Hadrian, after twenty-one years, paid the debt of nature,

1. Ibid., I. 68.   2. Ibid.

Antoninus called Pius succeeded to the Roman Empire. In his first year, Telesphorus departed this life in the eleventh year of his ministry, and Hyginus took over the office of Bishop of Rome. Irenaeus notes that Telesphorus died nobly as a martyr. In the same chapter he states that while Hyginus was bishop, Valentinus, who introduced a heresy of his own, and Cerdo, who was responsible for the Marcionite error, were both prominent in Rome. He writes:

11. Valentinus arrived in Rome in the time of Hyginus, reached his heyday under Pius, and remained till Anicetus. Cerdo, who preceded Marcion, also joined the Roman church and declared his faith publicly, in the time of Hyginus, the ninth bishop; then he went on in this way – at one time he taught in secret, at another he again declared his faith publicly, at another he was convicted of mischievous teaching and expelled from the Christian community.[1]

This comes from Book III of *Against Heresies*. In Book I we find this additional information about Cerdo:

One Cerdo, whose notions stemmed from the followers of Simon, had settled in Rome in the time of Hyginus, who held the ninth place in the episcopal succession from the apostles. He taught that the God proclaimed by the Law and the Prophets was not the Father of our Lord Jesus Christ; for the one was known, the other unknown; the one was righteous, the other gracious. He was succeeded by Marcion of Pontus, who inflated his teaching, blaspheming unblushingly.[2]

In another passage Irenaeus most effectively exposes the limitless depths of Valentinus' most erroneous system, and brings his wickedness, hidden out of sight like a reptile lurking in a hole, to the light of day. He further tells us about a contemporary of theirs, Marcus by name, a past-master in magical trickery, and writes of their senseless ceremonies and misbegotten mysteries, explaining them thus:

Some of them fit out a bridal chamber, and celebrate a mystery with invocations on those being initiated, declaring that what they are doing is

---

1. *Against Heresies*, III. 4. 2.   2. Ibid., I. 14.

a spiritual marriage on the pattern of the unions above; others take the candidates to water and baptize them, reciting this formula: 'Into the name of the unknown Father of the universe, into Truth the Mother of all things, into Him who came down into Jesus.' Others recite Hebrew words, in order to cause still more astonishment to those being initiated.[1]

After four years as Bishop of Rome Hyginus died, and Pius was chosen for the office. At Alexandria Mark was appointed pastor when Eumenes had completed thirteen years in all; ten years later, when Mark rested from his ministry, Celadion took over the ministry of the church at Alexandria. In Rome Pius passed away in the fifteenth year of his episcopate and Anicetus took charge of the community there. In his time Hegesippus settled in Rome, as he tells us himself, staying there till the episcopate of Eleutherus.

In their time Justin was at his most active; wearing the garb of a philosopher he proclaimed the divine message, and contended by means of his writings on behalf of the Faith. In a pamphlet which he wrote against Marcion he mentions that at the time when he was composing it the man was alive and in the public eye:

There was one Marcion of Pontus, who is still busy teaching his adherents to believe in some other god greater than the Creator. All over the world, with the help of the demons, he has induced many to speak blasphemously, denying that the Maker of his universe is the Father of Christ, and declaring that the universe was made by another, greater than He. All who base their belief on such doctrines are, as I said, called Christians, just as philosophers, even if they have no common principles, yet have one thing in common – the name 'philosopher'.

He adds a further note:

I have also written a book in answer to all the heresies that have appeared: if you would care to read it, I will present it to you.[2]

Justin's Defence: *Antoninus' letter to the Council of Asia*

Justin, in addition to his admirable work *Against the Greeks*,

1. Ibid., I. 14.   2. *Defence*, I. 26.

addressed other compositions containing *A Defence of our Faith* to the Emperor Antoninus, surnamed Pius, and to the Roman Senate: he had made his home in the capital. In the *Defence* he explains who he was and where he came from:

12. To the Emperor Titus Aelius Hadrianus Antoninus Pius Caesar Augustus, to Verissimus his son the philosopher, to Lucius, son by nature of the philosopher Caesar and by adoption of Pius, a passionate seeker after knowledge, and to the holy Senate and the entire People of Rome, on behalf of the men of every nation who are unjustly hated and abused, I, Justin, son of Priscus and grandson of Bacchius, of Flavia Neapolis in Palestine, being one of their number, have composed this address and petition.[1]

Petitioned also by Christians in Asia who were labouring under injuries of every kind at the hands of the local population, the same emperor was pleased to address this decree to the Council of Asia.

13. The Emperor Caesar Marcus Aurelius Antoninus Augustus Armenius, Pontifex Maximus, holding Tribunician Power the fifteenth time, Consul the third, to the Council of Asia, greeting. I know that the gods also take care that such persons should not go undetected: they are far more likely to punish those who will not worship them than you are. You get them into serious trouble by your accusations of atheism, and thereby strengthen their existing determination: and if accused they would choose apparent death rather than life, for the sake of their own god. And so they are the real winners, when they part with their lives rather than agree to carry out your commands. As regards the earthquakes which have been and still are occurring, it will not be out of place to draw your attention to the fact that whenever they happen your courage fails you, providing a painful contrast between our morale and theirs. They gain increased confidence in their god; whereas you, the whole of the time that you appear to be ignorant, neglect the other gods and the worship of the Immortal. But when the Christians worship Him you bully them and persecute them to death. On behalf of these people many of the provincial governors at an earlier date wrote to our most divine father, who sent them a reply forbidding them to take any action against these people

1. Ibid., I. 1.

unless it was clear that they were scheming against the Roman government. I too have received information about them from many quarters: I have replied in accordance with my father's wishes. But if anyone persists in starting legal proceedings against one of these people, simply because he is one of them, the accused shall be acquitted of the charge even if it is plain that he is one, and the accuser shall be liable to penalty. Published at Ephesus in the Council of Asia.

That this is how things happened we also gather from Melito, the eminent Bishop of Sardis at that time. So much is clear from what he says in the *Defence of our Doctrine* which he sent to the Emperor Verus.

The story of Polycarp, the pupil of the apostles

14. At this period, while Anicetus was head of the Roman church, Polycarp, who was still living, came to Rome and discussed with Anicetus some difficulty about the date of Easter. This we gather from Irenaeus, who tells us another story about Polycarp which must be included in the account of him that I am giving. Here it is:

FROM BOOK III OF AGAINST HERESIES, BY IRENAEUS

Polycarp was not only instructed by apostles and conversant with many who had seen the Lord, but was appointed by apostles to serve in Asia as Bishop of Smyrna. I myself saw him in my early years, for he lived a long time and was very old indeed when he laid down his life by a glorious and most splendid martyrdom. At all times he taught the things which he had learnt from the apostles, which the Church transmits, which alone are true. These facts are attested by all the churches of Asia and by the successors of Polycarp to this day – and he was a much more trustworthy and dependable witness to the truth than Valentinus and Marcion and all other wrong-headed persons. In the time of Anicetus he stayed for a while in Rome, where he won over many from the camp of these heretics to the Church of God, proclaiming that the one and only truth he had received from the apostles was the truth transmitted by the Church. And there are people who heard him describe how John, the Lord's disciple, when at Ephesus went to take a bath, but seeing Cerinthus inside rushed out of the building without taking a bath, crying: 'Let us get out of here, for fear the place falls in, now that Cerinthus, the enemy of truth, is inside!' Polycarp himself on one occasion came face to face with Marcion, and when Marcion said 'Don't you recognize me?' he replied: 'I do indeed: I recognize the firstborn of Satin!' So careful were the apostles and their disciples to avoid even exchanging words with any falsifier of the truth, in obedience to the Pauline injunction: 'If a man remains heretical after more than one warning, have no more to do with him, recognizing that a person of that type is a perverted sinner, self-condemned.[1]

There is also a most forceful epistle written by Polycarp to the Philippians, from which both the character of his faith and his preaching of the truth can be learnt by all who wish to do so and care about their own salvation.[2]

Such is Irenaeus' account. Polycarp in his letter to the Philippians, referred to above and still extant, has supported his views with several quotations from the First Epistle of Peter.

Martyrdom of Polycarp and others at Smyrna

Antoninus Pius, after a reign of twenty-two years, was succeeded by his son Marcus Aurelius Verus (or Antoninus) in association with his brother Lucius. 15. In this period Asia was thrown into confusion by the most savage persecutions, and Polycarp found fulfilment in martyrdom. As a written account of his end has come down to us, I am in duty bound to enshrine it in my pages. I refer to the letter, sent on behalf of the church over which he himself had presided, to inform the Christian communities everywhere of what happened to him. It begins thus:

The Church of God at Smyrna to the church of God at Philomelium and to all communities of the Holy Catholic Church everywhere – may mercy, peace, and love from God the Father and our Lord Jesus Christ be yours in abundance. We are writing, brethren, to tell you the story of those who have suffered martyrdom, especially blessed Polycarp, who as though he had set his seal on it by his martyrdom, brought the persecution to an end.

1. Titus iii. 10.   2. *Against Heresies*, III. 3. 4.

After this, before giving an account of Polycarp's death, they relate what happened to the other martyrs, vividly describing the heroism with which they faced their torments, to the amazement of the spectators on every side. Sometimes they were torn with scourges to the innermost veins and arteries, so that even the secret hidden parts of the body, the entrails and internal organs, were laid bare; sometimes they were forced to lie on pointed seashells and sharp spikes. After going through every kind of punishment and torture, they were finally flung to the beasts as food.

Special mention is made of the noble Germanicus, who by divine grace overcame his natural physical fear of death. The proconsul tried to dissuade him, stressing his youth and begging him as one still in the very prime of life to spare himself; but without a moment's hesitation he drew the savage beast towards him, wellnigh forcing and goading it on, the more quickly to escape from their wicked, lawless life. After his glorious death the whole crowd were so astounded by the heroism of God's beloved martyr, and the courage of Christian people everywhere, that a shout went up from all sides: 'Away with the godless! Fetch Polycarp!' The uproar that followed these shouts was so tremendous that a man named Quintus, newly arrived from Phrygia, on seeing the beasts and the threatened torments to follow broke down completely and ended by throwing away his salvation. It is plain from the text of the letter I have quoted that along with others this man dashed towards the tribunal with too much haste and without due thought, but when seized he gave everyone clear proof that it is fatal to risk such ventures in a reckless and thoughtless spirit. So ends the story of these men.

As for the wonderful Polycarp, when he first heard the news he remained unperturbed, preserving a firm and unshakeable demeanour, and wished to stay on in the city; but when his friends begged and besought him to make good his escape he was persuaded to go as far as a farm only a little distance away. There he remained with a few companions, devoting himself night and day to constant prayer to the Lord, pleading and imploring as he had always done that God would grant peace to the churches throughout the world. Three nights before his arrest, while at prayer he saw in a trance the pillow under his head burst into flames and burn to a cinder. He awoke at once and interpreted the vision to those present, opening the book of things to come and leaving his friends in no doubt that for Christ's sake he was to depart this life by fire. As the efforts of his pursuers went on relentlessly, the love and devotion of the brethren compelled him to move on to yet another farm. There he was soon overtaken: two of the farm servants were seized, and under torture one of them revealed Polycarp's quarters. Late in the evening they arrived and found him in bed upstairs. He might easily have moved to another house but he had refused, saying: 'God's will be done.' Indeed, when he heard that they had come, the account informs us, he came down and talked to them in the most cheerful and gentle manner, so that, never having seen him before, they could hardly believe their eyes when confronted with his advanced years and dignified confident bearing. Why, they wondered, was there such anxiety to arrest an old man of this kind? He meanwhile ordered the table to be laid for them immediately, and invited them to eat as much as they liked, asking in return a single hour in which he could pray unmolested. Leave being given, he stood up and prayed, full of the grace of the Lord, to the amazement of those whose were present and heard him pray, many of them indeed distressed now by the coming destruction of an old man so dignified and so godlike.

From that point the letter tells us the rest of the story as follows:

At last he ended his prayer, after mentioning all with whom at any time he had been associated, whether small or great, famous or unknown, and the whole Catholic Church throughout the world. The hour for departure had come, so they set him on an ass and brought him to the city. The day was a Great Sabbath. He was met by Herod the chief of police and his father Nicetes, who after transferring him to their carriage sat beside him and tried persuasion. 'What harm is there in saying "Lord Caesar" and sacrificing? You will be safe then.' At first he made no answer, but when they persisted he replied: 'I have no intention of taking your advice.' Persuasion having failed they turned to threats, and put him down so hurriedly that in leaving the carriage he scraped his shin. But without even looking round, as if nothing had happened, he set off happily and at a swinging pace for the stadium. There the noise was so deafening that many could not hear at all, but as Polycarp came into the arena a voice from heaven came to him: 'Be strong, Polycarp, and play the man.' No one saw the speaker, but many of our people heard the voice.

His introduction was followed by a tremendous roar as the news went round: 'Polycarp has been arrested!' At length, when he stepped forward, he was asked by the proconsul if he really was Polycarp. When he said yes, the proconsul urged him to deny the charge. 'Respect your years!' he exclaimed, adding similar appeals regularly made on such occasions: 'Swear by Caesar's fortune; change your attitude; say: "Away with the godless!"' But Polycarp, with his face set, looked at all the crowd in the stadium and waved his hand towards them, sighed, looked up to heaven, and cried: 'Away with the godless!' The governor pressed him further: 'Swear, and I will set you free: execrate Christ.' 'For eighty-six years,' replied Polycarp, 'I have been His servant, and He has never done me wrong: how can I blaspheme my King who saved me?' When the other persisted: 'Swear by Caesar's fortune,' Polycarp retorted: 'If you imagine that I will swear by Caesar's fortune, as you put it, pretending not to know who I am, I will tell you plainly, I am a Christian. If you wish to study the Christian doctrine, choose a day and you shall hear it.' The proconsul replied, 'Convince the people.' 'With you,' rejoined Polycarp, 'I think it proper to discuss these things; for we have been taught to render as their due to rulers and powers ordained by God such honour as casts no stain on us: to the people I do not feel it my duty to make any defence.' 'I have wild beasts,' said the proconsul. 'I shall throw you to them, if you don't change your attitude.' 'Call them,' replied the old man. 'We cannot change our attitude if it means a change from better to worse. But it is a splendid thing to change from cruelty to justice.' 'If you make light of the beasts,' retorted the governor, 'I'll have you destroyed by fire, unless you change your attitude.' Polycarp answered: 'The fire you threaten burns for a time and is soon extinguished: there is a fire you know nothing about – the fire of the judgement to come and of eternal punishment, the fire reserved for the ungodly. But why do you hesitate? Do what you want.'

As he said this and much besides, he was filled with courage and joy, and his features were full of grace, so that not only did he not wilt in alarm at the things said to him, but on the contrary the proconsul was amazed, and sent the crier to stand in the middle of the arena and announce three times: 'Polycarp has confessed that he is a Christian.' At this announcement the whole mass of Smyrnaeans, Gentiles and Jews alike, boiled with anger and shouted at the tops of their voices: 'This fellow is the teacher of Asia, the father of the Christians, the destroyer of our gods, who teaches numbers of people not to sacrifice or even worship.' So saying, they loudly demanded that the Asiarch Philip should set a lion on Polycarp. He objected that this would be illegal, as he had closed the sports. Then a shout went up from every throat that Polycarp must be burnt alive. For it was inevitable that the vision which appeared to him about the pillow should be fulfilled: he had seen it burning as he prayed, and turning to the faithful with him said prophetically: 'I must be burnt alive.'

The rest followed in less time than it takes to describe: the crowds rushed to collect logs and faggots from workshop and public baths, the Jews as usual joining in with more enthusiasm than anyone. When the pyre was ready, he took off all his outer garments, loosened his belt, and even tried to remove his shoes, though not used to doing this, because each of the faithful strove at all times to be the first to touch his person. Even before his hair turned grey he had been honoured in every way because of his virtuous life. There was no hesitation now. The instruments prepared for the pyre were put round him, but when they were going to nail him too, he cried: 'Leave me as I am: He who enables me to endure the fire will enable me, even if you don't secure me with nails, to remain on the pyre without shrinking.' So they bound him without nailing him. He put his hands behind him and was bound like a noble ram presented from a great flock as a whole burnt offering acceptable to God Almighty. Then he prayed: 'O Father of Thy beloved and blessed Son, Jesus Christ, through whom we have come to know Thee, the God of angels and powers and all creation, and of the whole family of the righteous who live in Thy presence, I bless Thee for counting me worthy of this day and hour, that in the number of the martyrs I may partake of Christ's cup, to the resurrection of eternal life of both soul and body in the imperishability that is the gift of the Holy Ghost. Among them may I be received into Thy presence today, a rich and acceptable sacrifice as Thou has prepared it beforehand, foreshadowing it and fulfilling it, Thou God of truth that canst not lie. Therefore for every cause I praise Thee, I bless Thee, I glorify Thee, through the eternal High Priest, Jesus Christ Thy beloved Son, through whom and with whom in the Holy Ghost glory be to Thee, both now and in the ages to come. Amen.'

When he had offered up the Amen and completed his prayer, the men in charge lit the fire, and a great flame shot up. Then we saw a marvellous sight, we who were privileged to see it and were spared to tell the others what happened. The fire took the shape of a vaulted room, like a ship's sail filled with wind, and made a wall round the martyr's body, which was in the middle not like burning flesh but like gold and silver refined in a furnace. Indeed, we were conscious of a wonderful fragrance, like a breath of frankincense or some other costly spice. At last, seeing that the body could not be consumed by the fire, the lawless people summoned a *confector* to come forward and drive home his sword. When he did so there came out a stream of blood that quenched the fire, so that the whole crowd was astonished at the difference between the unbelievers and the elect. To the elect belonged this man, the most wonderful apostolic and prophetic teacher of our time, bishop of the Catholic Church in Smyrna. For every word that he uttered was and shall be fulfilled.

But when the evil one, the enemy of the household of the righteous, saw the greatness of Polycarp's martyrdom and the blamelessness of his entire life, and how he had been crowned with the crown of imperishability and had carried off a prize beyond gainsaying, in jealousy and envy he saw to it that not even his poor body should be taken away by us, though many longed to do this and to have communion with his holy flesh. So Nicetes, Herod's father and Alce's brother, was induced to request the governor not to give up the body 'lest they should abandon the Crucified and start worshipping this fellow'. These suggestions were made under persistent pressure from the Jews, who watched us when we were going to take him out of the fire, not realizing that we can never forsake Christ, who suffered for the salvation of those who are being saved in the entire world, or worship anyone else. For to Him, as the Son of God, we offer adoration; but to the martyrs, as disciples and imitators of the Lord, we give the love that they deserve for their unsurpassable devotion to their own King and Teacher: may it be our privilege to be their fellow-members and fellow-disciples.

When the centurion saw that the Jews were determined to make trouble, he brought him into their midst in the usual way and burnt him. So later on we took up his bones, more precious than stones of great price, more splendid than gold, and laid them where it seemed right. When, if it proves possible, we assemble there, the Lord will allow us to celebrate with joy and gladness the birthday of his martyrdom, both to the memory of those who have contended in the past, and for the training and preparation of those whose time is yet to come.

Such was the story of blessed Polycarp. Counting those from Philadelphia, he was the twelfth to endure martyrdom at Smyrna, but he alone is specially remembered by all, so that even the heathen everywhere speak of him.

And such was the conclusion granted to the story of that wonderful and apostolic man. The record was set down by the brethren of the church at Smyrna in the letter which I have reproduced.

The document which tells us about Polycarp contains accounts of other martyrdoms which also took place at Smyrna at about the same period as his. Among them Metrodorus, who in Marcion's heretical sect passed for a presbyter, was consigned to the flames and put to death. One of the best-known and most celebrated matryrs of that time was Pionius. His repeated declarations of belief, his outspokenness, his defences of the Faith before the people and the authorities, his public lectures, as well as his friendly aid to those who had yielded to temptation in the persecution, and the encouraging words that he addressed in prison to the brother-Christians who visited him; the tortures that he later suffered, the agonies that these involved, the nailings, his endurance on the pyre, and to crown all his marvellous deeds his death – all these are described very fully in the *Martyrdom of Pionius*, which is included in my collection of *Early Martyrdoms* and which I can recommend to those interested.

Extant also are memoirs of others who were martyred in Pergamum, a city in Asia, Carpus and Papylus and a woman, Agathonice, who after many noble declarations of their belief found glorious fulfilment.

Justin the Philosopher martyred in Rome

16. At the same period, Justin, whom I mentioned a little way back, after presenting a second book in defence of our doctrines to the rulers already named, was honoured with a divine martyrdom, owing to the philosopher Crescens, a man who strove to make his life and conduct conform to his title of Cynic. It was he who devised the plot against Justin; for Justin had repeatedly refuted

him in debate with an audience present, and now at the last by his martyrdom bound on his brow the trophies of victory of the truth he ever proclaimed. That martyrdom he himself, truly the most philosophical of men, clearly foretold in the *Defence* referred to above, exactly as it was so soon to happen to him. This is what he wrote:

I too expect to be plotted against and clapped in the stocks by one of those I have named, or maybe by Crescens, who calls himself a philosopher yet is a lover not of wisdom but of showing off. He does not deserve the name of philosopher, seeing that he publicly criticizes what he does not understand, alleging that Christians are godless and impious, his object being to win the favour and applause of the deluded masses. For if he lashes out at us without studying Christ's teaching he is most unscrupulous and much worse than simple people, who as a rule refrain from arguing and making false statements on subjects they know nothing about: if he has studied it and failed to understand its greatness, or has understood it but for fear of being suspected behaves in this shameful way, there is all the more reason to call him ignoble and unscrupulous, yielding as he does to ignorant and senseless prejudice and suspicion. I would like you to know that by putting certain questions of this kind for him to answer I found out – in fact, proved – that he really is totally ignorant: to show that I am speaking the truth, if you have not been informed of our discussions, I am prepared even in your presence to discuss the questions again. This would be a task worthy of emperors. But if you are already acquainted with my questions and his answers, it must be obvious to you that he knows nothing of what we stand for: if he does know, but dare not say so for fear of the audience, then, as I said before, he is shown up as a lover not of wisdom but of glory: for he does not even honour the admirable precept of Socrates.[1]

These are Justin's words. That in accordance with his own prediction he was entrapped by Crescens, and found his fulfilment, is recorded by Tatian – a man who in his early years acquired considerable reputation by his lectures on Greek philosophy and science, and left a number of works for which he will long be remembered – in his work *Against the Greeks*:

That wonderful man, Justin, rightly declared that these people were no better than bandits.[2]

1. *Defence*, II.8.   2. *Against the Greeks*, 18.

Then, after further comments on the philosophers, he goes on:

Crescens, for instance, who made his lair in the great city, went beyond everyone in his offences against boys, and was passionately devoted to money-making. He urged others to depise death, but was so afraid of it himself that he did his best to compass the death of Justin – as though death was a calamity – simply because by preaching the truth Justin convicted the philosophers of gluttony and fraud.[1]

Such was the cause of Justin's martyrdom.

The martyrs mentioned in Justin's own writings

17. Before his own ordeal Justin, in his first *Defence*, refers to others martyred before him. His account bears on our subject:

There was a woman who lived with a dissolute husband. At first she was as dissolute as he was, but when she came to know Christ's teaching, she reformed her ways and tried to persuade her husband to reform his, passing on what she had learnt and warning him that there will be punishment in eternal fire for those who do not reform and order their lives aright. But he remained as dissipated as ever and by his actions estranged his wife. For she thought it wrong to go on sharing the bed of a man who in defiance of natural law and of morality tried to obtain the satisfaction of his desires in every possible way; so she planned to end the union. When, however, she was implored by her family, who urged her to remain with him still, in the hope that one day her husband would change, she forced herself to stay. But when her husband went off to Alexandria, and news came that he was behaving still worse, she determined not to be involved in his abominable misconduct by maintaining the marriage bond as sharer of his board and bed; so she gave him what you call the *repudium*, and regained her freedom.

That splendid fellow, her husband, ought to have been glad that she had finished with all that in the old days she had done so recklessly with servants and hirelings, delighting in drunken revels and vice of every kind, and that she wanted him to finish with them too. But no. She had left him against his wish, so he brought an accusation against her on the ground that she was a Christian. She then filed a petition with you, the Emperor, asking that she might be allowed first to put her affairs in order,

1. Ibid., 19.

and when that was done to answer the accusation. To this you agreed. Her former husband was no longer in a position to attack her, so he turned his attention to a man called Ptolemy, who had been her instructor in Christian doctrine and was punished by Urbicius. His method was simple. He persuaded a centurion friend to manacle Ptolemy, hold him tight, and ask him one question only – was he a Christian? When Ptolemy, a truthful man who hated deceit and falsehood, confessed himself a Christian, the centurion kept him manacled and tortured him for a long time in the prison. Finally, the poor fellow was brought before Urbicius and questioned as before on one point only – was he a Christian? Again, fully conscious of the benefits that came to him through Christ's teaching he confessed his schooling in divine virtues. For a man who denies anything either denies it because he condemns it, or avoids confession because he knows that he is unworthy and incapable of it. Neither of these is true of the real Christian.

When Urbicius ordered him to be led to execution, one Lucius, a Christian like Ptolemy, seeing the utter unreasonableness of the verdict said to Urbicius: 'Why have you punished this man, who is neither an adulterer, a fornicator, a homicide, a thief, nor a robber, and has not been found guilty of any offence, but merely confesses the name of Christian? Your verdict is discreditable to the Emperor Pius, to Caesar's philosopher son, and to the sacred Senate, Urbicius.' Urbicius made no reply except to say to Lucius: 'I think you're one of them yourself.' And when Lucius answered 'Indeed I am', he ordered him also to be led to execution. 'Thank you very much,' said Lucius. 'Now I'm free from such iniquitous masters, and I'm going to God, my gracious Father and King.' Then a third man stepped forward, and was condemned to the same punishment.[1]

From this Justin naturally goes on to add the words I quoted above:

I too expect to be plotted against by one of those I have named, etc.

The works of Justin that have come into my hands

18. Justin has left us many short works, the products of a cultured mind deeply versed in theology. They are full of good things, and I can recommend them to students, indicating those that have

1. *Defence*, II. 2.

come usefully to my knowledge. There is one work of his championing our doctrines, addressed to Antoninus Pius, his sons, and the Roman Senate, and another containing *A Second Defence of our Faith*, written for the enlightenment of that emperor's successor and namesake, Antoninus Verus, whose period I am dealing with at present. A third work is *Against the Greeks*, in which, after a very lengthy discussion of numerous questions debated both by ourselves and by the Greek philosophers, he expatiates on the nature of demons: these arguments there is no pressing need to quote at present. A second treatise of his in answer to the Greeks has come into my hands: this he entitled *A Refutation*. Then there is one called *The Sovereignty of God*, compiled not only from our own scriptures but from Greek books as well. Besides these there is a work entitled *The Harpist*, and a disputation on *The Soul*, in which he propounds various questions regarding the problem involved, and cites the opinions of the Greek philosophers: he promises to answer these and state his own opinion in a further treatise. Finally, he composed a *Dialogue against the Jews*, reproducing the argument that he had had in Ephesus with Trypho, one of the most eminent Hebrews of the day. In it he shows how God's grace guided him into the doctrine of the Faith, how keen he had once been on philosophic studies, and how fanatically he had striven to learn the truth.

Describing in the same work how the Jews contrived a plot against the teaching of Christ, he hurls these reproaches at Trypho:

Not only did you feel no remorse for your crimes, but you chose picked men at that time and dispatched them from Jerusalem to all parts of the world, saying that a godless sect of Christians had appeared, and retailing all the accusations which those who do not know us invariably bring against us, so that you corrupt not only yourselves but the entire human race.[1]

He also tells us that right up to his own time prophetic gifts were a conspicuous feature of the Church. He refers to the Revelation of John, stating explicitly that it was the work of the apostle. He also cites some passages from the prophets, proving

1. *Dialogue*, 17.

against Trypho that the Jews had actually cut them out of the Scriptures.

Numerous other books on which he laboured are in the possession of many Christian scholars, and so worthy of study did even the earlier writers think his writings that Irenaeus quotes passages from him. Book IV of *Against Heresies*, he makes this comment:

> Justin puts it neatly in his treatise against Marcion: 'I would not have believed the Lord Himself, if He had preached another god beside the Creator.'[1]

And in Book V of the same work he writes:

> Justin puts it neatly: 'Before the Lord's advent Satan never dared blaspheme God, since he did not yet know his condemnation.'[2]

All this had to be said to encourage students to pay careful attention to his books, and there we will leave him.

Prelates of Rome, Alexandria, and Antioch: Church writers of the time

19. When this reign was now in its eighth year Anicetus, who had completed eleven years as Bishop of Rome, was succeeded by Soter, and when Celadion had headed the see of Alexandria for fourteen years [20] Agrippinus took up the succession; while in the diocese of Antioch Theophilus, sixth from the apostles, was eminent. The fourth, appointed there after Hero, had been Cornelius, and after him in the fifth place Eros had succeeded to the bishopric.

21. It was at this period that a number of writers flourished in the Church. Hegesippus we have met already. There was also Bishop Dionysius of Corinth and Bishop Pinytus of Crete, as well as Philip, Apolinarius, Melito, Musanus, Modestus, and above all Irenaeus. In every case writings which show their orthodoxy and unshakeable devotion to the apostolic tradition have come into my hands.

---

1. *Against Heresies*, IV, 11. 2.   2. Ibid., V. 26. 3.

22. Hegesippus in the five short works that have come into my hands has left a very full acount of his own beliefs. In them he describes how when travelling as far as Rome he mixed with a number of bishops and found the same doctrine among them all. Listen to what he appends to some remarks about Clement's *Epistle to the Corinthians*:

The Corinthian church continued in the true doctrine until Primus became bishop. I mixed with them on my voyage to Rome and spent several days with the Corinthians, during which we were refreshed with the true doctrine. On arrival at Rome I pieced together the succession down to Anicetus, whose deacon was Eleutherus, Anicetus being succeeded by Soter and he by Eleutherus. In every line of bishops and in every city things accord with the preaching of the Law, the Prophets, and the Lord.

The same writer sketches the origins of the heresies of his day:

When James the Righteous had suffered martyrdom like the Lord and for the same reason, Symeon the son of his uncle Clopas was appointed bishop. He being a cousin of the Lord, it was the universal demand that he should be the second. They used to call the Church a virgin for this reason, that she had not yet been seduced by listening to nonsense. But Thebuthis, because he had not been made bishop, began to seduce her by means of the seven sects (to which he himself belonged) among the people. From these came Simon and his Simonians, Cleobius and his Cleobienes, Dositheus and his Dositheans, Gorthaeus and his Gorathenes, and the Masbotheans. From these were derived the Menandrianists, Marcionists, Carpocratians, Valentinians, Basilidians, and Saturnilians, every man introducing his own opinion in his own particular way. From these in turn came false Christs, false prophets, false apostles, who split the unity of the Church by poisonous suggestions against God and against His Christ.

Hegesippus also names the sects that once existed among the Jews:

There were various groups in the Circumcision, among the Children of Israel, all hostile to the tribe of Judah and the Christ. They were these – Essenes, Galilaeans, Hemerobaptists, Masbotheans, Samaritans, Sadducees, and Pharisees.

He wrote much else besides, to parts of which I have already referred, quoting his narrative whenever it was to the point. He also draws occasionally on the Gospel of the Hebrews, on the Syriac Gospel, and particularly on works in Hebrew, showing that he was a believer of Hebrew stock, and he mentions other matters as coming from Jewish oral tradition. And not only he but Irenaeus too, and the whole group of early writers, used to call Solomon's Proverbs the 'All-virtuous Wisdom'. And in discussing the apocryphal books, as they are called, he states that some of them were fabricated by heretics in his own time. But now I must move on to another writer.

The epistles of Bishop Dionysius of Corinth

23. First it must be said of Dionysius that when he had been enthroned as Bishop of Corinth he lavished his inspired industry without stint, not only on those under him but also on those in foreign lands, rendering the greatest service to all in the general epistles which he indited to the churches. Of these the one to the Spartans contains instruction in orthodoxy and an exhortation to peace and unity; the one to the Athenians is a rousing call to faith and to life according to the gospel. For their scorn of such a life, he takes them to task as virtual apostates from the word, since Publius their bishop had died a martyr's death in the persecutions of the time. He mentions that after Publius' martyrdom Quadratus was appointed their bishop, and testifies that through his endeavours they were brought together and their faith rekindled. He further informs us that Dionysius the Areopagite who, as related in the Acts,[1] was converted to the Faith by the apostle Paul, was the first to be appointed Bishop of Athens.

Another extant epistle of his is addressed to the Nicomedians. In this he joins battle with Marcion's heresy in defence of the standard of truth.

He also wrote to the church at Gortyna and the other communities in Crete, congratulating Philip, their bishop, on the

---

1. Acts xvii. 34.

many courageous acts credited to the church under him, but warning him to guard against the distortions of the heretics.

In a similar letter to the church at Amastris and to those in Pontus he mentions that Bacchylides and Elpistus had pressed him to write it. He then gives explanations of Holy Scripture, and refers by name to their bishop Palmas. The letter also contains a great deal of advice about marriage and celibacy, and a directive that those who returned to the fold after any kind of lapse, whether improper conduct or heretical error, should be warmly received.

Next on the list is an epistle to the Cnossians, in which he urges Pinytus, the bishop of the diocese, not to put on the brethren a heavy burden as being essential[1] – the rule of celibacy – but to remember that most people were weak creatures. To this Pinytus replies that he admires and esteems Dionysius, but urges him in his turn to provide more solid food in the near future and nourish his flock with a further letter, this time a more advanced one, so that they may not be kept all their lives on a diet of milky words and treated like babes till they grow old without knowing it. In this letter Pinytus' orthodoxy regarding the Faith, his anxiety to help those under him, his learning and grasp of theology, are mirrored to perfection.

There is also extant an epistle of Dionysius to the Romans, addressed to the then bishop, Soter. I cannot do better than quote the passage in which he commends the custom observed at Rome down to the persecution of our own day:

From the start it has been your custom to treat all Christians with unfailing kindness, and to send contributions to many churches in every city, sometimes alleviating the distress of those in need, sometimes providing for your brothers in the mines by the contributions you have sent from the start. Thus you Romans have observed the ancestral Roman custom, which your revered Bishop Soter has not only maintained but enlarged, by generously providing the abundant supplies distributed among God's people, and by encouraging with inspired words fellow-Christians who come to the city, as an affectionate father encourages his children.[2]

---

1. Matt. xxiii. 4 and Acts xv. 28.   2. I Thess. ii. 11.

In the same letter he refers to Clement's *Epistle to the Corinthians*, proving that from the very first it had been customary to read it in church. He says:

Today being the Lord's Day, we kept it as a holy day and read your epistle, which we shall read frequently for its valuable advice, like the earlier epistle which Clement wrote on your behalf.

Dionysius tells us that his own epistles had been tampered with:

When my fellow-Christians invited me to write letters to them I did so. These the devil's apostles have filled with tares,[1] taking away some things and adding others. For them the woe is reserved.[2] Small wonder then if some have dared to tamper even with the word of the Lord Himself, when they have conspired to mutilate my own humble efforts.

In addition to these there is an extant letter of Dionysius to Chrysophora, a devoted Christian woman. He writes most appropriately, and imparts to her the spiritual nourishment that she requires.

That is the complete list of Dionysius' writings.

Bishop Theophilus of Antioch

24. From the pen of Theophilus, already mentioned as Bishop of Antioch, three rudimentary treatises *To Autolycus* are extant, as is another with the title *Against the Heresy of Hermogenes*, in which he draws on the Revelation of John. Some *Manuals of Elementary Instruction* have also survived. At that time heretics were as busy as ever spoiling like tares the pure seed of the apostolic teaching; so the pastors of the churches everywhere, as though driving away savage beasts from Christ's sheep, strove to keep them at bay, now by warnings and admonitions to their congregations, now by more militant action, by subjecting the heretics to oral direct questioning and confutation, and finally by written polemics in which they employed the most unanswerable proofs to demolish their erroneous ideas. That Theophilus took the field against them

1. Matt. xiii. 25.   2. Rev. xxii. 18–19.

with the others is plain from an admirable work which he wrote in answer to Marcion, and which had been preserved till now along with the others I have named.

He was succeeded as Bishop of Antioch by Maximin, the seventh from the apostles.

Philip and Modestus: Melito and the contents of his books

25. Philip, whom we met in Dionysius' letter as Bishop of Gortyna, was author of another most effective answer to Marcion, as were Irenaeus and Modestus, who was more successful than anyone in pinpointing the man's errors and making them crystal clear. There are several others whose works are still to be found on the shelves of many Christians.

26. Contemporary with them were Bishop Melito of Sardis and Bishop Apolinarius of Hierapolis, who were at the peak of their fame, and who without reference to each other addressed defences of the faith to the Roman emperor of the time. Of their works the following have come to my knowledge.

By Melito: *The Easter Festival*, Books I and II, *Prophets and the Christian Way of Life*, *The Church*, and *The Lord's Day*; *The Faith of Man*, *Creation*, *Obedience to the Faith*, and *The Senses*; *Soul and Body*, and *Baptism, Truth, Faith, and the Birth of Christ*; his *Book of Prophecy*, *Soul and Body*, *Hospitality*, *The Key*, *The Devil*, *The Revelation of John*, and *God in Bodily Form*; and finally the *Petition to Antoninus*.

In *The Easter Festival* he begins by indicating the time of its composition:

When Servillius Paulus was proconsul of Asia, at the time when Sagaris died a martyr's death, there was a great deal of argument at Laodicea about the Easter festival, which fell due at that time; and this essay was written.

The work is quoted by Clement of Alexandria in his own *Easter Festival*, which was composed, he says, in consequence of Melito's.

In the *Petition* to the emperor he complains of the treatment we were receiving under his rule:

What never happened before is happening now – religious people as a body are being harried and persecuted by new edicts all over Asia. Shameless informers out to fill their own pockets are taking advantage of the decrees to pillage openly, plundering inoffensive citizens night and day . . . If this is being done by your authority, well and good: a just monarch would never follow an unjust course, and we are happy to accept the honour of such a death. But we ask you to grant this one favour: first be good enough to find out the truth about the authors of such strife, so that you can judge in accordance with the facts whether they deserve to be condemned and executed or to be acquitted and left in peace. But if you are not responsible for this policy or this new decree – which could not properly be directed even against foreign enemies – we appeal to you all the more earnestly not to leave us at the mercy of these marauding hooligans.

A little farther on he writes:

Our way of thought first sprang up in a foreign land, but it flowered among your own peoples in the glorious reign of your ancestor Augustus, and became to your empire especially a portent of good, for from then on, the power of Rome grew great and splendid. To that power you have most happily succeeded: it will remain with you and your son, if you protect the way of thought that began with Augustus and has grown to full stature along with the Empire. Your ancestors respected it, as they did the other cults, and the greatest proof that the establishment of our religion at the very time when the Empire began so auspiciously was an unmixed blessing lies in this fact – from the reign of Augustus the Empire has suffered no damage, on the contrary everything has gone splendidly and gloriously, and every prayer has been answered. Of all the emperors, the only ones ever persuaded by malicious advisers to misrepresent our doctrine were Nero and Domitian, who were the source of the unreasonable custom of laying false information against the Christians. But their ignorance was corrected by your religious predecessors, who constantly rebuked in writing all who ventured to make trouble for our people. It is clear, for instance, that your grandfather Hadrian wrote to many of his representatives, in particular the proconsul Fundanus, governor of Asia; and your father, while you were associated with him in the government of the world, wrote to the cities, for instance, Larissa, Thessalonica, and Athens and to all the peoples of Greece, forbidding them to make trouble for us. You, sir, hold the same views on this matter as they did, but with much more human sympathy and philosophic insight; so we are the more convinced that you will whole-heartedly accede to our request.

The foregoing passages are taken from the *Petition*. In the *Extracts* which he wrote the same author begins his introduction with a list of the recognized books of the Old Testament, a list which it is necessary to quote at this point:

Melito to Onesimus, his brother in Christ, greeting. In your devotion to the word you have repeatedly asked for extracts from the Law and the Prophets regarding the Saviour and the whole of our Faith, and you also wished to learn the precise facts about the ancient books, particularly their number and order. I was most anxious to do this for you, knowing your devotion to the Faith and eagerness to learn about the word, and how in your yearning for God you value these things more than all else, as you strive with might and main to win eternal salvation. So when I visited the east and arrived at the place where it all happened and the truth was proclaimed, I obtained precise information about the Old Testament books, and made out the list which I am now sending you. Here are the names.

Five books of Moses: Genesis, Exodus, Numbers, Leviticus, Deuteronomy;
Joshua son of Nun, Judges, Ruth;
Kings (four books), Chronicles (two);
The Psalms of David;
Solomon's Proverbs (Wisdom) Ecclesiastes, Song of Songs;
Job;
Prophets: Isaiah, Jeremiah, the Twelve in a single book, Daniel, Ezekiel;
Ezra.

From these I have taken the extracts arranged in six books.

Apolinarius and Musanus: Tatian's heresy

27. After Melito, Apolinarius. Numerous works of his are still to be found on the shelves of many persons, of which the following have come into my hands – the address to the emperor named above; *Against the Greeks* (five books); *Truth* I and II; *Against the Jews* I and II; and his subsequent writings against the Phrygian heresy, an innovation contrived a little later but then beginning to sprout, since Montanus with his false prophetesses was already beginning to go off the track.

28. Musanus, whose name appeared in the foregoing list, has left us a very pungent criticism which he wrote and sent to some Christians who had fallen away to the sect of the so-called Encratites, which was then beginning to spring up and was introducing an outlandish and pernicious false doctrine into the world.

29. There is evidence that the author of this error was Tatian, whose observations on 'that wonderful man Justin' I quoted a few pages back, remarking that he was a disciple of the martyr. This is stated by Irenaeus in *Against Heresies*, Book I, where, speaking of the man and his heresy, he writes:

Borrowing from Saturninus and Marcion, the so-called Encratites preached celibacy, setting aside the original creation of God and tacitly condemning Him who made male and female for the generation of human beings.[1] They also introduced abstention from 'animate things', as they call them, showing ingratitude to God who made all things. Again, they deny the salvation of the first created man. This notion they adopted quite recently: one Tatian was the first to introduce this blasphemy. He had been a pupil of Justin, and all the time that he was with him he suggested nothing of the kind; but after Justin's martyrdom he became an apostate from the Church, and elated at the thought of being a teacher, and puffed up by the conviction of his own superiority, gave instruction on peculiar lines – he romanced about invisible aeons, like the followers of Valentinus, and repudiated marriage as being depravity and fornication, just as Marcion and Saturninus had done; his one original idea was to deny salvation to Adam.[2]

This is what Irenaeus wrote at that time. But a little while later a man called Severus lent his weight to this sect, and in consequence its members have come to be called Severians after him. They make use of the Law, the Prophets, and the Gospels, interpreting in their own peculiar fashion the ideas contained in Holy Writ, but they ridicule Paul the Apostle, setting aside his epistles, and reject even the Acts of the Apostles. Their old leader Tatian produced a composite work by somehow combining the gospels, and called it the *Diatessaron*: some people still possess copies. It is said that he was bold enough to alter some of the Apostle's

1. Gen. i. 27.   2. *Against Heresies*, I. 26. 1.

expressions as though trying to rectify their phraseology. He has left a great many works, of which the one most generally familiar is his famous essay *Against the Greeks*, in which he discusses primitive times, showing that all the eminent writers of Greece belong to a much later period than Moses and the Hebrew prophets. This essay is, I think, the best and most helpful of all his writings.

Bardaisan the Syrian and his extant works

30. In the same reign heretical sects abounded in Mesopotamia. Bardaisan, a most able man and a highly skilled disputant in the Syriac language, composed dialogues against the followers of Marcion and other leaders of various doctrines, and wrote them down in his own language and script along with many other works of his. These dialogues his pupils, who were very numerous in view of his powerful defence of Christian truth, have translated from Syriac into Greek. Among them is his most effective dialogue with Antoninus, entitled *Destiny*, and many other works which he is said to have written in consequence of the current persecution. At an earlier stage he had belonged to the school of Valentinus, but later he condemned it and refuted many of its fanciful ideas, satisfied in his own mind that he had changed to the right way of thinking. For all that, the taint of the old heresy stuck to him to the end.

Finally, it was at that period that the death occurred of Soter, Bishop of Rome.

Book 5

It was in the eighth year of his rule that Bishop Soter of Rome passed away. He was succeeded by Eleutherus, twelfth from the apostles, it being the seventeenth year of the Emperor Antoninus Verus. At that period in some parts of the world the persecution of the Church flared up again more fiercely, and as the result of mob onslaughts in one city after another countless martyrs came to their glory, as can be gathered from what happened in a single province. Fortunately for posterity it was all written down, and it certainly deserves a permanent place in history. The entire document, containing a very full account of these things, has been inserted in my *Collection of Martyrs*. It contains not only the historical record but the lessons to be drawn from it. For the moment I will content myself with quoting such passages as are relevant to the present work.

Other historians have confined themselves to the recording of victories in war and triumphs over enemies, of the exploits of the commanders and the heroism of their men, stained with the blood of the thousands they have slaughtered for the sake of children and country and possessions; it is *peaceful* wars, fought for the very peace of the soul, and men who in such wars have fought manfully for truth rather than for country, for true religion rather than for their dear ones, that my account of God's commonwealth will inscribe on imperishable monuments; it is the unshakeable determination of the champions of true religion, their courage and endurance, their triumphs over demons and victories over invisible opponents, and the crowns which all this won for them at the last, that it will make famous for all time.

Gallic martyrs of Verus' reign

1. Gaul was the country in which the arena was crowded with people. Her capital cities, famous and held in higher repute than any in the land, are Lyons and Vienne, both situated on the River Rhône, whose broad stream flows through the whole area. A written account of the martyrs was sent by the most important churches there to those of Asia and Phrygia, relating what had happened in their midst as follows – I will quote their own words:

> The servants of Christ at Vienne and Lyons in Gaul to our brothers in Asia and Phrygia who have the same faith and hope of redemption as we: peace, grace, and glory from God the Father and Christ Jesus our Lord.[1]

Then, after completing their introductory remarks, they begin their story thus:

> The severity of our trials here, the unbridled fury of the heathen against God's people, the untold sufferings of the blessed martyrs, we are incapable of describing in detail: indeed no pen could do them justice. The adversary swooped on us with all his might, giving us now a foretaste of his advent, which undoubtedly is imminent.[2] He left no stone unturned in his efforts to train his adherents and equip them to attack the servants of God, so that not only were we debarred from houses, baths, and the forum: they actually forbade any of us to be seen in any place whatever. But against them the grace of God put itself at our head, rescuing the weak and deploying against our enemies unshakeable pillars,[3] able by their endurance to draw upon themselves the whole onslaught of the evil one. These charged into the fight, standing up to every kind of abuse and punishment, and made light of their heavy load as they hastened to Christ, proving beyond a doubt that the sufferings of the present time are not to be compared with the glory that is in store for us.[4]
>
> To begin with, they heroically endured whatever the surging crowd heaped on them, noisy abuse, blows, dragging along the ground, plundering, stoning, imprisonment, and everything that an infuriated mob normally does to hated enemies. Then they were marched into the forum

1. 2 Peter i. 1–2.   2. 2 Thess. ii. 7–9.   3. Gal. ii, 9 and 1 Tim. iii. 15.
4. Rom. viii. 18.

and interrogated by the tribune and the city authorities before the whole population. When they confessed Christ, they were locked up in gaol to await the governor's arrival. Later, when they were taken before him and he treated them with all the cruelty he reserves for Christians, Vettius Epagathus, one of our number, full of love towards God and towards his neighbour, came forward. His life conformed so closely to the Christian ideal that, young as he was, the same tribute might be paid to him as to old Zacharias: he had scrupulously observed all the commandments and ordinances of the Lord,[1] and was untiring in service to his neighbour, utterly devoted to God[2] and fervent in spirit.[3] As such he found the judgment so unreasonably given against us more than he could bear: boiling with indignation, he applied for permission to speak in defence of the Christians, and to prove that there was nothing godless or irreligious in our society. The crowd round the tribunal howled him down, as he was a man of influence, and the governor dismissed his perfectly reasonable application with the curt question: 'Are *you* a Christian?' In the clearest possible tones Vettius replied: 'I am.' And he, too, was admitted to the ranks of the martyrs. He was called the Christians' advocate, but he had in himself the Advocate,[4] the Spirit that filled Zacharias,[5] as he showed by the fullness of his love when he gladly laid down his own life in defence of his brother Christians.[6] For he was and is a true disciple of Christ, following the Lamb wherever He goes.[7]

Then the rest fell into two groups. It was clear that some were ready to be the first Gallic martyrs: they made a full confession of their testimony with the greatest eagerness. It was equally clear that others were not ready, that they had not trained and were still flabby, in no fit condition to face the strain of a struggle to the death. Of these some ten proved stillborn, causing us great distress and inexpressible grief, and damping the enthusiasm of those not yet arrested. However, in spite of the agonies they were suffering, these people stayed with the martyrs and did not desert them. But at the time we were all tormented by the doubts about their confessing Christ: we were not afraid of the punishments inflicted, but looking to the outcome and dreading lest anyone might fall away. But the arrests went on, and day after day those who were worthy filled up the number of the martyrs, so that from the two dioceses were collected all the active members who had done most to build up our

1. Luke i. 6.   2. Rom. x. 2.   3. Rom xii. 11 and Acts xviii. 25.
4. Paraclete: John xiv. 16.   5. Luke i. 67.   6. 1 Thess. ii. 8, 1 John iii. 16.
7. Rev. xiv. 4.

church life. Among those arrested were some of our heathen domestics, as the governor had publicly announced that we were all to be hunted out. These were ensnared by Satan, so that fearing the tortures which they saw inflicted on God's people, at the soldiers' instigation they falsely accused us of Thyestean banquets and Oedipean incest, and things we ought never to speak or think about, or even believe that such things ever happened among human beings. When these rumours spread, people all raged like wild beasts against us, so that even those who because of blood-relationship had previously exercised restraint now turned on us, grinding their teeth with fury. So was proved true the saying of our Lord: 'The time will come when whoever kills you will think he is doing a service to God.'[1] From then on the holy martyrs endured punishments beyond all description, while Satan strove to wring even from them some of the slanders.

The whole fury of crowd, governor, and soldiers fell with crushing force on Sanctus, the deacon from Vienne; on Maturus, very recently baptized but heroic in facing his ordeal; on Attalus, who had always been a pillar and support[2] of the church in his native Pergamum; and on Blandina, through whom Christ proved that things which men regard as mean, unlovely, and comtemptible are by God deemed worthy of great glory,[3] because of her love for Him shown in power and not vaunted in appearance. When we were all afraid, and her earthly mistress (who was herself facing the ordeal of martyrdom) was in agony lest she should be unable even to make a bold confession of Christ because of bodily weakness, Blandina was filled with such power that those who took it in turns to subject her to every kind of torture from morning to night were exhausted by their efforts and confessed themselves beaten – they could think of nothing else to do to her. They were amazed that she was still breathing, for her whole body was mangled and her wounds gaped; they declared that torment of any one kind was enough to part soul and body, let alone a succession of torments of such extreme severity. But the blessed woman, wrestling magnificently, grew in strength as she proclaimed her faith, and found refreshment, rest, and insensibility to her sufferings in uttering the words: 'I am a Christian: we do nothing to be ashamed of.'

Sanctus was another who with magnificent, superhuman courage nobly withstood the entire range of human cruelty. Wicked people hoped that the persistence and severity of his tortures would force him to utter

1. John xvi. 2.   2. 1 Tim. iii. 15.   3. A reminiscence of 1 Cor. i. 28.

something improper, but with such determination did he stand up to their onslaughts that he would not tell them his own name, race, and birthplace, or whether he was a slave or free; to every question he replied in Latin: 'I am a Christian.' This he proclaimed over and over again, instead of name, birthplace, nationality, and everything else, and not another word did the heathen hear from him. Consequently, the governor and his torturers strained every nerve against him, so that when they could think of nothing else to do to him they ended by pressing red-hot copper plates against the most sensitive parts of his body. These were burning, but Sanctus remained unbending and unyielding, firm in his confession of faith, bedewed and fortified by the heavenly fountain of the water of life that flows from the depths of Christ's being.[1] But his poor body was a witness to what he had suffered – it was all one wound and bruise, bent up and robbed of outward human shape, but, suffering in that body, Christ accomplished most glorious things, utterly defeating the adversary and proving as an example to the rest that where the Father's love is[2] nothing can frighten us, where Christ's glory is[3] nothing can hurt us. A few days later wicked people again put the martyr on the rack, thinking that now that his whole body was swollen and inflamed a further application of the same instruments would defeat him, unable as he was to bear even the touch of a hand; or that by dying under torture he would put fear into the rest. However, nothing of the sort happened: to their amazement his body became erect and straight as a result of these new torments, and recovered its former appearance and the use of the limbs; thus through the grace of Christ his second spell on the rack proved to be not punishment but cure.

Biblis again, one of those who had denied Christ, was handed over to punishment by the devil, who imagined that he had already devoured her[4] and hoped to damn her as a slanderer by forcing her to say wicked things about us, being – so he thought – a feeble creature, easily broken. But on the rack she came to her senses,[5] and, so to speak, awoke out of deep sleep, reminded by the brief chastisement of the eternal punishment in hell.[6] She flatly contradicted the slanderers: 'How could children be eaten by people who are not even allowed to eat the blood of brute beasts?'[7] From then on she insisted that she was a Christian, and so she joined the ranks of the martyrs.

1. A reminiscence of John vii. 38 and xix. 34.
2. A reminiscence of 1 John iv. 18.   3. 2 Cor. viii. 23.   4. 1 Peter v. 8.
5. 2 Tim. ii. 26.   6. Matt. xxv. 46.   7. Acts xv. 29.

When the tyrant's instruments of torture had been utterly defeated by Christ through the endurance of the blessed saints, the devil resorted to other devices – confinement in the darkness of a filthy prison; clamping the feet in the stocks, stretched apart to the fifth hole; and other agonies which warders when angry and full of the devil are apt to inflict on helpless prisoners. Thus the majority were suffocated in prison – those whom the Lord wished to depart in this way, so revealing His glory.[1] Some, though tortured so cruelly that even if they received every care it seemed impossible for them to survive, lived on in the prison, deprived of all human attention but strengthened by the Lord and fortified in body and soul, stimulating and encouraging the rest. But the young ones who had been recently arrested and had not previously undergone physical torture could not bear the burden of confinement and died in prison.

Blessed Pothinus, who had been entrusted with the care of the Lyons diocese, was over ninety years of age and physically very weak. He could scarcely breathe because of his chronic physical weakness, but was strengthened by spiritual enthusiasm because of his pressing desire for martyrdom. Even he was dragged before the tribunal, and though his body was feeble from age and disease, his life was preserved in him, that thereby Christ might triumph. He was conveyed to the tribunal by the soldiers, accompanied by the civil authorities and the whole populace, who shouted and jeered at him as though he were Christ Himself. But he bore the noble witness.[2] When the governor asked him 'Who is the Christians' god?', he replied: 'If you are a fit person, you shall know.' Thereupon he was mercilessly dragged along beneath a rain of blows, those close by assailing him viciously with hands and feet and showing no respect for his age, and those at a distance hurling at him whatever came to hand, and all thinking it a shocking neglect of their duty to be behind-hand in savagery towards him, for they imagined that in this way they would avenge their gods. Scarcely breathing, he was flung into prison, and two days later he passed away.

Then occurred a great dispensation of God, and the infinite mercy of Jesus was revealed to a degree rarely known in the brotherhood of Christians, but not beyond the skill of Christ. Those who when the first arrests took place had denied Him were gaoled with the others and shared their sufferings: on this occasion they gained nothing by their denial, for whereas those who declared what they were were gaoled as Christians, no

---

1. A reminiscence of John ii. 11.   2. An allusion to 1 Tim. vi. 13.

other charge being brought against them, the others were further detained as foul murderers and punished twice as much as the rest. For the faithful were relieved of half their burden by the joy of martyrdom and hope of the promises, and by love towards Christ and the Spirit of the Father, but the unfaithful were tormented by their conscience, so that as they passed they could easily be picked out from the rest by the look on their faces. The faithful stepped out with a happy smile, wondrous glory and grace blended on their faces, so that even their fetters hung like beautiful ornaments around them and they resembled a bride adorned with golden lace elaborately wrought,[1] they were perfumed also with the sweet savour of Christ,[2] so that some people thought they had smeared themselves with worldly cosmetics. The unfaithful were dejected, downcast, ill-favoured, and devoid of charm; in addition they were gibed at by the heathen as contemptible cowards; they were accused of homicide, and had lost the honourable, glorious, life-giving name. The sight of this stiffened the resistance of the rest: those who were arrested unhesitatingly declared their faith without one thought for the devil's promptings . . .

From that time on, their martyrdoms embraced death in all its forms. From flowers of every shape and colour they wove a crown to offer to the Father; and so it was fitting that the valiant champions should endure an everchanging conflict, and having triumphed gloriously should win the mighty crown of immortality. Maturus, Sanctus, Blandina, and Attalus were taken into the amphitheatre to face the wild beasts, and to furnish open proof of the inhumanity of the heathen, the day of fighting wild beasts being purposely arranged for our people. There, before the eyes of all, Maturus and Sanctus were again taken through the whole series of punishments, as if they had suffered nothing at all before, or rather as if they had already defeated their opponents in bout after bout and were now battling for the victor's crown. Again they ran the gauntlet of whips, in accordance with local custom; they were mauled by the beasts, and endured every torment that the frenzied mob on one side or the other demanded and howled for, culminating in the iron chair which roasted their flesh and suffocated them with the reek. Not even then were their tormentors satisfied: they grew more and more frenzied in their desire to overwhelm the resistance of the martyrs, but do what they might they heard nothing from Sanctus beyond the words he had repeated from the beginning – the declaration of his faith.

1. Ps. xiv. 13.   2. 2 Cor. ii. 15.

In these two, despite their prolonged and terrible ordeal, life still lingered; but in the end they were sacrificed, after being made all day long a spectacle to the world[1] in place of the gladiatorial contest in its many forms. But Blandina was hung on a post and exposed as food for the wild beasts let loose in the arena. She looked as if she was hanging in the form of a cross, and through her ardent prayers she stimulated great enthusiasm in those undergoing their ordeal, who in their agony saw with their outward eyes in the person of their sister the One who was crucified for them, that He might convince those who believe in Him that any man who has suffered for the glory of Christ has fellowship for ever with the living God. As none of the beasts had yet touched her she was taken down from the post and returned to the gaol, to be kept for a second ordeal, that by victory in further contests she might make irrevocable the sentence passed on the crooked serpent,[2] and spur on her brother Christians – a small, weak, despised woman who had put on Christ,[3] the great invincible champion, and in bout after bout had defeated her adversary and through conflict had won the crown of immortality.

Attalus too was loudly demanded by the mob, as he was a man of note. He strode in, ready for the fray, in the strength of a clear conscience, for he had trained hard in the school of Christ and had been one of our constant witnesses to the truth. He was led round the amphitheatre preceded by a placard on which was written in Latin 'This is Attalus the Christian', while the people were bursting with fury against him. But when the governor was informed that he was a Roman, he ordered him to be put back in gaol with the others, about whom he had written to Caesar and was awaiting instructions.

Their time of respite was not idle or unfruitful:[4] through their endurance the infinite mercy of Christ was revealed; for through the living the dead were being brought back to life; and martyrs were bestowing grace on those who had failed to be martyrs, and there was great joy in the heart of the Virgin Mother,[5] who was receiving her stillborn children back alive; for by their means most of those who had denied their Master travelled once more the same road, conceived and quickened a second time, and learnt to confess Christ. Alive now and braced up, their ordeal sweetened by God, who does not desire the death of the sinner but is gracious towards repentance,[6] they advanced to the tribunal to be again interrogated by the governor. For Caesar had issued a command that they

1. 1 Cor. iv. 9.   2. Is. xxvii. 1; cf. Gen. iii. 14.   3. Gal. iii. 27.
4. 2 Peter i. 8.   5. The Church.
6. A synthesis of Ex. xxxiii and 2 Peter iii. 9.

should be tortured to death, but any who still denied Christ should be released; so at the inauguration of the local festival, at which all the heathen congregate in vast numbers, the governor summoned them to his tribunal, making a theatrical show of the blessed ones and displaying them to the crowds. After re-examination, all who seemed to possess Roman citizenship were beheaded and the rest sent to the beasts. Christ was greatly glorified in those who had previously denied Him but now confounded heathen expectation by confessing Him. They were individually examined with the intention that they should be released, but they confessed Him and so joined the ranks of the martyrs. Left outside were those who had never had any vestige of faith or notion of the wedding-garment[1] or thought of the fear of God, but by their very conduct brought the Way into disrepute[2] – truly the sons of perdition.[3] But the rest were all added to the Church.[4]

During their examination, Alexander, a Phrygian by birth and a doctor by profession, who had lived for many years in Gaul and was known to nearly everyone for his love of God and his boldness of speech[5] – he had a large measure of the apostolic gift – stood by the tribunal and gestured to them to confess Christ. To those surrounding the tribunal it was plain that he was suffering birth-pangs. But the crowds, furious that those who had hitherto denied Christ were now confessing Him, shouted against Alexander as the person responsible. The governor made him come forward and demanded to know who he was; when he replied 'A Christian', he lost his temper and condemned him to the beasts. The next day he entered the arena with Attalus, whom the governor, to gratify the mob, was again giving to the beasts. The two men were subjected to all the instruments of torture assembled in the amphitheatre, and underwent a supreme ordeal. In the end they were sacrificed. Alexander uttered no cry, not so much as a groan, but communed with God in his heart, while Attalus, when he was put in the iron chair and was being burnt and the reek was rising from his body, called out to the spectators in Latin: 'Look! eating men is what *you* are doing: *we* neither eat men nor indulge in any malpractice.' When asked what name God had he answered: 'God hasn't a name like a man.'

To crown all this, on the last day of the sports Blandina was again brought in, and with her Ponticus, a lad of about fifteen. Day after day they had been taken in to watch the rest being punished, and attempts were made to make them swear by the heathen idols. When they stood

---

1. Matt. xxii. 11.   2. Acts xix. 9 and 2 Peter ii. 2.   3. John xvii. 12.
4. Acts ii, 47 and v. 14.   5. Acts iv. 29.

firm and treated these efforts with contempt, the mob was infuriated with them, so that the boy's tender age called forth no pity and the woman no respect. They subjected them to every horror and inflicted every punishment in turn, attempting again and again to make them swear, but to no purpose. Ponticus was encouraged by his sister in Christ, so that the heathen saw that she was urging him on and stiffening his resistance, and he bravely endured every punishment till he gave back his spirit to God. Last of all, like a noble mother who had encouraged her children and sent them before her in triumph to the King,[1] blessed Blandina herself passed through all the ordeals of her children and hastened to rejoin them, rejoicing and exulting at her departure as if invited to a wedding supper,[2] not thrown to the beasts. After the whips, after the beasts, after the griddle, she was finally dropped into a basket and thrown to a bull. Time after time the animal tossed her, but she was indifferent now to all that happened to her, because of her hope and sure hold on all that her faith meant, and of her communing with Christ. Then she, too, was sacrificed, while the heathen themselves admitted that never yet had they known a woman suffer so much or so long.

Not even this was enough to satisfy their insane cruelty to God's people. Goaded by a wild beast,[3] wild and barbarous tribes were incapable of stopping, and the dead bodies became the next object of their vindictiveness. Their defeat did not humble them, because they were without human understanding; rather it inflamed their bestial fury, and governor and people vented on us the same inexcusable hatred, so fulfilling the scripture: 'Let the wicked man be wicked still, the righteous man righteous still.[4] Those who had been suffocated in gaol they threw to the dogs, watching carefully night and day to see that no one received the last offices at our hands. Then they threw out the remains left by the beasts and the fire, some torn to ribbons, some burnt to cinders, and set a military guard to watch for days on end the trunks and severed heads of the rest, denying burial to them also. Some raged and ground their teeth at them, longing to take some further revenge on them; others laughed and jeered, magnifying their idols and giving them credit for the punishment of their enemies; while those who were more reasonable, and seemed to have a little human feeling, exclaimed with the utmost scorn: 'Where is their god?[5] and what did they get for their religion, which they preferred to their own lives?' Such were their varied reactions, while we were greatly distressed by our inability to give the bodies burial.

1. 2 Macc. vii. 21–41.   2. Rev. xix. 9.   3. The devil.
4. Rev. xxii. 11, reworded.   5. Ps. xlii. 3.

Darkness did not make it possible, and they refused all offers of payment and were deaf to entreaty; but they guarded the remains with the greatest care, regarding it as a triumph if they could prevent burial . . .

Thus the martyrs' bodies, after six days' exposure to every kind of insult and to the open sky, were finally burnt to ashes and swept by these wicked men into the Rhône which flows near by, that not even a trace of them might be seen on the earth again. And this they did as if they could defeat God and rob the dead of their rebirth,[1] 'in order,' they said, 'that they may have no hope of resurrection – the belief that has led them to bring into this country a new foreign cult and treat torture with contempt, going willingly and cheerfully to their death. Now let's see if they'll rise again, and if their god can help them and save them from our hands.'[2]

The martyrs' friendly aid for those fallen from grace in the persecution

2. Such were the experiences of the Christian churches under the emperor mentioned: from them one can easily guess what happened in the other provinces of the Empire. It will be worth while to add other extracts from the same document, in which the gentleness and humanity of those martyrs is described in the following words:

So eager were they to imitate Christ, who though He was in the form of God did not count it a prize to be on an equality with God,[3] that though they had won such glory and had borne a martyr's witness not once or twice but again and again, and had been brought back from the wild beasts and were covered with burns, bruises, and wounds, they neither proclaimed themselves martyrs nor allowed us to address them by this name: if any one of us by letter or word ever addressed them as martyrs he was sternly rebuked. For they gladly conceded the title of martyr to Christ, the faithful and true Martyr-witness and Firstborn of the dead and Prince of the life of God,[4] and they reminded us of the martyrs already departed: 'They indeed are martyrs, whom Christ judged worthy to be taken up as soon as they had confessed Him, sealing their martyrdom by their departure: we are nothing but humble confessors.'

1. Matt. xix. 28.   2. Dan. iii. 15.   3. Phil. ii. 6.
4. A conflation of Rev. 1. 5 and iii. 14 with Acts iii. 15.

They implored their brother-Christians with tears, begging that earnest prayers might be offered for their fulfilment. The *power* of martyrdom they proved by their actions, showing great boldness towards the heathen, and by their endurance and dauntless courage making their nobility evident to all, but the *title* of martyr they begged their fellow-Christians not to use, filled as they were with the fear of God . . .

They humbled themselves under the mighty hand, by which they have now been greatly exalted.[1] They defended all and accused none; they loosed all and bound none;[2] they prayed for those who treated them so cruelly, as did Stephen, the fulfilled martyr: 'Lord, do not charge them with this sin.'[3] If he pleaded for those who were stoning him, how much more for brother-Christians? . . .

This was the greatest war they fought against him through the reality of their love, that the Beast might be choked into bringing up alive those whom he thought he had swallowed already.[4] They did not crow over the fallen, but the things they themselves had in abundance they bestowed with motherly affection on those who lacked them. Shedding many tears on their behalf in supplication to the Father, they asked for life and He gave it to them.[5] This they shared with their neighbours when triumphantly victorious they departed to God. Peace they had ever loved; peace they commended to our care; and with peace they went to God, leaving no sorrow to their Mother,[6] no strife or warfare to their brothers, but joy, peace, concord, and love.

So much may profitably be said about the affection of those blessed ones for their brothers who had fallen from grace, in view of the inhuman and merciless attitude of those who later behaved so badly towards the members of Christ's body.[7]

The dream-vision of Attalus the martyr

3. The same record of these martyrs contains yet another story worth repeating: there can be no objection to my bringing it to the notice of my readers.

Among them was a certain Alcibiades, who made a practice of extreme austerity. Hitherto he had refused everything, partaking only of bread and water, and he tried to go on like this even in

1. Peter v. 6.   2. Matt. xvi. 19.   3. Acts vii. 60.   4. 1 Peter v. 8.
5. Ps. xxi. 4.   6. The Church.   7. The Donatists and Novatianists.

gaol. But after his first ordeal in the amphitheatre it was revealed to Attalus that Alcibiades was not doing well in rejecting what God had created and setting others a misleading example. Alcibiades saw the danger, and began to accept everything freely and to give God thanks.[1] For they were richly blest by the grace of God, and the Holy Spirit was their counsellor.

It was at that very time, in Phrygia, that Montanus, Alcibiades, Theodotus, and their followers began to acquire a widespread reputation for prophecy; for numerous other manifestations of the miraculous gift of God, still occurring in various churches, led many to believe that these men too were prophets. When there was a difference of opinion about them, the Gallic Christians again submitted their own careful and most orthodox conclusions on the question, attaching various letters from the martyrs fulfilled in their midst – letters penned while they were still in prison to their brothers in Asia and Phrygia, and also to Eleutherus, then Bishop of Rome, in an effort to ensure peace in the churches.

Irenaeus commended in a letter from the martyrs

4. The same martyrs commended Irenaeus, already a presbyter in the Lyons diocese, to the Bishop of Rome just mentioned, paying warm tribute to his character, as is clear from their words:

> Greeting once more, Father Eleutherus: may God bless you always. We are entrusting this letter to our brother and companion[2] Irenaeus to convey to you. We are anxious that you should hold him in high regard, as a man devoted to the covenant of Christ. For if we had thought that position conferred righteousness on anyone, we should have recommended him first as a presbyter of the Church, which indeed he is.

Need I go through the list of martyrs in the document we have been considering, distinguishing those who found fulfilment in decapitation from those thrown to the beasts for food and from those who fell asleep in gaol, or enumerate the confessors still surviving at the time? Anyone who so desires may easily find out

1. Tim. iv. 3–4.   2. Rev. i. 9.

all about them by looking up the actual letter, which, as I said before, is reproduced in full in my *Collection of Martyrs*.

Rain sent from heaven in answer to Christian prayers

5. While Antoninus was still on the throne, it is on record that when his brother Marcus Aurelius Caesar deployed his forces for battle with the Germans and Sarmatians, his men were parched with thirst and he was in a quandary. But the soldiers of the Melitene Legion, as it is called, through faith which has never wavered from that day to this, as they faced the enemy in their lines, knelt down on the ground, our normal attitude when praying, and turned to God in supplication. The enemy were astonished at the sight, but the record goes on to say that something more astonishing followed a moment later: a thunderbolt drove the enemy to flight and destruction, while rain fell on the army which had called on the Almighty, reviving it when the entire force was on the point of perishing from thirst.

The story can be found in the works of writers remote from our way of thinking, who have undertaken to record the reign of these monarchs; it has also been told by our own. The pagan chroniclers, being aliens to the Faith, have related the astonishing occurrence, but without acknowledging that it was the result of Christian prayers: our own, being lovers of truth, have described the event in a simple guileless fashion. Among these may be mentioned Apolinarius, who says that from then on the legion which by its prayers brought about the miracle received from the emperor a title appropriate to the occurrence, being called in Latin the Thundering Legion. A reliable witness of these facts is Tertullian, who in addressing to the Senate his Latin *Defence of the Faith*, to which I referred in the earlier section, confirmed the story with a stronger and clearer proof. What he had to say was this – letters from Marcus, the most sagacious of emperors, were still extant in which he himself testified that in Germany his army had been on the verge of destruction through lack of water, when it was saved by the Christians' prayer; and Marcus had threatened to execute any who attempted to accuse us. Tertullian continues:

What kind of laws are these, enforced against us alone by wicked, unprincipled, and brutal men? Laws which Vespasian disregarded, though he had conquered the Jews; which Trajan to a large extent set aside, when he forbade Christian-hunting; which neither Hadrian, in spite of his obsessive interest in all that was mysterious, nor Pius ever ratified.[1]

Everyone must make up his own mind about these matters; it is time for me to pass on to the next stage.

When Pothinus, at the age of ninety, had found fulfilment with the martyrs of Gaul, Irenaeus succeeded to the bishopric of Lyons, the diocese that had been headed by Pothinus. It appears that in his early youth he had listened to Polycarp. In Book III of his *Against Heresies* he sets out the succession of Bishops of Rome, giving the list as far as Eleutherus, whose period I am now discussing, the period in which Irenaeus was busy writing his work. He writes as follows:

The list of Bishops of Rome

6. Having founded and built the church, the blessed apostles entrusted the episcopal office to Linus, who is mentioned by Paul in the Epistles to Timothy;[2] Linus was succeeded by Anencletus; after him, in the third place from the apostles, the bishopric fell to Clement, who had seen the blessed apostles and conversed with them, and still had their preaching ringing in his ears and their authentic tradition before his eyes. And he was not the only one: there were still many people alive who had been taught by the apostles. In Clement's time a violent dispute broke out among the Christians at Corinth, and the church at Rome sent a very long letter to the Corinthians, bringing them together in peace and renewing their faith, and passing on to them the authentic tradition they had so recently received from the apostles . . .

Clement was succeeded by Evarestus, Evarestus by Alexander; then Xystus was appointed, the sixth from the apostles, followed by Telesphorus, who suffered glorious martyrdom; next came Hyginus, then Pius, and after him Anicetus. Anicetus was succeeded by Soter, and now, at the twelfth stage from the apostles, the position is filled by Eleutherus. In the same order and the same succession the authentic tradition received

1. *Defence*, 5.   2. 2 Tim. iv. 21.

from the apostles and passed down by the Church, and the preaching of the truth, have been handed on to us.[1]

Miraculous powers exercised down to those times by believers

7. In accord with the accounts which I have already given, Irenaeus demonstrates these facts in the five books entitled *Refutation and Overthrow of Knowledge Falsely so Called*, and in Book II of the same work he makes it clear that right down to his own time manifestations of divine and miraculous power had continued in some churches.

But they[2] fall far short of raising the dead, as the Lord raised them, and as did the apostles through prayer, and as among later Christians, because the need was so great and the whole of the local church besought God with much fasting and supplication, the spirit of the dead man has returned and his life has been granted to the prayers of God's people . . .

But if they suggest that the Lord has done these things only in appearance, I will refer them to the prophetic writings, and prove from them that all this had been foretold about Him and really happened, and that He alone is the Son of God. So it is that in His name those who truly are His disciples, having received grace from Him, put it to effectual use for the benefit of their fellow-men, in proportion to the gift each one has received from Him. Some drive out demons really and truly, so that often those cleansed from evil spirits believe and become members of the Church; some have foreknowledge of the future, visions, and prophetic utterances; others, by the laying-on of hands, heal the sick and restore them to health; and before now, as I said, dead men have actually been raised and have remained with us for many years. In fact, it is impossible to enumerate the gifts which throughout the world the Church has received from God and in the name of Jesus Christ crucified under Pontius Pilate, and every day puts to effectual use for the benefit of the heathen, deceiving no one and making profit out of no one: freely she received from God, and freely she ministers.[3]

Elsewhere Irenaeus writes:

Similarly, we hear of many members of the Church who have prophetic

---

1. *Against Heresies*, III. 3. 2f.   2. The adherents of Simon and Carpocrates.
3. *Against Heresies*, II, 49. 3, the last phrase adapted from Matt. x. 8.

gifts and by the Spirit speak with all kinds of tongues, and bring men's secret thoughts to light for their own good, and expound the mysteries of God.[1]

This will suffice to show that diversity of gifts continued among fit persons till the time I am speaking of.

Irenaeus' comments on Holy Scripture

8. At the beginning of the work I promised, when convenient, to quote passages in which the early presbyters and historians of the Church have transmitted in writing the traditions that had come down to them regarding the canonical scriptures. One of these was Irenaeus, so without more ado I will quote his remarks, beginning with those which concern the Holy Gospels.

Matthew published a written gospel for the Hebrews in their own tongue, while Peter and Paul were preaching the gospel in Rome and founding the church there. After their passing, Mark also, the disciple and interpreter of Peter, transmitted to us in writing the things preached by Peter. Luke, the follower of Paul, set down in a book the gospel preached by him. Lastly John, the disciple of the Lord, who had leant back on His breast,[2] once more set forth the gospel, while residing at Ephesus in Asia.[3]

Such are the statements of Irenaeus in Book III of the work mentioned. In Book V he makes a definite statement about the Revelation of John and the number of the antichrist's name:

Such then is the case: this number is found in all good and early copies and confirmed by the very people who saw John face to face, and reason teaches us that the number of the Beast's name is shown according to Greek numerical usage by the letters in it . . . I for one dare not risk making any positive assertion regarding the name of the antichrist. Had there been any need for his name to be openly announced at the present time, it would have been stated by the one who saw the revelations. For it was not seen a long time back, but almost in my own lifetime, at the end of Domitian's reign.[4]

1. *Against Heresies*, V. 6. 1, the last phrase adapted from 1 Cor. xii. 7–10 and xiv. 25.

2. John xxi. 20.   3. *Against Heresies*, III. 1. 2.   4. Ibid., V. 30. 1,3.

That is what Irenaeus has to say about the Revelation. He refers
also to 1 John, drawing much evidence from it, and similarly to 1
Peter. And he not only knows but accepts the 'Shepherd'.

Scripture is right in saying: 'First of all believe that God is one, the
Maker and Builder of all things, etc.'[1]

He makes use too of a few sayings from the Wisdom of
Solomon, which he quotes with fair accuracy:

The vision of God is the bestower of incorruption; and incorruption
brings men near to God.[2]

He refers also to short works by an apostolic presbyter, whose
name he omits to mention, and quotes comments of his on Holy
Writ. He had a good deal to say about Justin Martyr and Ignatius,
drawing his information as usual from their writings, and promises
that in a special work he will refute Marcion out of his own works.
  Regarding the translation by the seventy of the inspired scriptures,[3] let him speak for himself.

So God became man, and the Lord Himself saved us, giving the sign of
the Virgin, but not as suggested by some who in our day venture to
translate the text thus: 'Lo, the *young woman* shall be with child and bear a
son', as it was translated by Theodotion of Ephesus and Aquila of Pontus,
both Jewish proselytes, followed by the Ebionites, who argue that He was
Joseph's child . . .
Before the Romans established their empire, while the Macedonians
still held Asia, Ptolemy son of Lagus was anxious to equip the library he
had established in Alexandria with worth-while books from every quarter,
so he asked the people of Jerusalem to provide him with a copy of their
scriptures translated into Greek. Being at that time still subject to the
Macedonians, they sent him seventy men of mature age, the most skilled
they had in the scriptures and in both languages. Thus was God's purpose
fulfilled. Ptolemy wished to test them in his own way, fearing that they
might put their heads together and manipulate their translation to conceal
the true meaning of the scriptures. So he separated them from each other,
and told them they must all produce the same translation: he laid down

1. Ibid., IV. 34. 2 (quoting Hermas, *Mandates*, 1).
2. Ibid., IV. 63. 2 (quoting Wisdom vi. 18–19).   3. The Septuagint (LXX).

his rule for every one of the books. When they reassembled before Ptolemy and compared their respective versions, God was glorified and the scriptures were recognized as truly divine; they all said the same things in the same phrases and the same words from beginning to end, so that even the heathen who were present knew that the scriptures had been translated by the inspiration of God. Nor is it surprising that God made this possible, seeing that when Nebuchadnezzar took the people into captivity and the scriptures were destroyed, and then seventy years later the Jews returned to their own country, afterwards, in the reign of Artaxerxes the king of Persia, He inspired Ezra the priest of the tribe of Levi to re-create all the utterances of the old prophets and restore to the people the Law given by Moses.[1]

Bishops of Commodus' reign: Pantaenus the philosopher

9. When the reign of Antoninus had lasted nineteen years, Commodus stepped into his shoes. In his first year, Julian was entrusted with the archbishopric of the province of Alexandria, Agrippinus having reached the end of his twelve years' ministry.

10. At that time the school for believers in Alexandria was headed by a man with a very high reputation as a scholar, by name Pantaenus, for it was an established custom that an academy of sacred learning should exist among them. This academy has lasted till our own time, and I understand that it is directed by men of high standing and able exponents of theology, but we know that Pantaenus was one of the most eminent teachers of his day, being an ornament of the philosophic system known as stoicism. He is said to have shown such warm-hearted enthusiasm for the divine word that he was appointed to preach the gospel of Christ to the peoples of the East, and travelled as far as India. For there were, yes, there were even then many evangelists of the word eager to contribute an inspired fervour of apostolic pattern for the increase and building up of the divine word. Of these Pantaenus was one: it is stated that he went as far as India, where he appears to have found that Matthew's gospel had arrived before him and was in the hands of some there who had come to know Christ. Bar-

---

1. *Against Heresies*, III. 24. 1.

tholomew, one of the apostles, had preached to them and had left behind Matthew's account in the actual Hebrew characters, and it was preserved till the time of Pantaenus' mission. He himself, after doing great work, ended up as principal of the academy in Alexandria, where both orally and in writing he revealed the treasures of the divine doctrine.

Clement of Alexandria

11. In his time Clement was noted at Alexandria for his patient study of Holy Scripture. He bore the same name as the former head of the Roman church, the pupil of the apostles. In his *Outlines* he refers by name to Pantaenus as his teacher, and it seems to me that in Book I of the *Miscellanies* there is a covert allusion to that scholar. After indicating the more distinguished members of the apostolic succession to which he had been admitted, he says this:

This work is not a careful literary composition designed to impress, but notes stored up for my old age, a tonic for a bad memory, no more than a sketchy outline of those clear and vital words that I was privileged to hear, and of blessed and truly remarkable men. Of these one was in Greece (the Ionian), a second in south Italy, a third in the Lebanon, a fourth from Egypt. Others lived in the East and included one in Assyria, and one in Palestine of Hebrew origin. When I met the last – in ability, the first – by tracking him down in his Egyptian lair, I found rest. These men preserved the true tradition of the blessed teaching straight from Peter, James, John, and Paul, the holy apostle, son receiving it from father – how few are like their fathers! By the grace of God, they came right down to me, to deposit those ancestral apostolic seeds.[1]

Bishops of Jerusalem

12. In their time there was a noted bishop in Jerusalem who even now is famous almost everywhere – Narcissus, fifteenth in the succession from the time of the siege of the Jews under Hadrian. It

1. *Miscellanies*, I. 1. 11.

was then that the church there first consisted of Gentiles, who took the place of converts from the circumcision and were headed by the first Gentile bishop, Mark, as already explained. After him, as shown by the local succession-lists, came Bishop Cassian, followed by Publius, Maximus, Julian, Gaius, Symmachus, a second Gaius, then another Julian, followed by Capito, Valens, and Dolichian; finally Narcissus, the thirtieth from the apostles in unbroken succession.

Rhodo and the disagreement about Marcion which he records

13. At the same period, Rhodo, an Asian by birth and, as he himself relates, a disciple at Rome of Tatian, whose acquaintance we made earlier, composed various books, ranging himself with the others against Marcion's heretical sect. He tells us that in his day it split into dissentient groups, describes the people who caused the split, and effectively refutes the falsehoods invented by each of them. Listen to what he writes:

> Consequently, they no longer agree among themselves, but struggle to uphold irreconcilable views. One of their herd is Apelles, who prides himself on his mode of life and his grey hairs. He admits that there is a single Source, but says that the prophecies come from a hostile spirit, relying on the prophecies of a demoniac girl named Philumene. Others, like the captain himself, Marcion, introduce two Sources. These include Potitus and Basilicus, who followed the Pontic wolf, and failing, as he had done, to find an answer to the problem of evil, took the easy way out and announced two Sources, baldly and without proof. Others of them again plunged into still worse error and posited not merely two but three Natures! Their leading spirit is Syneros, according to those who claim membership of his school.

Rhodo also states that he conversed with Apelles:

> The old man Apelles, in a discussion with me, was shown to be guilty of many erroneous statements. He therefore began to suggest that it was far better not to argue about doctrine at all, and for each man to stick to his own beliefs: those who placed their hopes in the Crucified would be saved, he declared, so long as they continued in good works. The most

obscure part of his teaching, as I said before, was his doctrine of God, for he spoke of a single Source, as does our doctrine.

After a full statement of Apelles' position, Rhodo continues:

When I said to him 'What is your proof of this? how can you speak of a single Source? Please explain,' he replied that the prophecies refuted themselves, as they had never once told the truth: they were inconsistent, false, and mutually destructive. As to how there was a single Source, he said he did not know but simply inclined to that opinion. Then when I adjured him to tell the truth, he swore he was absolutely sincere in saying that he did not understand how there was one uncreated God, but that was his conviction. I laughed and condemned him, because he called himself a teacher and had no idea how to establish what he taught.

In the same work, addressing himself to Callistio, Rhodo admits that he was once a disciple of Tatian at Rome. Tatian had produced a book on *Problems*. In it he had promised to set out what was obscure and puzzling in Holy Writ, so Rhodo announces that in a special work he will furnish the answers to Tatian's problems. There is also extant an essay of his on *The Six Days of Creation*.

The egregious Apelles voiced innumerable profanities about the Mosaic Law, and in treatise after treatise blasphemed the inspired words, making the most determined efforts to refute them, as he imagined, and demolish them altogether.

The false prophet of Phrygia, and the schism of Blastus at Rome

14. Filled with hatred of good and love of evil the enemy of God's Church left no trick untried in his machinations against mankind, and did his best to make a fresh crop of heretical sects spring up to injure the Church. Some members of these crawled like poisonous reptiles over Asia and Phrygia, boasting of Montanus 'the Paraclete' and his female adherents Priscilla and Maximilla, alleged to have been his prophetesses.

15. Others flourished at Rome, led by Florinus, an unfrocked presbyter, along with Blastus who had been disgraced in the same

way. Between them they led many churchmen astray and got them under their thumb, each trying in his own way to pervert the truth.

Montanus and his band of false prophets

16. To counter the so-called Phrygian heresy, the Power which fights for truth raised up an effective and invincible weapon at Hierapolis, in the person of Apolinarius, already referred to in these pages. With him were associated many learned men of the day, who have left us ample material for reconstructing the history. At the beginning of his polemic against these heretics, one of these writers first indicates that he had also argued with them orally to refute their pretensions. His preface runs as follows:

My dear Avircius Marcellus,

It is now a very long time since you invited me to write some kind of treatise against the sect called after Miltiades, but I have been rather hesitant until now, not from inability to refute falsehood and witness to the truth, but as a precaution against the danger that some people might think I was adding another paragraph or clause to the wording of the New Covenant of the Gospel, to which nothing can be added, from which nothing can be taken away, by anyone who has determined to live by the Gospel itself. But a little while ago I visited Ancyra[1] in Galatia and found the local church deafened with the noise of this new craze – not prophecy, as they call it, but pseudo-prophecy, as I shall shortly prove. So far as I was able, the Lord helping me, I spoke out for days on end in the church about these matters, and replied to every argument they put forward. The church was delighted and confirmed in the truth, while the enemy were repulsed for the time being and the opposition demoralized So I was asked by the local presbyters, with the support of my fellow-presbyter Zoticus of Otrus, to leave them a summary of what I had said against the opponents of the word of truth. This I could not do, but I promised that if the Lord allowed me I would write it here and send it to them without delay.

After completing his explanation on these lines at the beginning

---

1. Gal. iii. 15, Phil. i. 27, Rev. ii. 18–19.

of his book, he goes on to describe the originator of this heretical sect, as follows.

Their opposition and their recent schismatic heresy in relation to the Church originated thus. There is, it appears, a village near the Phrygian border of Mysia called Ardabau. There it is said that a recent convert named Montanus, while Gratus was proconsul of Syria, in his unbridled ambition to reach the top laid himself open to the adversary, was filled with spiritual excitement and suddenly fell into a kind of trance and unnatural ecstasy. He raved, and began to chatter and talk nonsense, prophesying in a way that conflicted with the practice of the Church handed down generation by generation from the beginning. Of those who listened at that time to his sham utterances some were annoyed, regarding him as possessed, a demoniac in the grip of a spirit of error,[1] a disturber of the masses. They rebuked him and tried to stop his chatter, remembering the distinction drawn by the Lord, and His warning to guard vigilantly against the coming of false prophets.[2] Others were elated as if by the Holy Spirit or a prophetic gift, were filled with conceit, and forgot the Lord's distinction. They welcomed a spirit that injured and deluded the mind and led the people astray: they were beguiled and deceived by it, so that it could not now be reduced to silence. By some art, or rather by methodical use of a malign artifice, the devil contrived the ruin of the disobedient, and was most undeservedly honoured by them. Then he secretly stirred up and inflamed minds close to the true Faith, raising up in this way two others – women whom he filled with the sham spirit, so that they chattered crazily, inopportunely, and wildly, like Montanus himself. On those who were elated and exultant about him the spirit bestowed favours, swelling their heads with his extravagant promises. Sometimes it reproved them pointedly and convincingly to their faces, to avoid appearing uncritical – though few of the Phrygians were deceived. They were taught by this arrogant spirit to denigrate the entire Catholic Church throughout the world, because the spirit of pseudo-prophecy received neither honour nor admission into it; for the Asian believers repeatedly and in many parts of Asia had met for this purpose, and after investigating the recent utterances pronounced them profane and ejected the heresy. Then at last its devotees were turned out of the Church and excommunicated.

Having recorded these facts in his introduction, the author

1. 1 John iv. 6.   2. Matt. vii. 15.

continues throughout the book to refute their error. In Book II he
has this to say about their end:

> They called us 'prophet-killers' because we would not receive their
> garrulous prophets – according to them, the ones whom the Lord
> promised to send to the people – so let them answer before God. Is there
> one person, my good sirs, among those from Montanus and the women
> onwards who started the chatter, who was persecuted by the Jews or
> killed by the wicked? Not one. Or was any one of them seized and
> crucified for the Name? No indeed. Very well then: was one of the
> women ever whipped in Jewish synagogues or stoned? Never anywhere.[1]
> It was by a different death that Montanus and Maximilla are believed to
> have died. For it is thought that both of these were driven out of their
> minds by a spirit, and hanged themselves, at different times; and on the
> occasion of the death of each, it was said on all sides that this was how
> they died, putting an end to themselves just like the traitor Judas.[2] In the
> same way it is commonly asserted that Theodotus, that wonderful fellow,
> the first trustee, shall we say, of their 'prophecy', was once raised aloft and
> taken up to heaven, where he experienced an unnatural ecstasy and
> entrusted himself to the spirit of deception, only to be sent spinning and
> perish miserably. That at any rate is how they say it happened. But we
> must not imagine that without seeing them we know the truth about
> such things, my friend: it may be have been in this way, it may have been
> in some other way, that death came to Montanus, Theodotus, and their
> female associate.

Later in the same book he says that the holy bishops of the
time attempted to silence the spirit that was in Maximilla, but
were prevented by others, who were obviously in league with the
spirit:

> It will not do for the spirit which spoke through Maximilla to say in
> the same work of Asterius Urbanus: 'I am driven away like a wolf from the
> sheep. I am not a wolf; I am word and spirit and power.'[3] He must show
> clearly the power in the spirit and prove it, and by that spirit he must
> make himself acknowledged by those who were then present in order to
> test and converse with the spirit as it chattered – eminent men and
> bishops, Zoticus from the village of Cumane and Julian from Apamea –

1. See Matt. xxiii. 31, 34, 37 and 3 John 7.   2. Matt. xxvii. 5.
3. 1 Cor. ii. 4.

who were muzzled by Themiso and his henchmen, who would not allow them to silence the lying spirit which was leading the people astray.

In the same work again, after putting forward other arguments to dispose of Maximilla's prophecies, he indicates the time at which he was writing this, and in the same sentence refers to her predictions, in which she foretold wars and revolutions and which he exposes as false:[1]

Surely it is now obvious that this too is a lie? Today it is more than thirteen years since the woman's death, and there has been neither general nor local war in the world, but rather – even for Christians – continuous peace, by the mercy of God.

This passage is from Book II. From Book III also I will quote short passages in which, replying to those who boasted that they too had lost many by martyrdom, he has this to say:

When all their arguments have been disposed of and they have nothing to say, they try to take refuge in the martyrs, alleging that they have a great number and that this is a convincing proof of the power of what in their circles is called the prophetic spirit. But this seems to be as false as false can be, for some of the other heretical sects have immense numbers of martyrs, but this is surely no reason why we should approve of them or acknowledge that they have the truth. To take one instance – those who as sectaries of Marcion are called Marcionites claim an immense number of Christian martyrs, but they do not truly acknowledge Christ Himself . . . Hence whenever members of the Church called to martyrdom for the true Faith meet any of the so-called martyrs of the Phrygian sect, they part company with them and have nothing to do with them till their own fulfilment, because they will not be associated with the spirit that spoke through Montanus and the women. That this is true, and that it occurred in our own time in Apamea on the Maeander, in the case of Gaius and Alexander and the other martyrs from Eumenia, is perfectly clear.

Miltiades and the books which he wrote

17. In this work he also mentions Miltiades, a writer who was

1. Luke xxi. 9.

author of another polemic against the Montanist heresy. After quoting some of their sayings, he goes on:

> The statements which I have summarized I found in a publication of theirs attacking the work in which our brother Alcibiades shows that a prophet ought not to chatter in a state of ecstasy.

Later in the same work he gives a list of those who had prophesied under the New Covenant, among whom he includes a certain Ammia and Quadratus.

> But the pseudo-prophet speaks in a state of unnatural ecstasy, after which all restraint is thrown to the winds. He begins with voluntary ignorance and ends in involuntary madness, as stated already. But they cannot point to a single one of the prophets under either the Old Covenant or the New who was moved by the Spirit in this way – not Agabus or Judas or Silas or Philip's daughters;[1] not Ammia at Philadelphia or Quadratus; nor any others they may choose to boast about though they are not of their number . . . For if, as they claim, after Quadratus and Ammia at Philadelphia Montanus and his female disciples succeeded to the prophetic gift, let them tell us which of their number succeeded the followers of Montanus and the women. For the prophetic gift must continue in the whole Church until the final coming, as the apostle insists. But they point to no one, though this is the fourteenth year since Maximilla's death.

Let us turn now to Miltiades, who was referred to in one of these passages. He, too, has left us reminders of his own zeal for the oracles of God, in the works that he composed, *Against the Greeks* and *Against the Jews*, each subject being discussed separately in two books. In addition, he wrote a *Defence before the Rulers of this World* of the philosophy which he followed.

Apollonius' refutation of the Phrygians: his personal comments on some of them

18. While the so-called Phrygian sect was still flourishing in Phrygia itself, an orthodox writer named Apollonius embarked on a refutation, and produced a special polemic against them, proving point by point the fraudulent character of their 'prophecies' and

---

1. Acts xi. 28, xv. 32, xxi. 8–10.

revealing the sort of life lived by the leaders of the sect. Listen to his actual words about Montanus:

What sort of person this upstart teacher is, his own actions and teaching show. This is the man who taught the dissolution of marriages, who laid down the law on fasting, who renamed Pepuza and Tymion, insignificant towns in Phrygia, as Jerusalem, in the hope of persuading people in every district to gather there; who appointed agents to collect money, who contrived to make the gifts roll in under the name of 'offerings', and who has subsidized those who preach his message, in order that gluttony may provide an incentive for teaching it.

This is his summing-up of Montanus. A little farther on he has this to say of his prophetesses:

It is thus evident that these prophetesses, from the time they were filled with the spirit, were the very first to leave their husbands. How then could they lie so blatantly as to call Priscilla a virgin?

Next he goes on to say:

Don't you agree that all scripture debars a prophet from accepting gifts and money?[1] When I see that a prophetess has accepted gold and silver and expensive clothing, am I not justified in keeping her at arm's length?

Still farther on, he has this to say about one of their confessors:

Then there is Themiso, who is wrapped up in plausible covetousness, and who failed to raise aloft the standard of confession and bought his release by a heavy bribe. This ought to have made him feel small, but instead he vaunted himself as a martyr, and, copying the apostle, had the impudence to compose a 'general epistle' in which he instructed better Christians than himself, fought his battle with empty trumpetings, and blasphemed the Lord, the apostles, and Holy Church.

Again, about another of those whom they honour as martyrs he writes:

To confine ourselves to a single instance, let the prophetess tell us about Alexander, who calls himself a martyr, with whom she feasts, and whom many treat with profound respect. His robberies, and the other crimes for

1. Cf. *Didache*, 11. 6.

which he has been punished, there is no need for me to retail; they are filed in the record office. Who pardons whose sins? Does the prophet forgive the martyr's robberies, or the martyr the prophet's covetousness? The Lord said: 'Do not provide yourselves with gold or silver or two coats',[1] but these people have done the exact opposite – they have transgressed by providing themselves with these forbidden things. I can prove that their so-called prophets and martyrs rake in the shekels not only from the rich but from poor people, orphans, and widows. If they have the courage of their convictions, let them take their stand on this and settle the question, on this condition, that if convicted they will for the future refrain from transgressing, for the fruits of the prophet must be carefully examined, for from the fruit the tree is known.[2]

For the benefit of those interested in the history of Alexander – he was tried by Aemilius Frontinus, the proconsul at Ephesus, not because of the Name but because of his impudent robberies: there had been previous convictions. Then by a lying appeal to the name of the Lord he secured his release, having deceived the faithful there, but his own diocese from which he came would not receive him, because he was a robber. Any who want to know about him have the public archives of Asia to refer to. The prophet lived with him for years, and knows nothing about him, but I have exposed him, and in doing so have exposed the character of the prophet. I can show the same thing in the case of many others: if they dare, let them stand up to the exposure.

Again, elsewhere in the book he has this to say about their vaunted prophets:

If they deny that their prophets have accepted gifts, they will surely admit this, that if they are proved to have accepted them they are no prophets: I can provide endless proof of this. All the fruits of a prophet must be submitted to examination. Tell me, does a prophet dye his hair? Does a prophet paint his eyelids? Does a prophet love ornaments? Does a prophet visit the gaming tables and play dice? Does a prophet do business as a moneylender? Let them say plainly whether these things are permissible or not, and I will prove that they have been going on in their circles.

In the same work Apollonius informs us that he is writing it thirty-nine years after Montanus embarked on his career of spurious prophecy. He further states that while Maximilla was pretending

1. Matt. x. 9–10.   2. Matt. xii. 33.

to prophesy in Pepuza, Zoticus – who was mentioned by the previous writer – planted himself in front of her and tried to silence the spirit at work in her, but was prevented by her partisans. He also mentions one Thraseas as among the martyrs of that time. Furthermore, he states on the authority of tradition that the Saviour commanded His apostles not to leave Jerusalem for twelve years. He also makes use of evidences taken from the Revelation of John; and he relates how by divine power a dead man was raised by John himself at Ephesus. He makes other statements too, by which he has ably and fully demonstrated the error of the heresy under discussion. There we may leave Apollonius.

Serapion on the Phrygian heresy

19. The polemics of Apolinarius against the Phrygian heresy are referred to by Serapion, who, we have good reason to believe, was Bishop of Antioch in succession to Maximin in the period under discussion. He mentions him in a personal letter to Caricus and Pontius, in which he gives his own answer to the same heresy, and adds this:

In order that you may know this, that the working of the so-called New Prophecy of this fraudulent organization is held in detestation by the whole brotherhood throughout the world, I am sending you the writings of Claudius Apolinarius, Bishop of Hierapolis in Asia, of most blessed memory.

In this letter of Serapion's are preserved the signatures of various bishops, one of whom signed himself thus:

I, Aurelius Quirinius, a martyr, pray for your welfare,

Another, in this way:

I, Aelius Publius Julius, from Develtum, a colony in Thrace, Bishop. As God in heaven lives, blessed Sotas of Anchialus wished to drive out Priscilla's demon, and the hypocrites would not permit him.

The autograph signatures of several other bishops, who were of the same opinion, are preserved in the document we are discussing. And there we will leave them.

The correspondence of Irenaeus with the schismatics at Rome

20. In opposition to those at Rome who were falsifying the sound precepts of the Church, Irenaeus composed various letters, entitling one *To Blastus, on Schism*, another *To Florinus, on Sole Sovereignty, or God is not the Author of Evil* – a notion which Florinus seemed to be defending. Again, when Florinus was inveigled by the error of Valentinus, Irenaeus composed his masterpiece *The Ogdoad*, in which he also makes it clear that he himself was in the unbroken succession from the apostles. At the end of this work I have found a most graceful note of his which I cannot refrain from including in this book. Here it is:

If, dear reader, you should transcribe this little book, I adjure you by the Lord Jesus Christ and by His glorious advent, when He comes to judge the living and the dead,[1] to compare your transcript and correct it carefully by this copy, from which you have made your transcript. This adjuration likewise you must transcribe and include in your copy.

May it prove salutary that these words were spoken by him and are recorded by me, so that we may keep those truly saintly men of an earlier generation in mind, as a splendid example of meticulous accuracy.

In the letter *To Florinus* already mentioned, Irenaeus refers once more to his associations with Polycarp:

Such notions, Florinus, to put it mildly, do not indicate a sound judgement. Such notions are out of harmony with the Church, and involve those who accept them in beliefs well-nigh blasphemous. Such notions not even the heretics outside the Church have ever dared to propound. Such notions the presbyters of an earlier generation, those taught by the apostles themselves, did not transmit to you. When I was still a boy I saw you in Lower Asia in Polycarp's company, when you were cutting a fine figure at the imperial court and wanted to be in favour with him. I have a clearer recollection of events at that time than of recent happenings – what we learn in childhood develops along with

1. 2 Tim. iv. 1.

the mind and becomes a part of it – so that I can describe the place where blessed Polycarp sat and talked, his goings out and comings in, the character of his life, his personal appearance, his addresses to crowded congregations. I remember how he spoke of his intercourse with John and with the others who had seen the Lord; how he repeated their words from memory; and how the things that he had heard them say about the Lord, His miracles and His teaching, things that he had heard direct from the eye-witnesses of the Word of Life,[1] were proclaimed by Polycarp in complete harmony with Scripture. To these things I listened eagerly at that time, by the mercy of God shown to me, not committing them to writing but learning them by heart. By God's grace, I constantly and conscientiously ruminate on them, and I can bear witness before God that if any such suggestion had come to the ears of that blessed and apostolic presbyter he would have cried out and stopped his ears, exclaiming characteristically: 'Dear God, for what times Thou hast preserved me, that I should endure this!' And he would have fled from the very place where he had been sitting or standing when he heard such words. The letters he sent either to the neighbouring churches to stiffen them, or to individual Christians to advise and stimulate them, furnish additional proof of this.

Apollonius martyred at Rome

21. During the same period – the reign of Commodus – our situation became easier, and by God's grace peace came to the churches throughout the world. Then, too, the message of salvation began to lead every soul of every race of men towards the devout worship of the God of the universe, so that now many in Rome itself who enjoyed the advantages of birth and wealth were moving with all their household and kindred towards their own salvation. Needless to say, the demon, who hates what is good and is envious by nature, found this beyond endurance. Once more he stripped for the fight, and manifold were the devices he invented to destroy us. At Rome he dragged into court Apollonius, one of the most distinguished for learning and philosophy of the Christians of the time, having induced one of his servants – fit men for the task – to accuse him. But the wretched man brought the case

---

1 1 John i. 1.

at just the wrong time, for by an imperial decree those who informed on such matters were not allowed to live. His legs were at once broken, this sentence being passed on him by the judge Perennius. But God's most beloved martyr, when the judge pleaded with him long and earnestly, and pressed him to speak up for himself before the Senate, made before them all a most eloquent defence of the faith to which he was testifying, and by decree of the Senate found fulfilment in decapitation: under an old statute that still held good no other verdict was possible in the case of those who were once brought into court and refused to change their plea. Anyone who wishes to know what Apollonius said in court, the answers he gave when questioned by Perennius, and the whole of his defence to the Senate, will find it all in the register I have compiled of the early martyrs.

Notable bishops of the period

22. In the tenth year of Commodus' reign, after thirteen years' service as bishop, Eleutherus was succeeded by Victor. At the same time, Julian having completed his tenth year, responsibility for the Alexandrian province was entrusted to Demetrius. Contemporary with them was the Serapion already mentioned, eighth from the apostles as Bishop of Antioch, and quite outstanding. Caesarea in Palestine was headed by Theophilus, while Narcissus, already referred to in this book, was still responsible for the Jerusalem diocese. Other contemporary bishops were those of Corinth in Greece (Bacchyllus) and of the diocese of Ephesus (Polycrates). No doubt a great many others were prominent at the time: naturally it is those of whose orthodoxy I have found written proof that I have listed by name.

The controversy about the Easter festival

23. It was at that stage that a controversy of great significance took place, because all the Asian dioceses thought that in accordance with ancient tradition they ought to observe the fourteenth day of the lunar month as the beginning of the Paschal festival – the day

on which the Jews had been commanded to sacrifice the lamb: on that day, no matter which day of the week it might be, they must without fail bring the fast to an end. But nowhere else in the world was it customary to arrange their celebrations in that way: in accordance with apostolic tradition, they preserved the view which still prevails, that it was improper to end the fast on any day other than that of our Saviour's resurrection. So synods and conferences of bishops were convened, and without a dissentient voice, drew up a decree of the Church, in the form of letters addressed to Christians everywhere, that never on any day other than the Lord's Day should the mystery of the Lord's resurrection from the dead be celebrated, and that on that day alone we should observe the end of the Paschal fast. There is extant to this day a letter from those who attended a conference in Palestine presided over by Bishop Theophilus of Caesarea and Narcissus of Jerusalem; and from those at Rome a similar one, arising out of the same controversy, which names Victor as bishop. There are others from the Pontic bishops, presided over by Palmas as the senior; from the Gallic province, over which Irenaeus presided, and from the bishops in Osrhoene and the cities of that region. There are also personal letters from Bishop Bacchyllus of Corinth and very many more, who voiced one and the same opinion and judgment and gave the same vote. All these laid down one single rule – the rule already stated.

24. The Asian bishops who insisted that they must observe the custom transmitted to them long ago were headed by Polycrates, who in the letter which he wrote to Victor and the Roman church sets out in the following terms the tradition that he had received:

We for our part keep the day scrupulously, without addition or subtraction. For in Asia great luminaries sleep who shall rise again on the day of the Lord's advent, when He is coming with glory from heaven and shall search out all His saints – such as Philip, one of the twelve apostles, who sleeps in Hierapolis with two of his daughters, who remained unmarried to the end of their days, while his other daughter lived in the Holy Spirit and rests in Ephesus. Again there is John, who leant back on the Lord's breast, and who became a priest wearing the mitre, a martyr, and a teacher; he too sleeps in Ephesus. Then in Smyrna there is Polycarp, bishop and martyr; and Thraseas, the bishop and martyr from Eumenia, who also sleeps in Smyrna. Need I mention Sagaris, bishop and martyr, who sleeps in Laodicea, or blessed Papirius, or Melito the eunuch, who lived entirely in the Holy Spirit, and who lies in Sardis waiting for the visitation from heaven when he shall rise from the dead? All of these kept the fourteenth day of the month as the beginning of the Paschal festival, in accordance with the Gospel, not deviating in the least but following the rule of the Faith. Last of all I too, Polycrates, the least of you all, act according to the tradition of my family, some members of which I have actually followed; for seven of them were bishops and I am the eighth, and my family have always kept the day when the people put away the leaven. So I, my friends, after spending sixty-five years in the Lord's service and conversing with Christians from all parts of the world, and going carefully through all Holy Scripture, am not scared of threats. Better people than I have said: 'We must obey God rather than men.'[1]

Referring to the bishops who were with him when he wrote, and shared his opinion, he adds:

I could have mentioned the bishops who are with me and whom I summoned in response to your request. If I write their names, the list will be very long. But though they know what an insignificant person I am, they approve my letter, knowing that I have not frittered away my long life but have spent it in the service of Christ Jesus.

Thereupon Victor, head of the Roman church, attempted at one stroke to cut off from the common unity all the Asian dioceses, together with the neighbouring churches, on the ground of heterodoxy, and pilloried them in letters in which he announced the total excommunication of all his fellow-Christians there. But this was not to the taste of all the bishops: they replied with a request that he would turn his mind to the things that make for peace[2] and for unity and love towards his neighbours. We still possess the words of these men, who very sternly rebuked Victor. Among them was Irenaeus, who wrote on behalf of the Christians for whom he was responsible in Gaul. While supporting the view that only on the Lord's Day might the mystery of the Lord's resurrection be celebrated, he gave Victor a great deal of excellent

1. Acts v. 29.   2. Rom. xiv. 19.

advice, in particular that he should not cut off entire churches of God because they observed the unbroken tradition of their predecessors. This is how he goes on:

The dispute is not only about the day, but also about the actual character of the fast. Some think that they ought to fast for one day, some for two, others for still more; some make their 'day' last forty hours on end. Such variation in the observance did not originate in our own day, but very much earlier, in the time of our forefathers, who – apparently disregarding strict accuracy – in their naïve simplicity kept up a practice which they fixed for the time to come. In spite of that, they all lived in peace with one another, and so do we: the divergency in the fast emphasizes the unanimity of our faith.

This argument he illustrates with two anecdotes which I may with advantage quote:

Among these were the presbyters before Soter, who were in charge of the church of which you are the present leader – I mean Anicetus, Pius, Hyginus, Telesphorus, and Xystus. They did not keep it themselves or allow those under their wing to do so. But in spite of their not keeping it, they lived in peace with those who came to them from the dioceses in which it was kept, though to keep it was more objectionable to those who did not. Never was this made a ground for repulsing anyone, but the presbyters before you, even though they did not keep it, used to send the Eucharist to Christians from dioceses which did. And when Blessed Polycarp paid a visit to Rome in Anicetus' time, though they had minor differences on other matters too, they at once made peace, having no desire to quarrel on this point. Anicetus could not persuade Polycarp not to keep the day, since he had always kept it with John the disciple of our Lord and the other apostles with whom he had been familiar; nor did Polycarp persuade Anicetus to keep it: Anicetus said that he must stick to the practice of the presbyters before him. Though the position was such, they remained in communion with each other, and in church Anicetus made way for Polycarp to celebrate the Eucharist – out of respect, obviously. They parted company in peace, and the whole Church was at peace, both those who kept the day and those who did not.

Irenaeus, whose name means 'peaceable' and who by temperament was a peacemaker, pleaded and negotiated thus for the peace of the churches. He corresponded by letter not only with Victor

173

but with very many other heads of churches, setting out both sides of the question under discussion.

Unanimous decision on the question of Easter

25. The Palestinian bishops of whom I spoke a little while ago, Narcissus and Theophilus, with Bishop Cassius of Tyre, Clarus of Ptolemais, and the others assembled with them, composed a lengthy review of the tradition about the Easter festival which had come down to them without a break from the apostles, at the end of which they add this appeal:

Try to send a copy of our letter to every diocese, so that we may not fail in our duty to those who readily deceive their own souls. We may point out to you that in Alexandria they keep the feast on the same day as we do, for we send letters to them and they to us, to ensure that we keep the holy day in harmony and at the same time.

The admirably written works of Irenaeus which have come into my hands

26. In addition to the letters and other works of Irenaeus already quoted, there is extant a very succinct and highly convincing essay directed against the Greeks and entitled *Scientific Knowledge*; another, dedicated to a fellow-Christian named Marcian, on the *Exposition of the Apostolic Preaching*; and a collection of addresses on various subjects, in which he mentions the Epistle to the Hebrews and the 'Wisdom of Solomon', quoting several passages from them. That completes the list of works by Irenaeus that have come to my cognizance.

After thirteen years, Commodus reached the end of his reign and Severus took office as emperor, Pertinax having occupied the position for something less than six months following the death of Commodus.

The extant works of Irenaeus' contemporaries

27. Large numbers of short works composed with commendable zeal by churchmen of that early time are still preserved in many libraries. Those that I have read myself include Heraclitus on *The Epistles of Paul*; Maximus on the question so much discussed among the heretics, *The Origin of Evil*, and on *Matter the Result of a Creative Act*; Candidus on *The Six Days of Creation*; Apion on the same subject; also Sextus on *The Resurrection*; and an essay by Arabianus; and works by many other authors – lack of evidence make it impossible to give their dates or shed any light on their history. Finally, there are a number of others whom I cannot even name, whose writings have come into my hands – orthodox churchmen, as is clear from their respective interpretations of Holy Writ, but unknown to us all the same, as they are not named in their writings.

*Propagators of Artemon's heresy, their character, their
impudent corruption of Holy Scripture*

28. In a polemic composed by one of these against Artemon's heresy, which again in my own day Paul of Samosata has tried to revive, there is extant a discussion pertinent to the historical period under review. For the assertion of the heresy in question, that the Saviour was merely human, is exposed in this book as a recent invention, because those who introduced it were anxious to represent it as ancient and therefore respectable. After adducing many other arguments to refute their blasphemous falsehood, the writer continues:

They claim that all earlier generations, and the apostles themselves, received and taught the things they say themselves, and that the true teaching was preserved till the times of Victor, the thirteenth Bishop of Rome after Peter: from the time of his successor Zephyrinus the truth was deliberately perverted. This suggestion might perhaps have been credible if in the first place Holy Scripture had not presented a very different picture; and there are also works by Christian writers published before Victor's time, written to defend the truth against both pagan criticism and current heresies – I mean works by Justin, Miltiades, Tatian, Clement, and many more. In every one of these Christ is spoken of as God. For who does not know the books of Irenaeus, Melito, and the rest, which proclaim Christ as God and man, and all the psalms and hymns written from the beginning by faithful brethren, which sing of Christ as the Word of God and address Him as God? How then can it be true that when the mind of the Church had been proclaimed for so many years, Christians up to the time of Victor preached as these people say they did? And are they not ashamed to slander Victor in this way, knowing perfectly well that it was Victor who excommunicated Theodotus the shoemaker, the prime mover and father of this God-denying apostasy, when he became the first to declare that Christ was merely human? If Victor regarded their views in the way their slanderous statements suggest, how could he have thrown out Theodotus, the inventor of this heresy?

That is all I have to say about the events in Victor's time. When he had held office for ten years, Zephyrinus was appointed to succeed him, about the ninth year of Severus' reign.

The writer of the book just quoted about the founder of the heresy under discussion describes a further incident, which occurred in Zephyrinus' time. Here is the actual passage:

I will remind many of my brother-Christians of an event which occurred in my time and which I think, had it happened in Sodom,[1] would perhaps have warned even them. There was a confessor named Natalius, who lived not a long time ago but in my own lifetime. He was led astray by Asclepiodotus and by a second Theodotus, a banker. These two were disciples of Theodotus the shoemaker, the first to be excommunicated for thinking in this way – or rather for failing to think – by Victor, who as I said was bishop at the time. They persuaded Natalius to be known as bishop of this heretical sect, in return for a stipend which he was to receive from them of 150 denarii a month. After joining them, he was repeatedly warned by the Lord in visions; for our compassionate God and Lord, Jesus Christ, did not desire one who had witnessed to His own sufferings to perish outside the Church. He paid little attention to the visions, ensnared by his pre-eminence among them and by the love of ill-gotten gain that corrupts so many; but he was finally whipped all night long by holy angels, and suffered severely, so that he got up early, put on

---

1. Matt. xi. 23.

sackcloth, sprinkled himself with ashes, and without a moment's delay
prostrated himself in tears before Bishop Zephyrinus, rolling at the feet
not only of the clergy but of the laity as well, and moving with his tears
the compassionate Church of the merciful Christ. But though he begged
and besought them and displayed the weals left by the blows he had
received, it was only after much hesitation that he was readmitted to communion.

To this I will add some further comments on the same persons
from the same writer:

They have not hesitated to corrupt the word of God; they have treated
the standard of the primitive faith with contempt; they have not known
Christ. Instead of asking what Holy Scripture says, they strain every
nerve to find a syllogistic figure to bolster up their godlessness. If anyone
challenges them with a text from Divine Scripture, they examine it to see
whether it can be turned into a conjunctive or disjunctive syllogistic
figure. They put aside the sacred word of God, and devote themselves to
geometry – earth-measurement – because they are from the earth and
speak from the earth, and do not know the One who comes from above.[1]
Some of them give all their energies to the study of Euclidean geometry,
and treat Aristotle and Theophrastus with reverent awe; to some of them
Galen is almost an object of worship. When people avail themselves of
the arts of unbelievers to lend colour to their heretical views, and with
godless rascality corrupt the simple Faith of Holy Writ, it is obvious that
they are nowhere near the Faith. So it was that they laid hands unblushingly on the Holy Scriptures, claiming to have corrected them.

In saying this I am not slandering them, as anybody who wishes can
soon find out. If anyone will take the trouble to collect their several
copies and compare them, he will discover frequent divergencies; for
example, Asclepiades' copies do not agree with Theodotus'. A large
number are obtainable, thanks to the emulous energy with which disciples
copied the 'emendations' or rather perversions of the text by their
respective masters. Nor do these agree with Hermophilus' copies. As for
Apolloniades, his cannot even be harmonized with each other; it is
possible to collate the ones which his disciples made first with those that
have undergone further manipulation, and to find endless discrepancies.
The impertinence of this misconduct can hardly be unknown even to the
copyists. Either they do not believe that the inspired Scriptures were

1. John iii. 31.

177

spoken by the Holy Spirit – if so, they are unbelievers; or they imagine that they are wiser than He – if so, can they be other than possessed? They cannot deny that the impertinence is their own, seeing that the copies are in their own handwriting, that they did not receive the Scriptures in such a condition from their first teachers, and that they cannot produce any originals to justify their copies. Some of them have not even deigned to falsify the text, but have simply repudiated both Law and Prophets, and so under cover of a wicked, godless teaching have plunged into the lowest depths of destruction.

And there we will leave that subject.

Book 6

SEVERUS TO DECIUS: THE WORK OF ORIGEN
AND HIS CONTEMPORARIES:
WIDESPREAD PERSECUTION

The persecution under Severus

1. When Severus, in his turn, was instigating persecution of the churches, the champions of true religion achieved glorious martyrdoms in every land. These were most numerous at Alexandria, to which, as to a huge arena, God's noble champions were conducted from the whole of Egypt and the Thebaid. There, by their heroic endurance of every kind of torture and every form of death, they were wreathed with the crowns laid up with God. Among them was Leonides (usually referred to as the father of Origen), who was beheaded, leaving his son quite young. How devoted to the word of God Origen was from the start it will not be inappropriate to describe in brief, especially in view of the story about him that has received such wide publicity. 2. There would be a great deal to say if one tried to give a full-length account of his life in writing: the record of his doings would fill a whole book. However, for the present I shall cut down most parts of the story to the fewest possible words, and mention only a few features of his career. The facts here set forth are drawn from some of his letters and from the recollections of those of his friends who have lived on till my own time.

Origen's boyhood training; his early success as a preacher

Origen's story deserves, I think, to be told right from the cradle. It was the tenth year of Severus' reign; the governor of Alexandria and the rest of Egypt was Laetus; and as archbishop of that province Julian had just been succeeded by Demetrius. When the flames of persecution were fanned to a great blaze and untold numbers were being wreathed with martyrs' crowns, such a longing for martyrdom possessed the soul of Origen, boy as he was, that his one ambition was to come to grips with danger and charge headlong into the conflict. Indeed, he was within a hair's breadth of arriving at the end of his days, when for the benefit of mankind the providence of Almighty God used his mother to defeat his ambition. She first appealed to him in words, begging him to spare his mother's feelings for him; then, when the news that his father had been arrested and imprisoned filled his whole being with a craving for martyrdom, and she saw that he was more determined than ever, she hid all his clothing and compelled him to stay at home. He, in the grip of an ambition extraordinary in one so young, could not remain silent: he did the only thing possible, and sent his father a letter pressing him strongly on the subject of martyrdom, and advising him exactly in these words: 'Mind you don't change your mind on our account.'

This may serve as the first evidence of Origen's boyish sagacity and the perfect sincerity of his devotion to God. For already he had laid firm foundations for the understanding of the Faith, trained as he was from early childhood in the divine Scriptures. He had toiled at these assiduously, his father insisting that in addition to the normal curriculum he should pursue the study of Holy Writ with equal vigour. He constantly urged him not to give any time to secular subjects till he had steeped himself in religious studies, and every day required him to learn passages by heart and repeat them aloud. This was not at all distasteful to the boy: indeed, he gave himself up too completely to these tasks and, not content to read the sacred words in their simple and natural sense, looked for something more, and young as he was devoted himself to profounder investigation; so that he worried his father with questions as to the meaning and intention that underlay the inspired Scripture. His father would make a show of scolding him to his face, advising him not to look for anything beyond his understanding, or any meaning other than the obvious one, but in private he was delighted and profoundly grateful to God, the Author of all good things, who had deemed him worthy to father such a son. It is said that often when the boy was asleep he would bend over him and bare his breast, and as if it was the temple of a divine spirit would kiss it reverently and count himself blest in his promising child. These stories and others like them are told of Origen as a boy.

But when his father had found fulfilment in martyrdom he was left destitute with his mother and as many as six younger brothers while still in his seventeenth year. His father's property had been seized for the imperial treasury, so that he and the rest of his family now lacked even the necessities of life. But being deemed worthy of God's loving care, he was received into the comfortable house of a lady who was extremely wealthy and very distinguished in other ways; she was, however, a devotee of a notorious heretic, one of those then flourishing at Alexandria. An Antiochene by birth, he was the adopted son of the lady in question, who kept him at her house and was utterly devoted to him. Origen could not help associating with him, but from the start he gave clear proofs of his doctrinal orthodoxy. Crowds of heretics, and of our own people too, might gather to hear Paul, as the man was called, because his arguments seemed so convincing: never once was Origen induced to join with him in prayer, keeping from his earliest years the rule of the Church and 'abominating' – the very word he uses somewhere himself – all heretical teachings. Thanks to his father, he had made good progress in secular subjects: after his father's death he devoted himself entirely and with growing enthusiasm to the humanities, so that he acquired considerable ability as a literary man; in fact, his father had not long found fulfilment, before his devotion to these studies enabled him to enjoy a standard of life beyond the means of most young men.

3. So while Origen devoted himself to teaching, since at Alexandria there was no one dedicated to elementary Christian teaching (as they had all fled the threatened persecution), he was approached by some pagans who wished to hear the word of God. Of these the first to be named is Plutarch, whose noble life was crowned with divine martyrdom. The second was Plutarch's brother Heraclas, who by his own efforts furnished a remarkable example of the philosophic life and discipline, and was chosen Bishop of

Alexandria in succession to Demetrius. Origen was seventeen when he became principal of the school of elementary instruction: at the same period he came to the fore during the persecutions under Aquila the governor of Alexandria, when he won a resounding reputation among all adherents of the Faith by his eagerness to lend a helping hand to all the holy martyrs, known or unknown. For not only when they were in prison, or were being cross-examined, up to the final sentence, but even when they were afterwards led away to execution, he was at the side of the holy martyrs, displaying astonishing fearlessness and meeting danger face to face. As he boldly approached and fearlessly greeted the martyrs with a kiss, again and again the maddened crowd of pagans that surrounded him were on the point of stoning him, had he not found the right hand of God ever ready to help him, so that he escaped when it seemed impossible.

The same divine and heavenly grace protected him again and again on other occasions too many to count; for because of his fearlessness and extreme enthusiasm for the word of Christ he was at that time the target of plotters. So bitter was the hostility of unbelievers to him that they actually collected groups of soldiers and posted them round the house where he was living, because of the number of those whom he was instructing in the rudiments of the Holy Faith. Thus the persecution directed against him grew daily hotter, so that there no longer was room for him anywhere in the city. He moved from house to house, driven from pillar to post, in revenge for the number of those whom he had brought to hear his religious teaching. For in a quite amazing way his actions displayed to the full the fruits of the most genuine philosophy. His deeds matched his words, as the saying goes, and his words his deeds. That was the chief reason why, aided by the power of God, he led men in thousands to share his enthusiasm.

Responsibility for elementary instruction had been entrusted by Demetrius, prelate of the church, to Origen alone, who soon saw pupils coming to him in increasing numbers. He decided, however, that the teaching of literature did not harmonize with training in theology, and promptly broke off his lectures on literature, as useless and a hindrance to sacred studies. Then, with the worthy object of making himself independent of other people's assistance, he parted with all the volumes of ancient literature which had hitherto been his most cherished possessions, and if the purchaser brought him four obols a day he was satisfied.

For very many years he persisted in this philosophic way of life, putting away from him all inducements to youthful lusts, and at all times of the day disciplining himself by performing strenuous tasks, while he devoted most of the night to the study of Holy Scripture. He went to the limit in practising a life given up to philosophy; sometimes he trained himself by periods of fasting, sometimes by restricting the hours of sleep, which he insisted on taking never in bed, always on the floor. Above all, he felt that he must keep the gospel sayings of the Saviour urging us not to carry two coats or wear shoes[1] and never to be worried by anxiety about the future.[2] He displayed an enthusiasm beyond his years, and patiently enduring cold and nakedness went to the furthest limit of poverty, to the utter amazement of his pupils and the distress of the countless friends who begged him to share their possessions in recognition of the labours that they saw him bestow on his religious teaching. Not once did his determination weaken; it is said that for several years he went about on foot without any shoes at all, and for a much longer period abstained from wine and all else beyond the minimum of food, so that he ran the risk of upsetting and even ruining his constitution.

Pupils who became martyrs; Potamiaena

By setting such an example of the philosophic life to those who saw him he naturally kindled a similar enthusiasm in many of his pupils, so that even among pagan unbelievers and those who had been to schools and colleges there were persons of distinction who were won over by his teaching. Thanks to him, men like this with all their heart honestly embraced faith in the word of God, and came into prominence in the persecution that broke out at that time, some of them being arrested and finding fulfilment in martyrdom.

1. Matt. x. 10.   2. Matt. vi. 34.

4. The first of these was Plutarch, to whom I referred a little while ago. As he was on the way to execution, the subject of these pages stayed with him to the end, and again barely escaped lynching at the hands of the martyr's fellow-citizens, as being obviously to blame for his death, but on that occasion, too, God's will kept him safe. After Plutarch, the second of Origen's pupils to be revealed as a martyr was Serenus, who gave proof by fire of the faith he had received. From the same school the third to be martyred was Heraclides, who was still under instruction, and the fourth Hero, lately baptized: both were beheaded. In addition to these, a fifth member of the school was proclaimed a champion of true religion: a second Serenus, who – after showing the greatest patience under torture – died, there is reason to believe, under the axe. Of the women, Herais – still under instruction – received, as Origen himself records somewhere, the baptism of fire, and so departed this life.

5. Seventh among them must be reckoned Basilides, who led the renowned Potamiaena to execution. The praises of this woman are even today loudly sung by her own people. Endless the struggle that in defence of her chastity and virginity, which were beyond reproach, she maintained against lovers, for her beauty – of body as of mind – was in full flower. Endless her sufferings, till after tortures too horrible to describe she and her mother Marcella found fulfilment in fire. It is said that the judge, Aquila, subjected her whole body to dreadful agonies, and finally threatened to hand her over to the gladiators for bodily insult. She reflected for a moment, and when asked what she intended to do, gave an answer which offended their religious prejudices. She had hardly spoken when she heard sentence pronounced, and Basilides, a member of the armed forces, seized her arm and led her away to execution. As the crowd tried to plague her and insult her with obscene jests, Basilides thrust them back and drove them away, showing the utmost pity and kindness towards her. Potamiaena accepted his sympathy for her and gave him encouragement: when she had gone away she would ask her Lord for him, and it would not be long before she repaid him for all he had done for

her. This said, she faced her end with noble courage – slowly, drop by drop, boiling pitch was poured over different parts of her body, from her toes to the crown of her head. Such was the battle won by this splendid girl.

Not long afterwards Basilides was for some reason asked by his fellow-soldiers to take an oath, but he insisted that he was unable to swear in any circumstances,[1] as he was a Christian and made no secret of the fact. At first they thought he was joking, but when he stuck doggedly to his assertion he was brought before the magistrate, who, as he made no attempt to hide his convictions, committed him to prison. When his brothers in God visited him and asked the reason for this amazing impulse and determination, he is said to have declared that three days after her martyrdom Potamiaena stood before him in the night, put a wreath about his head, and said that she had prayed for him to the Lord, had obtained her request, and before long would place him by her side. At this the brethren bestowed on him the seal of the Lord,[2] and the next day, nobly witnessing for his Lord, he was beheaded. The records state that at this period many other citizens of Alexandria accepted the teaching of Christ in a body, as Potamiaena appeared to them in dreams and called them.

Clement of Alexandria: Jude the author

6. Pantaenus was succeeded by Clement, who remained principal of the school of instruction at Alexandria long enough to include Origen among his pupils. Observe that when he put together his *Miscellanies*, Clement set out a chronological table in Volume 1, making the death of Commodus a key date. It is clear then that he composed the work in the reign of Severus, whose times are the subject of these pages.

7. At the same period Jude, another author, wrote a treatise on Daniel's seventy weeks, bringing his account to an end in the tenth year of Severus. He believed that the much talked-of advent of

1. Matt. v. 34.   2. Baptism.

antichrist would take place at any moment – so completely had the persecution set in motion against us at that time thrown many off their balance.

Origen's headstrong act

8. About the same time, while responsible for the instruction at Alexandria, Origen did a thing that provided the fullest proof of a mind youthful and immature, but at the same time of faith and self-mastery. The saying 'there are eunuchs who made themselves eunuchs for the kingdom of heaven's sake' he took in an absurdly literal sense, and he was eager both to fulfil the Saviour's words and at the same time to rule out any suspicion of vile imputations on the part of unbelievers. For in spite of his youth he discussed religious problems before a mixed audience. So he lost no time in carrying out the Saviour's words, endeavouring to do it unnoticed by the bulk of his pupils. But however much he might wish it, he could not possibly conceal such an act, and it was not long before it came to the knowledge of Demetrius, as head of the diocese. He was amazed at Origen's headstrong act, but approving his enthusiasm and the genuineness of his faith he told him not to worry, and urged him to devote himself more keenly than ever to the work of instruction.

That was the line he took at the time, but when a little later the same worthy saw him prosperous, great, eminent, and universally esteemed, he yielded to human weakness and wrote to the bishops throughout the world in an attempt to make Origen's action appear outrageous, just when the most respected and outstanding bishops of Palestine, those of Caesarea and Jerusalem, judged him worthy of position in the Church and of the highest honour, and ordained him presbyter. As he had thus attained to a great name and reputation, and everyone everywhere esteemed him highly for his virtues and wisdom, Demetrius, for want of any other charge to bring against him, slandered him viciously for what he had done years before as a boy, and even dared to extend his accusations to those who had advanced him to the presbyterate.

This incident occurred somewhat later. At the time we are

speaking of, Origen was busy at Alexandria with the work of imparting religious knowledge to all without exception who came to him, night and day, and devoted the whole of his time unsparingly to religious teaching and the demands of his pupils.

Narcissus and Alexander

After eighteen years as master of the Empire, Severus was succeeded by his son Antoninus.[1] It was at this time that Alexander – one of those who faced persecution so manfully and openly confessed the Faith, yet by the providence of God were kept safe – was rewarded for his bold confessions of Christ by being appointed Bishop of the Jerusalem church, mentioned a few pages back. The appointment was made while his predecessor Narcissus was still alive.

9. Many stories of miracles wrought by Narcissus, handed down by generations of Christians, are told by members of the community. Among these they narrate the following tale of wonder. Once during the great all-night-long vigil of Easter, the deacons ran out of oil. The whole congregation was deeply distressed, so Narcissus told those responsible for the lights to draw water and bring it to him, and they obeyed him instantly. Then he said a prayer over the water, and instructed them to pour it into the lamps with absolute faith in the Lord. They again obeyed him, and, in defiance of natural law, by the miraculous power of God the substance of the liquid was physically changed from water into oil. All the years from that day to our own a large body of Christians there have preserved a little of it, as proof of that wonderful event.

Among the many interesting anecdotes from the life of Narcissus is recorded the following. His energy and conscientiousness were more than some insignificant nonentities could bear. Knowing themselves guilty of a long series of misdemeanours, they were afraid that conviction and punishment awaited them. To avoid this, they devised an intrigue against him and smirched him with a

---

1. Antoninus is better known as Caracalla.

horrid slander. Then, to convince their hearers, they bolstered up
their accusations with oaths. One swore: 'If it isn't true, may I be
burnt to death!' Another: 'May my body be wasted by a foul
disease!' A third: 'May I lose my sight!' But no amount of
swearing made any of the faithful take any notice, for no one
could fail to see the unshakeable integrity and blameless character
of Narcissus. But he himself was greatly distressed by their das-
tardly allegations, and in addition he had long ago embraced the
philosophic life; so, turning his back on the church community, he
fled into a remote and desert area, where he remained in hiding
for many years. However, the great eye of Justice did not remain
unmoved by these events, but very soon brought upon those
perjured scoundrels the curses with which they had bound themselves. The first saw the house which he occupied ablaze from top
to bottom for no other cause whatever than a tiny spark that
settled on the roof in the night, and he and all his family were
burnt to ashes; the second felt his entire body from head to toe
permeated by the very disease he had named as his penalty; the
third, seeing the fate of the others and dreading the inescapable
judgement of all-seeing God, publicly confessed his share in the
intrigue, but in his remorse he wore himself out with so many
lamentations, and poured out such a flood of tears, that he lost the
sight of both eyes. Such was the price these men paid for their lies.

10. As Narcissus had withdrawn, and there was no knowledge of
his whereabouts, the heads of the neighbouring churches decided
to proceed to the appointment of a new bishop. Dius was his
name. After a short time as prelate, he was followed by Germanion,
and he by Gordius. In his time Narcissus appeared from nowhere,
as if restored to life, and was invited by the brethren to resume his
prelateship, for he was admired by all even more than before
because of his withdrawal and philosophic life – above all because
of the judgement by which God had vindicated him.

11. When he had reached such an advanced age that he could no
longer carry out his duties, the Alexander already mentioned, then
holder of another bishopric, by the providence of God was
summoned to share the duties with Narcissus, by means of a

revelation given to him at night in a vision. Thereupon, as if in accordance with an oracle, he journeyed from Cappadocia, his original see, to Jerusalem, in order to worship there and to examine the historic sites. The Christian community welcomed him most warmly and would not let him return home again, for they, too, had received a revelation in the night, proclaiming a single unambiguous message to the most devout among them. It bade them go outside the city gates to welcome the man already chosen by God to be their bishop. This done, they forced him to remain, with the unanimous approval of the bishops who had charge of the churches round about. Alexander himself, in a personal letter to the Antinoites, which is still in my possession, mentions Narcissus as sharing the episcopal throne with him, using these exact words at the end of the letter:

> Narcissus, who preceded me as bishop of this diocese, and now at the age of 116 shares my responsibility for public worship, wishes to be remembered to you. He is as anxious as I am that you should agree among yourselves.

Serapion and his extant works

Turning now to Antioch, we note that when Serapion entered into rest he was succeeded as bishop by Asclepiades, who confessed his Lord with equal boldness during the persecution. His appointment, too, is mentioned by Alexander in a letter to the Antiochenes:

> Alexander, a servant and prisoner of Jesus Christ, to the blessed church of Antioch, greeting in the Lord. The Lord made my fetters light and easy to bear, when news reached me in my cell that by God's providence the bishopric of your holy church of Antioch had been entrusted to Asclepiades, an excellent choice in view of his wonderful faith.

This letter was conveyed by Clement, as is shown by the final sentences:

> I am sending you these lines, my dear brothers, by Clement the blessed presbyter, whom you have already heard of and will now get to know. The providence of the Master has so ordered it that during his stay with

us this virtuous and estimable man has both strengthened and enlarged the Church of the Lord.

12. It is probable that other short works from Serapion's pen are in the keeping of other people: none has come into my hands but those addressed to Domnus, a man who at the time of the persecution had fallen away from faith in Christ to Jewish will-worship,[1] and to the churchmen of Pontius and Caricus, together with letters to other people and a pamphlet of his composition entitled *The So-Called Gospel of Peter*. This he wrote to refute the lies in that document, which had induced some members of the Christian community at Rhossus to go astray into heterodox teachings. It will be worth while to quote from this work a few sentences which explain his attitude to the book:

We, my brothers, receive Peter and all the apostles as we receive Christ, but the writings falsely attributed to them we are experienced enough to reject, knowing that nothing of the sort has been handed down to us. When I visited you, I assumed that you all clung to the true Faith; so without going through the 'gospel' alleged by them to be Peter's, I said: 'If this is the only thing that apparently puts childish notions into your heads, read it by all means.' But as, from information received, I now know that their mind had been ensnared by some heresy, I will make every effort to visit you again; so expect me in the near future. It was obvious to me what kind of heresy Marcian upheld, though he contradicted himself through not knowing what he was talking about, as you will gather from this letter. But others have studied this same 'gospel', viz. the successors of those who originated it, known to us as Docetists and from whose teaching the ideas are mostly derived. With their comments in mind, I have been able to go through the book and draw the conclusion that while most of it accorded with the authentic teaching of the Saviour, some passages were spurious additions. These I am appending to my letter.

The works of Clement

13. Of Clement's works the *Miscellanies*, all eight books, are in my possession, bearing the title he chose for them – *Titus Flavius*

1. See Col. ii. 23.

Clemens' Miscellanies: Gnostic Publications in the Light of the True Philosophy. There are eight volumes again of the work he entitled *Outlines*, in which he names Pantaenus as his teacher. In these he has expounded his own interpretations of Scripture alongside the traditional. There is also a work of his addressed to the Greeks — the *Exhortation*; the three volumes of the work entitled *The Tutor*; *The Rich Man who finds Salvation*, as another work of his is entitled; the monograph on *The Easter Festival*; the discourses on *Fasting* and on *Slander*; the *Exhortation to Patience, or For the Newly Baptized*; and the work entitled *Canon of the Church, or An Answer to the Judaizers*, dedicated to Alexander, the bishop already mentioned.

In the *Miscellanies* he has woven a tapestry combining Holy Writ with anything that he considered helpful in secular literature. He includes any view generally accepted, expounding those of Greeks and non-Greeks alike, and even correcting the false doctrines of the heresiarchs, and explains a great deal of history, providing us with a work of immense erudition. With all these strands he has blended the arguments of philosophers, so that the work completely justifies the title *Miscellanies*. In it he has made use also of evidence drawn from the Disputed Writings — the 'Wisdom of Solomon', the 'Wisdom of Jesus the son of Sirach', the Epistle to the Hebrews, and those of Barnabas, Clement, and Jude; and he refers to Tatian's *Against the Greeks* and to Cassian, the compiler of another *Chronological Record* — also to Philo and Aristobulus, Josephus, Demetrius, and Eupolemus, Jewish authors whose writings all helped to prove that the first appearance of the Greeks did not go back as far as Moses and the Jewish people. Choice passages from many other writers fill the pages of this work. In Book 1 he shows that he himself was almost an immediate successor of the apostles: farther on he promises to write a commentary on Genesis.

In his work *The Easter Festival* he declares that his friends insisted on his transmitting to later generations in writing the oral traditions that had come down to him from the earliest authorities of the Church; he refers also to Melito, Irenaeus, and some others, whose statements he has reproduced.

14. In the *Outlines*, to put it briefly, he has summarized all canonical Scripture, even including the Disputed Books, namely the Epistle of Jude and the other Catholic Epistles, the Epistle of Barnabas, and the 'Revelation of Peter'. The Epistle to the Hebrews he attributes to Paul, but says that it was written for Hebrews in their own language, and then accurately translated by Luke and published for Greek readers. Hence, in the Greek version of this epistle we find the same stylistic colour as in the Acts. The usual opening – 'Paul, an apostle' – was omitted, with good reason. As Clement says:

> In writing to Hebrews already prejudiced against him and suspicious of him, he was far too sensible to put them off at the start by naming himself ... Now, as the blessed presbyter [1] used to say, the Lord, the apostle of the Almighty, was sent to the Hebrews; so through modesty Paul, knowing that he had been sent to the Gentiles, does not describe himself as an apostle of the Hebrews, first because he so reverenced the Lord, and secondly because he was going outside his province in writing to the Hebrews too, when he was an ambassador and apostle of the Gentiles.

In the same volumes Clement has found room for a tradition of the primitive authorities of the Church regarding the order of the gospels. It is this. He used to say that the earliest gospels were those containing the genealogies, while Mark's originated as follows. When, at Rome, Peter had openly preached the word and by the spirit had proclaimed the gospel, the large audience urged Mark, who had followed him for a long time and remembered what had been said, to write it all down. This he did, making his gospel available to all who wanted it. When Peter heard about this, he made no objection and gave no special encouragement. Last of all, aware that the physical facts had been recorded in the gospels, encouraged by his pupils and irresistibly moved by the Spirit, John wrote a spiritual gospel.

So much for Clement's writings. Clement himself is mentioned, along with Pantaenus, in a letter to Origen written by the Alexander referred to above, who knew them both. He writes as follows:

> This, as you know, is indeed God's will, that the friendship we have

1. Probably the author's teacher, Pantaenus.

inherited from our forebears should not wane, but rather grow warmer and more enduring. For we have found true fathers in those blessed ones who trod the road before us, with whom we shall soon be reunited – Pantaenus, my truly blessed friend, and holy Clement, my friend and helper, and others like them. Through them I came to know you, who are in every way my best friend and brother.

Origen's labours on Holy Writ· Symmachus the translator

When Zephyrinus was head of the Roman church, Adamantius – hitherto referred to as Origen – states in one of his writings that he himself visited Rome, anxious, as he says, to see the ancient Roman church. After a short stay in Rome he went back to Alexandria and took up again with enthusiasm his work of instruction there, as the bishop of the diocese, Demetrius, still pressed and almost begged him to continue unabated his efforts to assist the brethren. 15. But he saw that he could not find time himself for the more profound study of theology and the scrutiny and translation of sacred documents if he continued to instruct those who came to him and allowed him no time to breathe, batch after batch thronging his school from dawn to dusk. He therefore divided them up, and picking out Heraclas from his pupils, a keen theologian and in addition very well informed and a promising philosopher, gave him a share in the instruction. The introductory lessons for the beginners he entrusted to Heraclas: the higher education of the advanced pupils he reserved to himself.

16. So meticulous was the scrutiny to which Origen subjected the Scriptural books that he even mastered the Hebrew language, and secured for himself a copy, in the actual Hebrew script, of the original documents circulating among the Jews. Moreover, he hunted out the published translations of Holy Writ other than the Septuagint, and in addition to the versions in common use – those of Aquila, Symmachus, and Theodotion – he discovered several alternative translations. These had been lost for many years – I don't know where – but he hunted them out of their hiding-places and brought them to light. These were wrapped in mystery, and he had no idea who wrote them: the only thing he could say

was that he had found one at Nicopolis near Actium and the other at some similar place. Anyway, in his *Hexapla* of the Psalms, after the four familiar versions he placed in parallel columns not only a fifth but a sixth and seventh translation; in the case of one, he has added a note that it was found at Jericho in a jar during the reign of Antoninus, the son of Severus. All these he combined in one volume, breaking them up into clauses and setting them side by side in parallel columns, along with the original Hebrew text. Thus he has left us the copies of the *Hexapla*, as it is called. In a separate publication he put the versions of Aquila, Symmachus, and Theodotion alongside the Septuagint, in his *Tetrapla*.

17. Of these translators it should be observed that Symmachus was an Ebionite. The adherents of what is known as the Ebionite heresy assert that Christ was the son of Joseph and Mary, and regard Him as no more than a man. They insist also that the law ought to be kept more in the Jewish manner, as I mentioned earlier in this history. Pamphlets also by Symmachus are still extant, in which he inveighs against the Gospel according to Matthew, apparently in order to bolster up his heresy. These, together with other comments on Scripture by Symmachus, Origen states that he received from a woman called Juliana, on whom, he says, Symmachus had himself bestowed them.

Ambrose

18. At the same period, Ambrose – who shared the heretical opinions of Valentinus – was refuted by the truth which Origen expounded, and, as if light had dawned on his mind, accepted the orthodox teaching of the Church. Many other educated people were so impressed by Origen's universal renown that they came to his school to benefit by his skill in biblical exegesis; while innumerable heretics and a considerable number of the most eminent philosophers listened to him with close attention, as he instructed them not only in theology but to some extent in secular philosophy too, for he introduced any pupils in whom he detected natural ability to philosophic studies as well. First he taught them geo-

metry, arithmetic, and the other preparatory subjects; then he led them on to the systems of the philosophers, discussing their published theories and examining and criticizing those of the different schools, with the result that the Greeks themselves acknowledged his greatness as a philosopher. He found time also to give many less gifted persons a general grounding, declaring that it would stand them in very good stead for the examination and study of Holy Writ. He therefore thought it most important that he himself should be skilled in secular and philosophic studies.

References to Origen

19. Testimony to his success in these endeavours is paid by the Greek philosophers who flourished in his time, in whose writings I have found many references to him. Sometimes they dedicated their works to him, sometimes they submitted their own labours to him, as to a master, for criticism. Far more significant is the case of Porphyry, who in my own time settled in Sicily and in an attempt to traduce the Holy Scriptures published a long treatise attacking us, in which he refers to those who have interpreted them. He finds it quite impossible to bring any damaging accusation against our doctrines, so for lack of arguments he turns to abuse and traduces the interpreters. His special target is Origen, whom he claims to have known as a young man and attempts to traduce, little knowing that he is actually commending him. When he cannot help it, he tells the truth; when he thinks he will not be found out, he tells lies. Sometimes he accuses him as a Christian, sometimes he enlarges on his addiction to philosophic studies. Listen to his actual words:

In their eagerness to find, not a way to reject the depravity of the Jewish Scriptures, but a means of explaining it away, they resorted to interpretations which cannot be reconciled or harmonized with those scriptures, and which provide not so much a defence of the original authors as a fulsome advertisement for the interpreters. 'Enigmas' is the pompous name they give to the perfectly plain statements of Moses, glorifying them as oracles full of hidden mysteries, and bewitching the critical faculty by their extravagant nonsense ... This absurd method must be attributed to a man whom I met while I was still quite young, who enjoyed a great reputation and thanks to the works he has left behind him, enjoys it still. I refer to Origen, whose fame among teachers of these theories is widespread. He was a pupil of Ammonius, the most distinguished philosopher of our time. Theoretical knowledge in plenty he acquired with the help of his master, but in choosing the right way to live he went in the opposite direction. For Ammonius was a Christian, brought up in Christian ways by his parents, but when he began to think philosophically he promptly changed to a law-abiding way of life. Origen on the other hand, a Greek schooled in Greek thought, plunged headlong into un-Greek recklessness; immersed in this, he peddled himself and his skill in argument. In his life he behaved like a Christian, defying the law: in his metaphysical and theological ideas he played the Greek, giving a Greek twist to foreign tales. He associated himself at all times with Plato, and was at home among the writings of Numenius and Cronius, Apollophanes, Longinus, and Moderatus, Nicomachus, and the more eminent followers of Pythagoras. He made use, too, of the books of Chaeremon the Stoic and Cornutus, which taught him the allegorical method of interpreting the Greek mysteries, a method he applied to the Jewish Scriptures.

Such are the allegations made by Porphyry in the third book of his treatise against the Christians. He tells the truth about Origen's teaching and wide learning, but plainly lies – for opponents of Christianity are quite unscrupulous – when he says that he came over from the Greek camp, and that Ammonius lapsed from the service of God into paganism. For Origen clung firmly to the Christian principles his parents had taught him, as this record has already shown; and Ammonius' inspired philosophy remained pure and intact to the very end of his life. To this, surely, his literary labours bear witness, for the works that he bequeathed to posterity have won him a very wide reputation – for instance the book entitled *The Harmony of Moses and Jesus*, and the many other works treasured by discriminating readers.

These facts suffice to prove the untruthfulness of Origen's calumniator and his own perfect familiarity with Greek learning. Defending himself against critics who condemned his pre-occupation with such studies, he writes thus in one of his letters:

When I was giving all my time to the word, accounts of my ability went about, and brought sometimes heretics, sometimes men who had been trained in Greek learning, particularly philosophy; so I decided to examine the notions of the heretics, and also the supposed qualifications of philosophers for speaking about truth. In doing this I followed in the footsteps of one who helped many before my time – Pantaenus, a real expert in these questions; and of one who now has a seat in the presbytery of Alexandria – Heraclas, whom I found with the director of philosophical studies. He had already stayed with him five years before I attended my first lecture on the subject, and because of him he put off the normal dress he had hitherto worn, and donned a philosopher's garb, which he retains to this very day, while he devotes himself unceasingly and enthusiastically to the study of Greek literature.

That is what he says in defence of his Greek training. But at this period, when he was resident in Alexandria, one of the military arrived with letters from the ruler of Arabia to Demetrius, the bishop of the diocese, and to the governor of Egypt, asking them to send Origen at the earliest possible moment to confer with him. He did in fact visit Arabia, but he soon completed his business there and returned to Alexandria. Some time later a violent campaign blazed up in the city, so he slipped out of Alexandria and went to Palestine, where he settled in Caesarea. There he gave public lectures to the church on biblical exegesis, at the invitation of the bishops of the province, though not yet ordained to the presbyterate. The truth of this is evident from what Alexander and Theoctistus, bishops of Jerusalem and Caesarea, in writing about Demetrius, say in their own defence:

He included in his letter a statement that it was an unheard-of, unprecedented thing that where bishops were present laymen should preach – a statement that is glaringly untrue. In cases where persons are found duly qualified to assist the clergy, they are called on by the holy bishops to preach to the laity; e.g. in Laranda, Euelpius; in Iconium, Paulinus; in Synnada, Theodore were called on respectively by Neon, Celsus, and Atticus, our blessed brother-bishops. Probably there are other places too where this happens, unknown to us.

Such was the respect paid to Origen while still a young man, not only by his own countrymen but even by the bishops in another land. But when Demetrius sent first a letter recalling him, then deacons of the church to hasten his return to Alexandria, back he came and resumed his labours with all his old enthusiasm.

Works of the period: notable bishops

20. Prominent at that period were a number of learned churchmen, who penned to each other letters still surviving and easy of access, as they have been preserved to our own time in the library established at Aelia by the man who then presided over the church there, Alexander – the library from which I myself have been able to bring together the materials for the work now in hand. Of these writers Beryllus, Bishop of the Arabians at Bostra, in addition to letters left us compositions of the highest literary merit, as did Hippolytus – a prelate like Beryllus, though his see is unknown. I have also read a dialogue which Gaius, a man of the greatest learning, published at Rome in Zephyrinus' time as an answer to Proclus, the champion of the Phrygian heresy. In this, while reining in the audacity of his opponents in compiling new scriptures, he refers to only thirteen of the epistles of the holy Apostle, not including that to the Hebrews with the rest; for then as now there were some at Rome who did not think that it was the Apostle's.

21. When Antoninus had reigned seven years six months, he was succeeded by Macrinus. Macrinus having lasted only a year, the Roman Empire was next entrusted to another Antoninus.[1] In his first year, the Bishop of Rome, Zephyrinus, departed this life, after holding office eighteen years in all. After him Callistus took over the episcopate, but survived him by only five years, leaving his office to Urban. Alexander was the next to become sole ruler of the Roman Empire, Antoninus having lasted no more than four years. It was at this time that in the church of Antioch Asclepiades was succeeded by Philetus.

The emperor's mother Mamaea was one of the most religious and high-principled of women, and when the fame of Origen

1. Elagabalus.

spread so far that it came to her ears, she set her heart on securing an interview with him and testing his universally admired skill as a theologian. By good luck she was staying in Antioch, so she sent a bodyguard of soldiers to fetch him. He stayed with her for some time, revealing to her many things to the glory of the Lord and of the virtue of the divine message. Then he hurried back to his ordinary duties.

22. At that same period Hippolytus, author of many other short works, composed the essay *The Easter Festival*, in which he works out a system of dates and suggests a scheme for a sixteen-year cycle for Easter, relating his dates to the first year of Alexander's reign. Of his other essays I am acquainted with *The Six Days*, *The Sequel to the Six Days*, *Against Marcion*, *The Song*, *Parts of Ezekiel*, *The Easter Festival*, and *Against all the Heresies*. Many others are probably to be found in various private collections.

Origen's enthusiasm: his call to the presbyterate

23. It was at this period that Origen started work on his *Commentaries on Holy Scripture*, at the urgent request of Ambrose, who not only exerted verbal pressure and every kind of persuasion, but supplied him in abundance with everything needful. Shorthand-writers more than seven in number were available when he dictated, relieving each other regularly, and at least as many copyists, as well as girls trained in penmanship, all of them provided most generously with everything needful at Ambrose's expense. And not only that: in the devoted study of the divine teaching he brought to Origen his own immeasurable enthusiasm, the most powerful inducement to the composition of the *Commentaries*.

Meanwhile, after eight years as Bishop of the Roman Church, Urban was succeeded by Pontian, and at Antioch Philetus' place was filled by Zebennus. During their episcopate, the necessity of settling questions affecting the Church forced Origen to set out for Greece via Palestine. In Caesarea he was ordained presbyter by the Palestinian bishops. This made him the subject of an agitation on which the prelates of the churches passed judgement;

but like the impact which, having reached his prime, he made in other ways on the exposition of God's word, these matters deserve a book to themselves; so in the second volume of my *Defence of Origen* I have dealt with them at some length.

Commentaries written by him at Alexandria; references to the canonical Scriptures

24. To this I must add that in the sixth book of his *Commentary on John's Gospel* he mentions that he wrote the first five while still at Alexandria, but of his work on the whole of this same gospel only twenty-two books have come into my hands. And in the ninth book of his *Commentary on Genesis* – there are twelve altogether – he makes it clear that at Alexandria he wrote not only the first eight but also his *Commentary on Psalms i–xxv*, as well as the *Commentary on Lamentations*, of which I possess five books. In these he refers to his *Resurrection*, a work in two books. In addition he wrote his *On First Principles* before leaving Alexandria, and compiled the ten volumes entitled *Miscellanies* in the same city, while Alexander was on the throne, as is proved by the notes prefixed to them by the author himself.

25. In his commentary on Psalm i he wrote out a list of the Old Testament books, in the following terms:

It should be noted that the Canonical Books, according to Hebrew tradition, number twenty-two, like the letters of their alphabet . . . The twenty-two books of the Hebrew canon are these:

GENESIS, as we call it: the Hebrews (from the opening word) call it BRESITH (i.e. *in the beginning*)
EXODUS – OUELESMOTH (i.e. *these are the names*)
LEVITICUS – OUIKRA (*and he called*)
NUMBERS – AMMESPHEKODEIM
DEUTERONOMY – HELEADDEBARIM (*these are the words*)
JESUS SON OF NAVE – JOSHUA BEN NUN
JUDGES, RUTH – with the Hebrews, one book, SOPHETIM
KINGS I and 2 – with them a single book, SAMUEL (*the called of God*)

KINGS 3 and 4 – one book, OUAMMELCH DAVID (i.e. *the kingdom of David*)

THE OMITTED BOOKS 1 and 2 – one book, DABREIAMIN (i.e. *accounts of days*)

ESDRAS 1 and 2 – one book, EZRA (i.e. *helper*)

BOOK OF PSALMS – SPHARTHELLIM

PROVERBS OF SOLOMON – MELOTH

ECCLESIASTES – KOELTH

SONG OF SONGS (not, as sometimes thought, *Songs* of Songs) – SIR ASSIRIM

ESAIAS – IESSIA

JEREMIAS, *with* LAMENTATIONS and THE LETTER in one book – JEREMIAH

DANIEL – DANIEL

EZEKIEL – EZEKIEL

JOB – JOB

ESTHER – ESTHER

Excluded from the list is MACCABEES, entitled SARBETH SABANAIEL.

These statements he inserted in the treatise referred to above. In the first part of his *Commentary on Matthew*, when defending the canon of the Church, he testifies that he knows four gospels only. This is what he says:

I accept the traditional view of the four gospels which alone are undeniably authentic in the Church of God on earth. First to be written was that of the one-time exciseman who became an apostle of Jesus Christ – Matthew; it was published for believers of Jewish origin, and was composed in Aramaic. Next came that of Mark, who followed Peter's instructions in writing it, and who in Peter's general epistle was acknowledged as his son: 'Greetings to you from the church in Babylon, chosen like yourselves, and from my son Mark.'[1] Next came that of Luke, who wrote for Gentile converts the gospel praised by Paul. Last of all came John's.

In Book V of his *Commentary on John's Gospel* Origen has this to say about the epistles of the apostles:

1. 1 Peter i. 13.

The man who was enabled to become a minister of the New Covenant, not of the letter but of the spirit, Paul, proclaimed the gospel from Jerusalem, in a wide sweep as far as Illyricum.[1] But he did not write to all the churches he had taught; and to those to which he did write he sent only a few lines. Peter, on whom is built Christ's Church, over which the gates of Hades shall have no power,[2] left us one acknowledged epistle, possibly two – though this is doubtful. Need I say anything about the man who leant back on Jesus' breast, John? He left a single gospel, though he confessed that he could write so many that the whole world would not hold them.[3] He also wrote the Revelation, but was ordered to remain silent and not write the utterances of the seven thunders.[4] In addition, he left an epistle of a very few lines, and possibly two more, though their authenticity is denied by some. Anyway, they do not total a hundred lines between them.

Again, in his *Homilies on the Epistle to the Hebrews* he makes this comment:

In the epistle entitled *To the Hebrews* the diction does not exhibit the characteristic roughness of speech or phraseology admitted by the Apostle himself,[5] the construction of the sentences is closer to Greek usage, as anyone capable of recognizing differences of style would agree. On the other hand the matter of the epistle is wonderful, and quite equal to the Apostle's acknowledged writings: the truth of this would be admitted by anyone who has read the Apostle carefully ... If I were asked my personal opinion, I would say that the matter is the Apostle's but the phraseology and construction are those of someone who remembered the Apostle's teaching and wrote his own interpretation of what his master had said. So if any church regards this epistle as Paul's, it should be commended for so doing, for the primitive Church had every justification for handing it down as his. Who wrote the epistle is known to God alone: the accounts that have reached us suggest that it was either Clement, who became Bishop of Rome, or Luke, who wrote the gospel and the Acts.

Heraclas Bishop of Alexandria: what the bishops thought of Origen

26. It was in the tenth year of Alexander's reign that Origen made the move from Alexandria to Caesarea, leaving to Heraclas the

1. Rom. xv. 19.   2. Matt. xvi. 18.   3. John xxi. 25.   4. Rev. x 3–4.
5. 2 Cor. xi. 6.

school of elementary instruction for those in the city. Not long afterwards Demetrius, Bishop of the Alexandrian church, died, having completed forty-three years in that office; he was succeeded by Heraclas.

27. At this time Firmilian, Bishop of Caesarea in Cappadocia, paid a remarkable tribute to Origen, showing such admiration for him that at one time he would invite him to his own region to assist his churches, at another he would go all the way to Judaea to see him and spend some time with him, in order to deepen his own spiritual life. In the same way the head of the Jerusalem church, Alexander, and Theoctistus of Caesarea listened attentively to him at all times as their only teacher, leaving to him the interpretation of Holy Writ and all other branches of religious instruction.

Persecution under Maximin

28. When after reigning thirteen years the Roman emperor Alexander died, Maximin Caesar succeeded him. Through rancour against Alexander's house, which consisted mainly of believers, he instigated a persecution and ordered the leaders of the churches alone, as being responsible for the teaching of the gospel, to be destroyed. It was then that Origen composed his *Martyrdom*, dedicating his treatise to Ambrose and Protoctetus, a presbyter of the Caesarean diocese, both of whom had had a terrible time in the persecution, a time in which it is on record that they were fearless in the confession of their faith throughout Maximin's reign of three years only. This time for the duration of the persecution was noted by Origen in Section xxii of his *Commentary on John's Gospel*, and in various letters.

Fabian miraculously designated by God as Bishop of Rome

29. Gordian having succeeded Maximin as Roman emperor, Pontian, after six years as Bishop of the Roman church, was succeeded by Anteros, and he, after filling the office for a month, by Fabian. It is said that after Anteros's death Fabian came with a party from

the country and paid a visit to Rome, where by a miracle of divine and heavenly grace he was chosen to fill the place. When the brethren had all assembled with the intention of electing a successor to the bishopric, and a large number of eminent and distinguished men were in the thoughts of most, Fabian, who was present, came into no one's mind. But suddenly out of the blue a dove fluttered down and perched on his head (the story goes on), plainly following the example of the descent upon the Saviour of the Holy Spirit in the form of a dove. At this, as if moved by one divine inspiration, with the utmost enthusiasm and complete un-animity the whole meeting shouted that he was the man, and then and there seized him and set him on the bishop's throne.

At about the same time, Zebennus, Bishop of Antioch, departed this life, and Babylas succeeded to his position; while at Alexandria – where, following Demetrius, Heraclas had been appointed to the office – the school of elementary instruction was taken over by Dionysius, another of Origen's old pupils.

Men who became Origen's pupils

30. While Origen was performing his normal tasks at Caesarea, his services were in constant demand not only by the local people but also by innumerable foreign students who had left their own countries. The most distinguished names known to me are those of Theodore – who was none other than that illustrious bishop of my own day, Gregory – and his brother Athenodore. They were passionately devoted to Greek and Roman studies, but he im-planted in them a love of true philosophy and induced them to exchange their old enthusiasm for a theological training. Five whole years they spent with him, making such remarkable progress in theology that while still young both were chosen to be bishops of the churches in Pontus.

Africanus

31. At this time, Africanus – author of the work entitled *Cesti* – was another eminent writer. A letter which he wrote to Origen has

survived. In it he cast the gravest doubt on the authenticity of
the story of Susanna in Daniel. Origen wrote a very full reply.
From the same author there has also come into my hands a
five-volume *Dictionary of Dates*, compiled with unsparing devotion to accuracy. In it he says that he made a special journey to
Alexandria, in view of the great reputation of Heraclas, who –
as already stated – after showing himself an outstanding ex-
ponent of philosophy and other secular studies, had been elevated
to the bishopric of the church there. Another of his letters has
survived: it is addressed to Aristides, and deals with the alleged
discrepancy between Matthew and Luke on the subject of Christ's
genealogy. In it he demonstrates the harmony of the evangelists
most convincingly, from an account which has come down to
him and which I have found it convenient to reproduce earlier, in
Book 1 of the present work.

Commentaries written by Origen at Caesarea

32. Origen himself was busy at that time putting together his
Commentary on Isaiah, and at the same time that on *Ezekiel*. On the
third section of Isaiah, as far as the vision of the beasts in the
desert,[1] thirty books have come into my hands, and on Ezekiel
twenty-five, covering the entire book. It was during a visit to
Athens at that stage that he completed the *Commentary on Ezekiel*
and began that on the *Song of Songs*, getting as far as Book v
before leaving Athens and returning to Caesarea, where he wrote
the remaining five books. But this is not the time to give a
detailed list of all his works, which would be a task in itself. I have
already included one in my *Life of Pamphilus*, the holy martyr of
my own day, in which, to show the intensity of his devotion to
theology, I mentioned the list of books in the library he had
built up of the works of Origen and the other Church writers.
From these anyone who wishes can learn all about the extant
works of Origen. But now I must go on to the next stage in the
story.

1. Is. xxx. 6.

The deviation of Beryllus

33. Beryllus, who was mentioned some pages back as Bishop of Bostra in Arabia, perverted the true doctrine of the Church and tried to bring in ideas alien to the Faith, actually asserting that our Saviour and Lord did not pre-exist in His own form of being before He made His home among men, and had no divinity of His own but only the Father's dwelling in Him. Accordingly, a large number of bishops questioned and argued with him; then Origen was sent for, with several others. He began by getting into conversation with him, to find out what his ideas were. Then, having acquainted himself with his assertions, he straightened out his unorthodox ideas, and argued so convincingly that he set him on the right doctrinal path and brought him back to his former sound opinion. We still possess accounts of Beryllus and the synod that he made necessary; these, in addition to the questions put to him by Origen and the discussions held in his own see, record everything done at that time.

A great many other traditions about Origen have been passed on orally by the older men of our day, but I think I will omit them, as irrelevant to the present work. All that it is important to know about him can be gathered from the *Defence of Origen* written by myself and that holy martyr of our time, Pamphilus – a joint effort, a labour of love undertaken as an answer to carping critics.

The reign of Philip: Heraclas succeeded by Dionysius

34. After six years as Roman emperor Gordian died, and Philip along with a son of the same name succeeded him. He, there is reason to believe, was a Christian, and on the day of the last Easter vigil he wished to share in the prayers of the Church along with the people; but the prelate of the time would not let him come in until he made open confession and attached himself to those who were held to be in a state of sin and were occupying the place for penitents. Otherwise, if he had not done so, he would never have been received by him in view of the many accusations brought

against him. It is said that he obeyed gladly, showing by his actions the genuine piety of his attitude towards the fear of God

35. It was in Philip's third year that Heraclas departed this life, after presiding for sixteen years over the Alexandrian province, and Dionysius took office as bishop.

Other works written by Origen

36. At this period of rapid expansion of the Faith, when our message was being boldly proclaimed on every side, it was natural that Origen, now over sixty and with his abilities fully developed by years of practice, should, as we are told, have allowed his lectures to be taken down by shorthand-writers, though he had never before agreed to this. During the same period, he wrote his eight books to refute the attack made on us by Celsus the Epicurean in his *True Doctrine*; also the twenty-five books of his *Commentary on Matthew's Gospel*, and his *Commentary on the Minor Prophets*, of which I have laid my hand on twenty-five books only. We possess also a letter of his to the Emperor Philip himself, another to his consort Severa, and others to various other persons. These have been preserved here and there by various persons: all that I have succeeded in collecting I have stored methodically in separate bundles, to prevent them from being dispersed again. He also wrote to Bishop Fabian of Rome and to the heads of many other churches about his orthodoxy. You will find all this set out in Book VI of my *Defence of Origen*.

Unorthodox beliefs in Arabia: the Helkesaite heresy

37. While he was thus engaged, a new group appeared on the Arabian scene, originators of a doctrine far removed from the truth, namely, that at the end of our life here the human soul dies for a time along with our bodies and perishes with them; later, when one day the resurrection comes, it will return with them to life. At this crisis, a synod was convoked on a large scale, and Origen was again invited. On arrival he opened a public debate on

the question at issue, and argued so forcibly that he compelled those who had previously gone astray to change their views.

38. At the same time another distorted idea was started by the 'Helkesaite' sect, but it was no sooner started than it was extinguished. It is referred to in a published sermon by Origen on Psalm lxxxii:

A man has recently come forward who prides himself on his ability to uphold a blasphemous and most impious theory — known as that of the Helkesaites — which has lately reared its head against the churches. The pernicious suggestions of that theory I will make clear to you, for fear you may be carried away by it. It rejects parts of every book of the Bible, though it makes use of passages from every Old Testament book and every gospel: the Apostle it rejects altogether. It says that to deny the truth does not matter, and that in case of need the sensible man will deny it with his lips but not in his heart. They produce a book, alleging that it fell from heaven: anyone who hears it read and believes will receive forgiveness for his sins — forgiveness other than that which Jesus Christ won for us.

What happened under Decius

39. Philip, after a reign of seven years, was succeeded by Decius. Through hatred of Philip he started a persecution against the churches, in which Fabian found fulfilment in martyrdom at Rome, where Cornelius succeeded him as bishop.

In Palestine, Alexander, Bishop of the Jerusalem church, was again brought before the governor's court at Caesarea, and as for the second time he boldly confessed the Faith, he endured imprisonment, though crowned with ripe old age and venerable white hairs. After bearing splendid and glorious witness in the governor's court, he fell asleep in his prison, and Mazabanes was named as successor to the Jerusalem bishopric. Alexander's fate was not unique, for at Antioch Babylas confessed the Faith and departed this life in prison, Fabius being made head of the church there.

As for Origen, the terrible sufferings that befell him in the persecution, and how they ended, when the evil demon, bent on his destruction, brought all the weapons in his armoury to bear

and fought him with every device and expedient, attacking him
with more determination than anyone he was fighting at that time
– the dreadful cruelties he endured for the word of Christ, chains
and bodily torments, agony in iron and the darkness of his prison;
how for days on end his legs were pulled four paces apart in the
torturer's stocks – the courage with which he bore threats of fire
and every torture devised by his enemies – the way his maltreat-
ment ended, when the judge had striven with might and main at
all costs to avoid sentencing him to execution – the messages he
left us after all this, messages full of help for those in need of
comfort – of all these things a truthful and detailed account will be
found in his own lengthy correspondence.

What happened to Dionysius

40. What happened to Dionysius I will make clear by quoting his
letter directed against Germanus, in which he gives this account of
himself:

> I speak as in the presence of God, who knows whether I am lying. I did
> *not* act on my own judgement or without God when I made my escape;
> but even before that, when Decius announced his persecution, Sabinus
> then and there dispatched a *frumentarius* to hunt me out, and I stayed at
> home four days waiting for him to arrive. But though he went round
> searching every spot – roads, rivers, fields – where he guessed I was
> hiding or walking, he was smitten with blindness and did not find the
> house; he never imagined that when an object of persecution I should stay
> at home! It was only after four days, when God commanded me to go
> elsewhere, and by a miracle made it possible, that I set out along with the
> boys and many of the brethren. That this was indeed the work of divine
> providence was proved by what followed, when perhaps we were of use
> to some.

After dealing with various other matters, he describes what
happened to him after the flight:

> About sunset, my companions and I were caught by the soldiers and
> taken to Taposiris; but by the purpose of God it happened that Timothy

was absent and was not caught. When he arrived later, he found the house empty except for a guard of servants, and learnt that we had been captured without hope of release ... And how was God's wonderful mercy shown? You shall hear the truth. As Timothy fled distracted, he was met by one of the villagers on his way to attend a wedding-feast – which in those parts meant an all-night celebration – who asked why he was in such a hurry. He told the truth without hesitation, whereupon the other went in and informed the guests as they reclined at table. With one accord, as if at a signal, they all sprang to their feet, came as fast as their legs would carry them, and burst in where we were with such terrifying shouts that the soldiers guarding us instantly took to their heels. Then they stood over us, as we lay on bare mattresses. At first, God knows, I thought they were bandits who had come to plunder and steal, so I stayed on the bed. I had nothing on but a linen shirt; my other clothes that were lying near I held out to them. But they told me to get up and make a bolt for it. Then I realized what they had come for, and called out, begging and beseeching them to go away and let us be. If they wanted to do me a good turn, they had better forestall my captors and cut off my head themselves. While I shouted like this, they pulled me up by force, as the companions who shared all my adventures know. I let myself fall on my back on the floor, but they grasped me by hands and feet and dragged me out, followed by those who witnessed the whole scene, Gaius, Faustus, Peter, and Paul, who picked me up and carried me out of the village, set me on a donkey bareback, and led me away.

This is the account Dionysius gives us of his adventure.

Martyrs who suffered at Alexandria and elsewhere

41. In his letter to Bishop Fabius of Antioch, he gives this account of the ordeals of those who were martyred at Alexandria under Decius:

It was not the imperial edict that set the persecution in motion against us: it had already been going on for a whole year, and the nameless prophet and worker of mischief for this city was the first to stir up and incite the heathen masses against us, fanning the flames of their local superstition and working them up, till they seized on every available authority for their unholy deeds and convinced themselves that the only true religion was this demon-worship – thirst for our blood.

First they seized an old man named Metras, and ordered him to utter blasphemous words; when he refused, they beat him with cudgels, drove pointed reeds into his face and eyes, took him to the suburbs, and stoned him to death. Next they took a female convert named Quinta to the idol's temple and tried to make her worship. When she turned her back in disgust they tied her feet and dragged her right through the city over the rough paved road, bumping her on the great stones and beating her as they went, till they arrived at the same place, where they stoned her to death. Then they all ran in a body to the houses of the Christians, charged in by groups on those they know as neighbours, raided, plundered, and looted. The more valuable of their possessions they purloined; the cheaper wooden things they threw about, or they made a bonfire of them in the streets, making the city look as if it had been captured by enemies. The Christians retired and gradually withdrew; like those to whom Paul paid tribute, they took with cheerfulness the plundering of their belongings.[1] I do not know of anyone, except possibly one man who fell into their clutches, who up to now has denied the Lord.

Next they seized the wonderful old lady Apollonia, battered her till they knocked out all her teeth, built a pyre in front of the city, and threatened to burn her alive unless she repeated after them their heathen incantations. She asked for a breathing-space, and when they released her, jumped without hesitation into the fire and was burnt to ashes.

Serapion they arrested in his own house. They racked him with horrible tortures and broke all his limbs, then threw him down head first from the upper floor.

No road, no highway, no alley was open to us, either by night or by day; always and everywhere, everybody was shouting that anyone who did not join in their blasphemous chants must at once be dragged away and burnt. For a long time the terror remained intense, but the wretched men were suddenly plunged into faction and civil war, which turned the savagery of which we had been the victims against its authors. For a little while we breathed again, as they were too busy to vent their rage on us, but very soon the change from the reign that had been kinder to us became generally known, and the threat to our safety filled us with horrible foreboding. And the edict indeed arrived, almost exactly as foretold by our Lord in His truly terrifying words: 'So as, if possible, to trip up even the elect.'[2] Anyway, terror was universal, and of many public figures some at once came forward through fear, others who were in state employment were induced by professional reasons, others were

1. Heb. x. 34.   2. A slight misquotation of Matt. xxiv. 24.

dragged forward by the mob. Summoned by name, they approached the unclean, unholy sacrifices. Some came white-faced and trembling, as if they were not going to sacrifice but to be sacrificed themselves as victims to the idols, so that the large crowd of spectators heaped scorn upon them and it was obvious that they were utter cowards, afraid to die and afraid to sacrifice. Others ran more readily towards the altars, trying to prove by their fearlessness that they had never been Christians. Of these, the Lord had declared long before with complete truth that they would be saved with difficulty.[1] Of the rest, some followed each of these groups, others tried to get away; some were caught, and of these some allowed themselves to be chained and imprisoned (in some cases remaining confined for weeks), and then, even before coming into court, renounced their faith, while others held out for a time under torture but in the end gave up.

But the unbending, blessed pillars of the Lord, strengthened by Him and receiving power and endurance deservedly and in proportion to the vigorous faith that was in them, proved wonderful martyr witnesses of His kingdom. Of these the first was Julian, a sufferer from gout, unable to stand or walk, who was brought to trial with two others to bear him. One of the two at once denied his Master; the other, Cronion by name but nicknamed Goodfellow, and the aged Julian himself, confessed the Lord and were taken right through the city, which as you all know is immense, mounted on camels and whipped while perched aloft. Finally, while the whole population milled around, they were burnt up with quicklime. A soldier who was standing by as they were led away protested at the insults, and roused the mob to fury: he was brought to trial, Besas the gallant warrior of God, and having fought like a hero in the great war for the Faith, was beheaded. Another man, of Libyan stock, true both to his name Macar[2] and to the Beatitude, in spite of all the efforts of the judge to make him deny the Faith, stood firm and was burnt alive. After these came Epimachus and Alexander, who after remaining in prison a long time endured numberless agonies from scrapers and whips, and like the others were destroyed with quicklime.

With them were four women. Ammonarion, a most respectable young woman, in spite of the savage and prolonged torture inflicted on her by the judge because she had already made it clear beforehand that she would never say any of the things he ordered her to say, kept true to her promise and was led away. The others were Mercuria, a very dignified old lady,

1. An allusion to Matt. xix. 23.
2. A variant form of the first word of each Beatitude.

and Dionysia, the mother of a large family but just as devoted to her Lord. The governor was ashamed to go on torturing without results and to be defeated by women, so they died by the sword without being put to any further test by torture: this Ammonarion, foremost in the fight, had taken on herself for them all.

Three Egyptians, Hero, Ater, and Isidore, together with a boy of about fifteen called Dioscorus, were informed against. The judge began with the lad, trying to trick his unformed character with words, and to break down his feeble resistance by torture, but Dioscorus would neither obey nor give in. The others he tore in pieces with the utmost savagery, and when they held out they too were consigned to the flames. But Dioscorus behaved so splendidly in public, and gave such wise answers when questioned in private, that he astonished the judge, who let him go, saying that in view of his youth he would allow him time to come to his senses. And the saintly Dioscorus is with us still, having survived for a more prolonged ordeal and a more lasting conflict.

Nemesion, another Egyptian, was falsely reported to be in league with bandits. No sooner had he cleared himself before the centurion of such an absurd accusation than he was denounced as a Christian, and brought in chains before the governor. He, with gross injustice, subjected him to twice the tortures and floggings inflicted on the bandits, and burnt him between them, honouring him – blest indeed! – with a resemblance to Christ.

A whole squad of soldiers, Ammon, Zeus, Ptolemy, and Ingenuus, with an old man, Theophilus, were standing in court. When a man accused of being a Christian was on the point of denying Christ, they ground their teeth as they stood by, grimaced, stretched out their hands, and gestured with their bodies. All eyes were turned towards them, but before anyone could stop them they made a dash for the dock, saying that they were Christians. The governor and his fellow-judges were filled with alarm; in contrast to the panic on the bench, the accused all showed a complete disregard of the sufferings to come; they marched out of the court in triumph, proud of their witness, their fame gloriously spread abroad by God. 42. Many others in cities and villages were torn to pieces by the heathen. One example will suffice. Ischyrion was the salaried agent of one of the magistrates. His employer ordered him to sacrifice. When he refused, he insulted him; and when he persisted, he heaped abuse on him. Having failed to shift him, he took a stout stick, drove it through his bowels and internal organs, and so killed him.

Need I speak of the vast number who wandered over deserts and mountains¹ till hunger, thirst, cold, sickness, bandits, or wild beasts destroyed them? The survivors pay tribute to those chosen to be victors, but one incident I must bring to your notice as showing what kind of men they were. Chaeremon, the very aged Bishop of Nilopolis, fled with his wife to the mountain region of Arabia. He never came back, and despite a thorough search, the brethren failed to find either them or their remains. In that same mountain region very many were enslaved by the half-civilized Saracens. Some of them with difficulty and at great cost were ransomed; others never to this day.

This long account, brother, I have given in no idle spirit, but in order that you may know the extent of the terror to which we have been subjected. Those more deeply involved could tell you more about it . . .

Thus even the divine martyrs among us, who now sit by Christ's side as partners in His kingdom, share His authority, and are His fellow-judges, opened their arms to their fallen brethren who faced the charge of sacrificing. Seeing their conversion and repentance, they were sure that it would be acceptable to Him who does not in the least desire the death of a sinner, but rather his repentance; so they received them, admitted them to the congregation as 'bystanders', and allowed them to take part in services and feasts. What then, brothers, is your advice to us in this matter? What must we do? Shall we take our stand in full agreement with them, uphold their merciful decision, and deal gently with those they pitied? Or shall we condemn their decision as improper, and set ourselves up as judges of their attitude, wound their gentleness, and turn their practice upside down?

Novatus, his character and his heresy

43. Dionysius had good reason to argue thus, bringing up the question of those who had shown weakness at the time of the persecution, for Novatus, a presbyter of the Roman church, regarded them with lofty contempt: there was no hope of salvation for them now, even if they did everything in their power to prove their conversion sincere and their confession wholehearted. So he set himself up as leader of a new sect, whose members in the pride of their hearts entitled themselves the 'Pure'. To deal with the situation a synod on the largest scale was convened at Rome, and

1. A reminiscence of Hebrews xi. 38.

was attended by sixty bishops and a still greater number of presbyters and deacons, while in the other provinces of the Empire the local pastors considered separately what was to be done. The result was a unanimous decree that Novatus, his companions in presumption, and any who thought fit to approve his attitude of hatred and inhumanity to brother-Christians, should be regarded as outside the Church, but that those brothers who had had the misfortune to fall should be treated and cured with the medicine of repentance.

I have had access to a letter from Bishop Cornelius of Rome to Bishop Fabius of Antioch, giving an account of the Synod of Rome and the decisions reached by the representatives of Italy, Africa, and the neighbouring regions; and another, written in Latin, from Cyprian and his companions in Africa, making it clear that they too agreed that those who had been tempted should be helped, and that it was right and fair to expel from the Catholic Church the leader of the sect and to deal in the same way with all who had erred with him. Attached to these was a second letter from Cornelius, about the resolutions of the synod, and yet a third, about the conduct of Novatus; from this I will quote certain passages to enable readers of this book to know the facts about him. Enlightening Fabius as to the character of Novatus, Cornelius writes thus:

It is essential that you should know that years ago this fine fellow set his heart on becoming a bishop, and kept this consuming ambition of his bottled up inside, cloaking his crazy notion with the support that from the start the Confessors had given him. Maximus, one of our own presbyters, and Urban, who by confessing their faith had twice won the highest renown; Sidonius; and Celerinus, a man who by the mercy of God had endured torture of every kind with unshakeable determination, fortifying the weakness of the flesh by the strength of his faith, and had crushingly defeated the adversary – these four men observed him, and detecting his unscrupulousness and shiftiness, his perjuries and prevarications, his self-centredness and hollow pretence of friendship, returned to Holy Church. All the artifices and dirty tricks that he had long kept out of sight they revealed publicly in the presence of several bishops and presbyters and a crowd of laymen, weeping penitently for their folly in listening to this treacherous, malignant beast and for a time deserting the Church . . .

It is remarkable, dear brother, what a complete transformation we saw in him a little while later. This admirable person, who swore terrible oaths to convince us that to be a bishop was the last thing he desired, suddenly appears as a bishop as if he had been catapulted into our midst. For this doctrinal purist, this champion of the Church's teaching, in his attempt to grab and filch the bishopric not given to him from above, chose as his accessories two men who had renounced their own salvation, and sent them to an obscure corner of Italy to deceive three bishops of the region, uneducated and simple-minded men, and trick them into coming. He declared emphatically that their presence in Rome was urgently necessary, on the ground that the difference of opinion that had occurred might be completely resolved by their mediation, with the help of other bishops. As already stated, they were too simple-minded to cope with the schemes of unscrupulous rogues, so on their arrival they were shut up by some men as disorderly as himself, and in the late afternoon, when they were hopelessly drunk, he forcibly compelled them to make him a bishop, by a counterfeit and invalid consecration, so acquiring by craft and rascality an office not his by right. Not long afterwards one of the three returned to the Church, frankly and tearfully confessing his fault. We admitted him as a layman, since all the laity present pleaded for him. As for the other two, we appointed successors and sent them to occupy the vacant positions.

Thus the vindicator of the gospel was unaware that there can be only one bishop in a Catholic church, in which, as he knew perfectly well, there are forty-six presbyters, seven deacons, seven sub-deacons, forty-two acolytes, fifty-two exorcists, readers, and doorkeepers, and more than fifteen hundred widows and distressed persons. All these are supported by the Master's grace and love for men. But this vast community, so necessary to the church, a number by the providence of God both rich and growing, together with laymen too numerous to count, did not suffice to turn him from such a hopeless, crazy ambition and recall him to the Church . . .

Well now, I had better say next what activities or policies emboldened him to claim the episcopate. Did he make this claim because from the start he had spent his life in the Church, had endured many ordeals on her behalf, and had often been in the greatest danger for the sake of his religion? Not at all. The occasion of his becoming a believer came from Satan, who entered into him and stayed with him for a considerable time. While the exorcists were trying to help him he fell desperately ill, and since he was thought to be on the point of death, there as he lay in bed he received baptism by affusion – if it can be called baptism in the case of such a man. And when he recovered he did not receive the other things of which one should partake according to the rule of the Church, in particular the sealing by a bishop. Without receiving these how could he receive the Holy Ghost? . . .

The man who through cowardice and love of life at the time of the persecution denied that he was a presbyter! The deacons begged and besought him to come out of the chamber in which he had shut himself, and to help his brothers, in danger and in need of assistance, in every way right and possible for a presbyter; but so far was he from answering the deacons' appeal that he actually went right away in a rage, declaring that he did not want to be a presbyter any longer: he was in love with a different way of thought . . .

This fine fellow left the Church of God, in which after becoming a believer he was accepted for the presbyterate, by favour of the bishop who ordained him to presbyter's orders. The whole clerical body, and many laymen too, objected that the rules did not permit anyone baptized in bed by affusion owing to illness, as in the present case, to receive any orders, so the bishop asked leave to lay hands on this man only.

Now we come to something else, the vilest of the man's misdemeanours:

When he has made the offerings and is distributing to each his share and handing it over, he compels the unfortunate worshippers to take an oath instead of praising God. He takes the hands of those who have received in both his own, and does not let go until they take this oath – I quote his own words: 'Swear to me by the Blood and Body of the Lord Jesus Christ never to desert me and turn to Cornelius.' And the wretched man does not taste unless he first calls down a curse on his own head, and instead of saying Amen as he receives that Bread, he says: 'I will not go back to Cornelius.' . . .

You will be glad to learn that now he has been stripped of support and left by himself, as every day Christian people are deserting him and coming back into the Church. And when Moses, the blessed martyr who so recently bore noble and wonderful witness while yet in the world, saw his crazy impudence, he broke off all contact with him, and with the five presbyters who like him had cut themselves off from the Church

At the end of the letter he has listed the bishops who met at Rome and condemned the fatuity of Novatus, indicating both their names and their respective sees. Those who were absent from the Rome meeting but assented in writing to the decision of those already mentioned are also named, along with the cities from which they severally wrote. All this information was included in the letter from Cornelius to Bishop Fabius of Antioch.

Dionysius' story about Serapion

44. Fabius, who inclined a little towards the schism, received another communication – this time from Dionysius of Alexandria, who in his letter to him wrote a great deal about repentance, and described with particular care the ordeals of those recently martyred in Alexandria. In the course of his story he describes a quite amazing incident, which I must on no account omit:

I will tell you of one instance that occurred here. Among our number was an old believer named Serapion, whose conduct for most of his life had been beyond reproach, but who had lapsed when trial came. Again and again he pleaded, but no one listened – he had sacrificed. He fell sick, and for three days on end remained speechless and unconscious, but on the fourth day he was a little better, and called his grandson to his bedside. 'How long, child,' he asked, 'are you all determined to keep me alive? Do please hurry, and let me go quickly! You go yourself, and bring me one of the presbyters.' After saying this, he became speechless again. The boy ran to fetch the presbyter. But it was night time, and he was unwell and unable to come. I had, however, given instructions that those departing this life, if they desired it, and especially if they happened to have pleaded before, should be absolved, so that they could depart in sure hope; so he gave a portion of the Eucharist to the little boy, telling him to soak it and let it fall drop by drop into the old man's mouth. The boy returned with it to the house, but before he could enter, Serapion rallied again and said: 'Is that you, child? The presbyter could not come, but you must do as he told you, and let me depart.' The boy soaked it, and poured it into the mouth of the old man, who after swallowing a little immediately died. Was he not plainly preserved and kept alive until he was released and, his sin blotted out, could be honoured for his many good deeds?

Letters of Dionysius to Novatus and others

45. Now let us see the sort of letter the same Dionysius indited to Novatus at the time when he was upsetting the Roman brotherhood. When Novatus blamed his apostasy and schism on some of his fellow-Christians on the ground that they had coerced him into behaving thus, this is how Dionysius writes to him:

My dear Novatian,

If, as you say, you were led on unwillingly, you can prove it by retracing your steps willingly. You ought to have been ready to suffer anything whatever rather than split the Church of God, and martyrdom to avoid schism would have brought you as much honour as martyrdom to escape idolatry – I should say, more. For in the latter case a man is martyred to save his own single soul, in the former to save the whole Church. Even now if you were to persuade or coerce your fellow-Christians into unanimity, your fall would count for less than your recovery – the first will be forgotten, the second applauded. If they will not listen, and there is nothing you can do, by all means save your own soul.

Hold fast to peace in the Lord, and may every blessing be yours.

46. To the Egyptians he wrote a letter on repentance, in which he explained his views on those who had fallen into sin, distinguishing degrees of guilt. To Bishop Colon of Hermopolis he sent a personal letter, still extant, on repentance; another, calling for a change of heart, to his own flock at Alexandria. The surviving letters include the one to Origen on martyrdom. To the Christians of Laodicea under their bishop Thelymidres, and to those of Armenia, whose bishop was Meruzanes, he wrote further letters on repentance. In addition to all these, he wrote to Cornelius of Rome, after receiving his letter against Novatus. In this answer he made it plain that he had been invited by Bishop Helenus of Tarsus in Cilicia, and the others with him – Firmilian in Cappadocia and Theoctistus in Palestine – to attend the Antioch Synod, at which an attempt was being made to strengthen the schism of Novatus. He further stated that he had been informed that Fabius had fallen asleep, and that Demetrian had been chosen to succeed him as Bishop of Antioch. He also referred to the Bishop of Jerusalem, in the following terms:

That wonderful man Alexander was put in prison, and is now at rest with the blessed.

Next to this there is another extant letter, a helpful letter from Dionysius to the Romans, carried there by Hippolytus. To the same church he addressed a second on peace, and a third on repentance. He also sent one to the confessors there while they still adhered to the views of Novatus. This was followed by two more after their return to the Church. He communicated similarly by letter with many others, leaving a rich reward to those who still study his writing with attention.

Book 7

GALLUS TO GALLIENUS: THE WORK OF CYPRIAN
AND DIONYSIUS: THE HERESIES OF SABELLIUS,
NOVATUS, NEPOS, PAUL, AND THE MANICHEES

In writing Book 7 of my *History of the Church* I shall again enjoy
the cooperation of the great Bishop of Alexandria, Dionysius,
who in the letters that he left behind furnished an account in his
own words of the whole course of events in his time. From that
starting-point I will begin my narrative.

The criminal folly of Decius and Gallus

1. Decius had reigned rather less than two years, when he was
murdered, together with his sons, and was succeeded by Gallus. It
was at this time that Origen, now in his seventieth year, died.
Writing to Hermammon Dionysius has this to say about Gallus:

Nor did Gallus realize Decius' mistake or guard against what caused his
fall, but tripped over the same stone with his eyes open. When his reign
was proceeding smoothly and things were going to his liking, he drove
away the holy men who were praying God to grant him peace and
health. In banishing them, he banished their supplications on his behalf.

Bishops of Rome: the questions of baptism for penitent heretics:
Sabellianism

2. In the city of Rome the episcopate of Cornelius lasted about
three years. Lucius was chosen to succeed him, but after serving in
this ministry for less than eight months, he died, passing on his
office to Stephen. To him Dionysius addressed the first of his
letters on baptism, for a lively controversy had arisen at that time

as to whether those who abandoned a heresy of any kind ought to be cleansed by baptism. There was undoubtedly an old-established custom that in such cases all that was necessary was prayer combined with the laying on of hands [3] and Cyprian, pastor of the see of Carthage, was the first man of his time to maintain that only when cleansed by baptism ought they to be readmitted. But Stephen thought it wrong to introduce any innovation in defiance of the tradition established from the beginning, and protested vigorously.   4. So Dionysius communicated with him about this question in a very long letter, at the close of which he pointed out that now that the persecution had abated, the churches everywhere had turned their backs on the innovation of Novatus and resumed peace among themselves:

5. Now let me assure you, brother, that all the previously divided churches in the East and still farther away have been united, and all their prelates everywhere are at one, overjoyed at the unexpected return of peace – Demetrian at Antioch, Theoctistus at Caesarea, Mazabanes at Aelia, Marinus at Tyre (since Alexander fell asleep). Heliodorus at Laodicea (since Thelymidres went to his rest), Helenus at Tarsus with all the Cilician churches, Firmilian with all Cappadocia. I have named the more distinguished bishops only, for fear of making my letter too long and its contents wearisome. However, the whole of Syria and Arabia, which you assist at every opportunity and have now communicated with; Mesopotamia; Pontus; and Bithynia – in a word, everyone everywhere is delighted at the new spirit of harmony and brotherly love, and thankful to God.

When Stephen had fulfilled his ministry for two years, he was succeeded by Xystus. To him Dionysius indited a second letter on baptism, making clear the views held and expressed by Stephen and the other bishops, and speaking of Stephen as follows:

He had written previously with reference to Helenus, Firmilian, and all who came from Cilicia, Cappadocia, and of course Galatia and all the neighbouring countries, saying that he would have nothing to do with them, for this reason – they rebaptized heretics. Try to realize the seriousness of the situation. For it is a fact that resolutions about this question have been passed in the largest synods of bishops, if my information is correct, to the effect that those who come over from heresies are first instructed, then washed and cleansed afresh from the filth of the old unclean leaven. So I wrote appealing to him on all these questions . . . I also wrote two letters – the first brief, the second longer – to my dear fellow-presbyters Dionysius and Philemon, who at one time shared Stephen's view and wrote to me about this question.

6. In the same letter he mentions the Sabellian heretics, making it clear that they were numerous in his time:

The doctrine now being propagated at Ptolemais in Pentapolis is an impious one, characterized by shocking blasphemy against Almighty God, Father of our Lord Jesus Christ; utter disbelief in His only-begotten Son, the Firstborn of all creation, the Word made man; and indifference to the Holy Ghost. From both sides there came to me first manifestos, then adherents prepared to argue the question; so I wrote letters as well as I could, with God's help, dealing with the question in a rather professorial manner, I enclose copies of them for you.

The heretics' disgusting error: the rule of the Church: the heterodoxy of Novatus

7. In Dionysius's third letter on baptism, written to Philemon the Roman presbyter, we find the following story:

I myself studied the writings and teachings of the heretics, polluting my soul for a time with their disgusting ideas, but gaining this benefit from them that I disproved them for myself, and greatly increased my loathing. A brother-presbyter, indeed, tried to deter and frighten me from floundering in the mire of their wickedness, since I should harm my own soul. He was right, as I realized. But a vision sent by God came to strengthen me, and I heard a commanding voice say these very words: 'Study anything you lay your hand on; you are competent to examine and test everything – this gift was from the start the reason for your faith.' I accepted the vision, as agreeing with the apostolic precept directed to the more able: 'Prove yourselves sound bankers.'

Then, commenting on all the heresies, he continues.

This is the rule and principle I took over from our blessed pope Heraclas. Those who came over from the heretical sects had seceded from the Church. ('Seceded' is not the right word – they were still regarded as members of the congregation when they were reported as regular pupils of some heterodox teacher.) So he expelled them from the Church, shutting his ears to all pleas until they publicly confessed all that they had heard from our militant opponents.[1] Then he readmitted them without requiring them to be baptized again, as they had previously received holy baptism at his hands.

After dealing with the question at great length, he goes on:

I have learnt this too, that the practice is not of recent origin in Africa; a long while back, in the time of my episcopal predecessors, it was adopted in the most populous dioceses and in Church synods, at Iconium, Synnada, and many other places. I would not think of upsetting their arrangements and involving them in strife and contention. 'You shall not move your neighbour's boundaries, which were fixed by your ancestors.'[2]

The fourth of his letters on baptism was written to Dionysius of Rome, who had recently been ordained presbyter and was shortly to be consecrated bishop of the diocese. From its pages we can learn of the tribute paid to the learning and high character of this man too by Dionysius of Alexandria. After dealing with other matters, he refers to the business of Novatus thus:

8. Naturally, I feel bitter against Novatian. He has split the Church and drawn some of our brothers into profanity and blasphemy; he has brought in the most unholy teaching about God; he impudently suggests that our most kind Lord Jesus Christ was devoid of pity; and as if all this was not enough, he makes light of holy baptism, does away with the faith and confession that precede it, and even when there was some hope that the Holy Spirit would remain or even return to them, he banishes Him completely.

The heretics' perversion of baptism

9. His fifth letter was written to the Bishop of Rome, Xystus. In it he brings many charges against the heretics, and relates the following incident from his experience:

1. 2 Tim. ii. 25.   2. Deut. xix. 14.

My dear brother,

I really do need your advice, and I want you to give me your opinion about a problem I am faced with, for fear I am acting mistakenly. In the congregation there is a man regarded for a long time as a faithful Christian, whose membership goes back beyond my election, and I think beyond the appointment of the blessed Heraclas. After attending a recent baptism, and listening to the questions and answers, he came to me weeping, lamenting, and falling at my feet; confessing and protesting that the baptism he had received from the heretics was not like ours and had nothing in common with it: it was full of profanity and blasphemy. Now he was cut to the heart, and did not even dare to raise his eyes to God, after starting with such unholy words and ceremonies. And so he was anxious to receive this unalloyed cleansing and acceptance and grace. I could not presume to do this; I told him that his prolonged communion with us made it unnecessary. He had listened to the Eucharistic prayers and joined in the Amen; he had stood by the table and held out his hands to receive the holy food; he had received it, partaking of the body and blood of our Lord for long enough: I could not presume to rebuild him from the foundations. So I urged him to put his fears away, and with strong faith and confident hope to come forward and partake of the holy things. But he goes on grieving, and is too frightened to approach the table, and in spite of my invitation he can scarcely bring himself to join the 'bystanders' at the services.

In addition to the letters already mentioned as extant, there is another of his on baptism addressed by him and his diocese to Xystus and the Roman church. In it he discusses the subject in question with elaborate arguments and at great length. Another extant letter of his, sent to Dionysius of Rome, deals with Lucian.

Valerian and the persecution in his time

10. When Gallus and his associates had held sway for less than two years they disappeared from the scene, and Valerian with his son Gallienus took over the government. What Dionysius has to say about Valerian may be gathered from his letter to Hermammon, in which we find the following account:

John received a similar revelation. 'He was given,' says the writer, 'a mouth uttering boasts and blasphemy; he was given authority and forty-two months.'[1]

---

1. Rev. xiii. 5, slightly misquoted.

Both phases of Valerian's rule are astonishing, the first being especially remarkable in character: he was so wonderfully friendly and gentle to the people of God. Not one of the emperors before him – not even those who were supposed to have been avowed Christians – was so kindly and sympathetic in his attitude to them as was Valerian at first, when he received them publicly with all friendship and affection and filled his whole palace with godfearing people, making it a church of God. But what a change when he was induced to get rid of them by the teacher and and guild-leader of the magicians from Egypt, who urged him to kill or persecute pure and saintly men as rivals who hindered his own foul, disgusting incantations! For they are and were able, by being present and seen, and simply by breathing on them and speaking boldly, to frustrate the schemes of the wicked demons. He also induced him to perform devilish rites, loathsome tricks, and unholy sacrifices, to cut the throats of unfortunate boys, use the children of unhappy parents as sacrificial victims, and tear out the vitals of newborn babies, cutting up and mincing God's handiwork, as if these things would bring them happiness . . .

They[1] must have been delighted with the thank-offering Macrian brought them for his hoped-for empire. At first he held office as account-ant to the whole[2] imperial exchequer, but left Catholic principles wholly out of account. Now he has fallen under the prophetic curse: 'Woe to those who prophesy from the heart and do not see the whole.[3] For he had no idea of the catholicity of providence, and no suspicion of the judgement of One who is before all and through all and over all.[4] So he has made himself the enemy of His Catholic Church, and alienated and estranged himself from the mercy of God, and banished himself as far as he could from his own salvation, proving thus how well his name fits him![5] . . . Led by him into such courses, Valerian was subjected to insults and abuse, as was said to Isaiah: 'These have chosen their own ways and their own abominations; their soul delighted in them. I will choose their delusions, and for their sins I will repay them.'[6]

Macrian, mad to become emperor though quite unqualified, and unable to fit the imperial robes on his crippled body, put forward his two sons, who inherited their father's sins. For the prophecy uttered by God was unmistakably true of them: 'Visiting the fathers' sins on the children

1. The demons.   2. Greek 'catholic'; one of a series of puns.X
3. Ez. xiii. 3 (LXX).   4. A conflation of Eph. iv. 6 and Col. i. 17.
5. Macrian somewhat resembles a Greek word for 'far off'.   6. Is. lxvi. 3–4.

down to the third or fourth generation of those who hate me.'[1] In heaping his own evil ambitions – which came to nothing – on the heads of his sons, he wiped off on them his own wickedness and hatred of God.

How Dionysius and others fared under Valerian

11. As regards the persecution that raged so fiercely in his time, what Dionysius and others underwent because of their devotion to the God of the universe is vividly portrayed in the lengthy account that he directed against Germanus, a bishop of his time who was trying to blacken his character:

I am in danger of falling head first into utter silliness and stupidity, as I am compelled to recount God's amazing kindness to me. But as we are told that it is good to keep the secret of a king but honourable to reveal the works of God,[2] I will meet Germanus's attack.

I came before Aemilian, not alone but followed by my fellow-presbyter Maximus and the deacons Faustus, Eusebius, and Chaeremon; and one of the Christians from Rome came in with us. Aemilian did not open the proceedings by saying to me: 'You are not to hold meetings.' That would have been a waste of breath – the last thing he would say, when he was going back to the beginning. He did not talk about not holding meetings, but about not being Christians ourselves: he ordered me to abandon my beliefs, thinking that if I changed the rest would follow me. I gave a reasonable reply, on the lines of 'We must obey God rather than men.'[3] I told him outright that I worship the only God and no other, and would never change or cease to be a Christian. At that he ordered me to go right away to a village near the desert, called Cephro.

Perhaps you would care to hear the speeches on both sides, as they appear in the official records.

'When Dionysius, Faustus, Maximus, Marcellus, and Chaeremon were brought into court, Aemilian the acting governor said: "In an interview I spoke to you of the generosity our masters have shown you; they have given you a chance to go scot-free, if you are prepared to turn to what is natural and worship the gods who preserve their throne, and to forget those who are unnatural. What do you say to this? I suppose you will not

---

1. Ex. xx. 5.   2. Tobit xii. 7.   3. Acts v. 29.

be ungrateful for their generosity, as they are advising you for your own good."

'Dionysius: "Not all men worship all gods; each worships some – those he believes in. We believe in the one God and Creator of all things, who entrusted the throne to His most beloved emperors, Valerian and Gallienus; Him we both worship and adore, and to Him we continually pray that their throne may remain unshaken."

'Aemilian, the acting governor: "Who prevents you from worshipping him too, if he is a god, as well as the natural gods? You were ordered to worship gods, and gods known to all."

'Dionysius: "We worship no one else."

'Aemilian, the acting governor: "I see you are both ungrateful and blind to the leniency of our emperors; therefore you shall not stay in this city, but remove yourselves to Libya and remain in a place called Cephro. This is the place I have selected, by command of our emperors. On no account will you or anyone else be permitted either to hold assemblies or to enter the cemeteries, as you call them.[1] If anyone is shown not to have gone to the place I have named, or is found at any meeting, he will get himself into serious trouble. For you will be under careful and constant observation. You will therefore go at once to the place appointed."'

Even though I was ill he hurried me away, refusing to grant a single day's grace. So what time had I left to hold a meeting or anything else? . . .

But we did not refrain even from openly meeting together with the Lord, but I tried all the harder to bring together the Christians in the city as if I were with them – absent in body, as the Apostle said, but present in spirit.[2] At Cephro a large church formed itself round us, some following us from the city, others coming from various parts of Egypt. And there God opened to us a door for the word.[3] At first we were persecuted and stoned, but later quite a number of the heathen left their idols and turned to God. Never before had they received the word, but now at last through us it was sown among them. Surely it was for his purpose that God brought us to them, and when we had completed our mission took us away again.

Aemilian decided to remove us to what he thought rougher and more typically Libyan places, and ordered the Christians from every side to be concentrated in the district of Marea, allotting different villages in the area to the various groups. For us he chose a place closer to the road, so

1. 'Sleeping-places', a word used only by Christians.
2. 1 Cor. v. 3.   3. Col. iv. 3.

that we should be the first to be captured. Obviously, he was managing and arranging it so that whenever he decided to seize us he should find us easy to catch. In my own case, when I was ordered to go to Cephro I had no idea on which side the place lay – I had scarcely heard even the name before; however, I set off in good heart and made no fuss. But when I was told that I must go right away to the Colluthion district, those who were present know how badly I took it, for here I shall take myself to task. At first I was annoyed and very angry. It was true that these places happened to be better known and more familiar to me, but I was informed that there were no Christians or reputable people in the area, where travellers were exposed to annoyance and to bandit raids. But I felt happier when my friends reminded me that it was nearer the city, and that while Cephro allowed us to see a good deal of our friends from Egypt, so that our church was more broadly based, our new home was so much nearer to the city that we should have more opportunities to enjoy the sight of those we cared for most, our nearest and dearest. They would come and stay for a time, and as in the outer suburbs, there would be local meetings. And so it proved.

After giving further details of his adventures, he goes on as follows:

No doubt Germanus prides himself on a great many confessions of faith, and can tell of a great many things that he has had to bear; all the things he can list in my own case – court sentences, confiscations, proscriptions, plundering of property, relinquishing of privileges, contempt for worldly glory, indifference to praise or the reverse from governors and councils, patience in face of threats, outcries, dangers, persecutions, homelessness, distress, affliction of every kind; all of which were my lot under Decius and Sabinus, and are still my lot under Aemilian. But where did Germanus come in? What was said about him? But I must not make an utter fool of myself because of Germanus, so I will refrain from giving a detailed account of what occurred to friends who know about it already.

In his letter to Domitius and Didymus he again refers to the events of the persecution:

To give all the names of our people, who are so numerous and quite unknown to you, would be a waste of time, but I must tell you that men and women, youngsters and greybeards, girls and old women, soldiers and civilians, every race and every age, some the victims of scourges and the stake, others of the sword, came through their ordeal triumphantly and have received their crowns. In the case of others, not even a very long time sufficed for them to appear acceptable to the Lord, as indeed in my own case hitherto. No doubt I have been reserved for the proper time, known to Him who said: 'At an acceptable time I heard you, and in a day of salvation I succoured you.'[1] You ask about our affairs and want to know how we live. Well, you have heard of course that when we were being taken away as prisoners by a centurion and magistrates and the soldiers and servants with them – Gaius, Faustus, Peter, Paul, and myself – we were surprised by a party from Marea, who when we objected and refused to go with them dragged us off by force and carried us away. Now only Gaius, Peter, and I, bereft of our friends, are confined in a barren, parched spot in Libya, three days' journey from Paraetonium . . .

In the city four presbyters – Maximus, Dioscurus, Demetrius, and Lucius – have gone underground and secretly visit the Christians there. Those who are better known in the world, Faustinus and Aquila, are wandering about Egypt. Deacons who survived those who died on the island are Faustus, Eusebius, and Chaeremon – the Eusebius whom from the very first God inspired and equipped to attend so energetically to the needs of the confessors who were in prison, and perform the dangerous duty of laying out the bodies of the fulfilled and blessed martyrs. For even now the governor, as I said before, is relentlessly putting to a cruel death some of those who are brought before him; some he mangles on the rack; others he leaves to languish fettered in prison, forbidding anyone to come near them and watching to see if anyone is caught doing so. However, through the determination and perseverance of fellow-Christians God gives a breathing-space to the hard-pressed.

It should be noted that Eusebius, whom Dionysius here calls a deacon, a little later was appointed Bishop of Laodicea in Syria; while Maximus, to whom he refers as a presbyter at that time, succeeded Dionysius himself as head of the Alexandrian church; but that Faustus, who then made as noble a confession of faith as Dionysius himself, was preserved till the persecution of my own time, when in the evening of a very long life he found fulfilment as a martyr, in my own lifetime, by the headsman's axe.

1. 2. Cor. vi. 2, quoting Is. xlix. 8.

Martyrdoms at Caesarea in Palestine

12. During the same persecution of Valerian three men who at Caesarea in Palestine made a glorious confession of Christ were crowned with a divine martyrdom, becoming food for beasts. One was called Priscus and one Malchus, while the name of the third was Alexander. It is said that these men, while living in the country, at first accused themselves of apathy and indifference: they scorned the prizes which the times offered to those who craved for them with a heavenly longing, instead of grasping the martyr's crown with both hands. So when they had talked it over, they set out for Caesarea, where they presented themselves before the judge and met the end already described. It is also on record that in addition to these a woman, during the same persecution and in the same city, battled through a similar ordeal. But she is thought to have belonged to Marcion's sect.

The peace under Gallienus: contemporary bishops

13. Not long afterwards Valerian became the slave of the Persians. His son, who now found himself sole ruler, showed more prudence in his conduct of affairs. One of his first acts was to issue edicts ending the persecution against us. To those responsible for the word he granted freedom to perform their normal duties. This is the wording of the decree:

The Emperor Caesar Publius Licinius Gallienus Pius Felix Augustus to Dionysius, Pinnas, Demetrius, and the other bishops. The benefit of my bounty I have ordered to be proclaimed throughout the world. All places of worship shall be restored to their owners; you bishops, therefore, may avail yourselves of the provisions of this decree to protect you from any interference. The complete liberty of action which you now possess has long been granted by me; accordingly Aurelius Quirinius, my chief minister, will enforce the ordinance given by me.

To make the meaning clearer, the decree here quoted has been translated from the original Latin. We also possess another enactment of the same emperor addressed to other bishops, permitting them to recover the ground occupied by 'cemeteries'.

14. At that time the Roman church was still headed by Xystus, the Antioch church by Fabius' successor Demetrian, the church of Cappadocian Caesarea by Firmilian, and the Pontic churches by Gregory and his brother Athenodore, pupils of Origen. At Palestinian Caesarea, when Theoctistus died Domnus succeeded him as bishop; but Domnus lasted only a short time, and Theotecnus, my own contemporary, was chosen as his successor. He too came from Origen's school. Lastly at Jerusalem, when Mazabanes had gone to his rest, his throne was filled by Hymenaeus, who was prominent for so many years of my own lifetime.

Martyrdom of Marinus at Caesarea: the story of Astyrius

15. In their time the churches everywhere enjoyed peace; nevertheless at Caesarea in Palestine Marinus, who had served in the army with great distinction and was a man of good birth and great wealth, was beheaded for his witness to Christ. It came about thus. Among the Romans the vine-switch is a mark of honour, and those who win it, we are told, become centurions. A vacancy occurred, and by the order of seniority Marinus was entitled to be promoted to fill it. But when he was about to receive the honour, another man advanced to the tribune and declared that Marinus was debarred by old-established laws from holding rank in the Roman army, as he was a Christian and did not sacrifice to the emperors; so the office fell to himself. Reacting to this, the judge – his name was Achaeus – first asked what opinions Marinus held; when he saw that he stubbornly declared himself a Christian, he allowed him three hours to think it over.

As soon as he left the court, Theotecnus, the bishop of the diocese, came to him through the crowd, drew him aside, took him by the hand, and led him to the church. Inside, he placed him right in front of the altar, and drawing aside his cloak a little way pointed to the sword at his side. Then he fetched the book containing the divine gospels, placed it before him, and invited him to choose whichever of the two he preferred. Without a moment's hesitation, he put out his hand and took the divine book. 'Hold fast then,' said Theoctenus. 'Hold fast to God. May

you obtain what you have chosen, inspired by Him. Go in peace.'
No sooner had Marinus gone back than an usher called on him to
present himself before the court; the period of grace was now
over. He stood erect before the judge and displayed still greater
devotion to the Faith. Instantly, just as he was, he was taken to
execution and thus found fulfilment.

16. It was at Caesarea also that Astyrius is remembered for the
boldness by which he delighted the heart of God. A member of
the Roman Senate, and highly esteemed by emperors, he was in
the public eye because of his birth and affluence. He was present
when the martyr found fulfilment, and, shouldering the mortal
remains, he placed them on a magnificent costly robe, laid them
out in the most expensive fashion, and gave them fitting burial.

Many other stories are told about this man by acquaintances of
his, who have survived to my own time. They include the
following miraculous incident.

17. Near Caesarea Philippi, called Paneas by the Phoenicians, on
the skirts of the mountain called Paneum, they point to springs
believed to be the source of the Jordan.[1] Into these they say that
on a certain feast day a victim is thrown, and that by the demon's
power it disappears from sight miraculously. This occurrence
strikes the onlookers as a marvel to be talked of everywhere. One
day Astyrius was there while this was going on, and when he saw
that the business amazed the crowd he pitied their delusion, and
looking up to heaven pleaded through Christ with God who is
over all to refute the demon who was deluding the people and
stop them from being deceived. When he had offered this prayer,
it is said that the sacrifice instantly came to the surface of the
water. Thus their miracle was gone, and nothing marvellous ever
again happened at that spot.

The statue of the woman with a haemorrhage

18. As I have mentioned this city, I do not think I ought to omit a
story that deserves to be remembered by those who will follow us.

1. See Josephus: *Jewish War*, p. 230f.

The woman with a haemorrhage, who as we learn from the holy gospels was cured of her trouble by our Saviour,[1] was stated to have come from here. Her house was pointed out in the city, and a wonderful memorial of the benefit the Saviour conferred upon her was still there. On a tall stone base at the gates of her house stood a bronze statue of a woman, resting on one knee and resembling a suppliant with arms outstretched. Facing this was another of the same material, an upright figure of a man with a double cloak neatly draped over his shoulders and his hand stretched out to the woman. Near his feet on the stone slab grew an exotic plant, which climbed up to the hem of the bronze cloak and served as a remedy for illnesses of every kind. This statue, which was said to resemble the features of Jesus, was still there in my own time, so that I saw it with my own eyes when I resided in the city. It is not at all surprising that Gentiles who long ago received such benefits from our Saviour should have expressed their gratitude thus, for the features of His apostles Paul and Peter, and indeed of Christ Himself, have been preserved in coloured portraits which I have examined. How could it be otherwise, when the ancients habitually followed their own Gentile custom of honouring them as saviours in this uninhibited way?

The throne of Bishop James

19. The throne of James – who was the first to receive from the Saviour and His apostles the episcopacy of the Jerusalem church, and was called Christ's brother, as the sacred books show – has been preserved to this day. The Christians there, who in their turn look after it with such loving care, make clear to all the veneration in which saintly men high in the favour of God were regarded in time past and are regarded to this day.

Letters of Dionysius on the Easter festival and on events in Alexandria

20. In addition to the letters already quoted, Dionysius wrote at that time the 'festival letters', in which he expresses himself with

1. Mark v. 24–34.

unusual solemnity on the subject of the Easter festival. One letter
is addressed to Flavius, another to Domitius and Didymus. In the
latter he propounds a rule based on an eight-year cycle, and
demonstrates that at no time other than after the spring equinox is
it legitimate to celebrate Easter. Besides these, he indited another
to his fellow-presbyters at Alexandria and to others at the same
time in various places. These he wrote while the persecution was
still going on.

21. When peace was almost established, he returned to Alexandria; but when faction fighting broke out there anew, it was
impossible for him to keep a fatherly eye on all the Christians in
the city, divided as they were between the two warring camps. So
when Easter came he was again forced, like someone in a foreign
country, to communicate with them by letter from Alexandria
itself. Then to Hierax, a bishop in Egypt, he wrote another festival
letter, in which he speaks as follows of the current dissension in
Alexandria:

  In my own case, is there any wonder if it is difficult to communicate
even by letter with those living at a distance, when it has become almost
beyond me even to converse with myself or think things over in my own
mind? I am most anxious to send letters to those who mean so much to
me, the brothers who belong to the same family, who are of the same
mind, who are members of the same church; but to get such letters
through to them seems impossible. It would be easier to make one's way,
not merely into a foreign land but from farthest east to farthest west, than
to reach Alexandria from Alexandria itself. The great trackless desert that
took Israel two generations to cross was less difficult and impassable than
the street through the very middle of the city! The sea which divided and
formed a wall on either side providing them with a carriage way, a high
road on which the Egyptians disappeared under the water, foreshadowed
only too clearly our calm and waveless harbours, which from the murders
committed in them have so often resembled a Red Sea. The river that
flows past the city at one time appeared drier than the waterless desert,
more parched than the one in crossing which Israel was so thirsty that
Moses cried out, and from the only Doer of wonders drink poured for
them out of the flinty rock. At another time it rose so high that it flooded
the whole neighbourhood, roads and fields alike, threatening us with the

rush of water that occurred in Noah's time. At all times it flows polluted with blood and murders and drownings, such as under the hand of Moses it became for Pharaoh, when it changed to blood and stank. What other water could there be to cleanse the water that cleanses everything? How could the mighty ocean impassable to man, if poured over it, clear the filth from this dreadful sea? How could the great river that flows out of Eden, if it channelled the four heads into which it divides into one, the Gihon,[1] wash away the filthy gore? When would the air, fouled by the poisonous exhalations rising on every side, be purified? Such vapours are given off from the land, such winds from the sea, such breezes from the rivers, such mists from the harbours, that it is the discharges from dead bodies rotting in all their component parts that form the dew. And then people are surprised and puzzled as to the source of the continual epidemics, the serious illnesses, the variety of pestilences, the changing forms and high rate of human mortality, and unable to see why this immense city no longer contains as big a number of inhabitants, from infant children to those of extreme age, as it used to support of those described as hale old men. As for those from forty to seventy, they were then so much more numerous that their total is not reached now, though we have counted and registered as entitled to the public food ration all from fourteen to eighty; and those who look the youngest are now reckoned as equal in age to the oldest men of our earlier generation. Men see the human race upon earth constantly shrinking and wasting thus, yet they do not turn a hair, while its complete destruction comes daily nearer.

22. Later, when a severe epidemic followed the war just as the festival was approaching, he again communicated in writing with the Christian community, revealing the horrors of the disaster:

Other people would not think this a time for festival: they do not so regard this or any other time, even if, so far from being a time of distress, it is a time of unimaginable joy. Now, alas! all is lamentation, everyone in mourning, and the city resounds with weeping because of the number that have died and are dying every day. As Scripture says of the firstborn of the Egyptians, so now there has been a great cry: there is not a house in which there is not one dead – how I wish it had been only one!

Many terrible things had happened to us even before this. First we were set on and surrounded by persecutors and murderers, yet we were the only ones to keep festival even then. Every spot where we were

---

1. Gen. ii. 10–14; the Fathers identified Gihon with the Nile.

attacked became for us a place for celebrations, whether field, desert, ship, inn, or prison. The most brilliant festival of all was kept by the fulfilled martyrs, who were feasted in heaven. After that came war and famine, which struck at Christian and heathen alike. We alone had to bear the injuries they did us, but we profited by what they did to each other and suffered at each other's hands; so yet again we found joy in the peace which Christ has given to us alone. But when both we and they had been allowed a tiny breathing-space, out of the blue came this disease, a thing more terrifying to them than any terror, more frightful than any disaster whatever, and as a historian of their own [1] once wrote: 'the only thing of all that surpassed expectation'. To us it was not that, but a schooling and testing as valuable as all our earlier trials; for it did not pass over us, though its full impact fell on the heathen . . .

Most of our brother-Christians showed unbounded love and loyalty, never sparing themselves and thinking only of one another. Heedless of the danger, they took charge of the sick, attending to their every need and ministering to them in Christ, and with them departed this life serenely happy; for they were infected by others with the disease, drawing on themselves the sickness of their neighbours and cheerfully accepting their pains. Many, in nursing and curing others, transferred their death to themselves and died in their stead, turning the common formula that is normally an empty courtesy into a reality: 'Your humble servant bids you good-bye.' The best of our brothers lost their lives in this manner, a number of presbyters, deacons, and laymen winning high commendation, so that death in this form, the result of great piety and strong faith, seems in every way the equal of martyrdom. With willing hands they raised the bodies of the saints to their bosoms; they closed their eyes and mouths, carried them on their shoulders, and laid them out; they clung to them, embraced them, washed them, and wrapped them in grave-clothes. Very soon the same services were done for them, since those left behind were constantly following those gone before.

The heathens behaved in the very opposite way. At the first onset of the disease, they pushed the sufferers away and fled from their dearest, throwing them into the roads before they were dead and treating unburied corpses as dirt, hoping thereby to avert the spread and contagion of the fatal disease; but do what they might, they found it difficult to escape.

After this letter, when the people in the city were at peace, he again sent a festival letter to the Egyptian community, following it

1. Thucydides, describing the plague of Athens (II. 64. 1).

up with several others. A letter of his on the Sabbath and another on religious training have also been preserved.

The reign of Gallienus

Communicating again by letter with Hermammon and the Egyptian community, he has much to say about the criminal folly of Decius and his successors, and recalls the peace under Gallienus. 23. It will be worth while to hear what he has to say about these things:

Macrian, after goading one of his emperors and attacking the other, suddenly disappeared root and branch with his whole family, and Gallienus was proclaimed and recognized by all. He was both an old emperor and a new: he both preceded and followed them. For, in accordance with the message given to the prophet Isaiah: 'See, the earliest things have come about, and new things shall now arise.'[1] You know how a cloud sweeps under the sun's rays and for a time screens and darkens it and is seen in its place; then when the cloud has gone by or melted, the sun reappears, shining as it did before. In the same way Macrian, after pushing himself forward and insinuating himself into the imperial prerogatives of Gallienus, is no more (he never was!), while Gallienus is just as he was before, and as if it had cast off its old age and purged away its former dross, the monarchy flourishes now as never before, is seen and heard over a wider sweep, and spreads in all directions.

He goes on to indicate the time at which he wrote this:

It occurs to me to take another look at the length of the various reigns. I observe that the wicked emperors who once were famous have been quickly forgotten, while the one who became more religious and devoted to God has passed the seven-year mark and is now completing a ninth year, in which we may indeed keep festival.

Nepos and his schism

24. Beside all this letter writing, he found time to produce the two pamphlets *On Promises*. These were occasioned by Nepos, one of

1. Is. xlii. 9.

the Egyptian bishops, who taught that the promises made to the
saints in holy scripture would be fulfilled more in accordance with
Jewish ideas, and suggested that there would be a millennium of
bodily indulgence on this earth. Thinking that he could draw on
the Revelation of John to prove his peculiar notion, he wrote a
book on the subject and entitled it *The Allegorists Refuted.* To this
Dionysius replied in his two pamphlets: in the first he expounds
his own opinion about the doctrine; in the second he discusses the
Revelation of John, after referring to Nepos at the start in the
following terms:

They put forward a treatise by Nepos, on which they rely completely
as proving incontrovertibly that Christ's kingdom will be on earth. Now
in general I respect and love Nepos for his faith and industry, his careful
study of the Scriptures, and his rich hymnody, which is still a source of
comfort to many of our fellow-Christians, and I am most unwilling to
criticize him, especially now that he has gone to his rest. But more than
anything we must love and reverence truth, and while it is right to give
ungrudging praise and approval to every statement that is correct, it is
our duty to examine and criticize any piece of writing that appears
unsound. If Nepos were here now and putting forward his ideas in
speech alone, conversation with nothing in writing would suffice, using
question and answer as means to persuade and win over our militant
opponents.[1] But a work has been published which some people find
most convincing, and certain teachers regard the Law and the Prophets
as worthless, discourage the following of the gospels, make light of
the apostolic epistles, and make extravagant claims for the teaching of
this treatise as if it was some great and hidden mystery. They do not
allow our simpler brethren to have lofty noble thoughts, either about
the glorious and truly divine epiphany of our Lord or about our
own resurrection from the dead, when we shall be gathered together and
made like Him;[2] they persuade them to expect in the kingdom of God
what is trifling and mortal and like the present. How then can we do
otherwise than thrash the matter out as if our brother Nepos were here
with us? . . .

When I arrived in the district of Arsinoe, where as you know this
notion had long been widely held, so that schisms and secessions of entire
churches had taken place, I called a meeting of the presbyters and teachers

1. 2 Tim. ii. 25.   2. Mark xiii. 27 and I John iii. 2.

of the village congregations, with any laymen who wished to attend, and urged them to thrash out the question in public. So they brought me this book as positive and irrefutable proof, and I sat with them for three days on end from dawn to dusk, criticizing its contents point by point. In the process I was immensely impressed by the essential soundness, complete sincerity, logical grasp, and mental clarity shown by these good people, as we methodically and good-temperedly dealt with questions, objections, and points of agreement. We refused to cling with pig-headed determination to opinions once held even if proved wrong. There was no shirking of difficulties, but to the limit of our powers we tried to grapple with the problems and master them; nor were we too proud, if worsted in argument, to abandon our position and admit defeat: conscientiously, honestly, and with simple-minded trust in God, we accepted the conclusions to be drawn from the proofs and teachings of Holy Writ. In the end, the author and originator of this doctrine, Coracion by name, in the hearing of all present assured and promised us that for the future he would not adhere to it, argue about it, mention it, or teach it, as he was completely convinced by the arguments on the other side. Of the rest, some were delighted with the discussion, and with the all-round spirit of accommodation and concord.

The Revelation of John

Farther on he has this to say about the Revelation of John:

25. Some of our predecessors rejected the book and pulled it entirely to pieces, criticizing it chapter by chapter, pronouncing it unintelligible and illogical and the title false. They say it is not John's and is not a revelation at all, since it is heavily veiled by its thick curtain of incomprehensibility: so far from being one of the apostles, the author of the book was not even one of the saints, or a member of the Church, but Cerinthus, the founder of the sect called Cerinthian after him, who wished to attach a name commanding respect to his own creation. This, they say, was the doctrine he taught – that Christ's kingdom would be on earth; and the things he lusted after himself, being the slave of his body and sensual through and through, filled the heaven of his dreams – unlimited indulgence in gluttony and lechery at banquets, drinking-bouts, and wedding feasts, or (to call these things by what he thought more respectable names) festivals, sacrifices, and the immolation of victims. But I myself would never dare to reject the book, of which many good Christians have a very high

opinion, but realizing that my mental powers are inadequate to judge it
properly, I take the view that the interpretation of the various sections is
largely a mystery, something too wonderful for our comprehension. I do
not understand it, but I suspect that some deeper meaning is concealed
in the words; I do not measure and judge these things by my own
reason, but put more reliance on faith, and so I have concluded that they
are too high to be grasped by me; I do not condemn as valueless what I
have not taken in at a glance, but rather am puzzled that I have not taken
it in.

After examining the whole book of the Revelation and proving
the impossibility of understanding it in the literal sense, he goes
on:

On arriving almost at the end of his prophecy, the prophet blesses those
who observe it, and indeed himself too: 'Blessed is the man who keeps the
words of the prophecy in this book, and I John, the man who saw and
heard these things.' [1] That he was called John, and that this work is John's,
I shall therefore not deny, for I agree that it is from the pen of a holy and
inspired writer. But I am not prepared to admit that he was the apostle,
the son of Zebedee and brother of James, who wrote the gospel entitled
According to John and the general epistle. On the character of each, on
the linguistic style, and on the general tone, as it is called, of Revelation, I
base my opinion that the author was not the same. The evangelist
nowhere includes his name or announces himself in either the gospel or
the epistle . . . but John nowhere, in either first or third person; whereas
the writer of the Revelation puts himself forward at the very beginning:
'The Revelation of Jesus Christ, which He gave Him to show to His
servants at once; and He sent and signified it by His angel to His servant
John, who testified to the word of God and to His testimony, to
everything that he saw.' [2] Next he writes a letter: 'John to the seven
churches in Asia: grace to you and peace.' [3] But the evangelist did not
prefix his name to the general epistle either, but without any preliminaries
began with the solemn mystery of the divine revelation: 'What was from
the beginning; what we have heard, what we have seen with our own
eyes.' [4] It was on this revelation that the Lord congratulated Peter:
'Blessed are you, Simon Bar-Jonah; for flesh and blood have not revealed
it to you, but my Father in heaven.' [5] Nor again in the second and third

1. Rev. xxii. 7–8.   2. Rev. i. 1–2.   3. Rev. i. 4.
4. 1 John i. 1.   5. Matt. xvi. 17.

extant epistles of John, though they are so short, is John named. he is mentioned anonymously as 'the presbyter'. But this writer did not even think it enough, after naming himself once for all, to go on with his story, but goes back to it again: 'I John, your brother and partner in the oppression and kingdom and in the patience of Jesus, was in the island called Patmos because of the word of God and the testimony of Jesus.'[1] Again, at the end he speaks thus: 'Blessed is the man who keeps the words of the prophecy in this book, and I John, the man who saw and heard these things.'

That the writer was John he himself states, and we must believe him. But which John? He does not say here, as so often in the gospel, that he was the disciple loved by the Lord, the one who leant back on His breast, the brother of James, the eyewitness and earwitness of the Lord. He would surely have used one of these descriptions, had he wished to reveal his identity. But he uses none of them, merely calling himself our brother and partner, a witness of Jesus, blessed in seeing and hearing the revelations. Many, I imagine, have had the same name as John the apostle, men who because they loved, admired, and esteemed him so greatly, and wished to be loved as he was by the Lord, were more than glad to be called after him, just as Paul and Peter are favourite names for the children of believers. We find, too, another John in the Acts of the Apostles, John surnamed Mark, whom Barnabas and Paul took with them,[2] and who is referred to again in the words: 'They had John as their attendant.'[3] Was he the writer? I should say not. For he did not go as far as Asia with them, as the record shows: 'Setting sail from Paphos, Paul and his companions came to Perga in Pamphylia; but John left them and went back to Jerusalem.'[4] I think there was another John among the Christians of Asia, as there are said to have been two tombs at Ephesus, each reputed to be John's.

From the ideas too, and from the words used and the way they are put together, we shall readily conclude that this writer was different from the other. There is complete harmony between the gospel and the epistle, and they begin alike. The one says 'In the beginning was the Word', the other 'What was from the beginning'. The one says: 'And the Word became flesh and made His home in our midst: and we gazed on His glory, glory such as an only son receives from his father.' The other, the same thing in slightly different words: 'What we have heard, what we have seen with our own eyes; what we gazed on and our hands touched, concerning the Word of life – the life was manifested.' The reason for this prelude is, as

1. Rev. i. 9.   2. Acts xii. 25.   3. Acts xiii. 5.   4. Acts xiii. 13.

he shows in what follows, that his target is those who declare that the Lord has not come in the flesh. So he carefully added: 'We have seen and bear witness and proclaim to you the eternal life, which was with the Father and was manifested to us; what we have seen and heard we proclaim to you also.' He is consistent and adheres to his plan, setting out everything under the same headings and in the same language. I will give you some brief examples.

The careful reader will find in both books again and again the Life, the Light, Turning away from darkness, Truth, Grace, Joy, the Flesh and the Blood of the Lord, Judgement, Forgiveness of sins, God's love for us, the Commandment 'love one another', the obligation to keep all the Commandments; the Convicting of the world, the devil, antichrist; the promise of the Holy Ghost; the Adoption of sons by God; the Belief that is constantly required of us; the Father and the Son (*passim*). To sum up, anyone who examines their characteristics throughout will inevitably see that Gospel and Epistle have one and the same colour. But there is no resemblance or similarity whatever between them and the Revelation; it has no connexion, no relationship with them; it has hardly a syllable in common with them. Nor shall we find any mention or notion of the Revelation in the Epistle (let alone the Gospel), or of the Epistle in the Revelation. How different from Paul, who in his epistles gives us a glimpse of his revelations,[1] which he did not write down by themselves.

By the phraseology also we can measure the difference between the Gospel and Epistle and the Revelation. The first two are written not only without any blunders in the use of Greek, but with remarkable skill as regards diction, logical thought, and orderly expression. It is impossible to find in them one barbarous word or solecism, or any kind of vulgarism. For, by the grace of the Lord, it seems their author possessed both things, the gift of knowledge and the gift of speech. That the other saw revelations and received knowledge and prophecy I will not deny; but I observe that his language and style are not really Greek: he uses barbarous idioms, and is sometimes guilty of solecisms. There is no need to pick these out now; for I have not said these things in order to pour scorn on him — do not imagine it — but solely to prove the dissimilarity between these books.

The letters of Dionysius

26. In addition to these letters of Dionysius, many others are

1. 2 Cor. xii. 1–4, Eph. iii. 3, and Col. i. 26.

preserved, e.g. those denouncing Sabellius, sent to Ammon, Bishop of Bernice, and letters to Telesphorus, Euphranor, Ammon again, and Euporus. He was also the author of four pamphlets on the same subject addressed to his namesake at Rome. Many more letters of his are in my collection, as well as lengthy documents in letter form, e.g. those on Nature addressed to his boy Timothy, and the one on temptation dedicated to the same Euphranor. Besides these, when writing to Basilides, Bishop of Pentapolis, he says that he has written a commentary on the beginning of Ecclesiastes, and he has left us various other letters to the same correspondent.

Paul of Samosata starts a heresy at Antioch

Now let us pass on to another subject, and describe for the benefit of future generations the character of our own.

27. When Xystus had been head of the Roman church for eleven years he was succeeded by the Bishop of Alexandria's namesake, Dionysius. At the same period Demetrian departed this life at Antioch, and the bishopric went to Paul of Samosata. As he held low, degraded opinions about Christ, in defiance of the Church's teaching, regarding Him as in His nature just an ordinary man, Dionysius of Alexandria was invited to attend the synod; but, excusing himself on the ground of both age and sickness, he put off his coming and sent a letter expressing his own view of the question. The other pastors of the churches, however, gathered from every direction to deal with this destroyer of Christ's flock, all hastening to Antioch.

Famous bishops of the time

28. Pre-eminent among these was Firmilian, Bishop of Cappadocian Caesarea; the brothers Gregory and Athenodore, pastors of the Pontic communities; Helenus, Bishop of Tarsus, and Nicomas, Bishop of Iconium; and of course Hymenaeus of the Jerusalem church and Theotecnus of its neighbour, my own church of

Caesarea. I must name one more – Maximus, who was shepherding the Christians of Bostra with such distinction. It would be easy to reckon up many, many more, together with presbyters and deacons, who assembled in Antioch for the same purpose, but the most eminent were those I have named. They all met on many different occasions, and at every meeting questions were raised and arguments put forward, Paul and his friends endeavouring all the time to hide and cover up his heterodox ideas, while the others did all they could to lay bare and bring into the open his heresy and blasphemy against Christ.

Meanwhile Dionysius died, in the twelfth year of Gallienus, after being head of the Alexandrian church for seventeen years. His successor was Maximus. When Gallienus had completed fifteen years as emperor, he was succeeded by Claudius, who at the termination of his second year left his throne to Aurelian.

Paul excommunicated; the bishops' letter condemning him

29. During his reign a final meeting of the synod was held, attended by a very large number of bishops, who exposed and at last, explicitly and unanimously, condemned for heterodoxy the originator of the Antioch heresy, who was excommunicated from the Catholic Church throughout the world. The person who did most to call him to account and to pin him down, wriggle as he might, was Malchion, a man of great learning who was principal of a school of rhetoric, one of the centres of Hellenic education at Antioch, and in view of the utter genuineness of his faith in Christ had been appointed presbyter of that community. He arranged for shorthand writers to take notes as he embarked on an argument with Paul which we know to be extant to this day; he and he alone succeeded in exposing the crafty dissembler.

30. Accordingly, a single letter expressing their united judgement was drafted by the assembled pastors: nominally addressed to Bishop Dionysius of Rome and Maximus of Alexandria, it was sent out to all the provinces of the Empire. In it they made clear to all the trouble they had taken, the perverse heterodoxy of Paul,

and the arguments and questions they had put to him; they also gave a survey of his whole life and character. To make sure that the facts are not forgotten, it would be well at this point to reproduce what they said:

Helenus, Hymenaeus, Theophilus, Theotecnus, Maximus, Proclus, Nicomas, Aelian, Paul, Bolanus, Protogenes, Hierax, Eutychius, Theodore, Malchion, Lucius, and all the other members of our communities in the neighbouring cities and countries – bishops, presbyters, deacons, and Christian congregations – to their beloved brothers in the Lord, Dionysius, Maximus, and all our fellow-ministers in every land – bishops, presbyters, and deacons – and to the entire Catholic Church throughout the world – greeting . . .

We sent invitations to many even of the more distant bishops to join in putting right this deadly teaching, for instance Dionysius at Alexandria and Firmilian of Cappadocia, both of blessed memory. Dionysius wrote to Antioch, disregarding the existence of the originator of the error, and addressing his letter not to him but to the diocese as a whole: we enclose a copy. Firmilian, who actually came twice, condemned Paul's modernistic notions, a fact for which we who were present can vouch, and which is known to many others; but when Paul promised to change, Firmilian, trusting and believing that without any reproach to the word the matter would be happily settled, adjourned the proceedings, duped by a man who denied his God and Lord and had abandoned the belief that he himself had previously held. And Firmilian was on the point of crossing to Antioch a third time, and had got as far as Tarsus, having seen too much of the God-denying wickedness of this man. But meanwhile, when we had met together and were sending for him and waiting till he arrived, he reached the end of his days.

Farther on they describe the tenor of his life:

Whereas he has forsaken the canon and deviated to spurious and bastard doctrines, there is no need to judge the actions of one who is outside the Church, even in the case of a man who once was nearly penniless, having neither inherited a competence from his forebears nor acquired one by the labour of hand or brain, but who now has amassed immense wealth by committing illegalities, robbing churches, and blackmailing his fellow-Christians. He deprives the injured of their rights, promising them help if they will pay for it but breaking his word to them, and makes easy money out of the readiness of those entangled in court proceedings to buy relief from their persecutors. In fact, he regards religion as a way of making money.[1]

Nor did we judge him because he is ambitious and arrogant, decking himself out with worldly honours and anxious to be called *ducenarius* rather than bishop, and swaggers in city squares,[2] reading letters aloud or dictating them as he walks in public surrounded by a numerous body-guard, some in front and some behind. The result is that the Faith is regarded with distaste and hatred because of his self-importance and inflated pride.

Nor need we judge the way this charlatan juggles with church assemblies, courting popularity and putting on a show to win the admiration of simple souls, as he sits on the dais and lofty throne he has had constructed for him (how unlike a disciple of Christ!) or in the *secretum*, as he calls it, which he occupies in imitation of the rulers of the world. He slaps his thigh and stamps on the dais. Some do not applaud and wave their handkerchiefs as in a theatre, or shout and spring to their feet like his circle of partisans, male and female, who form such a badly behaved audience: they listen, as in God's house, in a reverent and orderly manner. These he scolds and insults. Those who have departed this life, but once preached the word, he assails in a drunken, vulgar fashion in public, while he boasts about himself as if he were not a bishop but a trickster and mountebank.[3]

All hymns to our Lord Jesus Christ he has banned as modern compositions of modern writers, but he arranges for women to sing hymns to himself in the middle of the church on the great day of the Easter Festival: one would shudder to hear them! And he allows the fawning bishops of the neighbouring districts and towns, and presbyters too, to talk in the same way when preaching to the people. He will not admit that the Son of God came down from heaven – as we shall explain more fully later, not merely stating the fact but proving it from passage after passage of the attached notes, especially where he says that Jesus Christ is 'from below'. Yet those who sing hymns and praises to him in the congregation say that their blasphemous teacher is an angel come down from heaven; and he allows this to go on even when he is there to hear, such is his vanity. And what of his 'spiritual brides', as the Antioch people call them? and those of his presbyters and deacons, with whom he joins in concealing this and their other incurable sins, though he knows all about them, so as to have them under his thumb, too frightened on their own account to accuse him of his offences in word and deed? He has even enriched them, thus

1. 1 Tim. vi. 5.   2. A reminiscence of Demosthenes.   3. Demosthenes again.

securing the loyalty and admiration of those who are the same way inclined.

But why should we put these things in writing? We know, dear brothers, that the bishop and entire priesthood ought to be an example to the people of all good works; we are aware also how many through taking 'spiritual brides' have fallen, while others have become suspect. Even if we grant that he does nothing licentious, he should at least have taken care to avoid the suspicion to which such practices give rise, so as not to lead someone else astray and make others imitate him. How could he reprove another man, or advise him not to associate any longer with a 'bride', for fear of a slip – as Scripture warns us [1] – when he has dismissed one already and now has two in his house, both young and pretty, whom he takes round with him whenever he leaves home, living, I may add, in luxury and surfeiting? Small wonder that all weep and groan in secret; for so frightened are they of this tyrannical power that they dare not accuse him. Yet, as we said before, a man could be called to account for these things, if only he had a catholic mind and was one of our number.[2] But when he burlesqued the mystery [3] and paraded with the filthy sect of Artemas (it is our unpleasant duty to name his father), we do not feel called upon to ask for an explanation of all this . . .

We were therefore obliged, as he ranged himself against God and would not yield, to excommunicate him and appoint another bishop in his place for the Catholic Church. By the providence of God, as we feel sure, we chose Domnus, the son of Demetrian of blessed memory who once presided with such distinction over the same diocese. He possesses all the excellent qualities required in a bishop, and we are informing you of his appointment in order that you may write to him and receive from him a letter establishing communion. But this fellow had better write to Artemas, then Artemas and his gang can be in communion with him.

When Paul had lost both the orthodoxy of his faith and his bishopric, Domnus, as already stated, took over the ministry of the Antioch church. But Paul absolutely refused to hand over the church building; so the Emperor Aurelian was appealed to, and he gave a perfectly just decision on the course to be followed: he ordered the building to be assigned to those to whom the bishops of the religion in Italy and Rome addressed a letter. In this way the man in question was thrown out of the church in the most ignominious manner by the secular authority.

1. Eccles. ix. 8–9.   2. Acts i. 17.   3. A reminiscence of Lucian.

Such was the treatment we received from Aurelian at that time. But as his reign went on, he changed his attitude towards us and was now pressed by some of his advisers to instigate a persecution against us, and this became the subject of much comment on every side. But when he was on the point of doing so and was almost in the act of signing the decrees against us, divine justice struck, seizing him in an iron grip to frustrate the attempt – clear proof for all to see that it would never be easy for the rulers of this world to resist the churches of Christ, unless the protecting hand, as a divine and heavenly judgement to chasten and reform us, should at times of its own choosing allow this to be done. Anyway, Aurelian had reigned only six years when he was succeeded by Probus who held sway for about as long and was followed by Carus, in association with his sons Carinus and Numerian. They lasted less than three years, and the government next fell to Diocletian and those later co-opted. Under them the persecution of my own time took place, and with it the destruction of the churches.

Shortly before this the Bishop of Rome, Dionysius, after holding this office for nine years, was succeeded by Felix.

The heterodox deviation of the Manichees, then starting

31. Meanwhile, the maniac whose name[1] reflected his demon-inspired heresy was arming himself with mental derangement, since the demon, God's adversary Satan himself, had put him forward for the ruin of many. A barbarian in mode of life, as his speech and manners showed, and by nature demonic and manic, he acted accordingly, and tried to pose as Christ: at one time he announced himself as the Paraclete, the Holy Ghost himself, being a maniac and a boaster too; at another he imitated Christ, and chose twelve disciples as partners of his crazy ideas. Bringing together false and blasphemous doctrines from the innumerable long-extinct blasphemous heresies, he made a patchwork of them, and brought from Persia a deadly poison with which he infected our own world. From him came the unholy name of Manichee,

1. Mani.

which is still in common use. Such then is the basis of this Knowledge falsely so called, which grew up at the period mentioned.

Distinguished churchmen of my own time

32. At that period too, Felix, head of the Roman church for five years, was succeeded by Eutychian. He lasted less than ten months and left his office to Gaius, my own contemporary, who governed the see for about fifteen years. Marcellinus was chosen to succeed him, but has since fallen victim to the persecution.

In their time the bishopric of Antioch passed from Domnus to Timaeus, who was succeeded by my contemporary Cyril. In this time I made the acquaintance of Dorotheus, a learned man who had been ordained to the presbyterate at Antioch. Enraptured with the study of divinity, he mastered the Hebrew language so thoroughly that he was able to read and understand the precious Hebrew scriptures; he was equally at home in the most liberal studies and Greek elementary education. He was however a natural eunuch, having been such from birth: the emperor, seeing in this a kind of miracle, honoured him with his friendship and graciously appointed him manager of the dye-works at Tyre. I heard him expounding the Scriptures in church very sensibly.

After Cyril, Tyrannus succeeded to the bishopric of Antioch: it was in his day that the attack on the churches reached its peak.

As head of the diocese of Laodicea, Socrates was followed by Eusebius, who came from Alexandria. The reason for his move was the question of Paul. On this account he came to Syria, where eager students of divinity detained him. He was one of the most lovely examples of true religion in my time, as may easily be seen from the remarks of Dionysius already quoted. Anatolius was appointed his successor, one good man following another, as the saying goes. Anatolius was by birth an Alexandrian, and for his learning, secular studies, and philosophy was in the first rank of the most eminent men of my time; indeed in arithmetic, geometry, astronomy, and the other sciences, physical or metaphysical, and in the speaker's art too, he had climbed to the summit. It was apparently on this account that he was invited by the citizens there to found the school of the Aristotelian succession at Alexandria. Countless exploits of his during the siege of the Bruchium at Alexandria are recorded: a unique privilege among the officials was unanimously conferred on him. I shall mention one incident only. It is said that when the defenders had run out of wheat, so that now the enemy without were less terrible than hunger within, our hero devised the following scheme.

The other half of the city was fighting on the Roman side and so was not besieged. Eusebius, who was still there before his move to Syria, was in this half, and had won such fame and such an outstanding reputation that even the Roman commander was impressed. Anatolius sent to Eusebius a full account of the starving victims of the siege. On receiving it, he asked the Roman general as an act of the greatest kindness to promise immunity to deserters from the enemy: having obtained his request, he informed Anatolius. When the promise reached him, Anatolius at once convened a council of Alexandrians and began by appealing to them all to give the right hand of friendship to the Romans. When he saw that they were angered by the suggestion, he went on: 'Well, I don't think you would say no if I advised you to allow those who are superfluous and of no use to us, old men and women and young children, to go outside the gates whichever way they like. Why do we hold on to these people to no purpose, when they are on the point of death? Why do we let the maimed and crippled die of starvation, when we ought to support only men and youths and ration our precious wheat to those capable of defending the city?'

With arguments on these lines he convinced the meeting, and was the first to stand up and give his vote that the whole mass of men and women incapable of military service should be free to leave the city, because if they continued to stay there uselessly they could not hope to survive, as hunger would destroy them. When the whole council agreed to this proposal, he succeeded in saving nearly everyone inside the gates. He saw to it that first the members of the Church, and then the rest of those in the city, whatever their age, should escape, not only those covered by the vote but countless others pretending to be so, who disguised themselves in women's clothing and in accordance with his plan slipped out of the gates and hurried towards the Roman lines. There they were all welcomed by Eusebius, who like a father and a doctor looked after them, much the worse for the long siege, with every care and attention. Such were the two pastors whom the church of Laodicea was privileged to have in succession: by divine providence they had come there from Alexandria after the war described above. No very great number of works came from Anatolius' pen, but enough have come into my hands to demonstrate his learning and varied knowledge. In these he presents in particular his views on the Easter festival. It will be desirable at this point to quote the following:

FROM THE CANONS OF ANATOLIUS ON THE EASTER FESTIVAL

It was therefore in the first year the new moon of the first month, which begins the whole nineteen-year cycle – according to the Egyptians on 26 Phamenoth, according to the Macedonian calendar 22 Dystrus, by Roman reckoning 22 March. On this day the sun is found not only to have reached the first sign of the Zodiac, but to be already passing through the fourth day within it. This sign is generally known as the first of the twelve, the equinoctial sign, the beginning of months, head of the cycle, and start of the planetary course. But the sign before that is the last of the months, the twelfth sign, last stage, and end of the planetary circuit. For this reason I am convinced that those who place the first month in it, and fix the Paschal 'fourteenth day' accordingly, make a great and indeed an extraordinary mistake. This is not my own suggestion: the Jews were aware of the fact long ago, even before Christ's time, and observed it carefully. We can learn it from the statements of Philo, Josephus, and Musaeus, and not them only but still earlier writers, the two Agathobuli, famous as the teachers of Aristobulus the Great. He was one of Seventy who translated the sacred and inspired Hebrew Scriptures for Ptolemy Philadelphus and his father; he also dedicated commentaries on the Mosaic Law to the same kings. These authorities, in explaining the problems of the Exodus, state that the Passover ought invariably to be sacrificed after the spring equinox, at the middle of the first month; and that this occurs when the sun is passing through the first sign of the solar, or as some of them call it, the zodiacal cycle. Aristobulus adds that it is necessary at the Passover Festival that not only the sun but the moon as well should be passing through an equinoctial sign. There are two of these signs, one in spring, one in autumn, diametrically opposite each other, and the day of the Passover is assigned to the fourteenth of the month, after sunset; so the moon will occupy the position diametrically opposite the sun, as we can see when the moon is full: the sun will be in the sign of the spring equinox, the moon inevitably in that of the autumnal. I am familiar with many other of their statements, in some cases probable, in others claimed as final proofs, by which they try to show that the festival of the Passover and Unleavened Bread ought always to be kept after the equinox. But I decline to demand such a structure of proof from those from whom has been removed the veil on the Law of Moses; for them it remains now with face unveiled at all times to reflect like a mirror Christ and the life of Christ,[1] His lessons and sufferings.[2] That the first month according to the Hebrews includes the equinox can be shown also by reference to Enoch.[3]

Anatolius has also left us an *Elements of Arithmetic*, complete in ten parts, as well as evidence of his lifelong study of divinity. He had first been consecrated bishop by Theotecnus, Bishop of Palestinian Caesarea, who was anxious to secure him as his successor in his own diocese after his death, and indeed for some little time they both administered the same church. But he was summoned to Antioch by the synod that dealt with Paul, and as he passed through Laodicea the Christians there took possession of him, Eusebius having fallen asleep.

When Anatolius too departed this life, his episcopate passed to Stephen, the last bishop before the persecution. For his attainments in philosophy and other secular studies he was widely admired; but he was not equally devoted to the divine Faith, as was shown in the course of the persecution, in which he stood revealed as a dissembler and a spiritless coward rather than a true philosopher. However, the church was not to be ruined because of him; she was set on her feet again by one whom God Himself, the universal Saviour, at once chose to be bishop of that diocese – Theodotus, who by his very acts proved his own name[4] and that of bishop true. In the science of bodily healing he was very highly qualified; in the curing of souls he was without a rival, such were his

1. See 2 Cor. iii. 15–18.   2. Heb. v. 8.
3. The uncanonical book quoted in Jude 14.   4. *Theodotus* means 'God-given'.

kindness, genuine sympathy, and active interest in those who asked him for help; he also put a great deal of effort into the study of divinity. Such was his character in a nutshell.

At Caesarea in Palestine Theotecnus, after carrying out his episcopal duties most conscientiously, was succeeded by Agapius. I know that he too worked very hard, and showed a most genuine regard for the welfare of his people, ministering with a generous hand to the poor most of all. In this time I made the acquaintance of a most remarkable man, a true philosopher in his life, who was chosen for the presbyterate in that diocese – Pamphilus. To discuss his background and character would be too big an undertaking; all the details of his life, the school he founded, his ordeals in successive confessions of his faith during the persecution, and the crown of martyrdom which he won at last, I have recorded in a work devoted to him alone. He was the most wonderful of the people there, but among the men of my time there were certainly two of the rarest merit – one of the Alexandrian presbyters, Pierius, and Meletius, bishop of the Pontic province. Pierius had been noted for his life of absolute poverty and for his philosophical studies. He was exceptionally well versed in the science and exposition of theology, and was a first-rate popular preacher. Meletius – Mellifluous,[1] as the learned called him – was the sort of man who might be described as the complete all-round scholar. His excellence as an orator cannot be sufficiently admired, though it might be said that this came to him as a gift from nature. But who could rival his excellence as a lifelong and profound scholar? You had only to meet him to discover that in every kind of intellectual activity he was the most accomplished and well informed person alive. No less remarkable was the excellence of his character. I observed him at the time of the persecution, when he was chased all over Palestine for seven years.

In the Jerusalem church, following Hymenaeus, the bishop mentioned a little while back, Zabdas took over the ministry. Very soon he fell asleep, and Hermo, last of the bishops up to the

---

1. Greek 'the honey (*meli*) of Attica'.

persecution of my time, ascended the apostolic throne preserved there to this day.

At Alexandria, Maximus, who for eighteen years after the death of Dionysius had been bishop, was succeeded by Theonas. In his time Achillas was ordained to the presbyterate at Alexandria, along with Priscus, and was greatly esteemed. The school of the holy Faith was entrusted to his hands, for he had shown unusual and unrivalled abilities as a philosopher, and a character in true accord with the gospel way of life. When Theonas had done his utmost for nineteen years, he was succeeded in the diocese of Alexandria by Peter, who in his turn did splendid work for twelve years. He administered the church for not quite three years before the persecution; for the rest of his life he subjected himself to a harsher discipline, and his care for the common good of the churches was evident to all. The result was that in the ninth year of the persecution he was beheaded, and so was honoured with the crown of martyrdom.

In these books I have dealt fully with the subject of the successions from our Saviour's birth to the destruction of our places of worship, a story covering 305 years. Well now, for the information of future generations, I had better next record the continual and terrible ordeals of those who in my time fought so manfully for true religion.

Book 8

Having dealt fully with the apostolic succession in seven books, in this eighth section it is surely a matter of the highest importance that for the enlightenment of future generations I should set down the events of my own day, calling as they do for a most careful record. That shall be the starting-point for my account.

Events before the persecution of my time

1. How great, how unique were the honour, and liberty too, which before the persecution of my time were granted by all men, Greeks and non-Greeks alike, to the message given through Christ to the world, of true reverence for the God of the universe! It is beyond me to describe it as it deserves. Witness the goodwill so often shown by potentates to our people; they even put into their hands the government of the provinces, releasing them from the agonizing question of sacrificing, in view of the friendliness with which they regarded their teaching. What need I say about those in the imperial palaces and about the supreme rulers? Did they not permit the members of their households – consorts, children, and servants – to embrace boldly before their eyes the divine message and way of life, hardly minding even if they boasted of the liberty granted to the Faith? Did they not hold them in special esteem, and favour them more than their fellow servants? I might instance the famous Dorotheus, the most devoted and loyal of their servants, and on that account much more honoured than the holders of offices and governorships. With him I couple the celebrated Gorgonius, and all who because of God's word were held in the same honour as these two. And what approbation the rulers in

every church unmistakably won from all procurators and governors! How could one describe those mass meetings, the enormous
gatherings in every city, and the remarkable congregations in
places of worship? No longer satisfied with the old buildings, they
raised from the foundations in all the cities churches spacious in
plan. These things went forward with the times and expanded at a
daily increasing rate, so that no envy stopped them nor could any
evil spirit bewitch them or check them by means of human
schemes, as long as the divine and heavenly hand sheltered and
protected its own people, as being worthy.

But increasing freedom transformed our character to arrogance
and sloth; we began envying and abusing each other, cutting our
own throats, as occasion offered, with weapons of sharp-edged
words; rulers hurled themselves at rulers and laymen waged party
fights against laymen, and unspeakable hypocrisy and dissimulation
were carried to the limit of wickedness. At last, while the gatherings were still crowded, divine judgement, with its wonted mercy,
gently and gradually began to order things its own way, and with
the Christians in the army the persecution began. But alas! realizing
nothing, we made not the slightest effort to render the Deity
kindly and propitious; and as if we had been a lot of atheists, we
imagined that our doings went unnoticed and unregarded, and
went from wickedness to wickedness. Those of us who were
supposed to be pastors cast off the restraining influence of the fear
of God and quarrelled heatedly with each other, engaged solely in
swelling the disputes, threats, envy, and mutual hostility and hate,
frantically demanding the despotic power they coveted. Then,
then it was that in accordance with the words of Jeremiah, the
Lord in His anger covered the daughter of Zion with a cloud, and
cast down from Heaven the glory of Israel; He remembered not
the footstool of His feet in the day of His anger, but the Lord also
drowned in the sea all the beauty of Israel, and broke down all his
fences.[1] So also, as foretold in the Psalms, He overthrew the
covenant of His bondservant and profaned to the ground (through
the destruction of the churches) his sanctuary and broke down all

---

1. A conflation of parts of Lam. ii. 1–2 with Ps. lxxxix. 40.

his fences; He made his strongholds cowardice. All that passed by
the way despoiled the multitudes of the people; moreover, he
became a reproach to his neighbours. For He exalted the right
hand of his enemies, and turned back the aid of his sword and did
not assist him in the war. But He also cut him off from cleansing
and threw down his throne to the ground, and shortened the days
of his time, and finally covered him with shame.[1]

The destruction of the churches

2. Everything indeed has been fulfilled in my time; I saw with my
own eyes the places of worship thrown down from top to
bottom, to the very foundations, the inspired holy Scriptures
committed to the flames in the middle of the public squares, and
the pastors of the churches hiding disgracefully in one place or
another, while others suffered the indignity of being held up to
ridicule by their enemies – a reminder of another prophetic
saying: for contempt was poured on rulers, and He made them
wander in a trackless land where there was no road.[2] But it was
not for me to describe their wretched misfortunes in the event:
nor is it my business to leave on record their quarrels and inhumanity to each other before the persecutions, so I have made up my
mind to relate no more about them than enough to justify the
divine judgement. I am determined therefore to say nothing even
about those who have been tempted by the persecution or have
made complete shipwreck of their salvation[3] and of their own
accord flung themselves into the depths of the stormy sea; I shall
include in my overall account only those things by which first we
ourselves, then later generations, may benefit. Let me therefore
proceed from this point to describe in outline the hallowed ordeals
of the martyrs of God's word.

It was the nineteenth year of Diocletian's reign and the month
Dystrus, called March by the Romans, and the festival of the
Saviour's Passion was approaching, when an imperial decree was

1. A free adaptation of Ps. lxxxix. 39–45.   2. Ps. cvii. 40.
3. A reminiscence of 1 Tim. i. 19.

published everywhere, ordering the churches to be razed to the ground and the Scriptures destroyed by fire, and giving notice that those in places of honour would lose their places, and domestic staff, if they continued to profess Christianity, would be deprived of their liberty. Such was the first edict against us. Soon afterwards other decrees arrived in rapid succession, ordering that the presidents of the churches in every place should all be first committed to prison and then coerced by every possible means into offering sacrifice.

Ordeals endured in the persecution: God's glorious martyrs

3. Then, then it was that many rulers of the churches bore up heroically under horrible torments, an object lesson in the endurance of fearful ordeals; while countless others, their souls already numbed with cowardice, promptly succumbed to the first onslaught. Of the rest, each was subjected to a series of different tortures, one flogged unmercifully with the whip, another racked and scraped beyond endurance, so that the lives of some came to a most miserable end. But different people came through the ordeal very differently: one man would be forcibly propelled by others and brought to the disgusting, unholy sacrifices, and dismissed as if he had sacrificed, even if he had done no such thing; another, who had not even approached any abomination, much less touched it, but was said by others to have sacrificed, would go away without attempting to repudiate the baseless charge. Another would be picked up half dead, and thrown away as if already a corpse; and again a man lying on the ground might be dragged a long way by his feet, though included among the willing sacrificers. One man would announce at the top of his voice his determination not to sacrifice, another would shout that he was a Christian, exulting in the confession of the Saviour's Name, while yet another insisted that he had never sacrificed and never would. These were struck on the mouth and silenced by a formidable body of soldiers lined up for the purpose: their faces and cheeks were battered and they were forcibly removed. It was the one object in life of the enemies of true religion to gain credit for having finished the job.

But no such methods could enable them to dispose of the holy martyrs. What could I say that would do full justice to them? 4. I could tell of thousands who showed magnificent enthusiasm for the worship of the God of the universe, not only from the beginning of the general persecution, but much earlier when peace was still secure. For at long last the one who had received the authority was as it were awaking from the deepest sleep, after making attempts – as yet secret and surreptitious – against the churches, in the interval that followed Decius and Valerian. He did not make his preparations all at once for the war against us, but for the time being took action only against members of the legions. In this way he thought that the rest would easily be mastered if he joined battle with these and emerged victorious. Now could be seen large numbers of serving soldiers most happy to embrace civil life, in order to avoid having to repudiate their loyalty to the Architect of the universe. The commander-in-chief, whoever he was,[1] was now first setting about persecuting the soldiery, classifying and sorting those serving in the legions, and allowing them to choose either to obey orders and retain their present rank, or alternatively to be stripped of it if they disobeyed the enactment. But a great many soldiers of Christ's kingdom without hesitation or question chose to confess Him rather than cling to the outward glory and prosperity they enjoyed. Already here and there one or two of them were suffering not only loss of position but even death as the reward of their unshakeable devotion: for the time being the man behind the plot was acting cautiously and going as far as bloodshed[2] in a few cases only; he was apparently afraid of the number of believers, and shrank from launching out into war with them all at once. But when he stripped more thoroughly for battle, words are inadequate to depict the host of God's noble martyrs whom the people of every city and every region were privileged to see with their own eyes.

1. Veturius.   2. Reminiscent of Heb. xii. 4.

Martyrs in Nicomedia and in the imperial palaces

5. When the edict against the churches was issued at Nicomedia and posted up in a conspicuous public place, a well-known person,[1] by worldly standards of pre-eminence a man of the greatest distinction, was so stirred by religious enthusiasm and carried away by burning faith that he promptly seized it and tore it to shreds, as something unholy and utterly profane − and that, when two emperors were there in the same city, the most senior of them all and the one who held the fourth place in the government.[2] But he was only the first of many who at that time distinguished themselves in this way and suffered the natural consequences of such bold conduct, preserving a cheerful, confident bearing to their very last breath.   6. Of all those who have at any time been praised in song for their virtues and lauded for their courage, among Greeks and non-Greeks alike, none was ever more remarkable than the divine martyrs produced by this occasion − Dorotheus and the imperial servants who followed his lead. They had been most highly honoured by their imperial masters and treated by them as if they had been their own children, but they accounted reproaches and sufferings for religion, and the many kinds of death invented against them, as in truth greater riches than worldly fame and luxury.[3] I shall describe the death that one of them met, and leave it to my readers to infer from that case what happened in the others.

In the city named above, the rulers in question brought a certain man into a public place and commanded him to sacrifice. When he refused, he was ordered to be stripped, hoisted up naked, and his whole body torn with loaded whips till he gave in and carried out the command, however unwillingly. When in spite of these torments he remained as obstinate as ever, they next mixed vinegar with salt and poured it over the lacerated parts of his body, where the bones were already exposed. When he treated these agonies too with scorn a lighted brazier was then brought forward, and as if it were edible meat for the table, what was left of his body was consumed by the fire, not all at once, for fear his

1. Euethius.   2. Diocletian and Galerius.   3. Freely adapted from Heb. xi. 26.

release should come too soon, but a little at a time; and those who placed him on the pyre were not permitted to stop till after such treatment he should signify his readiness to obey. But he stuck immovably to his determination, and victorious in the midst of his tortures, breathed his last. Such was the martyrdom of one of the imperial servants, a martyrdom worthy of the name he bore – it was Peter.

The heroism of the others was just as great, but to preserve the proportions of this book I shall pass it over, only recording that Dorotheus and Gorgonius, with many more of the imperial household, went through a succession of ordeals and finally were put to death by strangling, carrying off the prizes of their inspired victory.

It was at that period that Anthimus, then head of the Nicomedian church, bore witness to Christ and was beheaded. He was followed by a number of martyrs at once, for somehow or other at that very time there was a conflagration in the palace at Nicomedia, and through a groundless suspicion word went round that our people were responsible. By imperial command God's worshippers there perished wholesale and in heaps, some butchered with the sword, others fulfilled by fire; it is on record that with an inspired and mystical fervour men and women alike leapt on to the pyre. A number of others were bound by the public executioners, dumped in small boats, and thrown into the depths of the sea. As for the imperial servants already dead and committed to the ground with fitting ceremony, they were dug up by their so-called masters, who thought it advisable to start again and throw them too into the sea, with the absurd notion that as they lay in their graves some people would worship them in the belief that they were gods!

Such was the state of affairs at Nicomedia in the early stages of the persecution. But when a little later, in the district of Melitene and all over Syria as well, attempts were being made to attack the empire, an imperial decree was circulated that the heads of the churches everywhere should be fettered and imprisoned. The spectacle of what happened after this beggars description: in every town great numbers were locked up, and everywhere the gaols built long before for homicides and grave-robbers were crowded with bishops, presbyters and deacons, readers and exorcists, so that now there was no room in them for those convicted of crimes.

It was not long before the first decree was followed by another, in which it was laid down that if the prisoners offered sacrifice they should be allowed to go free, but if they refused they should be mutilated by endless tortures. Now once more, how could one count the number of martyrs in every province of the Empire, especially those in Africa and Mauretania, in the Thebais and Egypt? From Egypt at this time some went off to other cities and provinces, where they showed their worth by martyrdom.

Egyptian martyrs in Phoenicia, in Egypt itself, and in the Thebais

7. At any rate we know those of them who became shining lights in Palestine, and we know those at Tyre in Phoenicia. Did any man see them without being amazed at the merciless floggings and the endurance displayed under them by these truly astounding champions of pure religion; at the ordeal with man-eating beasts which came directly after the floggings, when they were attacked by panthers, bears of different kinds, wild boars, and bulls goaded with red-hot irons; at the unflinching courage of these noble people in the face of every one of the beasts? When these things were going on I was there myself, and there I witnessed the ever-present divine power of Him to whom they testified, our Saviour Jesus Christ Himself, visibly manifesting itself to the martyrs. For some time the man-eaters did not dare to touch or even approach the bodies of God's beloved, but rushed at the others who apparently were irritating and provoking them from outside; only the holy champions; as they stood naked, and in accordance with their instructions waved their hands to attract the animals to themselves, were left quite unmolested: sometimes when the beasts did start towards them, they were stopped short as if by some divine power, and retreated to their starting-point. When this went on for a long time it astounded the spectators, so that in view of the ineffectiveness of the first a second and third beast were set on to one and the same martyr.

Nothing could be more amazing than the fearless courage of these saints under such duress, the stubborn, inflexible endurance in youthful bodies. You would see a youngster not yet twenty standing without fetters, spreading out his arms in the form of a cross, and with a mind unafraid and unshakeable occupying himself in the most unhurried prayers to the Almighty: not budging in the least and not retreating an inch from the spot where he stood, though bears and panthers breathing fury and death almost touched his very flesh. Yet by some supernatural, mysterious power their mouths were stopped, and they ran back again to the rear. Again you would have seen others – there were five altogether – thrown to an infuriated bull. When others approached from outside he tossed them with his horns into the air and mangled them, leaving them to be picked up half-dead; but when in his fury he rushed head down at the lonely group of holy martyrs, he could not even get near them, but stamped his feet and pushed with his horns in all directions. Provoked by the hot irons he breathed rage and threats, but divine providence dragged him back. So, as he too did his intended victims no harm whatever, other beasts were set on them. At last, when these animals had launched their terrible varied assaults, the martyrs were one and all butchered with the sword, and instead of being buried in the earth were given to the waves of the sea.

8. Such was the ordeal of the Egyptians who championed the faith so gloriously at Tyre. But we should feel equal admiration for those of them who were martyred in their own country, where immense numbers of men, women, and children, despising this transient life, faced death in all its forms for the sake of our Saviour's teaching. Some were scraped, racked, mercilessly flogged, subjected to countless other torments too terrible to describe in endless variety, and finally given to the flames; some were submerged in the sea; others cheerfully stretched out their necks to the headsman's axe; some died under torture; others were starved to death; others again were crucified, some as criminals usually are, some with still greater cruelty nailed the other way up, head down, and kept alive till they starved to death on the very cross.

9. But words cannot describe the outrageous agonies endured by the martyrs in the Thebais. They were torn to bits from head to foot with potsherds like claws till death released them. Women were tied by one foot and hoisted high in the air, head downwards, their bodies completely naked without a morsel of clothing, presenting thus the most shameful, brutal, and inhuman of all spectacles to everyone watching. Others again were tied to trees and stumps and died horribly; for with the aid of machinery they drew together the very stoutest boughs, fastened one of the martyr's legs to each, and then let the boughs fly back to their normal position; thus they managed to tear apart the limbs of their victims in a moment. In this way they carried on, not for a few days or weeks, but year after year. Sometimes ten or more, sometimes over twenty were put to death, at other times at least thirty, and at yet others not far short of sixty; and there were occasions when on a single day a hundred men as well as women and little children were killed, condemned to a succession of ever-changing punishments.

I was in these places, and saw many of the executions for myself. Some of the victims suffered death by beheading, others punishment by fire. So many were killed on a single day that the axe, blunted and worn out by the slaughter, was broken in pieces, while the exhausted executioners had to be periodically relieved. All the time I observed a most wonderful eagerness and a truly divine power and enthusiasm in those who had put their trust in the Christ of God. No sooner had the first batch been sentenced, than others from every side would jump on to the platform in front of the judge and proclaim themselves Christians. They paid no heed to torture in all its terrifying forms, but undaunted spoke boldly of their devotion to the God of the universe and with joy, laughter, and gaiety received the final sentence of death: they sang and sent up hymns of thanksgiving to the God of the universe till their very last breath.

Wonderful as these were, far, far more wonderful were those who were conspicuous for their wealth, birth, and reputation, and for learning and philosophy, yet put everything second to true religion and faith in our Saviour and Lord Jesus Christ. One was

Philoromus, who had been entrusted with an important office in the imperial administration at Alexandria, and with his authority and Roman rank had a military bodyguard and conducted judicial investigations every day. Another was Phileas, Bishop of Thmuis, a man esteemed for his patriotic activities and public services, and for his work as a philosopher. Great numbers of relations and friends implored them, as did prominent officials, and the judge himself appealed to them to pity themselves and spare their wives and children; yet all this was not enough to make them yield to love of life and despise our Saviour's warning about confessing and denying Him. So with manly and philosophic determination, or rather with heartfelt devotion and love of God, they stood like rocks against all the judge's threats and insults, and were both beheaded.

Phileas the martyr's written account of events at Alexandria

10. Since I have said that Phileas made his mark by his secular learning too, let him come forward as his own witness, to make clear what sort of man he was and at the same time to describe, more accurately than I could and in his own words, the martyrdoms that took place at Alexandria in this day.

EXCERPT FROM THE LETTER OF PHILEAS TO THE THMUITES

With all these examples and precedents and trustworthy signposts before their eyes in the inspired and holy Scriptures, the blessed martyrs among us did not hesitate, but directing the eye of the soul [1] with all earnestness towards the Almighty, and resolved to die for their faith, they clung firmly to their vocation, aware that our Lord Jesus Christ became man for our sakes, in order to destroy every kind of sin and make it possible for us to enter into eternal life. For He did not regard it as a prize to be on an equality with God, but emptied Himself, taking the form of a bondservant, and appearing in human shape submitted humbly to death, and death on the cross. [2] So, eagerly desiring the greater gifts, [3] the Christ-bearing martyrs endured every kind of suffering and every outrage that iniquity could invent, not once but twice in some cases; and then their armed

1. Cf. Plato, *Republic*, 533D.   2. Phil. ii. 6–8, slightly abridged.   3. 1 Cor. xii. 31.

guards competed not only in making all sorts of threats against them, but also in carrying them out, they never wavered, because perfect love casts out fear.[1]

What words would suffice to recount their heroic courage under every torture? Liberty was given to all who wished to insult them, and some struck them with cudgels, some with sticks, some with whips, others with straps, and yet others with rope-ends. The spectacle of these outrages was constantly changing and abominable through and through. Some, with their hands tied behind them, were hung from the gibbet and all their limbs were pulled apart by machines; then the torturers were ordered to get to work on every part of their helpless bodies, not as with murderers applying their instruments of correction to sides alone, but even to belly, legs, and cheeks. Others were hung by one hand from the porch and hauled up: no agony could have been so horrible as the stretching of their joints and limbs. Others were bound to pillars, facing inwards, with their feet off the ground and the weight of the body drawing the ropes tighter and tighter. This they endured, not only while the governor was busy haranguing them, but almost all day long. Whenever he went on to another group, he left subordinate officials to keep an eye on the first, in case anyone succumbed to the tortures and seemed to be giving in. He instructed them to add unsparingly to their bonds, and then when they were at the last gasp to cut them down and drag them away. They were not to show the least consideration for us but to regard us and treat us as if we no longer existed, this being the second torture devised by our adversaries in addition to the floggings. Some, even after these outrageous sufferings, were put in the stocks with their feet stretched out all four holes apart, so that they were forced to lie on their backs, incapacitated by the open wounds with which the blows had covered their entire bodies. Others were hurled to the ground and lay helpless as a result of the concentrated onslaught of the torturers, presenting to the spectators a sight more horrible than the torture itself, as they bore in their bodies marks of the elaborate and unlimited ingenuity of the torturers.

In this state of affairs some died under their tortures, shaming their adversary by their unshakeable determination; others were locked up in prison half dead, and a few days later were overcome by their agonies and so found fulfilment; the rest responded to treatment and time, and their stay in prison restored their confidence. So when the order was given, they were invited to choose between touching the abominable sacrifice (in which case they would go unmolested, receiving from their persecutors

1. 1 John iv. 18.

the freedom that brought a curse with it) and refusing to sacrifice and so incurring the supreme penalty. Without hesitating a moment, they went gladly to their death, knowing what Holy Scripture has laid down for us: 'He who sacrifices to other gods shall be utterly destroyed',[1] and 'You shall have no gods other than Me'.[2]

Such was the message that the martyr, truly both lover of wisdom and lover of God, sent to the Christians of his diocese before the final sentence, while he was still undergoing imprisonment, explaining his own situation and at the same time urging them on to hold firmly, even after his approaching fulfilment, to true religion in Christ.

Martyrs in Phrygia; various ordeals of many others of both sexes

But why need I tell a long story, piling up examples of the victories won by devoted martyrs all over the world, especially those who were attacked now not under common law but as enemies in war? 11. For example a little Christian town in Phrygia was encircled by legionaries, who set it on fire and completely destroyed it, along with the entire population – men, women, and children – as they called on Almighty God. And why? Because all the inhabitants of the town without exception – the Mayor himself and the magistrates, with all the officials and the whole populace – declared themselves Christians and absolutely refused to obey the command to commit idolatry.

There was also a man whom the Romans had raised to high office, Adauctus by name. He came from a distinguished Italian family, and had progressed through all the offices tenable under the emperors, giving complete satisfaction in the general administration of what the Romans call *magistratus* or the ministry of finance. As in addition to all this he set a shining example by the splendid things he did in his religious fervour, and by his bold confession of the Christ of God, he was adorned with the crown of martyrdom: he was still serving as finance minister when he faced his ordeal for his religion's sake.

1. Ex. xxii. 20.   2. Ex. xx. 3.

12. Need I now mention the rest by name, or count all the men, or depict the constantly changing outrages suffered by the amazing martyrs? Sometimes they were killed with the axe, as it happened to those in Arabia; sometimes their legs were broken – the fate of those in Cappadocia. Sometimes they were hung up by the feet head down over a slow fire, so that the smoke rising from the burning wood choked them, as was done to those in Mesopotamia; sometimes noses, ears, and hands were severed, and the other parts and portions of the body cut up like meat – the procedure at Alexandria.

Need I rekindle the memory of the martyrs at Antioch, who were roasted over lighted braziers, not roasted to death but subjected to prolonged torture? Or of others who plunged their hands right into the fire sooner than touch the abominable sacrifice? Some of them were unable to face such a trial, and before they were caught and came into the hands of their would-be destroyers, threw themselves down from the roofs of tall houses, regarding death as a prize snatched from the scheming hands of God's enemies.

At Antioch there was a saintly person [1] whose woman's body housed an indomitable spirit. Universally respected for wealth, birth, and good judgement, she had brought up on religious principles a couple of unmarried daughters in the full flower of their girlish charm. These aroused a great deal of envy: as a result every effort was made to track them to their hiding-place; and when it was discovered that they were living abroad they were purposely summoned to Antioch, and were at the mercy of the soldiers. Seeing that her daughters and herself were in dire peril she opened their eyes to the dreadful things they must expect at human hands, and of all dreadful things the most unbearable – the threat to their chastity. She impressed on the girls and herself too the necessity of shutting their ears to any such suggestion, declaring that to surrender their souls to be enslaved by demons was worse than any death and any destruction, and putting it to them that the only way to escape from it all was to take refuge with the

1. Domnina.

Lord. All three agreed on this, so they arranged their garments
neatly about them, and when they had travelled exactly half way
they modestly requested the guards to excuse them a moment, and
threw themselves into a river that flowed by.

These three made away with themselves. But there was another
couple of girls, again at Antioch, Christians in every respect and
sisters indeed, aristocratic by birth, splendid in their lives, young in
years, charming in appearance, serious in their outlook, religious
in their conduct, admirable in their devotion; but as if such
perfection was too much for the earth to support, they were
thrown into the sea by command of the demon's devotees.

Things that would make the hearer shudder were done to
others in Pontus. Pointed reeds were driven into the fingers of
both hands under the ends of the nails; in other cases lead was
melted over a fire and the boiling seething mass poured down
their backs, roasting the vital parts of the body; others endured in
their private parts and bowels sufferings shameful, merciless, and
unmentionable, which the noble judges, upholders of the law,
showing off their brutality as proof of their cleverness, most
ingeniously devised: by constantly inventing new outrages, as if
they were taking part in a prize competition, they tried their
hardest to put each other in the shade.

These miseries came to an end when, worn out at last by their
ghastly wickedness, tired of killing, satiated and surfeited with
bloodshed, they turned to what seemed to them kindness and
humanity: they thought they were no longer doing us any harm.
It was not in good taste, they said, to pollute the city with the
blood of people of their own race, or to lay the highest levels of
government open to the charge of cruelty, a government mild and
gentle to all; rather ought the beneficence of the humane imperial
authority to be extended to everybody, no one henceforth being
punished with death: they had already ceased to impose this
penalty on us, thanks to the emperor's humanity. Orders were
then issued that eyes should be gouged out and one leg maimed.
That is what they meant by 'humanity' and 'the lightest of
punishments' inflicted on us. As a result of this 'humanity' shown
by God's enemies, it is no longer possible to count the enormous

number of people who first had the right eye hacked out with a
sword and cauterized with fire, and the left foot rendered useless
by branding-irons applied to the joints, and then were condemned
to the province's copper mines, not so much to secure their
services as to subject them to ill-treatment and physical hardship, to
say nothing of the various other ordeals that befell them and were
too numerous to list, for their heroic achievements went beyond
all reckoning.

In these trials the splendid martyrs of Christ let their light so
shine over the whole world that they everywhere astounded the
eyewitness of their courage – and small wonder: they furnished in
themselves unmistakable proof of our Saviour's truly divine and
ineffable power. To mention each one by name would be a
lengthy task – nay, an impossibility.

*Church leaders who by their blood proved the religion they
preached genuine*

13. Of leading churchmen martyred in important cities the first
whose name we must blazon on monuments to God's faithful
servants as a martyr of Christ's kingdom was Bishop Anthimus of
Nicomedia, who was beheaded. Of the martyrs at Antioch the
one who was noblest throughout his life was a local presbyter,
Lucian, who at Nicomedia, when the emperor himself was there,
had proclaimed the heavenly kingdom of Christ, first by a spoken
defence of the Faith, then by deeds as well. Of the martyrs in
Phoenicia the most famous are surely God's altogether beloved
pastors of the spiritual nurslings of Christ – Tyrannion, bishop of
the church at Tyre, Zenobius, presbyter of the church at Sidon,
and Silvanus, Bishop of Emesa and the neighbouring churches.
Silvanus became food for beasts with others at Emesa itself, and
was taken up into the choirs of martyrs; the other two glorified
the word of God in Antioch by enduring to the last. One of them,
the bishop, was thrown into the depths of the sea, while Zenobius,
the best of physicians, died bravely under the torments applied to
his sides. Of the martyrs in Palestine, Silvanus, Bishop of Gaza and

the neighbouring churches, was beheaded at the copper mines in Phaeno, with thirty-nine others. There also two Egyptian bishops, Peleus and Nilus, with several others, were burnt at the stake.

And now also mention must be made of the chief glory of the Caesarean community, Pamphilus, a presbyter and the most wonderful man of my time, the marvel of whose heroic achievements I shall describe when the moment is opportune. Of those at Alexandria and throughout the Thebais and the rest of Egypt who found glorious fulfilment, I must mention first Peter, Bishop of Alexandria itself, a splendid example of the teachers of true religion in Christ; of the presbyters with him, Faustus, Dius, and Ammonius, fulfilled martyrs of Christ; and Phileas, Hesychius, Pachymius, and Theodore, bishops of the Egyptian churches. Besides these there were countless other prominent persons who are commemorated by the churches to their area and locality.

To commit to writing the ordeals of those who battled all over the world for the true worship of the Deity, and to set out in detail everything that happened to them, are no tasks for me: they are surely reserved for those who saw the events with their own eyes. But the struggles I myself witnessed I shall put on record, for the benefit of future generations, in another work. However, in the present book I shall follow up my record with the recantation of the measures taken against us and all the events that followed the opening of the persecution, matters of very great moment to my readers.

As regards the state of the Roman government before the war against us, in every period when the emperors were friendly to us and peaceably disposed, it is beyond the power of words to describe the harvest and abundance of good things that it enjoyed, when the supreme rulers of the world-wide empire, on reaching their tenth and twentieth year, spent their time in festivities and public gatherings, in the gayest of banquets and jollifications, with complete and stable peace. But as there was no obstacle to the growth of their authority, which daily became more inflated, they suddenly abandoned their peaceful attitude to us and launched an implacable campaign. The second year of this kind of activity had not yet run its course, when a shock at the centre of affairs turned the whole system upside down. An unfortunate illness struck down the most senior of the four emperors,[1] resulting in mental derangement; so, together with the one next to him in order of precedence,[2] he returned to normal private life. And this had not yet come about when the whole empire was split in two, a thing that had never happened before, if memory serves.

Not very long afterwards the Emperor Constantius, who throughout his life showed a gentle and kindly spirit towards his subjects and a friendly attitude to the divine teaching, after appointing his lawful son Constantine Emperor and Augustus in his place, paid his debt to nature, and so became the first of the four to be proclaimed one of the gods by the Romans, the recipient of every posthumous honour that could be bestowed on an emperor, and the kindest and mildest of emperors. He was the only one in my time who spent the whole of his reign in a manner worthy of his exalted position. In all ways he showed himself most considerate and benevolent towards everyone: above all he took no part in the campaign against us – indeed he saved God's servants among his subjects from injury and ill-usage, and he neither pulled down church buildings nor caused us any other mischief. So he achieved a conclusion to his life that was happy and supremely blest; for he alone while still emperor died in an atmosphere of goodwill and glory, to be succeeded by a lawful son in every way most prudent and most religious.

His son Constantine was immediately proclaimed Absolute Ruler and Augustus by the legions – and long before them by the Supreme Ruler, God Himself; and he determined to emulate his father's reverent attitude to our teaching.

Later Licinius, by common vote of the princes, was declared Emperor and Augustus. This was a bitter blow to Maximin, who was everywhere still entitled only Caesar. So, being a tyrant to the marrow, he impudently usurped the honour and became a self-appointed Augustus. Meanwhile, it was discovered that a plot to kill Constantine had been hatched by the man who, as already explained, had abdicated and then resumed office, and he died a

1. Diocletian.   2. Maximian.

most ignominious death: he was the first whose complimentary inscriptions and statues, and everything else that it is customary to set up, were thrown down as being reminders of a foul monster.

The conduct of the enemies of true religion

14. His son Maxentius, who assumed autocratic power in Rome, began by making a pretence of our faith in order to gratify and flatter the citizens. He commanded his subjects to cease persecuting the Christians, putting on the guise of religion and trying to appear considerate and much gentler than his predecessors. But what people hoped he would be was very different from what he turned out to be. He plunged into every kind of depravity, and there was not one filthy, dissolute act of which he was innocent, given up as he was to adultery and sexual corruption in all its forms. He would take respectable married women away from their husbands, insult and grossly dishonour them, and send them back to their husbands; and he took care not to victimize unknown or obscure persons, but to make the most outstanding of the senior members of the Roman Senate the chief recipients of his besotted attentions. The whole city cowered before him, common people and magistrates, well known and unknown, worn down by his cruel tyranny: not even when they stayed quiet and made doormats of themselves was there any escape from the tyrant's bloodthirsty cruelty. With a trivial excuse he once handed the people over to be massacred by his bodyguard, and thousands of Roman citizens were killed in the heart of the city, not by Scythians or other foreigners, but by their fellow-citizens in full military array. How many senators were massacred because of designs on their property cannot possibly be determined: for one fabricated reason or other hundreds were put to death. The culmination of the tyrant's crimes was his resort to witchcraft: full of magical notions, he sometimes ripped up pregnant women, sometimes scrutinized the entrails of new-born babies, slaughtered lions, and invented unspeakable rites to call up demons and avert the threat of war; for in these practices lay all his hope of emerging victorious.

What this man did while lording it at Rome to enslave his subjects defies description: they were reduced to such desperate

straits for lack of even essential food as my contemporaries inform
me have never once been known at Rome.

The eastern despot Maximin, as if he were tarred with the same
brush, made a secret alliance with Maxentius in Rome, and for a
long time imagined that no one was any the wiser. (Actually he
was later found out and paid the penalty he deserved.) It was
wonderful what blood-brothers in crime the two of them
appeared, or rather how Maximin robbed his opposite number of
the first prize for villainy. Quacks and impostors held the highest
place in his esteem; terrified at every sound, and horribly superstiti-
ous, he was at the mercy of his illusions about idols and demons.
Without divinations and oracles he could not bring himself to
move a hair's breadth. The result was that he devoted himself to
the persecution against us with more vehemence and determination
than his predecessors, ordering temples to be built in every city
and the sacred precincts which had gone to ruin with the lapse of
time to be carefully restored; he appointed priests of idols in every
locality and city, and over these a high priest of every province
chosen from the public servants of the first rank and distinguished
in every branch of civic life, with a bodyguard of armed soldiers;
and with utter recklessness he rewarded all impostors, as the pious
darlings of the gods, with governorships and the highest
privileges.

From that time on he tortured and oppressed not one city or
district, but the provinces under him, whole and complete, by
exactions of gold and silver and goods without stint, and by very
heavy impositions and a variety of judicial penalties. Robbing the
wealthy of the property their ancestors had bequeathed to them he
lavished unbounded wealth and mountains of goods on his circle
of flatterers. His drunken orgies he carried to such a pitch that in
his cups he went crazy and out of his mind, and issued orders
when drunk which he regretted next day when sober. In de-
bauchery and wild self-indulgence he brooked no rival, appointing
himself a teacher of wickedness to those round him, both rulers
and ruled. He induced the army to grow soft through utter self-
indulgence and wantonness, and invited governors and army
commanders to ruin their subjects with plundering and extortion,

as if they were his co-tyrants. Need I recall his crimes of lust, or count the host of women he seduced? He was incapable of passing through a town without leaving a trail of dishonoured wives and ravished maidens. These things went as he wanted with all except Christians, who laughed at death and snapped their fingers at his vile tyranny. The men endured fire and sword and crucifixion; wild beasts and submersion in the sea; severance of limbs and branding; stabbing and gouging out of eyes; mutilation of the entire body; and, in addition, starvation, fetters, and the mines – they were prepared to endure anything for religion's sake, rather than give to idols the reverence due to God. As for the women, schooled by the divine word, they showed themselves as manly as the men. Some underwent the same ordeals as the men, and shared with them the prize of valour; others, when dragged away to dishonour, gave up their souls to death rather than their bodies to that dishonour. Alone among those whom the tyrant tried to seduce at Alexandria, a Christian woman of the greatest eminence and distinction[1] won the victory by her heroic spirit over the lustful and wanton soul of Maximin. Famed for her wealth, birth, and education, she put everything second to modesty. In spite of his constant advances and her willingness to die, he could not put her to death, because desire was stronger than anger; but he exiled her as a punishment, and appropriated all her possessions. Numberless others were assailed by provincial governors, but refusing even to listen to a threat of sexual relations, underwent every kind of punishment: they were racked and tortured till they died.

Wonderful as were these, the palm goes to a woman at Rome[2] – like them a Christian – who was quite the noblest and most modest of all the intended victims of the besotted tyrant there, Maxentius, whose conduct was only too like Maximin's. When she was told that the tyrant's pandars were at her door, and that her husband – a Roman prefect at that – through fear had given them leave to seize her and take her away, she begged to be excused a moment, as if to dress herself for the occasion. Then she went into her own room, shut the door, and stabbed herself to the

---

1. Dorothea.   2. Sophronia.

heart, dying instantly. Her dead body she left to the emperor's pimps; but by deeds that spoke more loudly than any words she proclaimed to all men then living or yet to come that the only unconquerable and indestructible possession was a Christian's virtue. So far could vileness be carried, as practised at one and the same time by the two tyrants who had divided east and west between them. Would anyone who sought the reason for these crimes fail to put his finger on the persecution against us? Particularly as this appalling state of confusion did not come to an end until Christians got back their freedom.

What happened to those outside the Church

15. Throughout the ten-year period of the persecution, their plotting and campaigning against each other continued without intermission. The seas were unnavigable, and wherever people sailed from they could not avoid being subjected to outrages of every sort: they were racked, and had their sides torn open, and were interrogated with the aid of an endless variety of tortures, on the pretext that they might be enemy agents; finally they were subjected to crucifixion or to punishment by fire. Then again the manufacture of shields and breastplates, and the preparation of javelins, spears, and other munitions of war, not to mention warships and naval equipment, went on apace everywhere, and no one could look for anything but an enemy attack any day. On them, too, fell the famine and pestilence that followed. I shall give the necessary details at the proper time.

The change for the better

16. Such were the conditions that persisted throughout the persecution, which in the tenth year by the grace of God came to a complete end, having begun to die down after the eighth. For when it became evident that we were in the kindly, beneficent keeping of divine and heavenly grace, an amazing thing happened – our rulers, the very people who had long been the driving force behind the campaign against us, changed their minds in a most

astonishing manner and solemnly recanted, extinguishing by means of decrees sympathetic to us and ordinances of the mildest character the fire of persecution which had raged so fiercely. It was no human initiative that brought this about – no pity, as might be suggested, or humanity on the part of the rulers. Anything but that: they were from the start daily devising against us still further measures yet more drastic; by multifarious and constantly changing schemes they were for ever inventing new ways of outraging us. It was a manifest visitation of divine providence, which became reconciled to the common people but took action against the perpetrator of these crimes,[1] indignant with him as being primarily responsible for the whole iniquitous persecution. It was indeed inevitable that these things should come about as a divine judgement, but 'Woe', the Scripture says, 'to the man through whom the stumbling-block comes'.[2] He was pursued by a divinely ordained punishment, which began with his flesh and went on to his soul. Without warning, suppurative inflammation broke out round the middle of his genitals, then a deep-seated fistular ulcer: these ate their way incurably into his inmost bowels. From them came a teeming indescribable mass of worms, and a sickening smell was given off; for the whole of his hulking body, thanks to over-eating, had been transformed even before his illness into a huge lump of flabby fat, which then decomposed and presented those who came near with a revolting and horrifying sight. Of the doctors, some were unable to endure the overpowering and extraordinary stench, and were executed on the spot; others, unable to be of any assistance now that the entire mass had swollen up and deteriorated beyond hope of recovery, were put to death without mercy.

The recantation of the emperors

17. As he wrestled with this terrible sickness, he was filled with remorse for his cruel treatment of God's servants. So he pulled himself together, and after first making open confession to the

1. Galerius.   2. Paraphrased from Luke xvii. 1.

God of the universe, he called his court officials and ordered them to lose no time in stopping the persecution of Christians, and by an imperial law and decree to stimulate the building of churches and the performance of the customary rites, with the addition of prayers for the Emperor's Majesty. Action immediately followed the word, and imperial ordinances were published in all the cities, setting forth in the following terms the recantation by the emperors of our time:

The Emperor Caesar Galerius Valerius Maximianus Invictus Augustus, Pontifex Maximus, Germanicus Maximus, Egyptiacus Maximus, Thebaicus Maximus, Sarmaticus Maximus five times, Persicus Maximus twice, Carpicus Maximus six times, Armeniacus Maximus, Medicus Maximus, Adiabenicus Maximus, Holder of Tribunician Authority for the twentieth time, Imperator for the nineteenth, Consul for the eighth, Pater Patriae, Proconsul; the Emperor Caesar Flavius Valerius Constantinus Pius Felix Invictus Augustus, Pontifex Maximus, Holder of Tribunician Authority, Imperator for the fifth time, Consul, Pater Patriae, Proconsul; and the Emperor Caesar Valerius Licinianus Licinius Pius Felix Invictus Augustus, Pontifex Maximus, Holder of Tribunician Authority for the fourth time, Imperator for the third, Consul, Pater Patriae, Proconsul – in the people of their several provinces, greeting.

Among the other steps that we are taking for the advantage and benefit of the nation, we have desired hitherto that every deficiency should be made good, in accordance with the established law and public order of Rome; and we made provision for this – that the Christians who had abandoned the convictions of their own forefathers should return to sound ideas. For through some perverse reasoning such arrogance and folly had seized and possessed them that they refused to follow the path trodden by earlier generations (and perhaps blazed long ago by their own ancestors), and made their own laws to suit their own ideas and individual tastes and observed these; and held various meetings in various places.

Consequently, when we issued an order to the effect that they were to go back to the practices established by the ancients, many of them found themselves in great danger, and many were proceeded against and punished with death in many forms. Most of them indeed persisted in the same folly, and we saw that they were neither paying to the gods in heaven the worship that is their due nor giving any honour to the god of the Christians. So in view of our benevolence and the established custom by which we invariably grant pardon to all men, we have thought proper

279

in this matter also to extend our clemency most gladly, so that Christians may again exist and rebuild the houses in which they used to meet, on condition that they do nothing contrary to public order. In a further letter we shall explain to the justices what principles they are to follow. Therefore, in view of this our clemency, they are in duty bound to beseech their own god for our security, and that of the state and of themselves, in order that in every way the state may be preserved in health and they may be able to live free from anxiety in their own homes.

So ran the edict in the original Latin, which I have turned into Greek to the best of my ability. What happened subsequently it is now time to consider.

APPENDIX

The author of the edict had no sooner made this confession, than he was released from his bodily torments; but in a very little while he was dead. It is on record that he had been the prime mover in the calamitous persecution, for long before the other emperors made a move he had used physical violence to pervert the Christians in the armed forces, after starting with the members of his own household. Some he had deprived of their military rank, some he had insulted most shamefully, others he had actually threatened with death. Finally, he had incited the fellow-emperors to undertake a worldwide persecution.

It would not be proper to pass over the deaths of these men in silence. Of the four who had shared worldwide rule, the two who were senior in years and status [1] abdicated less than two years after the start of the persecution, as I have already explained, and after passing the rest of their lifetimes like any ordinary citizens, met their end as follows. The one who had reached first place in status and years [2] succumbed to a prolonged and very painful physical disease. The one who held second place strangled himself, thereby fulfilling a demon-inspired prediction, for he had been guilty of innumerable atrocities. Of the junior pair, the occupant of the last place, [3] who as already stated was the person behind the whole

---

1. Diocletian and Maximian.   2. Diocletian.   3. Galerius.

persecution, suffered the fate described above, but his immediate superior, the kindest and mildest of emperors, Constantius, spent the whole of his reign in a manner worthy of his exalted position. In all ways he showed himself most considerate and benevolent towards everyone; above all, he stayed outside the campaign against us and saved God's servants among his subjects from injury and ill-usage, and he neither pulled down the church buildings nor caused us any other mischief whatever. So he truly achieved a conclusion to his life that was happy and supremely blest; for he alone while still emperor died in an atmosphere of goodwill and glory, to be succeeded on the throne by a lawful son in every way most prudent and religious. He was immediately proclaimed Absolute Ruler and Augustus by the legions, and he determined to emulate his father's reverent attitude to our teaching.

Such were the ways in which, one by one, the lives of the four men of whom I have written above came to an end. Last of them to survive was the man of whom I wrote a little way back.[1] He, with those later admitted to the highest office,[2] in the document reproduced above published for all to read the confession which I have described.

1. Galerius.   2. Maximin, Constantine, and Licinius.

Book 9

The pretence of relaxation

1. The recantation of the imperial will set forth above was published up and down the whole of Asia and in the adjoining provinces of the empire. When this task had been accomplished, Maximin, tyrant in the east – a bitter enemy of religion if ever a man was, and most hostile to the worship of the God of the universe – found what was written little to his liking; instead of circulating the letter set forth above, he gave oral instructions to his subordinate officials to relax the campaign against us. As he could find no other way to reverse the decision of his superiors, he put on one side the ordinance set forth above, and making sure that in the areas under his control it should never be brought to light, he issued verbal instructions to his subordinate officials to relax the persecution against us. They put the order in writing for each other's information. For example, the man they had honoured with the title of His Excellency the Prefect, Sabinus, informed the provincial governors of the emperor's wishes in a letter written in Latin, the translation of which is as follows:

With the most shining and dedicated zeal the Divinity of our most divine masters, the Emperors, has long been resolved to lead the thoughts of all men to the holy and right way of life, in order that even those who apparently follow customs alien to the Romans might render to the immortal gods the worship that is their due. But the opposition and fierce resistance of some was so extreme that the sound logic of the order failed to shake their fixed purpose, and the threatened punishment had no terrors for them. Since therefore the result of such behaviour was that many were involving themselves in danger, the Divinity of our masters, the most mighty potentates, in accordance with the habitual grandeur of their devotion to the gods, deeming it alien to their own most divine purpose that for such a cause they should involve the men in so great danger, issued a command that through my Dedicatedness your Sagacity should be informed in writing that if any of the Christians were found practising the religion of his own people, you must safeguard him from molestation and from danger, and must not on these grounds hold any man guilty of a punishable offence, inasmuch as in the course of so long a time it has become evident that it is impossible to persuade them by any means whatever to abandon their determined opposition. It is therefore your Vigilance's duty to write to the sheriffs, magistrates, and *praepositi* of every urban district, in order that they may realize that it is incumbent on them to take no action that goes beyond what is here laid down.

Thereupon the provincial governors, having decided that the recommendations in the letter they had received were genuine, wrote to the sheriffs, magistrates, and rural commissioners explaining the imperial decision. It was not only in writing that they gave effect to this policy, but much more by action. To make sure that the imperial will was carried out, they saw to it that all whom they were keeping shut up in prison because of their confession of the Deity were brought out and set free; indeed, they released those prisoners who as a punishment were shackled in the mines — for in their innocence they believed this to be what the emperor really intended.

When these recommendations had been carried out, it was as if all at once a light had shone out of a dark night. In every town could be seen crowded churches, overflowing congregations, and the appropriate ceremonies duly performed. This dumbfounded all the unconverted heathen, who were astonished at the miracle of this transformation and loudly proclaimed that the Christians' God was alone great and true. Of our own people, those who had faithfully and manfully fought through the ordeal of the persecutions again held their heads high in the sight of all; those whose faith had been sickly and their souls storm-tossed made earnest efforts to be made well, begging and imploring those who had stood firm to hold out the right hand of deliverance, and beseeching God to be merciful to them. Then, too, the gallant champions of true religion were released from the misery of the mines and allowed to return to their homes, exulting and beaming as they passed through every town, full of unspeakable joy and a confidence beyond description. Long columns of men and women went on their way, singing psalms and hymns of praise to God in the middle of the highways and city squares. Those who a little while ago had been prisoners, driven from their homeland and punished most cruelly, could be seen with happy, smiling faces regaining their own hearths, so that even those who had earlier been athirst for our blood, when they saw this marvellous thing, so utterly unexpected, shared our joy at what had happened.

The subsequent change for the worse: the idol at Antioch: resolutions attacking us: the forged 'Memoranda'

2. All this was more than could be borne by the tyrant who as I have said ruled the eastern region, for everything noble was hateful to him and all good men were objects of his enmity; in fact, he did not tolerate this state of affairs for as long as six months. He did all he could think of to overthrow the peace. First, he found a pretext for trying to stop us from meeting in the cemeteries; then, through the agency of a number of scoundrels, he sent embassies to himself to appeal against us, having instigated the citizens of Antioch to ask him to grant them a very great favour by absolutely forbidding any Christian to live in their country, and to work it so that others suggested the same thing. The man behind all this belonged to Antioch itself – one Theotecnus, a clever unprincipled trickster who belied his name.[1] Apparently he was the city sheriff.

3. Time after time this man campaigned against us. He left no method untried in his determination to hunt our people out of hiding-places as if they were thieving scoundrels; he employed every device to defame and calumniate us; he engineered the deaths of thousands; finally he set up an image of Zeus the Friendly, with tricks and illusions; invented devilish rites, unholy

---

1. *Theotecnus* means 'God's child'.

initiations, and loathsome purifications; and even in the emperor's presence displayed his magic arts by spurious oracular utterances. In fact, by subtle flattery of the emperor, this man aroused the demon against the Christians: the god, he said, had commanded 'the emperor's enemies', to be cleared right out of the city and its neighbourhood.

4. This man was the first to follow his bent, but all the other authorities in the cities under the same rule lost no time in following his lead: the provincial governors had seen at once that the emperor approved of such a course, and they had advised their subjects to act in this very way. The tyrant was most happy to approve their resolutions, by means of a rescript; so the persecution against us blazed up all over again.

Priests, if you please, were appointed in every town by Maximin himself – priests of the images, and high priests too – men of the greatest note in political life and continuously in the public eye, who were filled with enthusiasm for the worship of the gods they served. The absurd superstition of the emperor, in short, was inducing all under him, rulers and ruled alike, to seek his favour by an all-out attack on us. This was the greatest favour that they could bestow on him, in return for the benefits they expected at his hands – to thirst for our blood and show their spite against us in novel ways.

5. They actually forged *Memoranda* of Pilate and our Saviour, full of every kind of blasphemy against Christ. These, with the approval of their superior, they sent to every district under his command, announcing in edicts that they were to be publicly displayed in every place, whether hamlet or city, for all to see, and that they should be given to children by their teachers instead of lessons, to study and learn by heart.

While these steps were being put into effect, an army officer – called *dux* by the Romans – at Damascus in Phoenicia arranged for some disreputable women to be removed by force from the city square, and threatened to torture them. In this way he compelled them to sign a statement to the effect that they had once been Christians and were aware of breaches of the law by

Christians, who in their very churches were guilty of immoral practices and everything else he wished the women to say in defamation of the Faith. What they said he set down in a report which he passed to the emperor, and at his command he published the document in every city and district.   6. But not long afterwards he, the officer, committed suicide and so paid the penalty of his malignity.

Martyrdoms at this time

For us there was a resumption of banishments and harsh persecution, and of bitter attacks on us by all the provincial governors. As a result, some of the most notable preachers of the world were sentenced to death, with no right of appeal. Three of these in Emesa, a Phoenician town, confessed themselves Christians and were given to wild beasts as food. Among them was a bishop, Silvanus, a very old man who had filled this office for forty years. At the same time Peter, who had presided over the Alexandrian churches most admirably – a splendid example of a bishop in the nobility of his life and his intimate knowledge of Holy Scripture – was suddenly arrested for no reason and without warning, marched off then and there without explanation, and beheaded, as if by Maximin's command. With him many other Egyptian bishops suffered the same fate.

Lucian, a man of the highest character, self-disciplined and steeped in divinity, a presbyter of the Antioch diocese, was taken to Nicomedia, where the emperor then happened to be staying. Before the ruler he put forward his defence of the doctrine he upheld, and was sent to prison and to death.

So swift an onslaught did Maximin, in his hatred of all that is good, direct against us, that the earlier persecution seemed trifling in comparison with this.   7. In the middle of the cities – an unheard of thing – resolutions from cities attacking us, and rescripts embodying imperial decisions on the questions raised, were engraved on bronze tablets and posted up; and the children in the schools daily repeated the names of Jesus and Pilate and the insolent forged *Memoranda.*

Here I find it necessary to insert the actual document set up on tablets by Maximin, in order that the swaggering, arrogant presumption of this enemy of God may be clear to all, and with it the divine justice following hard on his heels with its unsleeping detestation of evil in the wicked. This it was that soon afterwards drove him to treat us in exactly the opposite way, and publish written laws declaring his policy.

COPY OF A TRANSLATION OF MAXIMIN'S RESCRIPT IN
REPLY TO THE RESOLUTIONS ATTACKING US, TAKEN FROM
THE TABLET IN TYRE

At last the feeble presumption of the human mind has succeeded in shaking off and scattering all the black fog of error that till now had wrapped the senses of men not so much wicked as unfortunate in the fatal darkness of ignorance, and was still assailing them; at last it has realized that the beneficent providence of the almighty gods governs it and keeps it secure. It is beyond me to express my extreme gratitude, pleasure, and delight at the magnificent proof you have given of your devout disposition; for even before this no one was unaware of the wonderful reverence and piety you always showed towards the immortal gods, evincing not a faith of bare and empty words but a constant and astonishing flow of notable deeds. And therefore your city deserves to be called the temple and abode of the immortal gods: there are many evidences to prove that it is the residence there of the celestial gods that causes it to flourish.

So it is that your city completely disregarded its private interests and did not press its earlier requests with reference to its own affairs, and when it saw that the adherents of that damnable folly were again beginning to spread – like a neglected and smouldering pyre which when it burns up again becomes a huge blazing mass – instantly and without a moment's delay it fled for refuge to our piety as to a mother-city of all religious feelings, appealing for some remedy and assistance. This salutary thought was undoubtedly planted in you by the gods because of the faith shown by your devotion to them. He therefore it was, he the most high and mighty Jupiter, the guardian of your most glorious city, the protector of your ancestral gods, of your women and children, of your hearth and homes, from all destruction and decay, who inspired your breasts with this wholesome resolve, clearly revealing how wonderful and glorious and salutary it is with due reverence to approach the worship and sacred ceremonies of the immortal gods.

Who could be found so stupid or devoid of all sense as not to see that it is thanks to the beneficent activity of the gods that the soil does not refuse the seeds committed to it and disappoint the hopes and expectations of the farmer? and that the form of impious war does not rise up irresistibly upon the earth while the balmy air of heaven grows foul and men's bodies covered with filth are dragged off to death? and that the sea does not rage and swell under the blasts of the squally winds? and that typhoons do not burst without warning, bringing destruction in their wake? and again that the earth, nurse and mother of all, does not sink down from her deepest hollows with a frightful tremor and the mountains that rise from her face disappear into the chasms thus formed? All these things, and things more terrible still, have in days gone by happened over and over again, as we all know. And all of them happened at once as a result of the fatal error implicit in the empty folly of these immoral people, when it enslaved their minds and by its shameful deeds came near to making the entire world suffer . . .

Let them cast their eyes on the wide plains, where already the crops are ripe with waving ears of corn, and the meadows, thanks to abundance of rain, are bright with flowering plants, and the weather we enjoy is temperate and very mild. Let them rejoice also, every one of them, that through our piety, our sacrifices, and our adoration, the power of the most mighty and most unyielding air has been propitiated; and let them therefore rejoice that they benefit by the most tranquil peace in security and repose. As for all those who have been brought safely out of the blind error in which they wandered, and restored to a right and satisfactory state of mind, let them the more rejoice, as if they had been rescued from a sudden tempest or from a grave illness and were henceforth gathering from life a rich harvest. But if they persist in their damnable folly, let them be thrown out as you requested, and driven right away from your city and neighbourhood, in order that thereby, in accordance with your praiseworthy enthusiasm in this matter, your city may be purged of all contamination and impiety, and in pursuit of its set purpose may with due reverence give itself to the regular worship of the immortal gods.

That you may know how welcome your request in this matter has been to us, and how anxious our mind is, apart from resolutions and entreaties, and of its own accord, to exercise beneficence, we permit your Dedicatedness to ask whatever munificence you wish in return for this your devout purpose. Make up your minds now to do this and receive your reward: it will be yours without the least delay. The fact of its being granted to your city will provide evidence for all time of your devoted piety towards the immortal gods.

This attack on us was engraved on tablets in every province of the Empire, depriving us of any hope, humanly speaking, so that in full accordance with the divine saying, if possible these things should trip up even the elect.[1] Indeed, generally speaking, in the majority expectation was fainting,[2] when all at once, while those in charge of the document attacking us were on their way, with a few miles still to go in some districts, God, the Defender of His own Church, curbing the loud boasting of the tyrant against us, revealed Himself as our ally in heaven.

Famine, pestilence, and war

8. It was the winter season, and the usual rains and showers were withholding their normal downpour, when without warning famine struck, followed by pestilence and an outbreak of a different disease – a malignant pustule, which because of its fiery appearance was known as a carbuncle. This spread over the entire body, causing great danger to the sufferers; but the eyes were the chief target for attack, and hundreds of men, women, and children lost their sight through it.

Besides this, the tyrant had to cope with the war against the Armenians, people who from a very early date had been friends and allies of Rome. They were Christians and zealous adherents of the Deity; so the God-hater attempted to force them to sacrifice to idols and demons, thereby turning them from friends into foes and from allies into enemies.

The conjunction of all these things at one and the same time disproved the presumptuous tyrant's loud boasting against the Deity, for he had had the effrontery to declare that his devotion to the idols and his attack on us prevented any famine or plague or even war from occurring in his time. These things, coming on

---

1. Cf. Matt. xxiv. 24.   2. A very free paraphrase of Luke xxi. 26.

him together and at the same time, formed the prelude to his own downfall. In the Armenian war the emperor was worn out as completely as his legions: the rest of the people in the cities under his rule were so horribly wasted by famine and pestilence that a single measure of wheat fetched 2,500 Attic drachmas. Hundreds were dying in the cities, still more in the country villages, so that the rural registers which once contained so many names now suffered almost complete obliteration; for at one stroke food shortage and epidemic disease destroyed nearly all the inhabitants. Some, indeed, thought fit to sell their most precious possessions to those who were better off, in return for a tiny quantity of food; others parted with their treasures one at a time till they were driven by want to desperate straits; while some ruined their bodily health by chewing small fragments of cattle fodder and recklessly swallowing poisonous plants, with fatal results. As for the women, some leaders of city society were driven by their straits to such shameless necessity that they went out to beg in the public squares, showing signs of their gentle nurture in their shy looks and the care with which they were dressed.

Some people, shrunken like ghosts and at death's door, tottered and slipped about in all directions till, unable to stand, they fell to the ground; and as they lay face down in the middle of the streets, they implored passers-by to hand them a tiny scrap of bread, and with their life at its last gasp they called out that they were hungry – anything else than this anguished cry was beyond their strength. Others – men classed as well-to-do – were astounded by the number of beggars, and after giving to scores, they adopted for the future a hard and merciless attitude, in the expectation that very soon they themselves would be no better off; so that in the middle of public squares and narrow streets dead and naked bodies lay about unburied for days on end, furnishing a most distressing sight to all who saw them. Indeed some even became food for dogs, and it was mainly for this reason that the survivors turned to killing the dogs, for fear they might go mad and begin devouring human flesh. No less terrible was the pestilence which consumed every household, particularly those which were so well off for food that famine could not wipe them out. Men of great wealth, rulers, governors, and numberless officials, left by the famine to the epidemic disease as if on purpose, met a sudden and very swift end. Lamentations filled the air on every side, and in all the lanes, squares, and streets there was nothing to be seen except processions of mourners with the usual flute-playing and beating of breasts. In this way death waged war with these two weapons of pestilence and famine, swallowing whole families in a few moments, so that two or three dead bodies could be seen carried to the graveyard by a single group of mourners.

Such was the reward for Maximin's loud boasts and the cities' resolutions against us, while the fruits of the Christians' limitless enthusiasm and devotion became evident to all the heathen. Alone in the midst of this terrible calamity they proved by visible deeds their sympathy and humanity. All day long some continued without rest to tend the dying and bury them – the number was immense, and there was no one to see to them; others rounded up the huge number who had been reduced to scarecrows all over the city and distributed loaves to them all, so that their praises were sung on every side, and all men glorified the God of the Christians and owned that they alone were pious and truly religious: did not their actions speak for themselves?

At the end of all this, when God, the great and heavenly Defender of Christians, had by such means displayed his wrath as a warning to all men in return for the cruel wrongs they had done us, He again restored to us the kindly, cheering radiance of His providence towards us. As if in black darkness, He most wonderfully illumined us with the light of peace from Himself, making it plain to all that God himself had been watching over us throughout: at first He had scourged His people, and by severe trials had in due time corrected them; then again, after sufficient chastisement, He had shown Himself gracious and kind to all whose hopes were fixed on Him.

The victory of God's beloved emperors

9. Thus Constantine, an emperor and son of an emperor, a religious man and son of a most religious man, most prudent in every way,

as stated above – and Licinius the next in rank, both of them honoured for their wise and religious outlook, two men dear to God – were roused by the King of kings, God of the universe, and Saviour against the two most irreligious tyrants and declared war on them. God came to their aid in a most marvellous way, so that at Rome Maxentius fell at the hands of Constantine, and the ruler of the East[1] survived him only a short time and himself came to a most shameful end at the hands of Licinius, who at that time was still sane.

The senior in imperial rank and position, Constantine, was the first to feel pity for the victims of tyranny at Rome. Calling in prayer on God in heaven and on His Word, Jesus Christ Himself, the Saviour of all, to come to his aid, he advanced at the head of all his forces, intent on recovering for the Romans the liberty of their ancestors. Maxentius, for his part, pinned his faith more to the wiles of a trickster than to the goodwill of his subjects, and could not pluck up courage to go an inch beyond the city gates. Instead he employed a vast host of heavy infantry and countless centuries of legionaries to garrison every region, district, or city, in the neighbourhood of Rome or anywhere in Italy, that he had reduced to slavery. The emperor who clung to God for aid attacked the first, second, and third of the tyrant's concentrations, completely defeated them all, overran a great part of Italy, and arrived almost at the gates of Rome. Then, to save him from the necessity of fighting Romans because of the tyrant, God Himself as it were dragged the tyrant with chains a long way from the city gates; and the words enshrined long ago in Holy Writ as a warning to the wicked – words regarded as mythical by most and disbelieved, but to believers worthy of all belief – by their unmistakable truth compelled the belief of practically everyone, believer or unbeliever, when he saw the miracle before his eyes. In the time of Moses himself and the godfearing nation of the ancient Hebrews,

> The chariots of Pharaoh and his hosts He hurled into the sea;
> His picked horsemen, his captains, He swallowed up in the Red Sea;
> With the deep He covered them.

1. Maximin.

In just the same way Maxentius and his bodyguard of infantry and
pikemen

> Went down into the depths like a stone[1]

when he turned back before the God-given might of Constantine,
and began to cross the river in his path, having himself constructed
a perfectly sound bridge of boats from one bank to the other,
contriving thus an instrument for his own destruction. And so we
might say

> He made a pit and dug it,
> And shall fall into the ditch that he fashioned.
> His labour shall return on to his own head,
> And on his own crown shall his unrighteousness come down.[2]

In this way, through the breaking of the floating bridge, the
crossing collapsed, and in a moment the boats, men and all, went
to the bottom, and first the prime villain, then his bodyguard of
picked men, in the way foretold by the inspired sayings

> Sank like lead in the mighty waters.[3]

Thus, if not in words at any rate in deeds, like the great servant
Moses and his companions, the men who with God's help had
won the victory might well sing the same hymn as was sung
about the villainous tyrant of old:

> Let us sing to the Lord, for gloriously has He been glorified:
> Horse and rider He threw into the Sea.
> The Lord became my helper and protector, to my salvation.[4]

And

> Who is like Thee among the gods, Lord? who is like Thee?
> Glorified among saints, marvellous in praises, doing wonders?[5]

These things, and many others akin to them and just like them,
Constantine by his very deeds sang as a hymn to the universal
Lord, the author of his triumph, God. Then he rode into Rome
with songs of victory, and together with women and tiny children,
all the members of the Senate and citizens of the highest distinction

1. Ex. xv. 4–5.   2. Ps. vii. 15–16.   3. Ex. xv. 10.   4. Ex. xv. 1–2.
5. Ex. xv. 11.

in other spheres, and the whole populace of Rome, turned out in force and with shining eyes and all their heart welcomed him as deliverer, saviour, and benefactor, singing his praises with insatiate joy. But he, as if he possessed an innate reverence for God, was not in the least excited by their shouts or elated by their plaudits, fully aware that his help came from God: at once he ordered a trophy of the Saviour's Passion to be set up under the hand of his own statue – indeed, he ordered them to place him in the most frequented spot in Rome, holding the sign of the Saviour in his right hand, and to engrave this inscription in Latin. I reproduce it exactly:

By this saving sign, the true proof of courage, I saved your city from the yoke of the tyrant and set her free; furthermore I freed the Senate and People of Rome and restored them to their ancient renown and splendour.

After this, Constantine himself and with him the Emperor Licinius – whose mind was not yet unhinged by the mania which later took possession of him – first made things right with God, the author of all their successes; then both with one will and intent formulated on behalf of the Christians a most thoroughgoing law in the fullest terms. Next, an account of the wonders that God had performed for them, of their triumph over the tyrant, and of the law itself, was sent to Maximin, who was still master of the eastern provinces and posing as their friend. He, tyrant that he was, was very upset by what he learnt. He did not wish it to appear that he was giving way to others; on the other hand, he dared not suppress the order, for fear of those who had issued it. So, as if on his own initiative, he perforce indited to the governors under him this first missive on behalf of the Christians; in it he lays claim to actions he had never yet taken, lying about himself.

COPY OF A TRANSLATION OF THE TYRANT'S LETTER

Jovius Maximinus Augustus to Sabinus. I am satisfied that it is obvious to Your Steadfastness and to everybody else that our masters Diocletian and Maximian, our fathers, when they realized that nearly everyone had abandoned the worship of the gods and associated himself with the people known as Christians, were justified in giving orders that all who withdrew from the worship of their own immortal gods should by public correction and punishment be recalled to the worship of the gods. But when I first arrived so auspiciously in the east I was informed that in some localities a great number of people capable of service to the community were for the reason already given being deported by judges, so I gave instructions to each of the judges that for the future none of them was to treat the provincials harshly, but rather by coaxing and persuasion recall them to the worship of the gods. The immediate result was that in conformity with my order the judges carried out their instructions and no one in the eastern region was either deported or interfered with, but rather as a result of the leniency with which they were treated they were recalled to the worship of the gods.

Later, however, when last year I paid an auspicious visit to Nicomedia and was staying there, some of the citizens presented themselves before me, bringing images of the gods and earnestly requesting that in no circumstances should such people be allowed to live in their city. But when I was informed that large numbers of men who practised that same religion lived in that very region, I gave them this answer: I thanked them heartily for their request, but saw that it was by no means unanimous. So, if there were some who persisted in the same superstition, each must keep to his purpose in accordance with his own choice, and if they wished they could acknowledge the worship of the gods. Notwithstanding, to the people of Nicomedia and the other cities which with such enthusiasm have made the same request to me – that none of the Christians should live in their cities – I had no option but to give a friendly answer; for this very principle had been maintained by all my predecessors from the beginning, and the gods themselves, without whom all mankind and the whole administration of the Empire would perish, willed that such a request, put forward on behalf of the worship of their Deity, should be confirmed by me.

The position therefore is this. Particular instructions have in the past been sent in writing to Your Dedicatedness, and express commands have similarly laid it down that provincials who have made up their mind to adhere to such a custom must be treated not harshly, but with forbearance and restraint. Nevertheless, to prevent their suffering insults or blackmail at the hands of *beneficiarii* or anyone else, I have thought it desirable to send this further letter to draw the attention of Your Steadfastness to the advantages of coaxing and persuading the provincials into a proper regard for the gods. If therefore anyone decides by his own choice that the worship of the gods must be acknowledged, such persons may appropriately be welcomed; but if some choose to follow their own worship, you will please leave them free to do so.

My final recommendation to Your Dedicatedness is that you adhere to these instructions, and that you give no one authority to subject our provincials to insults and blackmail; for, as already stated, it is by persuasion and coaxing that our provincials can more appropriately be recalled to the worship of the gods. And in order that this our command may come to the knowledge of all our provincials you are requested to issue an edict of your own, and so give publicity to what we have commanded.

As it was under the compulsion of necessity and not in accordance with his own wishes that he sent out these commands, it was now universally recognized that he was neither truthful nor trustworthy, for already on a previous occasion, after making a similar concession, his attitude had been inconsistent and hypocritical. So none of our people ventured to hold a meeting or appear in public, because not even this was allowed him by the letter, which merely permitted us to be protected from deliberate cruelty, and gave no encouragement to the holding of meetings or building of churches or performance of any of our normal practices. And yet the advocates of peace and true religion had sent him written instructions to allow these very things, and by laws and decrees had conceded them to all their subjects. But this unprincipled scoundrel had made up his mind not to budge an inch – till he found himself in the grip of divine Justice and at long last driven willy-nilly to give way.

Close of the tyrant's life

10. His downfall was brought about by the following circumstance. The burden of the government with which he had so undeservedly been entrusted was too heavy for his shoulders, and for want of a prudent and imperial mentality he was clumsy in his handling of affairs; above all, he was senselessly elated by arrogance and boastfulness, even at the expense of his colleagues in the Empire, who were vastly superior to him in birth, upbringing,

and education, in character and intellect, and in the most important thing of all – prudence and reverence for the true God. He began to display presumption and effrontery, publicly proclaiming himself first in rank. Then, pushing his madness to the point of utter dementia, he broke the treaty he had made with Licinius and brought about a war to the death. It was not long before he had produced universal confusion and set every city in a turmoil. He concentrated all available forces, forming an army of immense size, and set out in battle array to challenge Licinius, pinning his hopes to demons whom, if you please, he regarded as gods, and supremely confident, in view of the immense numbers of his infantry forces.

When the armies met, he found himself deprived of God's assistance, and it was to his rival, who was still on the throne, that the one and only God of all Himself assigned the victory. First to perish was the heavy infantry on which he had placed such reliance; then his personal bodyguard deserted him, leaving him utterly defenceless, and went over to his conqueror. So the wretched man lost no time in stripping off the imperial insignia, of which he was so unworthy, and unmanly, craven coward as he was, slipped unnoticed into the crowd. Then he ran this way and that, hiding in fields and villages. But though he tried so hard to save his skin, he only just succeeded in eluding his pursuers, proving by his own straits the absolute trustworthiness and truth of the inspired sayings:

> No king is saved by great power,
> And a giant will not be saved by the fulness of his strength;
> Vain is a horse for safety.
> And by the fulness of his power he will not be saved.
> Lo, the eyes of the Lord are on those that fear Him.
> Those that hope in His mercy,
> To deliver their souls from death.[1]

In this very way the tyrant, full of shame, reached his own territory. There in his insane fury he began by seizing many priests and prophets of the gods whom he had once so revered and whose oracles had inflamed his warlike ardour, and – on the ground that

---

1. Ps. xxxiii. 16–19.

they had tricked and deceived him, and above all that they had betrayed his safety – he put them to death. Next, he paid tribute to the Christians' God, and to safeguard their freedom drew up a law that went the whole way to meet their case. But the sands had run out, and in a few days his life came to a miserable end.

The law issued by him was as follows:

COPY OF THE TYRANT'S ORDINANCE IN FAVOUR OF THE CHRISTIANS, TRANSLATED FROM LATIN INTO GREEK

The Emperor Caesar Gaius Valerius Maximinus, Germanicus Sarmaticus, Pius Felix Invictus Augustus. That in every way we devote our constant attention to the benefit of our provincials, and desire to furnish them with those things by which the advantage of all is most fully secured, with all such things as are to the advantage and benefit of the community as a whole, tending to the public advantage and meeting the wishes of each individual, is a truth of which all are aware, for everyone who looks at the facts themselves must realize without a shadow of doubt that it is so – of that I am convinced. Whereas therefore before this it has come to our knowledge that with the excuse that orders had been given by Diocletian and Maximian, our most divine fathers, that Christian assemblies were prohibited, blackmail and robbery had been practised on a large scale by public employees, and that with the passage of time this was causing increasing hurt to our provincials – whose interests we strongly desire to be carefully considered – as their own personal possessions were being whittled away: we have sent letters to the governors of each province in the past year, decreeing that if any man chose to follow such a custom or the same form of worship, he might without hindrance hold on to his purpose and be hindered or prevented by none, and that they should have freedom, without any fear or suspicion, to do exactly as each man pleased. But even so it has not escaped our notice that some of the judges have been disregarding our commands and causing our people to feel doubts about our instruction, making them more hesitant to participate in those acts of worship that accorded with their desires.

In order therefore that for the future all suspicion or doubt due to fear may be done away, we have decreed that this ordinance shall be promulgated, making it clear to all that everyone who chooses to follow this sect and form of worship may, in accordance with this our indulgence and in fulfilment of his own choice and desire, participate in such acts of worship as he was accustomed and wishful to practise. Permission to build 'the Lord's houses', as they call them, has also been accorded. Moreover, in order that our indulgence may be yet greater, we have thought it good to make this further decree: if any houses and lands which before this were the legal property of the Christians have through the command of our predecessors passed into the ownership of the Treasury, or been confiscated by any city council – whether these have been publicly auctioned or bestowed as a favour on an individual – all these shall by our command be restored to their former legal owners, the Christians, in order that in this also our piety and loving care may be apparent to all.

These were the tyrant's words, coming less than a year after the posting on tablets of his anti-Christian ordinances. The very man by whom such a little while before we had been judged impious and godless and ruinous to public life – so that we were not permitted to live in the country or the desert, much less in a city – was now drawing up pro-Christian ordinances and decrees; and those who so recently were being destroyed by fire and sword and given as food for beasts and birds before his eyes, and were undergoing every kind of punishment and torture and death – as if, poor wretches, they were godless and impious – are now allowed by the same man to practise their form of worship and permitted to rebuild the Lord's houses; and the tyrant himself allows that they have legal rights!

When he had allowed all this he received a reward, of a sort, for doing so; at any rate, he got a great deal less than his deserts when he was struck all at once by God's scourge, and in the second encounter of the war met his end. The character of his end was not such as befalls the general at the head of his army, who for the sake of his friends and the right again and again plays the man and fearlessly meets a glorious fate in battle, but like an impious enemy of God, while his army still held its position on the field he stayed at home in hiding, till he paid the penalty that fitted his crimes. All at once he was struck by God's scourge over his whole body, so that he was plagued with terrible, agonizing pain and fell prone; he was wasted by hunger, and the whole of his flesh was consumed by an invisible fire sent from God, so that all the contours of his former shape disintegrated and disappeared, and nothing but a collection of dry bones, like a phantom reduced by long years to a skeleton, was left, so that the onlookers could imagine nothing else than that his body had become the grave of his soul, which was interred in what was already a corpse and completely disintegrated. As the fever that consumed him blazed up ever more fiercely from the depths of his marrow, his eyes stood out of his head and fell from their sockets, leaving him blind. But even in this condition he could still breathe, and made open confession to the Lord, begging for death. So at long last he acknowledged that he deserved these torments because of his furious onslaught on Christ, and all was over.

Final destruction of the enemies of true religion

11. The way had now been left clear by Maximin, the last survivor of the enemies of true religion and unmistakably the worst. So the re-establishment of the churches from the foundations was by the grace of Almighty God taken in hand, and the message of Christ, making itself clearly heard to the glory of the God of the universe, was preached with greater freedom than before, while the anti-religious activities of the enemies of true religion were covered with the utmost shame and dishonour. For Maximin had been the first to be proclaimed by the supreme rulers a common enemy of all and posted in public notices as a most anti-religious, abominable, and God-hated tyrant. Of the portraits set up in every city in his honour and his children's, some were flung from a height to the ground and smashed, others had their faces blacked out with dark paint and were damaged beyond repair. The many statues, too, that had been erected in his honour were similarly thrown down and smashed, and lay there an object of jesting and horseplay to all who wished to insult and abuse them.

The next step was to strip the other enemies of the true religion of all their honours, and to execute all Maximin's sympathizers especially those in government circles who had held office under him, and as a sop to him had poured violent and irresponsible

abuse on our teaching. Such was the man who was higher in his
favour and more respected than anyone else, the most trustworthy
of his friends, Peucetius, consul a second and a third time and by
Maximin's appointment chief finance minister; another was Culcianus, who had held every office in turn, a man who had prided
himself on the murder of innumerable Christians in Egypt; to say
nothing of many others who had been chief contributors to the
strengthening and extending of Maximin's tyranny.

Theotecnus too was called to account, for justice was determined
that what he had done to the Christians should never pass into
oblivion. For when he set up the idol at Antioch he had seemed to
be on top of the world, and indeed was rewarded with a governorship by Maximin, but when Licinius arrived at Antioch, he hunted
out the impostors and tortured the prophets and priests of the
newly made idol, to find out the means by which they perpetrated
their frauds. When these tortures made it impossible to hide the
truth, and they revealed that the whole mystery was a fraud
contrived by the arts of Theotecnus, Licinius gave all of them their
deserts: first Theotecnus himself and then his partners in imposture
were subjected to elaborate tortures and handed over to the executioner.

To these were added the sons of Maximin, who had already
made them partners in his imperial honours, with their features
publicly displayed in painted portraits. Those who hitherto had
vaunted their kinship with the tyrant and arrogantly attempted to
lord it over all and sundry suffered the same fate, with every
circumstance of shame; for they did not receive correction[1] or
know or understand the precept in the inspired books:

> Put not your trust in princes,
> In the sons of men, in whom is no salvation.
> His breath shall go forth and he shall return to his earth;
> In that day shall perish all their thoughts.[2]

Thus the wicked were purged away, and the imperial powers
that had been theirs were preserved stable and undisputed for
Constantine and Licinius and for them alone. They made it their

---

1. A reminiscence of Zeph. iii. 2.   2. Ps. cxlvi. 3-4.

first duty to purge the world of enmity towards God, and recognizing the blessings He had lavished upon them, they showed their high purpose and love of God, their devotion and gratitude to the Deity, by their decree in favour of the Christians.

Book 10

PEACE AND RECOVERY OF THE CHURCH: VICTORY OF CONSTANTINE

The peace bestowed on us by God

1. Thanks be to God, the Almighty, the King of the universe, for all His mercies; and heartfelt thanks to the Saviour and Redeemer of our souls, Jesus Christ, through whom we pray that peace from troubles outside and troubles in the heart may be kept for us stable and unshaken for ever.

Together with my prayers I now add Book 10 of the *History of the Church* to its predecessors. This I shall dedicate to you, my most worshipful Paulinus, calling on you to set the seal on the entire work; and it is appropriate that in a perfect number I should here set out the perfect account in celebration of the re-establishment of the churches, obeying the Divine Spirit when He exhorts us thus:

> Sing to the Lord a new song, for He has done marvellous things;
> His right hand and His holy arm have wrought salvation for Him.
> The Lord has made known His salvation;
> In the sight of the heathen He has revealed His righteousness.[1]

As these inspired lines command me, let me now obediently sing aloud the new song, because after those terrifying darksome sights and stories I was now privileged to see and celebrate such things as in truth many righteous men and martyrs of God before us desired to see on earth and did not see, and to hear and did not hear.[2] But they, hastening with all speed, attained far better things in the heavens, caught up in a paradise of divine pleasure;[3] whereas I, acknowledging that even my present lot is better than I deserve, have been more than amazed at the bountiful grace of its

1. Ps. xcviii. 1-2.   2. Adapted from Matt. xiii. 17.   3. See 2 Cor. xii. 4.

Author, and am duly filled with wonder, worshipping Him with my whole soul's strength, and testifying to the truth of the written prophecies which declare:

> Come hither and behold the works of the Lord,
> What wonders He has wrought in the world,
> Making wars cease to the ends of the world:
> The bow He will break and will shatter the weapon,
> And the shields He will burn up with fire.[1]

Happy that all this has been clearly fulfilled in my own time let me proceed with the next part of my story.

Destruction, in the way described, had overtaken the whole brood of God's enemies, and at one stroke had blotted them out from human sight. Thus yet another inspired saying had been fulfilled:

> I saw the wicked high exalted,
> And lifted up like the cedars of Lebanon.
> And I passed by, and lo, he was not;
> And I sought his place, and it was not found.[2]

From that time on a day bright and radiant, with no cloud overshadowing it, shone down with shafts of heavenly light on the churches of Christ throughout the world, nor was there any reluctance to grant even those outside our community the enjoyment, if not of equal blessings, at least of an effluence from and a share in the things that God had bestowed on us.

Re-establishment of the churches

2. Thus all men living were free from oppression by the tyrants; and released from their former miseries, they all in their various ways acknowledged as the only true God the Defender of the godly. Above all for us who had fixed our hopes on the Christ of God there was unspeakable happiness, and a divine joy blossomed in all hearts as we saw that every place which a little while before

1. Ps. xlvi. 8–9.   2. Ps. xxxvii. 33–6.

had been reduced to dust by the tyrants' wickedness was now, as if from a prolonged and deadly stranglehold, coming back to life; and that cathedrals were again rising from their foundations high into the air, and far surpassing in magnificence those previously destroyed by the enemy.

Emperors too, the most exalted, by a succession of ordinances in favour of the Christians, confirmed still further and more surely the blessings that God showered upon us; and a stream of personal letters from the emperor reached the bishops, accompanied by honours and gifts of money. I shall take the opportunity at the proper place in my account to inscribe in this book as on a sacred tablet these communications, translated from Latin into Greek, in order that all who come after us may bear them in remembrance.

Dedication ceremonies everywhere

3. The next stage was the spectacle prayed and longed for by us all – dedication festivals in the cities and consecrations of the newly built places of worship, convocations of bishops, gatherings of representatives from far distant lands, friendly intercourse between congregation and congregation, unification of the members of Christ's body conjoint in one harmony. In accordance with a prophet's prediction, which mystically signified beforehand what was to be, there came together bone to bone [1] and joint to joint, and all that in riddling oracles the scripture infallibly foretold. There was one power of the divine Spirit coursing through all the members, one soul in them all, [2] the same enthusiasm for the faith, one hymn of praise on all their lips. Yes, and our leaders performed ceremonies with full pomp, and ordained priests the sacraments and majestic rites of the Church, here with the singing of psalms and intoning of the prayers given us from God, there with the carrying out of divine and mystical ministrations; while over all were the ineffable symbols of the Saviour's Passion. And together, the people of every age, male and female alike, with all their powers of mind, rejoicing in heart and soul, gave glory through

1. Ez. xxxvii. 7. Eusebius has added the 'joints' to secure the play upon words.
2. Acts iv. 32.

prayers and thanksgiving to the Author of their happiness, God Himself.

Every one of the dignitaries of the Church present delivered a public oration according to his ability, inspiring the great audience. 4. One of the moderately capable came forward into their midst with a prepared discourse. It was a church assembly, and the many pastors present gave him a quiet and orderly hearing. Addressing himself personally to a single bishop, an admirable man and one dear to God, through whose initiative and enthusiasm the most magnificent cathedral in Phoenicia had been built at Tyre, he delivered the following address.

FESTIVAL ORATION ON THE BUILDING OF THE CHURCHES, ADDRESSED TO PAULINUS, BISHOP OF TYRE

Friends of God, and priests[1] clothed with the sacred vestment and the heavenly crown of glory, the divine unction and priestly garments of the Holy Spirit; and you, so young yet the pride of the holy temple of God, honoured with ripe wisdom from God yet renowned for the precious works and deeds of virtue in its youthful prime, on whom the God who holds the entire universe in His hand has Himself bestowed the supreme honour of building His house upon earth and re-establishing it for Christ, His only begotten and firstborn Word, and for Christ's holy and majestic bride – shall I call you a new Bezalel,[2] the master builder of a divine tabernacle, or a Solomon, king of a new and far nobler Jerusalem, or a new Zerubbabel, who adorned the temple of God with the glory that was far greater than the old?[3] And you too, nurslings of the sacred flock of Christ, home of good words, school of self-discipline, and university of true religion, earnest and dear to God.

Long ago, as the inspired records of miraculous signs from God and the wonders performed by the Lord in the service of men were read aloud in our hearing, we might well send up hymns and songs to God; for we were taught to say:

O God, with our ears have we heard, our fathers have told us,
The work which Thou didst in their days, in ancient days.[4]

---

1. Eusebius here writes not *presbyteroi* but *hiereis*, equivalent to Latin *sacerdotes*; he uses the corresponding adjective just below.
2. Ex. xxxv. 30.   3. Hag. ii. 9.   4. Ps. xliv. 1.

But now it is no longer by hearing the spoken word that men learn of the uplifted arm and the heavenly right hand of our God, All-gracious and King of all; but by deeds, if we may put it so, and with our very eyes we see that the traditions of an earlier age were trustworthy and true. And so we may raise our voices in a second hymn of victory and cry aloud:

> As we have heard, so also we have seen
> In the city of the Lord of Hosts, in the city of our God.[1]

And in what city but this new-made city built by God? It is the Church of the Living God, the pillar and basis of truth,[2] and of it another inspired saying joyously declares:

> Glorious things have been spoken of thee,
> O city of God.[3]

And since in this city God the All-Gracious has brought us together through the grace of His Only-begotten, let each of the invited guests sing, nay shout,

> I was glad when they said to me
> 'Into the house of the Lord we will go'

and

> Lord, I have loved the beauty of Thy house,
> And the dwelling-place of Thy glory.[4]

It is not only for each by himself, but for all of us together with one spirit and one soul, to give glory and praise, saying:

> Great is the Lord and highly to be praised
> In the city of our God, in His holy mountain.[5]

For great He is in truth, and great is His house, lofty and stretching far, and lovely in beauty beyond the sons of men.[6] Great is the Lord, who alone does wondrous things; great is He who does things great and unsearchable, glorious and marvellous things of which there is no number;[7] great is He who changes times and seasons, removing kings and setting them up, raising the poor man from the ground and from the dunghill lifting up the needy.[8] He has pulled down princes from their thrones and exalted the humble from the ground; the hungry He has

---

1. Ps. xlviii. 8.   2. 1 Tim. iii. 15.   3. Ps. lxxxvii. 3.
4. Ps. cxxii. 1 and xxvi. 8.   5. Ps. xlviii. 1.   6. Baruch iii. 24 and Ps. xlv. 2.
7. Ps. lxxii. 18 and Job ix. 10.   8. Dan. ii. 21 and Ps. cxiii. 7.

filled with good things and the arms of the proud He has broken.[1] Not only for believers but also for unbelievers has He proved true the record of the ancient narratives, He the Doer of wonders, the Doer of great things, the Master of the universe, the Fashioner of the whole world, the Almighty, the All-Gracious, the one and only God. To Him then let us sing the new song with this as the background to our thought:

> To Him who alone does wondrous things
> (For everlasting is His mercy);
> To Him who smote great kings,
> And slew mighty kings
> (For everlasting is His mercy).
> For in our low estate He remembered us,
> And redeemed us from our adversaries.[2]

The Father of the universe may we praise aloud in such strains without ceasing. The second source of our blessings, our Guide to the knowledge of God, the Teacher of true religion, the Destroyer of the wicked, the Tyrannicide, the Reformer of our life, our Deliverer from despair, Jesus, let us glorify, His name ever on our lips. For He alone, being an All-Gracious Father's unique, All-Gracious Son, in fulfilment of His Father's love for man, most willingly put on the nature of us men who lay far below, doomed to perish. A devoted physician, to save the lives of the sick, sees the horrible danger yet touches the infected place, and in treating another man's troubles brings suffering on himself:[3] but we were not merely sick, or afflicted with horrible ulcers and wounds already festering, but actually lying among the dead, when He by his own efforts saved us from the very abyss of death, because no one else in heaven was strong enough to minister unscathed to the salvation of so many. Alone He took hold of our most painful perishing nature; alone endured our sorrows; alone He took upon Him the retribution for our sins.[4] When we were not half dead, but lying in tombs and graves and by now altogether foul and stinking,[5] He raised us up; and as He did long ago, so now in His eager love for men He surpasses all the hopes of ourselves or anyone else, saving us and giving us His Father's blessings without stint – He the Lifegiver, the Lightbringer, our great Physician and King and Lord, the Christ of God. Then, once for all, seeing that the entire human race was buried in gloomy night and deep darkness through the deceitfulness of

---

1. Luke i. 52–3 and Job xxxviii. 15. 2. Ps. cxxxvi. 4, 17–18, 23–4.
3. Hippocrates, *Breaths*, 1. 4. Adapted from Is. liii. 4–5.
- A reminiscence of John v. 28 and xi. 39.

wicked demons and the activities of accursed spirits, by nothing but His appearing He tore asunder – as easily as the sun's rays melt wax – the imprisoning bonds of our sins.

And now, as a result of this wonderful grace and bounty, the envy that hates good, the demon that loves evil, bursting with rage, lined up all his lethal forces against us. At first he was like a mad dog that closes his jaws on the stones thrown at him and vents on the inanimate missiles his fury against those who are trying to keep him away: he directed his ferocious madness against the stones of the places of worship and the inanimate timbers of the buildings, bringing, as he himself imagined, ruin on the churches. Then he uttered terrible hissings and his own serpent-like sounds, at one time in the threats of godless tyrants, at another in the blasphemous decrees of impious rulers. Again, he vomited forth his own deadly venom, and by his noxious, soul-destroying poisons he paralysed the souls enslaved to him, almost annihilating them by his death-bringing sacrifices to dead idols, and letting loose against us every beast in human shape and every kind of savagery.

But once again the Angel of great counsel, God's great Commander-in-Chief,[1] after the thoroughgoing training of which the greatest soldiers in His kingdom gave proof by their patience and endurance in all trials, appeared suddenly and thereby swept all that was hostile and inimical into oblivion and nothingness, so that its very existence was forgotten. But all that was near and dear to Him He advanced beyond glory in the sight of all, not men only but the heavenly powers as well – sun, moon, and stars, and the entire heaven and earth. So now as never before the most exalted emperors of all, aware of the honour they had been privileged to receive from Him, spit in the faces of dead idols, trample on the lawless rites of demons, and laugh at the old lies handed down by their fathers. But as the one only God they recognize the common Benefactor of themselves and all men, and Christ they acknowledge as Son of God and sovereign Lord of the universe, naming Him 'Saviour' on monuments, and inscribing in royal characters in the middle of the city that is queen of the cities on earth an indelible record of His triumphs and His victories over the wicked. So it is that alone since time began Jesus Christ our Saviour is not acknowledged as an ordinary human king – even by the most exalted on earth – but worshipped as the true Son of the God of the universe and as Himself God.

And no wonder. For which of the kings who ever lived achieved such greatness as to fill the ears and mouths of all men on earth with his name?

1. Joshua v. 14.

What king established laws so just and impartial, and was strong enough to have them proclaimed in the hearing of all mankind from the ends of the earth and to the furthest limit of the entire world? Who made the barbarous, uncivilized customs of uncivilized races give place to his own civilized and most humane laws? Who was for whole ages attacked on every side, yet displayed such super-human greatness as to be for ever in his prime and to remain young throughout his life? Who so firmly established a people unheard-of from the beginning of time that it is not hidden in some corner of the earth but is found in every place under the sun? Who so armed his soldiers with the weapons of true religion that their souls proved tougher than steel in their battles with their opponents? Which of the kings wields such power, leads his armies after death, sets up trophies over his enemies, and fills every place, district, and city, Greek or non-Greek, with votive offerings – his own royal houses and sacred temples, like this cathedral with its exquisite ornaments and offerings?

These things are indeed awe-inspiring and overwhelming, astonishing and amazing, and serve as clear proofs that our Savour is King; for now too

> He spoke, and they were made;
> He commanded, and they were created.[1]

What indeed could withstand the will of the sovereign Lord and Ruler, the Word of God Himself? These things, again, call for a lengthy exposition of their own, if we are to examine them carefully and interpret them. But less importance attaches to the efforts of those who have laboured, in the eyes of Him whom we name God, when He looks at the live temple consisting of us all, and views the house of living and immovable stones,[2] well and securely based on the foundation of the apostles and prophets, Jesus Christ Himself being the chief cornerstone.[3] This stone was rejected by the master builders not only of that old building which no longer exists, but also of the building that still stands and consists of most of mankind – bad builders of bad buildings. But it was accepted by the Father, who laid it then to be for all time the head of the corner of this our common Church. This temple built of you yourselves, a living temple of a living God, the greatest truly majestic sanctuary, I say, whose innermost shrines are hidden from the mass of men and are in truth a Holy Place and a Holy of Holies, who would dare to examine and describe? Who could ever look inside the surrounding

---

1. Ps. xxxiii. 9 and cxlviii. 5.   2. 1 Peter ii. 4.   3. Eph. ii. 20–1.

temple buildings, except the Great High Priest of the universe, who alone is permitted to search out the secrets of every rational soul?

But perhaps there is one other for whom, alone among equals, it is possible to take the second place after Him. I mean the commander at the head of this army, whom the first and great High Priest [1] Himself has honoured with second place in the priestly offices here performed, the shepherd of your spiritual flock, who by the allotment and judgement of the Father was set over your people, as if He had Himself appointed him His votary and interpreter, the new Aaron or Melchizedek, made like the Son of God, [2] abiding and guarded by Him continually through the common prayers of you all. Let him then be permitted alone after the first and greatest High Priest, if not in the first place at any rate in the second, to see and examine the innermost recesses of your souls; for through long experience he has made a thorough test of every man, and by his enthusiasm and attentiveness he has disposed you all in the order and teaching of true religion; and of all men he is best able to give an account to match his deeds of all that by divine power he has accomplished.

Our first and great High Priest tells us that whatever He sees the Father doing, that the Son does likewise. [3] This one looks to the First as a teacher, with the pure eyes of the mind, and whatever he sees Him doing, that he takes as an archetype and pattern, and like an artist he has moulded its image, to the best of his ability, into the closest likeness. In no respect is he inferior to the Bezalel whom God Himself filled with a spirit of wisdom and understanding, and with technical and scientific knowledge, and close to the architect of the temples that symbolized the heavenly types. In the same way this man, having the whole Christ, the Word, the Wisdom, the Light, impressed upon his soul, has built this magnificent shrine for God Most High, resembling in its essence the pattern of the better one as the visible resembles the invisible. Words cannot do justice to his generosity, to his liberal hand, so insatiable in its determination, or to the eagerness of you all, to the generous scale of your contributions, as in splendid rivalry you strove to be in no way behind him in this same purpose.

This site, to put first things first, which by the machinations of our opponents had been buried under a heap of filthy rubbish, he did not disregard or abandon to the malignity of those responsible, though he could have gone to any of the innumerable sites that abounded in the city, and so found an easy solution of the problem and a means of avoiding trouble. Instead, he first braced himself to his task, then roused all

1. Heb. iv. 14.   2. Heb. vii. 1, 3.   3. John v. 19.

Christian people by his enthusiasm, gathered them all together in one great body, and launched his first campaign; for he felt that the church which had been assailed by her enemies, which had suffered before the rest and had endured the same persecutions as we, but before they came to us, and which was like a mother bereft of her children, should be the first to share the enjoyment of the All-Gracious God's munificence. For when the Great Shepherd[1] had driven away the wild beasts and wolves and every kind of savage creature, and had, as the word of God declares, broken the teeth of the lions,[2] deeming it good that His sons should again come together, it was most proper that he should erect the fold of the flock, in order to shame the enemy and avenger and publicly condemn the crimes of the sacrilegious enemies of God.

Now these men no longer exist, these enemies of God – in fact they never did; for after bringing distress on other people and on themselves too, they paid to justice a penalty not to be laughed at, utterly ruining themselves, their friends, and their families. Thus the predictions inscribed so long ago on sacred tablets have been proved trustworthy by events. In them the voice of God speaks the truth throughout, but listen to these declarations about them.

> A sword have the wicked drawn, they have bent their bow,
> To cast down the poor and needy,
> To slay the upright in heart.
> May their sword enter their own hearts,
> And may their bows be broken.[3]

And again:

> Their memorial has perished with a resounding crash,
> And their name Thou hast blotted out for ever and for ever and ever.[4]

For indeed, when they were in trouble,

> They cried, and there was none to save;
> To the Lord, and He did not listen to them.
> They were bound hand and foot and fell;
> But we have risen and have been set upright.[5]

And listen to this prophecy:

1. Heb. xiii. 20.   2. Ps. lviii. 6.   3. Ps. xxxvii. 13–14.
4. Ps. ix. 6, 5.   5. Ps. xviii. 41, xx. 8.

Lord, in Thy city Thou shalt set their image at nought.[1]

The truth of that statement has been established for all to see.

These men, like the giants of old,[2] joined battle with God and have brought their lives to this miserable end. By contrast, the Church that was desolate and rejected by men has by her inspired endurance won the victory we have seen, so that the prophetic voice of Isaiah calls aloud to her thus:

> Be glad, thirsty desert;
> Let the desert rejoice, and blossom as a lily;
> The desert places shall blossom forth and rejoice.
> Be strong, weak hands and feeble knees:
> Take courage, you that are timid at heart;
> Be strong, do not fear.
> Lo, our God dispenses justice and will dispense;
> He will come and save us.
> For (says he) in the desert water broke out,
> And a channel in thirsty soil;
> And the dry ground shall become lush meadows,
> And on the thirsty soil shall be a spring of water.[3]

These things were foretold in words long ago, and set down in sacred books; but the fulfilment has reached us no longer by hearsay but in fact. This desert, this dry ground, this defenceless widow – they cut down her gates with axes as in a thicket of trees, together breaking her down with hatchet and stonemason's hammer; they destroyed her books and set on fire the sanctuary of God; they profaned to the ground the dwelling-place of His name; all that passed by the way plucked her fruit, having first broken down her fences; the boar from the thicket ravaged her and the solitary wild beast devoured her – yet by the miraculous power of Christ, now when He wills it, she has become like a lily. At that time by His command, as of a father who cares, she was disciplined:

> For whom the Lord loves, He disciplines,
> And He whips every son whom He acknowledges.[4]

In moderation, then, she was suitably corrected; and now once more she is commanded to rejoice again, and she blossoms like a lily and breathes her sweet divine odour on all mankind; for, as the Scripture says, in the

---

1. Ps. lxxiii. 20.   2. A reference to the Greek legend, but cf. Gen. vi. 1–4 (LXX).
3. Is. xxxv. 1–7.   4. Prov. iii. 12 and Heb. xii. 6.

desert water broke out, the stream of the divine regeneration by the saving baptism; and now what a little while ago was desert has become lush meadows, and on the thirsty soil has gushed a spring of living water. Strength has indeed come to hands that before were weak; and to the strength of those hands these great and splendid works bear witness. The once diseased and sagging knees have recovered their normal movement, and march straight forward along the road to the knowledge of God, in haste to rejoin the flock of the All-Gracious Shepherd. If the tyrants' threats have reduced some souls to torpor, even they are not passed over by the Saving Word as incurable: to them He freely gives the healing medicine, urging them on towards the divine comfort:

> Take courage, you that are timid at heart;
> Be strong, do not fear.

The word which foretold that she whom God had allowed to become desolate should enjoy these blessings was heard and readily understood by this new and splendid Zerubbabel of ours, after that bitter captivity and the abomination of desolation.[1] He did not pass the body over as dead, but he made it his very first task, by means of entreaties and prayers, to propitiate the Father, with the warm approval of you all. Taking the only Quickener of the dead as ally and co-worker, he raised up the fallen church, after first cleansing her and curing her sickness; and he clothed her with a garment – not the old one she had had from the first, but one that accorded with the further instructions of the divine oracles which emphatically declare: 'The final glory of this house shall be greater than the former.'[2]

Accordingly, the whole area that he took in was much larger, and he gave the outer enclosure the protection of a wall surrounding the whole, to provide the maximum safety from the entire structure. Then he opened up a gateway, wide and towering high, to receive the rays of the rising sun, thus providing even those who stood outside the sacred precincts with an unlimited view of the interior, and as it were turning the eyes even of strangers to the Faith towards the first entrances, so that no one should hurry past without being profoundly moved by the thought of the former desolation and the miraculous transformation now: he hoped that perhaps emotion at the mere sight would turn people and propel them towards the entrance.

He does not permit a man who has passed inside the gates to go at once with unhallowed and unwashed feet into the holy places within; he has left a very wide space between the church proper and the first entrances,

1. Dan. xii. 11 and Matt. xxiv. 15.   2. Hag. ii. 9.

adorning it all round with four colonnades at right angles, so that the outer walls turn the site into a quadrangle and pillars rise on every side. The space between these he has filled with wooden screens of trellis work to a proportionate height. In the middle he left a clear space where the sky can be seen, so that the air is bright and open to the sun's rays. There he placed symbols of sacred purifications, constructing fountains exactly in front of the cathedral: these with their ample flow of fresh water enable those who are proceeding towards the centre of the sacred precincts to purify themselves. For all who enter, this is the first stopping-place, lending beauty and splendour to the whole and at the same time providing those still in need of elementary instruction with the station they require.

Passing beyond this wonderful sight, he opened passages to the cathedral through still more numerous gateways inside the court. In the full blaze of the sun once more, he sited three gates on one side: the centre one he dignified with height and breadth far exceeding those of the outside pair, and by providing bronze plates bound with iron, and elaborate reliefs, he gave it breathtaking loveliness, so that it looks like a queen between two humble bodyguards. In the same way he determined the number of the gateways to the colonnades along both sides of the whole edifice: over the colonnades, to admit still more light, he designed separate openings into the buildings; and these he ornamented elaborately with exquisite wood-carvings.

The basilica itself he built solidly of still richer materials in abundance, never for a moment counting the cost. This is not, I think, the time to state the precise measurements of the building, or to describe in full its dazzling beauty, the incredible vastness, the brilliant appearance of the workmanship, the towering walls that reach for the sky, and the costly cedars of Lebanon that form the ceiling. Even about them the inspired word has something to tell us.

> The trees of the Lord shall be glad,
> The cedars of Lebanon which He planted.[1]

I need not go into details now about the perfection of the overall design and the superlative beauty of the individual parts, for the evidence of our eyes makes instruction through the ears unnecessary. But I will say this: after completing the great building I have described, he furnished it with thrones high up, to accord with the dignity of the prelates, and also with benches arranged conveniently throughout. In addition to all this, he placed in the middle the Holy of Holies – the altar – excluding the general public from this part too by surrounding it with wooden trellis-

---

1. Ps. civ. 16.

work wrought by the craftsmen with exquisite artistry, a marvellous sight for all who see it.

Not even the floor was overlooked by him. This he made bright with marble laid in wonderful patterns, going on next to the outside of the building, where he constructed halls and chambers along both sides on a great scale, skilfully uniting them with the fabric of the basilica so that they share the openings that let light into the central building. These, too, were provided for those still in need of cleansing and sprinkling with water and the Holy Ghost, and were the work of our most peaceful Solomon, who built the temple of God, so that the prophecy I quoted earlier is no longer mere words but plain fact; for the final glory of this house has become and now in truth is greater than the former.

It was natural and right that – as her Shepherd and Lord had once for all accepted death on her behalf, and after His Passion had changed the foul body which for her sake He had put on into His dazzling glorious body, and brought the very flesh that was dissolved from perishability to imperishability[1] – so in her turn the Church should reap the benefit of the Saviour's labours. For having received from Him the promise of much better things than these,[2] she longs to receive permanently and for all time the much greater glory of the regeneration in the resurrection of an imperishable body, with the choir of the angels of light in the kingdom of God beyond the skies, and with Christ Jesus Himself, the great Benefactor and Saviour. Meanwhile, in the present she who was once widowed and desolate has by God's grace been wreathed with these blossoms, and has become in truth like a lily, as the prophecy declares; and having donned her bridal dress and put on the garland of loveliness, she is taught by Isaiah to dance, so to speak, offering her thanks to God the King in words of praise. Listen to what she says:

Let my soul rejoice in the Lord;
For He has clothed me with the mantle of salvation and the tunic of
   gladness;
He has wreathed me like a bridegroom with a chaplet,
And like a bride He has adorned me with ornaments,
And like the ground that grows its blossom,
And as a garden will cause what is sown in it to spring up,
So the Lord, the LORD , has caused righteousness and rejoicing
   to spring up before all the heathen.[3]

1. 1 Cor. xv. 42.   2. An allusion to Heb. xi. 39–40.   3. Is. lxi. 10–11.

With such words on her lips she dances. And how does the Bridegroom, the heavenly Word, Jesus Christ Himself, answer her? Listen to His words:

Do not fear because you have been put to shame,
Or tremble because you have been reproached;
For your everlasting shame you will forget,
And the reproach of your widowhood you will remember no more.
Not as a wife forsaken and without hope has the Lord called you,
Nor as a woman hated from her youth, says your God.
For a little while I forsook you,
And with great mercy will I comfort you.
With a little wrath I turned my face from you,
And with everlasting mercy will I comfort you,
Says your Deliverer, the Lord.
Awake, awake!
You who have drunk from the hand of the Lord the cup of His wrath;
For the cup of staggering, the bowl of my wrath, you have drained and emptied.
There was none to comfort you out of all the children whom you bore,
And there was none to take your hand.
Lo, I have taken from your hand the cup of staggering, the bowl of my wrath;
And never again shall you drink it:
I will put it into the hands of those who wronged you and humbled you.
Awake, awake! put on your strength, put on your glory:
Shake off the dust and stand up.
Sit down: loose the band from your neck.
Raise your eyes and look about you, and see your children gathered together:
Lo, they are gathered together and have come to you.
As I live, says the Lord, you will put them all on as an ornament,
And wrap them about you like the ornaments of a bride.
For your desolate, destroyed, and ruined places will be too narrow for your inhabitants,
And those who swallow you up will be removed far from you.
For the sons you have lost will say in your ears,

'The place is too narrow for me: give me a place where I may dwell.'
And you will say in your heart, 'Who has begotten me these?
I am childless and a widow: who has brought these up for me?
I was left alone: these my children, whence came they?' [1]

These things Isaiah foretold, these things had long ago been set down
about us in sacred books, but it was necessary, was it not, that their truth
should one day be shown by facts. And since this is the way in which the
Bridegroom, the Word, speaks to His Bride, the Sacred and Holy
Church, it was with good reason that this escort of the Bride stretched
out *your* hands in the common prayers of you all, and woke and raised up
the desolate one who lay dead, despaired of by men, by the will of God
the universal King and by the manifestation of the power of Jesus Christ;
and when he had raised her he made her such as the precepts of the sacred
oracles taught him she should be.

This cathedral is a marvel of beauty, utterly breathtaking, especially to
those who have eyes only for the appearance of material things. But all
marvels pale before the archetypes, the metaphysical prototypes and
heavenly patterns of material things – I mean the re-establishment of the
divine spiritual edifice in our souls. This edifice the Son of God Himself
created in His own image, and in every way and in every respect He
endowed it with the divine likeness, an imperishable nature, a non-
physical spiritual essence, remote from any earthly matter and actively
intelligent. Once for all, at the first He transformed it from non-existence
to existence, making it a holy bride and a most sacred temple for Himself
and the Father. This He Himself plainly reveals in this confession:

> I will dwell in them and walk in them:
> And I will be their God, and they shall be my people. [2]

Such is the perfect and cleansed soul, begotten from the beginning so as to
bear the image of the heavenly Word.

But when, through the envy and jealousy of the demon that loves evil,
she became by her own free choice a lover of sensuality and evil, the
Deity withdrew from her, and bereft of a protector, she was soon
captured, proving an easy prey to the inveiglements of those so long
bitter against her. Overthrown by the battering-rams and engines of her
unseen and spiritual foes, she came crashing to the ground, so that not

1. Is. liv. 4–8, li. 17–23, lii. 1–2, xlix. 18–21.
2. 2 Cor. vi. 16; a conflation of Lev. xxvi. 12 and Ez. xxxvii. 27.

even one stone of her virtue remained standing on another in her; she lay full length on the ground dead, her natural thoughts about God gone without trace. As she lay prostrate, made as she was in the image of God,[1] she was ravaged not by that boar out of the wood[2] visible to us, but by some destroying demon and spiritual beasts of the field, who inflamed her with sensual passions as if with blazing arrows of their own wickedness,[3] and set on fire the truly divine sanctuary of God, profaning to the ground the dwelling-place of His name.[4] Then they buried the unfortunate under a great heap of earth, and robbed her of the last hope of salvation.

But when she had paid the just penalty of her sins, the Protector, the Word, the divinely bright and saving One, restored her once more, obedient to the benevolent spirit of His Father, the All-Gracious. First He chose the souls of the supreme emperors, most dear to Him, and by their means He purged the whole world of all the wicked and pernicious people, and of the terrible God-hating tyrants themselves. Then He brought out into the open His own disciples, who all their lives had been dedicated to Him but, as in a storm of evils, secretly concealed under His sheltering wings, and with His Father's munificence He gave them a worthy reward. Again by their means He purged the souls which a little while before were fouled and heaped with rubbish of every sort and the debris of impious decrees: He cleansed them with pickaxes and two-pronged hoes – the penetrating lessons that He taught; and when He had made the place of the understanding of you all bright and shining, thenceforth He entrusted it to this leader, so wise and dear to God. An acute and discriminating judge of other matters, he is well able to appreciate and evaluate the character of the souls entrusted to his care; and from almost the first day he has never yet ceased to build, finding the right place, now for the shining gold, now for the tested, pure silver and the precious, costly stones among you all. So once more a sacred, mystic prophecy is fulfilled in what he has done for you – the prophecy that says:

> Lo, I prepare for you the carbuncle for your stone,
> And for your foundations the sapphire,
> And for your battlements the jasper,
> And for your gates stones of crystal,
> And for the enclosing wall choice stones,
> And all your sons taught of God,
> And in perfect peace your children;
> And in righteousness shall you be built.[5]

1. Gen. i. 27.   2. Ps. lxxx. 13.   3. A reminiscence of Eph. vi. 16.
4. Ps. lxxiv. 7.   5. Is. liv. 11–14.

Building truly in righteousness, he equitably divided the whole people in accordance with their powers. With some, he walled round the outer enclosure – that was enough for them – making unwavering faith the protective barrier. This accounted for far the greater part of the people, who were not strong enough to support a greater edifice. To some he entrusted the entrances to the church proper, giving them the task of waiting at the doors to guide those entering, since he justifiably regarded them as gateways to the house of God. Others he made under-props to the first outer pillars that form a quadrangle round the court, bringing them for the first time into touch with the letter of the four gospels. Others he joined to the basilica along both sides, still under instruction and in process of advancing, but not very far removed from the divine vision that the faithful enjoy of what is innermost. From these last he chooses the undefiled souls, purified like gold by divine washing; these he makes under-props to pillars much grander than the outer ones, drawing on the innermost mystic teaching of Holy Writ, while others he illumines with openings towards the light. With one huge gateway, consisting of the praise of our Sovereign Lord, the one only God, he adorns the whole cathedral; and on both sides of the Father's supreme power he supplies the secondary beams of the light of Christ, and the Holy Ghost. As to the rest, from end to end of the building he reveals in all its abundance and rich variety the clear light of the truth in every man, and everywhere and from every source he has found room for the living, securely-laid, and unshakeable stones of human souls. In this way he is constructing out of them all a great and kingly house, glowing and full of light within and without, in that not only their heart and mind, but their body too, has been gloriously enriched with the many-blossomed adornment of chastity and temperance.

There are also in this shrine thrones and an infinite number of benches and seats, all the souls, on which rest the Holy Spirit's gifts, just as in olden time, they appeared to the holy apostles, and others with them, to whom were revealed dividing tongues like flames of fire, fire which rested on each one of them.[1] In the ruler of them all[2] we may say that the entire Christ Himself has found a resting-place, and in those who take second place to him proportionately, according to each man's capacity to receive the power of Christ and the Holy Spirit divided among them.[3] The souls of some might be benches for the angels assigned to each man with a view to his instruction and protection. As to the solemn, great, and unique altar, what could it be if not the spotless Holy of Holies of the

1. Acts ii. 3.   2. Paulinus.   3. Heb. ii. 4.

common Priest of them all – His soul? Standing beside it on the right-hand side,[1] the great High Priest of the universe,[2] Jesus Himself, the only begotten of God, receives with shining eyes and upturned hands the sweet-smelling incense of all the worshippers, and the bloodless and immaterial prayer-sacrifices, and transmits them to the Father in heaven, the God of the universe. He Himself first adores the Father, and alone renders Him the honour due; then He beseeches Him to continue favourable and propitious towards us for ever.[3]

Such is the great cathedral which throughout the whole world under the sun the great Creator of the universe, the Word, has built, Himself again fashioning this spiritual image on earth of the vaults beyond the skies, so that by the whole creation and by rational beings on earth His Father might be honoured and worshipped. As for the realm above the skies and the patterns there of things here on earth, the Jerusalem above, as it is called,[4] the heavenly Mount Zion and the celestial city of the Living God, in which countless hosts of assembled angels and the church of the first-born enrolled in heaven give glory with praises beyond our utterance or understanding to their Maker, the supreme Ruler of the universe – these things no mortal can worthily hymn; for indeed eye has not seen and ear has not heard, and into the heart of man there have not entered, these very things which God has prepared for those that love Him.[5] Of these things we have now in part been found worthy; so let us all – men, women, and children, small and great together, with one spirit and one soul – everlastingly give thanks and praise to the Author of all the blessings we enjoy. He is very merciful to all our iniquities, He cures all our diseases, He redeems our life from destruction, He crowns us with pity and compassion, He satisfies our desire with good things. He has not dealt with us according to our sins or rewarded us according to our iniquities; for as far as the east is from the west, He has removed our iniquities from us. Just as a father pities his sons, the Lord has pitied those who fear Him.[6]

Let us now and for all time to come rekindle the memory of these things; and let the Author of the present assembly and of this joyous and most glorious day, the Lord of the festival Himself, be before the eyes of our mind night and day at every hour and, may I say, at every breath. Let us love and reverence Him with all the power of our soul; and let us now

---

1. Luke i. 11.   2. Heb. iv. 14.   3. Rom. viii. 34 and Heb. vii. 25.
4. Gal. iv. 26.   5. 1 Cor. ii. 9, slightly modified.
6. Ps. ciii. 3–5, 10–13, slightly modified.

stand up and with a loud voice of supplication beseech Him to shelter us in His fold and preserve us to the end, bestowing on us His own unbreakable, unshakeable, and everlasting peace in Christ Jesus our Saviour, through whom be glory to Him for ever and ever. Amen.

Copies of imperial laws

5. At this point it would be well to reproduce also the imperial ordinances of Constantine and Licinius in translations from the Latin.

COPY OF IMPERIAL ORDINANCES, TRANSLATED FROM LATIN

For a long time past we have made it our aim that freedom of worship should not be denied, but that every man, according to his own inclination and wish, should be given permission to practise his religion as he chose. We had therefore given command that Christians and non-Christians alike should be allowed to keep the faith of their own religious beliefs and worship. But in view of the fact that numerous conditions of different kinds had evidently been attached to that rescript, in which such a right was granted to those very persons, it is possible that some of them were soon afterwards deterred from such observance.

When with happy auspices I, Constantinus Augustus, and I, Licinius Augustus, had arrived at Milan, and were enquiring into all matters that concerned the advantage and benefit of the public, among the other measures directed to the general good, or rather as questions of highest priority, we decided to establish rules by which respect and reverence for the Deity would be secured, i.e. to give the Christians and all others liberty to follow whatever form of worship they chose, so that whatsoever divine and heavenly powers exist might be enabled to show favour to us and to all who live under our authority. This therefore is the decision that we reached by sound and careful reasoning: no one whatever was to be denied the right to follow and choose the Christian observance or form of worship; and everyone was to have permission to give his mind to that form of worship which he feels to be adapted to his needs, so that the Deity might be enabled to show us in all things His customary care and generosity. It was desirable to send a rescript stating that this was our pleasure, in order that after the complete cancellation of the conditions contained in the earlier letter[1] which we sent to Your Dedicatedness about the Christians, the procedure that seemed quite unjustified and alien to our clemency should also be cancelled, and that now every individual still desirous of observing the Christian form of worship should without any interference be allowed to do so. All this we have decided to explain very fully to Your Diligence, that you may know that we have given the said Christians free and absolute permission to practise their own form of worship. When you observe that this permission has been granted by us absolutely, Your Dedicatedness will understand that permission has been given to any others who may wish to follow their own observance or form of worship – a privilege obviously consonant with the tranquillity of our times – so that every man may have permission to choose and practise whatever religion he wishes. This we have done to make it plain that we are not belittling any rite or form of worship.

With regard to the Christians, we also give this further ruling. In the letter sent earlier to Your Dedicatedness precise instructions were laid down at an earlier date with reference to their places where earlier on it was their habit to meet. We now decree that if it should appear that any persons have bought these places either from our treasury or from some other source, they must restore them to these same Christians without payment and without any demand for compensation, and there must be no negligence or hesitation. If any persons happen to have received them as a gift, they must restore the said places to the said Christians without loss of time; provided that if either those who have bought these same places or those who have received them as a gift wish to appeal to our generosity, they may apply to the prefect and judge of the region, in order that they also may benefit by our liberality. All this property is to be handed over to the Christian body immediately, by energetic action on your part, without any delay.

And since the aforesaid Christians not only possessed those places where it was their habit to meet, but are known to have possessed other places also, belonging not to individuals but to the legal estate of the whole body, i.e. of the Christians, all this property, in accordance with the law set forth above, you will order to be restored without any argument whatever to the aforesaid Christians, i.e. to their body and local associations, the provision mentioned above being of course observed, namely, that those persons who restore the same without seeking compensation, as we mentioned above, may expect to recoup their personal losses from our generosity.

1. The Edict of Galerius.

In all these matters you must put all the energy you possess at the service of the aforesaid Christian body, in order that our command may be carried out with all possible speed, so that in this also our liberality may further the common and public tranquillity. For by this provision, as was mentioned above, the divine care for us of which we have been aware on many earlier occasions will remain with us unalterably for ever. And in order that the pattern of this our enactment and of our generosity may be brought to the notice of all, it is desirable that what we have written should be set forth by an edict of your own and everywhere published and brought to the notice of all, so that the enactment giving effect to this our generosity may be known to every citizen.

COPY OF A SECOND STATUTE ISSUED BY THE EMPEROR MAKING IT CLEAR THAT ONLY TO THE CATHOLIC CHURCH WAS THE FAVOUR GRANTED

Greeting, Anulinus, Your Excellency.

It is in keeping with our benevolence that when things belong by right to another man we wish them not only to suffer no damage, but also to be restored, Your Excellency Anulinus. Accordingly it is our wish that when you receive this letter you will see to it that if any of the former property of the Catholic Church of the Christians in the several cities or other places is now in the possession either of citizens or of any other persons, it shall be restored forthwith to the said churches, inasmuch as we have determined that whatever the said churches formerly possessed shall be restored to its rightful owners. Since therefore Your Faithfulness sees plainly that the purport of this our command is perfectly clear, you must take energetic steps to ensure that gardens, houses, and everything else of which the said churches were the rightful owners shall in their entirety be restored to them at the earliest possible moment, so that we may be duly informed that this our command has been meticulously carried out by you. Our compliments to you. Anulinus, Your most Esteemed Excellency.

COPY OF AN IMPERIAL LETTER ORDERING AN EPISCOPAL SYNOD TO BE HELD AT ROME WITH A VIEW TO THE UNITY AND CONCORD OF THE CHURCHES

Constantinus Augustus to Miltiades, Bishop of Rome, and Mark.

In view of the nature of the missives sent to me repeatedly by Anulinus, the Illustrious Proconsul of Africa, which convey the intelligence that Caecilian, Bishop of Carthage, is accused by some of his colleagues in Africa of numerous misdemeanours, I feel it to be a very serious matter that in those provinces which divine providence has freely entrusted to My Dedicatedness, and where the population is very large, the general public should be found persisting in the wrong course as if it were splitting in two, and the bishops divided among themselves. I have therefore decided that Caecilian himself, with ten of the bishops who apparently are accusing him, and ten others regarded by him as essential to his case, shall sail for Rome. There in the presence of yourselves and of Reticius, Maternus, and Marinus, your own colleagues whom I have instructed to proceed at once to Rome for this purpose, he will be granted a hearing in such conditions as you will judge proper under the most sacred law. To ensure that you shall be fully acquainted with all the circumstances of the case, I am enclosing with my letter copies of the reports sent to me by Anulinus, and am dispatching them to your colleagues named above. When you have read them, Your Steadfastness will decide what procedure will be most appropriate for investigating the aforementioned case and reaching a just verdict; for, as Your Diligence is well aware, such is the regard I pay to the lawful Catholic Church that I desire you to leave no schism or division of any kind anywhere.

May the divine power of the great God keep you all safe for many years, Your Excellency.

COPY OF AN IMPERIAL LETTER COMMANDING A SECOND SYNOD TO BE HELD WITH A VIEW TO THE HEALING OF ALL DIVISIONS BETWEEN THE BISHOPS

Constantinus Augustus to Chrestus, Bishop of Syracuse.

When on an earlier occasion base and perverted motives led certain persons to begin creating divisions regarding the worship of the holy and heavenly Power and the Catholic Religion, I determined to cut short such quarrels among them. I therefore gave instructions for certain bishops to be sent from Gaul, and for those men who had taken sides and were engaged in persistent and unrelenting strife to be summoned from Africa, and for the Bishop of Rome to be present also: in this way the questions which had apparently been raised would be enabled by their presence to be thoroughly examined in all its implications and finally settled. But as it happens, certain persons have forgotten both their own salvation and the respect due to their most holy religion, and have not ceased even now to keep alive their private enmities: they refuse to accept the decision already reached, and allege that only a few persons expressed their views and opinions, or that without first subjecting all points that required investigation to careful scrutiny they were in far too great a hurry to pass judgement. In consequence of all this it has come about that the very persons who ought to display brotherly unity and concord are estranged from each other in a way that is disgraceful if not positively sickening; and to people whose minds are strangers to this most holy religion they give a pretext for mockery. It therefore became incumbent on me to provide that what ought after the judgement already passed to have been ended by voluntary agreement should now at last by the presence of many persons be terminated once and for all.

Inasmuch therefore as we have ordered a very large number of bishops from various places beyond counting to assemble at Arles by the first of August, we have decided to write specially to you. Be good enough to obtain from the Illustrious Latronian, my *corrector* in Sicily, a public carriage; attach to yourself two others in presbyter's orders, chosen entirely by yourself; take with you three servants who will be able to look after your comfort on the journey; and present yourself by the appointed day at the place named above. We have likewise ordered those who are now at variance with each other to be present. When all their arguments have been heard, it will be possible for Your Steadfastness, together with the united and harmonious wisdom of the others there assembled, to see that this latest dispute – which owing to inexcusable contentions has most regrettably survived till this present time – may be transformed, however belatedly, into genuine religious feeling, faith, and brotherly concord.

May God Almighty keep you in good health for many years.

COPY OF AN IMPERIAL LETTER MAKING GRANTS OF MONEY TO THE CHURCHES

6. Constantinus Augustus to Caecilian, Bishop of Carthage.

Inasmuch as I have resolved that in all provinces, namely, Africa, Numidia, and Mauretania, certain named ministers of the lawful and most holy Catholic Religion should receive some contribution towards expenses, I have sent a letter to Ursus, the Eminent Finance Officer of Africa, informing him that he must arrange the transfer to Your Steadfastness of 3000 *folles* in cash. Your task on receipt of this sum of money will be to see that it is distributed among all the persons named above according to the schedule supplied to you by Hosius. If later you find that you still lack means to carry out my intentions in this matter in respect of them all, you must not hesitate to ask Heraclides our procurator for whatever you find necessary. I have given him orders in person that if Your Steadfastness should ask him for any sum, he is to arrange for its transfer to you without question.

And whereas I have learnt that certain persons of unstable character desire to lead astray the laity of the most holy Catholic Church by disreputable enticements, this is to inform you that I have given full instructions to Anulinus the Proconsul and also to Patricius the Prefects' *Vicarius* in person, that in all matters, and particularly in this, they are to make the appropriate arrangements and are on no account to overlook such incidents. If therefore you observe any such persons persisting in this insane conduct, you must without hesitation apply to the aforementioned judges and refer the matter to them, so that, as I have instructed them in person, they may bring pressure to bear.

May the divine power of the great God keep you safe for many years.

COPY OF AN IMPERIAL LETTER COMMANDING THE HEADS OF THE CHURCHES TO BE EXEMPTED FROM ALL PUBLIC DUTIES

7. Greeting, Anulinus, Your Excellency.

Many facts combine to prove that the sad neglect of religious observances, by which the highest reverence for the most holy, heavenly Power is preserved, has brought great dangers upon the community, and that the lawful restoration and preservation of the same has conferred the greatest good fortune on the Roman name, and wonderful prosperity on all mankind – blessings conferred by divine benevolence. I have accordingly decided that those men who with due holiness and constant attention to this law give their services to the conduct of divine worship shall receive the rewards of their own labours, Anulinus, Your Excellency. So in the province entrusted to you, in the Catholic church over which Caecilian presides, I desire those who give their services to these sacred observances – the people commonly known as clergymen – once and for all to be kept entirely free from all public duties. This will ensure that by no error or sacrilegious fall from grace will they be drawn away from the worship owed to the Godhead; rather will they be completely free to serve their own law at all times. In thus rendering wholehearted service to the Deity, it is evident that they will be making an immense contribution to the welfare of the community.

Our compliments to you, Anulinus, Your Most Esteemed Excellency

The criminal folly of Licinius, and his calamitous end

8. Such then were the boons conferred on us by the divine, heavenly grace of the manifestation of our Saviour; so great was the abundance of good things won for all men through the peace we enjoyed. And thus our new life was inaugurated with festivities and celebrations. But in the eyes of evil-minded envy and of the malignant demon the sight of what was going on was beyond endurance, and in the same way Licinius could not be brought to a sensible frame of mind by the fact of the tyrants already mentioned.[1] He had been honoured with sovereign power in time of prosperity; he had ranked next after the great Emperor Constantine, and had become brother-in-law and kinsman of the most exalted person living; yet he turned his back on the examples of good men and emulated the wickedness and criminal folly of the evil tyrants; and he chose to follow the same path as those whose life he had with his own eyes seen ending in calamity, rather than remain on terms of friendship and esteem with his superior. Madly envious of the universal benefactor, he launched an unholy, all-out war against him, paying no respect to natural laws and trampling underfoot solemn pledges, ties of blood, and treaties. For, like the all-gracious emperor that he was, Constantine had given him tokens of real goodwill, not grudging kinship with himself or refusing him the privilege of a brilliant marriage with his sister. Again, he honoured him with a share in his ancestral nobility and the imperial blood he had inherited, and conferred on him, as brother-in-law and joint emperor, the privilege of enjoying sovereign power, giving him an equal part of the lands under Roman sway to govern and administer.

But Licinius responded by behaving in the opposite way: he devised scheme after scheme to injure his superior, and invented plan after plan in his efforts to return evil for good. At first he attempted to conceal his intrigues, and posed as a friend, in the hope that by making constant use of trickery and deception he would most easily achieve his purpose. But in God Constantine had a true Friend, Protector, and Guardian, who brought to light

1. Maxentius and Maximin.

the plots devised in darkness and secrecy and frustrated them: so powerful is the great weapon of godliness for the repulse of the enemy and the preservation of its own safety. Thus protected, our Emperor, God's dearly beloved, escaped the plots of this infamous twister. The latter saw that his stealthy intrigue was not going at all according to plan, for God made every trick and fraud manifest to His beloved emperor; so, being unable to remain hidden any longer, he made war openly. Having resolved to fight it out with Constantine, he was already rushing into conflict with the God of the universe too, whom he knew that his rival worshipped. So – quietly and cautiously at first – he planned an attack on the ministers of God among his subjects, though they had never yet shown the least disloyalty to his rule. The motive for this was the terrible blindness forced upon him by his inborn vileness. Thus he failed to keep before his eyes the memory either of those who had persecuted Christians before him, or of those whom he had taken it upon himself to punish and destroy because of their iniquitous activities. But he turned his back on prudence and commonsense, lost his sanity altogether, and determined to match his strength against God Himself, as Constantine's Protector, rather than against the person protected.

He began by dismissing every Christian from his household, robbing himself, poor fool, of the supplication to God for him which their fathers had taught them to make for all men.[1] Next, he ordered the soldiers, city by city, to be picked out and deprived of their rank if they did not choose to sacrifice to demons.

These were mere trifles, judged by comparison with more drastic measures. There is no need to mention one by one the separate acts of this enemy of God, and how laws that were unlawful were invented by this most lawless of men. One actually laid down that where men were languishing in prison no one might give them food as an act of humanity, or pity those who were fettered and starving to death: no one was to show any kind feeling at all, and no kind act was to be done even by those who were compelled by their own nature to show fellow-feeling for their neighbours. Among his laws one was undisguisedly shameless

1. 1 Tim. ii. 1.

and most cruel, excluding every civilized sentiment: it ordained that those who showed pity should suffer the same punishment as those who aroused it, and that any who performed humane services should be fettered and flung into prison, to share the punishment of those already undergoing it. Such were the orders of Licinius.

Need I enumerate his innovations with regard to marriage, or his startling changes affecting those who departed this life? He had the impudence to rescind the ancient Roman laws, so well and wisely laid down, replacing them with barbarous, uncivilized substitutes, laws unquestionably unlawful and contrary to law. Then there were the innumerable demands that he concocted at the expense of subject peoples, the constant exactions of gold and silver, the revaluations of land, the pocketing of fines imposed on country-dwellers no longer alive but long since departed. In addition, this hater of his fellow-men devised means of banishing persons entirely innocent, and of arresting men of good birth and high reputation, whose lawful wives he removed and handed over to filthy menials to be insulted and humiliated; while he himself, the besotted old dotard, used countless married women and unwedded girls to satisfy his own unbridled lust. But why should I dwell on these things, when the extravagance of his ultimate behaviour makes the earlier seem trifling and negligible?

In the later stages of his madness he took action against the bishops. As the servants of the God who is over all, he felt them to be obstacles to his misdeeds; so he began to plot against them, not openly at first, for fear of his superior, but secretly as usual and guilefully; and enlisting the help of the governors he put the most influential of them to death. The way they were murdered was a novel one, till then unheard of. The things done at Amasea and the other Pontic cities outranged the most extravagant cruelty. Some of the churches of God there were again thrown down from roof to foundations; others were locked up, to prevent any of the regular congregation from meeting and giving to God the worship due to Him. And why? Because he did not believe that the prayers were offered on his behalf – the suggestion sprang from his guilty conscience – but was convinced that it was for the Emperor

whom God loved that we did everything and made our supplications to Him. That was what brought down his wrath upon our
heads. Among the governors were flatterers who – in the conviction that they were doing what the wretched man wanted –
subjected some of the bishops to the penalties reserved for criminals, men completely innocent being arrested and executed without pretext as if they were murderers. Others suffered an even
more unprecedented form of death: their bodies were hacked with
a sword and carved up like butcher's meat; then, after this savage,
horrifying spectacle, they were thrown into the depths of the sea
to feed the fishes. This led to a new flight of the ministers of God,
and once more the fields, once more the deserts, valleys, and hills
became the refuge of Christ's servants.

When the evil emperor had achieved his purpose in this way
also, he next turned his attention to indiscriminate persecution. His
design was in his power, and there was no obstacle to its being
carried out, had not the threatened danger been speedily foreseen
by God, the defender of the souls that are His, who in the black
darkness and utter gloom of night all at once kindled a great
beacon light, a saviour for them all, with uplifted arm leading
His servant Constantine to the spot. 9. On him, as the due
reward of his devotion, God bestowed from heaven above the
trophies of victory over the wicked; but the guilty one He
threw down, with all his counsellors and friends, prone beneath
Constantine's feet.

Victory of Constantine; the benefits he conferred on his subjects

When Licinius had rushed headlong to the limit of madness, this
seemed no longer endurable to the emperor, God's friend, who –
reasoning along sound lines and tempering the rigidity of justice
and humanity – determined to rescue the tyrant's victims, and by
putting a few destroyers out of the way made haste to save the
bulk of the human race. He had treated Licinius with nothing but
kindness hitherto, and had shown mercy where no sympathy was
deserved. But Licinius grew no better: his wickedness continued
unabated, and he raged more and more madly against his subject

peoples; while for his victims there remained no hope of escape, with a wild beast tyrannizing over them.

And so, his love of goodness blended with a hatred of evil the champion of the good set out with his son Crispus, that most humane emperor, by his side, holding out a saving hand to all who were perishing. Then, taking God the universal King, and God's Son the Saviour of all, as Guide and Ally, father and son together divided their battle array against God's enemies on every side, and easily carried off the victory: every detail of the encounter was made easy for them by God, in fulfilment of His purpose. Suddenly in less time than it takes to say it, those who a day or two before had been breathing death and threats were no more, and even their name was forgotten; their portraits and tributes were swept into merited oblivion; and the very things that Licinius with his own eyes had seen befall the wicked tyrants who preceded him he underwent himself, because he did not allow himself to be disciplined or learn wisdom from the blows that fell on his neighbours; and having pursued the same path of wickedness as they, he deservedly toppled over the identical cliff.

His adversary thus finally thrown down, the mighty victor Constantine, pre-eminent in every virtue that true religion can confer, with his son Crispus, an emperor most dear to God and in every way resembling his father, won back their own eastern lands and reunited the Roman Empire into a single whole, bringing it all under their peaceful sway, in a wide circle embracing north and south alike from the east to the farthest west. Men had now lost all fear of their former oppressors; day after day they kept dazzling festival; light was everywhere, and men who once dared not look up greeted each other with smiling faces and shining eyes. They danced and sang in city and country alike, giving honour first of all to God our Sovereign Lord, as they had been instructed, and then to the pious emperor with his sons, so dear to God. Old troubles were forgotten, and all irreligion passed into oblivion; good things present were enjoyed, those yet to come eagerly awaited. In every city the victorious emperor published decrees full of humanity and laws that gave proof of munificence and true piety. Thus all tyranny had been purged away, and the kingdom that was theirs was preserved securely and without question for Constantine and his sons alone. They, having made it their first task to wipe the world clean from hatred of God, rejoiced in the blessings that He had conferred upon them, and, by the things they did for all men to see, displayed love of virtue and love of God, devotion and thankfulness to the Almighty.

Bibliography

General

L. Duchesne, *Histoire ancienne de l'Eglise* (3 vols., Paris, 1906–10; Eng. tr., 1909–24).

H. Chadwick, *The Early Church* (Pelican History of the Church, vol. 1; Harmondsworth, 1967).

Robin Lane Fox, *Pagans and Christians* (London, 1986; Harmondsworth, 1988).

P. Nautin, *Lettres et Écrivains chrétiens des IIe et IIIe siècles* (Patristica, 2; Paris, 1961).

   Origène. Sa vie et son oeuvre (Christianisme antique, 1; Paris, 1977).

(The two volumes by P. Nautin contain much stimulating critical discussion of the evidence, especially that provided by Eusebius, for the history of the Church in the second and third centuries. Much of it is, however, very speculative.)

On Eusebius

J. B. Lightfoot, 'Eusebius (23) of Caesarea', in *Dictionary of Christian Biography*, ed. W. Smith and H. Wace, vol. 2 (1880), pp. 308–48 (with separate article on the *Chronicle* by G. Salmon, pp. 348–55).

E. Schwartz, 'Eusebios' in *Real-Encyclopädie der classischen Altertumswissenschaft*, ed. A. Pauley and G. Wissowa, VI, part 1 (1907), cols. 1370–439.

H. J. Lawlor, *Eusebiana* (Oxford, 1912).

J. Stevenson, *Studies in Eusebius* (Cambridge, 1929).

D. S. Wallace-Hadrill, *Eusebius of Caesarea* (London, 1960).

T. D. Barnes, *Constantine and Eusebius* (Cambridge, Mass., and London, 1981).

G. F. Chesnut, *The First Christian Histories* (Théologie Historique, 46; Paris, 1977).

J. Sirinelli, *Les vues historiques d'Eusèbe de Césarée durant la période prénicéenne* (Dakar, 1961).

R. A. Markus, 'Church history and the early church historians' in *The Materials, Sources and Methods of Ecclesiastical History*, ed. D. Baker (Studies in Church History, 11; Oxford, 1975).

J. Quasten, S. J., *Patrology*, vol 3 (Utrecht, 1986), pp. 309–45.

Frances Young, *From Nicaea to Chalcedon* (London, 1983), pp. 1–23.

(The last two works both contain bibliographies.)

Principal references in the 'Who's Who'

A New Eusebius	J. Stevenson, *A New Eusebius*, (London, 1957)
Charlesworth	*The Old Testament Pseudepigraphia*, ed. J. H. Charlesworth, 2 vols., (London, 1983–5).
Early Christian Writings	*Early Christian Writings: The Apostolic Fathers*, trans. Maxwell Staniforth, revised edn. Andrew Louth (Harmondsworth, 1987).
Foerster	W. Foerster, *Gnosis: A Selection of Gnostic Texts*, English tr. ed. R. McL. Wilson, 2 vols., (Oxford, 1972–4).
Hennecke and Schneemelcher	*New Testament Apocrypha*, ed. E. Hennecke and W. Schneemelcher, English tr. ed. R. McL. Wilson, 2 vols., (London 1963–5).
James	M. R. James, *The Apocryphal New Testament*, (Oxford, 1924).
Jewish War	Josephus, *The Jewish War*, trans. G. A. Williamson, revised edn. E. Mary Smallwood, (Harmondsworth, 1981).
Lane Fox	Robin Lane Fox, *Pagans and Christians*, (Harmondsworth, 1988).

Bibliography

Musurillo   *The Acts of the Christian Martyrs*, trans. and ed. H. Musurillo, (Oxford, 1972).

Schürer   E. Schürer, *A History of the Jewish People in the Age of Jesus Christ*, new English version, rev. and ed. G. Vermes, F. Millar, and M. Goodman, 3 vols., (Edinburgh, 1973–87).

The World of Eusebius

Who's Who in Eusebius

The following 'Who's Who' has entries for all the people who appear in the pages of *The History of the Church* (with the exception of a very few people mentioned in quotations from Josephus and of no importance to Eusebius' story). It also contains articles on a few other matters – e.g., Easter, the Septuagint, groups such as the 'Seventy' (disciples), the Apostles, the gnostics, the docetists – which also require comment. Each article includes a list of the places in *The History of the Church* (by Book and chapter: IX. 2 = Book 9, chapter 2) where they are mentioned, as well as brief comment, which often supplements and sometimes corrects what Eusebius tells us. Dates are given when it is possible to be specific: in the case of the bishops of the great sees of Rome, Alexandria, Antioch and Jerusalem (Aelia), except for Rome, (where there is confirmation independent of Eusebius) dates are not given, and the reader is recommended to consult Appendix A. Almost all geographical places mentioned by Eusebius can be found on the map opposite. Other information can be found in the appendices.

ABGAR (I. 13; II. 1). King (toparch) of Edessa in Osrhoene. The legend of the correspondence between Jesus and Abgar is fabulous, though Abgar V Uchama ('the Black') was king in Edessa during Jesus' ministry in Palestine. The legend perhaps reflects the favour to Christians in Edessa shown by Abgar IX the Great (179–214). The parallel version of the legend in the fifth-century *Doctrine of Addai* (Addai = Thaddaeus (q.v.) in *The History of the Church*) relates that Abgar not only received a letter from Jesus, but also acquired a portrait of him: of this Eusebius knows nothing. J. B. Segal, *Edessa, 'The Blessed City'* (Oxford, 1970), pp. 62–81.

ABRAHAM (I. 2, 4). Jewish patriarch (Gen. xii–xxv).

ACHAEUS (VII. 15). *Legatus* of Syria and Palestine *c.* 260/1.

ACHILLAS (VII. 32). Presbyter of Alexandria under Theonas, the head of the Catechetical School. He succeeded Peter as bishop of Alexandria.

ADAUCTUS (VIII. 11). Roman official martyred under Diocletian.

ADOPTIONISTS. Heretics who believed that Jesus was a mere man whom God had adopted as his son ('mere man' = *psilos anthropos* in Greek; hence adoptionism is sometimes called 'psilanthropism').

AELIAN (VII. 30). Member of the synod that condemned Paul of Samosata.

AEMILIAN (VII. 11). Lucius Mussius Aemilianus, Deputy-Prefect of Egypt in 257 and later Prefect. After the capture of Valerian he conspired unsuccessfully against Gallienus, and was besieged in Alexandria.

AFRICANUS (I. 6, 7; VI. 31). Sextus Julius Africanus, probably born in Jerusalem, he later settled at Emmaus. On its behalf he went on an embassy to the Emperor Elagabalus, which led to its restoration as Nicopolis. He was friendly with the royal house of Edessa, and had connexions with Heraclas and Origen in Alexandria. Under the Emperor Alexander Severus he was involved in the building of a public library in the Pantheon at Rome. A lay Christian writer, he compiled a *Chronography* (Dictionary of Dates), according to which the world was to last for 6,000 years, the birth of Christ having occurred in 5500, and a major work (in twenty-four books) called *Cesti* ('embroidered girdles', a fanciful name for a miscellany, like *Stromateis* – 'carpet bags'): of these only fragments survive. Two letters survive, one to Origen on the authenticity of the story of Susanna (interpolated in the Greek Septuagint version of Daniel), in which he produces cogent reasons for its having been composed in Greek (to which Origen replies unconvincingly), and another to Aristides, which seeks to reconcile the divergent genealogies of Christ in the gospels of Matthew and Luke. Both letters manifest an astute critical intelligence. His reconciliation of Matthew's and Luke's genealogies was widely accepted: the same method is found (with some amplification) in the eighth-century compendium of Byzantine theology, John Damascene's *On the Orthodox Faith*, 87.

AGABUS (II. 3, 8; V. 17). The Christian prophet from Judaea, mentioned in Acts xi. 28, xxi. 10.

AGAPIUS (VII. 32). Bishop of Caesarea after Theotecnus, late third century; probably succeeded by Eusebius.

AGATHOBULI (VII. 32). The two Agathobuli are said by Anatolius to have been the teachers of Aristobulus the Great.

AGATHONICE (VI. 15). Martyr, the account of whose martyrdom survives: see Carpus.

AGRIPPA I (II. 4, 9, 10, 19). Herod Agrippa I, grandson of Herod the Great, he reigned 37–44. He was the Herod of Acts who had James the apostle beheaded, and died consumed by worms, the account of which is given by Luke in Acts xii and by Josephus (which Eusebius reproduces).

AGRIPPA II (II. 19, 23; III. 10). Son of Agrippa I, reigned 50–*c*. 93, he was the 'king Agrippa' before whom Paul the apostle appeared (Acts xxv. 13ff.)

AGRIPPA CASTOR (IV. 7). Earliest recorded Christian writer against heresy, he wrote against the Gnostic Basilides: of him we know no more than Eusebius tells us.

AGRIPPINUS (IV. 20; V. 9). Bishop of Alexandria.

ALBINUS (II. 23). Procurator of Judaea 62–4.

ALCE (IV. 15). Apparently a prominent Christian of Smyrna, conceivably the same lady greeted by Ignatius of Antioch forty years earlier (Ignatius' *Smyrneans*, 13; *Polycarp*, 8). Her brother and nephew were pagans, but not apparently hostile to Polycarp.

ALCIBIADES (V. 3). Christian converted from Encratism in prison.

ALCIBIADES (V 3). Montanist leader not mentioned elsewhere; it may be that the name Miltiades was intended, and 'Alcibiades' is a slip of the pen, caused by the mention of Alcibiades a few lines earlier.

ALEXANDER (II. 5). Brother of Philo (q.v.). He held the post of *alabarch*, i.e. (probably) superintendent of customs on the Arabian side of the Nile.

ALEXANDER (IV. 1; V. 6). Bishop of Rome 105–15.

ALEXANDER (V. 1). Martyred in the persecution at Lyons and Vienne.

ALEXANDER (V. 16). One of the martyrs from Eumenia in Phrygia, martyred at Apamea.

ALEXANDER (V. 18). Montanist self-styled martyr, presented by Apollonius (Eusebius' source) as a fraud.

ALEXANDER (VI. 8, 11, 14, 19, 20, 27, 39, 46). A friend of the two philosopher-theologians who taught at Alexandria, Pantaenus and Clement, he became a friend and supporter of Origen. He was twice a confessor, being imprisoned during persecution for several years at the beginning of the third century, and finally dying in prison during the Decian persecution. Already bishop of an unknown see in Cappadocia, *c.* 212 he visited Jerusalem and was chosen as coadjutor to the bishop Narcissus, whom he succeeded on his death. His is the first recorded example both of the appointment of a coadjutor and of the translation of a bishop from one see to another (the latter practice forbidden, ineffectually, by the Council of Nicaea). He established a library at Jerusalem, which Eusebius used in compiling *The History of the Church.* He defended Origen against the accusations of his bishop, Demetrius, and together with Theoctistus, bishop of Caesarea, ordained him to the priesthood. He wrote several letters, from which Eusebius quotes some passages.

ALEXANDER (VI. 21, 24, 26, 28). Marcus Aurelius Severus Alexander, Emperor 222–235, probably thought by Eusebius (implausibly) to have been a Christian (cf. VII. 10).

ALEXANDER (VI. 41). Martyred at Alexandria in the Decian persecution.

ALEXANDER (VII. 11). Martyred in Caesarea in the reign of Valerian.

ALOGI. The name given by Epiphanius to heretics who opposed Montanism and rejected the Fourth Gospel and the Revelation, ascribing them to the heretic Cerinthus. They flourished in Asia Minor towards the end of the second century. Their name (from a = not and logos = reason or word) means 'irrational' and was probably also meant to suggest opponents of reason (in theology) and of the Logos or Word of God (this name figures prominently in the Johannine Literature). Gaius of Rome may have been associated with them.

AMBROSE (VI. 18, 23, 28). A rich and cultured man of noble birth, whom Origen reclaimed from heresy *c.* 211. He became Origen's patron and encouraged him in his writing and research, making it possible for Origen to devote himself to the study of the Scriptures at the school he set up in Caesarea (231), where Ambrose joined Origen. He was apparently ordained deacon, and suffered as a confessor at Caesarea *c.* 235, which prompted Origen's *Exhortation to Martyrdom*. He died *c.* 250.

AMMIA (V. 17). Christian prophetess mentioned by Miltiades.

AMMON (VII. 41). Soldier martyr at Alexandria in the Decian persecution.

AMMON (VIII. 26). Bishop of Bernice in Pentapolis, to whom Dionysius of Alexandria wrote several letters against Sabellius.

AMMONARION (VI. 41). Martyred at Alexandria in the Decian persecution.

AMMONIUS (VIII. 13). Presbyter of Alexandria, martyred in the Great Persecution.

AMMONIUS SACCAS (VI. 19). Alexandrian philosopher, the teacher of Longinus and Plotinus, as well as Origen. Brought up a Christian, according to Porphyry, he became a pagan. Died *c.* 243.

ANATOLIUS (VII. 32). An Alexandrian philosopher of considerable learning who established a school of Aristotelian philosophy at Alexandria. He played a notable role during a siege of the Greek quarter (the *Brucheum*) of Alexandria, probably during the revolt of the Prefect Aemilian (262). Soon afterwards he was consecrated bishop by Theotecnus, bishop of Caesarea, presumably as coadjutor, but in 268, on his way to the synod at Antioch which condemned Paul of Samosata, was made bishop of Laodicea. Eusebius quotes a long passage from his treatise on the date of Easter (q.v.), which introduced a nineteen-year cycle for calculating the date: this cycle is essentially that still used. He also wrote a ten-part work, *Elements of Arithmetic*; the fragments that remain, however, are probably not authentic. Died *c.* 282.

ANDREW (III. 1, 25, 39). The apostle. Eusebius says that he went to Scythia. The tradition that he preached in Achaia, and was martyred at Patras, is late and unreliable, and even more so the tradition that he was crucified on a 'St Andrew's cross' (in the form of an X). Eusebius also mentions the spurious *Acts of St. Andrew*, which he asserts is heretical. For the *Acts*, see James, pp. 337–63, and Hennecke and Schneemelcher, II, pp. 390–425.

ANENCLETUS (III. 13, 15, 21; V. 6). Bishop of Rome, also called (not in Eusebius) Anacletus and Cletus (conventional dates: 76–88).

ANICETUS (IV. 11, 14, 19, 22; V. 6, 24). Bishop of Rome 155–66.

ANNAS (I. 9f). (Called, correctly, Ananus by Josephus.) Jewish high priest A.D. 6/7–15, when he was deposed by the Prefect, Valerius Gratus, and later succeeded by his son-in-law, Caiaphas. Luke (and Acts) and John speak of Annas *and* Caiaphas as high priests, perhaps reflecting the conviction of some Jews that Annas could not be deposed. Eusebius is very confused, and tries to make out that Annas was high priest at the beginning of Jesus' ministry, Caiaphas at the end, Jesus' ministry having lasted almost four years (something Eusebius seeks to establish elsewhere: see III. 24). This involves a curious interpretation of the passage he quotes from Josephus: there may have been barely four years between the deposition of Annas and the appointment of Caiaphas, but Caiaphas seems to have been high priest for almost twenty years.

ANNIANUS (II. 24; III. 14, 21). First bishop of Alexandria after the evangelist Mark, though Eusebius studiously avoids the term 'bishop'.

ANONYMOUS (V. 16f.). Eusebius does not give the name of one of his main sources for Montanism, though he quotes from him extensively. He is consequently referred to as the 'Anonymous'. We know nothing about him, though from the way he refers to Zoticus as 'our fellow-presbyter' (V. 16.5; cf. 1 Peter v. 1) and his authoritative tone, it has been argued that he must have been a bishop.

ANTEROS (VI. 29). Bishop of Rome 22 November 235–3 January 236.

ANTHIMUS (VIII. 6, 13). Bishop of Nicomedia, martyred in 303 at the beginning of the Great Persecution.

ANTINOUS (IV. 8). Favourite page of the Emperor Hadrian, who was drowned in the Nile 130 or 131. He was deified by Hadrian, who founded Antinoopolis in the Thebais in his honour. His deification is mentioned often by the second-century apologists as an example of the origin of the pagan gods: a theory often called Euhemerism (after Euhemerus, a Sicilian writer, *c.* 315 B.C.).

ANTIPAS (I. 9–11; II. 4). Herod Antipas (called Herod by Eusebius), son of Herod the Great, tetrarch of Galilee and Peraea 4 B.C.–A.D. 39, who married Herodias, his brother's wife, thus incurring the wrath of John the Baptist, whose execution he ordered (see Mark vi. 14–29). He is the 'Herod' of the Crucifixion (Luke xxiii. 6–12).

ANTIPATER (I. 6f.). Father of Herod the Great.

ANTONINUS PIUS (II. 13; IV. 10–12, 14, 18). Titus Aurelius Fulvus Boionius Antoninus Pius, Emperor 10 July 138–7 March 161. Eusebius is very confused about the Antonines, so it is sometimes unclear which Emperor he has in mind: he evidently regarded Antoninus Pius as friendly towards the Christian Church (see Marcus Aurelius).

ANULINUS (X. 5–7). Proconsul of Africa after Constantine's conversion (if not before), who had to deal with the early stages of the Donatist controversy.

APELLES (V. 13). Disciple of Marcion, who broke away from his master's teaching, rejecting his dualism and his Docetism, but retaining his hostility to the Old Testament. Apart from Eusebius, our main source is Tertullian, who refers to him in his *On the Prescription of Heretics* and devoted to him a treatise (now lost). The discussion between Rhodo and Apelles, which we know of from Eusebius, was called by the great Church historian A. von Harnack 'the most important religious discussion in Church history'. He wrote a long book, *Syllogisms*, devoted to proving the worthlessness of the Old Testament, fragments of which are preserved in Ambrose's treatise *On Paradise*.

APION (V. 27). A contemporary of Irenaeus who wrote a treatise (now lost), *The Six Days of Creation*.

APOLINARIUS (IV, 21, 26, 27; V. 5, 16, 19). Claudius Apolinarius, bishop of Hierapolis and Christian writer. We know no more than Eusebius tells us. As he wrote an apology to Marcus Aurelius (alone), he must have flourished 170–80. He seems to have been a prominent opponent of Montanism. He is also one of Eusebius' sources for the story of the Thundering Legion (q.v.).

APOLLONIA (VI. 41). Martyred at Alexandria in the Decian persecution.

APOLLONIADES (V. 28). Probably disciple of Theodotus (the cobbler or the banker q.v.), adoptionist heretic.

APOLLONIUS (V. 18). Anti-Montanist writer, perhaps writing as late as 200. He is said (on no very reliable authority) to have been bishop of Ephesus. According to Jerome, his attack on Montanism provoked a response from Tertullian (now lost).

APOLLONIUS (V. 21). A senator (according to Jerome) martyred in Rome under Commodus. The *Acts* of his martyrdom survive in a late and unreliable version, which makes Apollonius an Alexandrian and the magistrate Perennius proconsul of Asia. See Musurillo, pp. 90–105.

APOLLOPHANES (VI. 19). Antiochene Stoic (third century B.C.).

APOLOGISTS. The name given to those Christian writers (mainly of the second century) who wrote *Defences* (*Apologies*) of Christianity, often addressed to the Emperor. They were pleas that Christians did not deserve to be persecuted, and answered the suspicions often raised against Christians: suspicions of atheism (denial of the existence of the gods) and immorality (especially 'Oedipean incest and Thyestean banquets' – Oedipus made love to his mother, Thyestes had a meal of his children). The first charge was met by the explanation that Christians were monotheists, the second by the explanation that it was a misunderstanding of the Christian Eucharist and the fraternal love of the Christian community.

Eusebius once suggests that the charge of immorality is justly levelled against the Gnostic sects with whom pagans confuse Christians (IV. 7). The charge of Thyestean feasts and Oedipean incest is mentioned as having been made against Christians in the letter about the persecution at Lyons and Vienne (V. 1. 14). The apologists drew on Greek (mostly Platonic) philosophy in their attempts to explain Christianity to the pagan world.

APOSTLES. Name given to the most important leaders in the first-generation Church. Luke (in Acts) attempts to limit the number of apostles to the twelve disciples of Jesus, Matthias being chosen to fill the place vacated by Judas Iscariot; Paul seems unaware of the twelve *apostles* (though he knows of the Twelve: see 1 Cor. xv. 5–7) but fiercely defends his own right to the title of apostle (see the beginning of all his epistles). The *Didache* (see below) seems to envisage the apostles as itinerant missionaries, as opposed to the settled ministry of bishops and deacons. Eusebius makes what he can of this evidence (and seems not to have any more): apostles belonged to the first generation of the Church; the name refers primarily to the Twelve, but by extension to a 'large number', including Paul (I. 12). Eusebius mentions the *Didache* (the 'Teachings of the Apostles') as a spurious work, not to be included in the canon (q.v.). This work, probably very ancient, was rediscovered in the last century, and is a kind of primitive Church Order: see *Early Christian Writings*, pp. 187–99.

AQUILA (V. 8; VI. 16). Biblical translator. A native of Sinope in Pontus, he lived under the Emperor Hadrian. He was a proselyte to Judaism, and produced an extremely literal translation of the Hebrew Bible into Greek, intended to replace the Septuagint which the Christians had adopted. Only a few fragments survive, but Origen and Jerome admitted its fidelity to the Hebrew original. It occupied the third column of Origen's *Hexapla*.

AQUILA (VI. 3, 5). Subatianus Aquila, Prefect of Egypt 203–10.

AQUILA (VII. 11). Alexandrian presbyter (probably) mentioned in one of Dionysius of Alexandria's letters.

ARABIANUS (V. 27). An essay of his mentioned. Otherwise unknown.

ARCHELAUS (I. 6, 8). Son of Herod the Great; ethnarch of Judaea, Idumaea and Samaria 4 B.C.–A.D. 6.

ARISTARCHUS (II. 22). Fellow-prisoner of Paul (Col. iv. 10).

ARISTEAS (V. 8). The letter of Aristeas is a pseudepigraphical letter, written in Greek, supposedly by Aristeas, an official at the court of Ptolemy Philadelphus (285–247 B.C.), giving a miraculous account of translation of the Septuagint (q.v.). Charlesworth, II, pp. 7–34.

ARISTIDES (I. 7: VI. 31). Recipient of letter from Africanus on the genealogy of Christ.

ARISTIDES (IV. 3). A Christian apologist from Athens who wrote the earliest extant *Apology*. For centuries it was believed lost. Towards the end of the last century part of an Armenian translation was discovered, then a complete Syriac version: this led J. A. Robinson to detect the original Greek version behind an episode in the Greek novel ascribed to John Damascene, *Barlaam and Josaphat*. Eusebius ascribes the *Apology* to the reign of Hadrian, but there are strong reasons for thinking that it was addressed to Antoninus Pius, early in his reign. *The Apology of Aristides*, ed. and trans. J. Rendel Harris (Texts and Studies, I/1; 2nd edn, 1893; repr. 1967).

ARISTION (III. 39). Mentioned alongside John the presbyter by Papias. An Armenian manuscript of the Gospels, dated 986, discovered by F. C. Conybeare in 1891, attributes Mark xvi. 9–20 (the 'longer ending') to the 'elder Aristion'. This may refer to Papias' Aristion, and may be correct.

ARISTO OF PELLA (IV. 6). The learned John of Scythopolis (sixth century) tells us (in a passage preserved in the scholia on *The Mystical Theology* of Dionysius the Areopagite attributed to Maximus the Confessor) that Aristo of Pella was the author of the Dialogue between Jason (a Christian) and Papiscus (a Jew). It was known to Celsus (whose mockeries of it Origen attacked: *Contra Celsum* IV. 52) and it quotes a verse from the version of Aquila. It must have been written therefore between 140 and *c*. 180; these dates fit with what Eusebius tells us, that Aristo wrote an account of the destruction of the Temple under Hadrian.

ARISTOBULUS (VI. 13; VII. 32). Great Jewish philosopher who lived in the time of Ptolemy VI Philometor (i.e., about 180–145 B.C.) in Alexandria. Anatolius is certainly wrong in regarding him as one of the seventy translators of the Septuagint (VII. 32). Schürer, III, pp. 579–87.

ARISTOTLE (V. 28). Greek philosopher, 384–322 B.C.

ARMENIA (IX. 8). Eusebius mentions that the Armenians had become Christians by 312, but he seems to know no more. The 'apostle of Armenia' was Gregory the Illuminator, of royal descent, who had been brought up a Christian while an exile in Cappadocia. On his return to Armenia, he succeeded in converting the king, Tiridates (*c.* 238–314), to the Christian faith. He himself was consecrated bishop (Catholicos) by the metropolitan of Caesarea in Cappadocia *c.* 290 and lived to *c.* 328.

ARTEMON (V. 28; VII. 30). Artemon (who seems to be identical with Artemas) was an adoptionist (q.v.). He was named by the synod of Antioch (268), which condemned Paul of Samosata, as the father of the heresy, and seems to have been alive at the time. In V. 28, Eusebius quotes from a work Theodoret tells us was called the *Little Labyrinth* (q.v.), as if it were directed against Artemon. The passages quoted, however, do not mention Artemon, but rather concern the two Theodoti (the cobbler and the banker, q.v.), Asclepiodotus and Natalius, and describe events in Rome during the time of pope Victor (189–99) and pope Zephyrinus (199–217): probably too early for one who was alive and influential in the region of Antioch in 268.

ASCLEPIADES (VI, 11, 21). Bishop of Antioch.

ASCLEPIODOTUS (V. 28). Also called Asclepiades, unless that is someone else. An adoptionist attacked by name in the *Little Labyrinth* (q.v.). He belonged to the Rome of pope Zephyrinus (199–217), and is accused of heavy-handed emendation of the Scriptures as well as adoptionism.

ASTERIUS URBANUS (V. 16). Montanist, probably the compiler of Maximilla's oracles.

ASTYRIUS (VII. 16, 17). Senator of Caesarea, prominent opponent of paganism, who buried the body of the soldier–martyr Marinus.

ATER (VI. 41). An Egyptian (i.e., a Copt, not a Greek), martyred at Alexandria during the Decian persecution.

ATHENODORE (VI. 30; VII. 14, 28). Brother of Gregory Thaumaturgus. Like him, he studied rhetoric as a pagan, became a Christian, studied under Origen at Caesarea, and returned to Pontus, where he became a bishop. As a bishop, he participated in the synod of Antioch (268) which condemned Paul of Samosata.

ATTALUS (V. 1, 3). A Christian from Pergamum, martyred in the persecution at Lyons and Vienne, by being thrown to the wild beasts. V. 3 records a vision he had in a dream.

ATTICUS (III. 32). Provincial Governor in Judaea, who had been a Consul: perhaps Sextus Attius Suburanus, who was Consul in 104.

ATTICUS (VI. 19). Bishop of Synnada in Phrygia.

AUGUSTUS (I. 5f., 9). Gaius Julius Caesar Octavianus (Augustus from 27 B.C.), great-nephew of Julius Ceasar; Emperor 23 B.C.–A.D. 14. (Eusebius dates his reign from 44 B.C., the year of Julius Caesar's death.)

AURELIAN (VII. 28, 30). Lucius Domitius Aurelianus, Emperor 270–5. The Christians of Antioch appealed to him to remove Paul of Samosata after their failure to acquire possession of the church in Antioch. According to Eusebius, he contemplated a renewed persecution of Christians, but died before he could put it into effect.

AURELIUS QUIRINIUS (V. 19). A bishop-signatory to a (synodical?) letter by Serapion of Antioch. He signs himself 'martyr': i.e., witness or confessor.

AVILIUS (III. 14. 21). Second bishop of Alexandria, though Eusebius avoids the term 'bishop'.

AVIRCIUS MARCELLUS (V. 16). Recipient of the anonymous treatise against Montanism. A Greek epitaph, discovered in 1883 by W. M. Ramsey, now in the Vatican Museum, mentions the travels of an Abercius Marcellus, bishop of Hieropolis in Phrygia Salutaris, to Rome and Nisibis, and bears witness in allusive symbolic language to the universal celebration of the Eucharist. The text of this epitaph is incorporated in an early fifth-century life of St Abercius, which makes much of his miraculous powers. There seems little doubt that this Abercius is Eusebius' Avircius, and it seems that the anti-Montanist leader was not only well travelled during his lifetime, but after his death was held in such esteem that two centuries later he was still venerated as a notable miracle-worker.

BABYLAS (VI. 29, 34, 39). Bishop of Antioch, who died a confessor in prison during the Decian persecution. According to Chrysostom, it was Babylas who insisted that the Emperor Philip, wishing to take part in the Easter Vigil, make open confession of Christianity and consent to be enrolled with the penitents (the story related in VI. 34): though the story itself is hardly credible.

BACCHYLIDES (IV. 23). A Christian of Corinth, very likely the same as Bacchyllus (see next entry).

BACCHYLLUS (V. 22, 23). Bishop of Corinth at the end of the second century, who, together with Polycrates of Ephesus and Theophilus of Caesarea, took a leading part in the Quartodeciman controversy (q.v.).

BARCABBAS and BARCOPH (IV. 23). Prophets of the Gnostic Basilides (Barcoph's name is spelled Parchor by Clement of Alexandria).

BAR COCHBA (IV. 6, 8). The leader of the Jewish rebellion in Palestine in A.D. 132. He was hailed as messiah by Rabbi Akiba, but his revolt was ultimately unsuccessful. The name 'Bar Cochba' means 'Son of a star' and has messianic connotations (cf. Num. xxiv. 17). It only occurs in Christian sources: Jewish sources call him Simon Bar Kosiba ('Son of a lie'), repudiating any such claims.

BARDAISAN (IV. 30). A Syriac writer, born in Edessa in 154 of pagan parents, he became a Christian and wrote polemics against Marcionism; later he fell out with the bishop of Edessa and was excommunicated. He fled to Armenia *c.* 216 and died 222. Eusebius regards him as one who had been a Valentinian Gnostic, but had renounced heresy and become a more or less orthodox defender of Christianity. Other Christians (notably, Hippolytus) regarded him as a leader of oriental Gnosticism. Porphyry knew him as a learned champion of Christianity with a special interest in other religions. He certainly seems to have denied the doctrine of the resurrection of the body. His followers maintained their existence as a sect for some centuries. Ephrem (fourth-century Syriac writer) regarded Bardaisan as one who opened the door to Mani and his doctrine.

BARNABAS (I. 12; II. 3, 12; III. 25; VI. 14). Companion of Paul the apostle on his first missionary journey (Acts xiii–xiv). Eusebius says that he was one of the Seventy (q.v.). He also mentions the *Epistle of Barnabas*, which he regards as spurious. Although it does not claim to be written by Paul's companion, it was regarded as his as early as Clement of Alexandria. For the epistle, see *Early Christian Writings*, pp. 155–84.

BARSABAS (I. 12; III. 39). Joseph Barsabas, who was unsuccessful in the lottery to choose the successor as apostle for Judas (Acts i. 15–26). Eusebius says he was one of the Seventy (q.v.).

BARTHOLOMEW (V. 10). One of the apostles, who, according to Pantaenus, had preached in 'India' (a vague term referring to any country east of Ethiopia) and founded a Christian community there.

BASILICUS (V. 13). Follower of Marcion.

BASILIDES (IV. 7, 22). Gnostic theologian who taught at Alexandria in the second quarter of the second century. Accounts of his teaching – strikingly divergent – are preserved by Irenaeus and Hippolytus. He seems, unlike most Gnostics, to have had genuine philosophical interests. Foerster, I, pp. 59–83.

BASILIDES (VI. 5). Soldier, sympathetic to Christianity, who was involved in the martyrdom of Potamiaena and later martyred himself. He was a pupil of Origen's in the Catechetical School.

BENJAMIN (IV. 5). Sixth bishop of Jerusalem.

BERYLLUS (VI. 20, 33). Bishop of the Arabians in Bostra. Eusebius is enthusiastic about his literary work, but tells us nothing of it. He fell into some form of adoptionism, from which he was rescued by Origen.

BESAS (VI. 41). Soldier martyred at Alexandria after showing sympathy for Christians.

BIBLIS (V. 1). Martyred in the persecution at Lyons and Vienne. She first apostasized, but then, under torture to make a confession damning to the Christians, rallied and accepted martyrdom. Her rejection of the charge of cannibalism seems to suggest that Christians abstained from animal blood, as required by the apostolic decree of Acts xv. 19f.

BLANDINA (V. 1). Slave-girl martyred in the persecution at Lyons and Vienne.

BLASTUS (V. 15, 20). Roman schismatic presbyter, against whom Irenaeus wrote. Another source says that he was a Quartodeciman.

BOLANUS (VII. 30). Member of the synod that condemned Paul of Samosata.

'BYSTANDERS' (VI. 42; VII. 9). The highest order of penitents, allowed to be present throughout the Eucharistic liturgy, but not allowed to receive communion (Latin: *consistentes*). The penitential discipline of the early Church required those Christians guilty of grave sin and wishing to be restored to full membership of the Church as communicants to undergo a (usually long) period of exclusion from the liturgy, until they were deemed ready to receive communion again.

CAECILIAN (X. 5, 6, 7). Bishop of Carthage 311–*c*. 345. His consecration as bishop by Felix, bishop of Aptunga, who was accused (probably falsely) of being a *traditor*, led to the Donatist schism, which afflicted the North African Church for many years. The Donatists held that as Felix was a *traditor*, i.e., one who had handed over Scriptures and/or sacred vessels during the persecution, he could no longer validly consecrate.

CAIAPHAS (I. 10). Jewish High Priest *c*. 18–37, and therefore the high priest involved in the Crucifixion. Son-in-law of Annas (q.v.).

CALIGULA (II. 4–8). Gaius Julius Caesar Germanicus, Emperor 37–41 (called Gaius by Eusebius).

CALLISTIO (V. 13). Addressee of Rhodo's account of his disputation with Apelles.

CALLISTUS (VI. 21). A former slave who was bishop of Rome 217–*c.* 222. He was attacked by Hippolytus for both Sabellianism and laxity in admitting to communion those guilty of adultery and fornication. It is not clear what the truth is behind Hippolytus' charges. Eusebius seems to know nothing about it.

CANDIDUS (V. 27). A contemporary of Irenaeus who wrote a treatise (now lost), *The Six Days of Creation*.

CANON (III. 25). Eusebius lists the 'writings of the New Testament' in three categories: (i) those which are acknowledged by all: the four Gospels, the Acts of the Apostles, the Epistles of Paul (at III. 3 he specifies that there are 14, though he recognizes that the Roman Church denies that Hebrews is by Paul: at III. 38 he mentions the notion that Paul wrote the Epistle to the Hebrews in Hebrew and that the Greek version is a translation, either by Luke or, which Eusebius finds more convincing, by Clement of Rome), I John, I Peter, to which he adds, with doubts, the Revelation of John; (ii) those which are disputed: five of the Catholic Epistles – James, Jude, II Peter, and II and III John; (iii) the spurious books: the Acts of Paul, the Shepherd of Hermas, the Revelation of Peter, the Epistle of Barnabas, the Teachings of the Apostles (the *Didache*), and the Revelation of John (if it does not belong in class i). Eusebius also mentions as a possible candidate for class iii the Gospel of the Hebrews. Additionally, he lists works that are simply heretical, falsely ascribed to the apostles: the gospels of Peter, Thomas, Matthias, and the acts of Andrew, John, 'and other apostles'. This gives a vivid picture of the fluid nature of the New Testament canon at the beginning of the fourth century. Indeed the canon of the New Testament developed only gradually: it begins to take shape towards the end of the second century (spurred on as a response to Marcion's truncated canon), and becomes relatively settled only in the course of the fourth century. See H von Campenhausen, *The Formation of the Christian Bible*, trans. J. A. Baker (London, 1972).

CAPITO (V. 12). Tenth Gentile bishop of Jerusalem.

CARACALLA (VI. 8, 16, 21). Marcus Aurelius Antoninus, nicknamed Caracalla, elder son of Septimius Severus; Emperor 212–17 (called Antoninus by Eusebius).

CARICUS (V. 19. VI. 12). Correspondent of Serapion of Antioch.

CARINUS (VII. 30). Marcus Aurelius Carinus, elder son of Carus, he became Augustus on his death, and was killed, having been defeated in battle by Diocletian, in 285.

CARPOCRATES (IV. 7, 22). Gnostic. Eusebius says that Carpocrates was 'father of another heresy known as that of the Gnostics'; Irenaeus, whom he claims in support, says simply that the Carpocratians *called themselves* Gnostics.

CARPUS (IV. 15). Eusebius remarks that the accounts of the martyrdom of Carpus, Papylus and Agathonice survive. They were discovered late last century: see Musurillo, pp. 22–37.

CARUS (VII. 30). Marcus Aurelius Carus. Rebelled against Probus and became Emperor in 282. He invaded Persia and captured Ctesiphon but was killed in Persia.

CASSIAN (V. 12). Second Gentile bishop of Jerusalem.

CASSIAN (VI. 13). Julius Cassian, a second-century writer whose views were Encratite and Docetic. Eusebius refers to his *Chronography*. He is usually mentioned (as here) in tandem with Tatian. We know more about him from Clement who quotes from several works of his.

CASSIUS (V. 25). Bishop of Tyre, late second century.

CELADION (IV. 11, 19). Bishop of Alexandria (though not called bishop).

CELERINUS (VI. 43). A layman, one of the Confessors (q.v.); he seems to have been a Carthaginian.

CELSUS (VI. 19). Bishop of Iconium.

CELSUS (VI. 36). Author of the first-known pagan polemic against Christianity, called the *True Doctrine*. Eusebius calls him an Epicurean, but he was almost certainly a Platonist. His attack, which belongs to the late second century and was probably directed against Justin Martyr, produced a massive response from Origen in the middle of the third century. His fundamental charge against

Christians was one of sedition, coupled with that of innovation upon and corruption of ancient tradition. See *Origen: Contra Celsum*, translated with introduction and notes by H. Chadwick (Cambridge, 1953).

CEPHAS (I. 12). Eusebius, following Clement of Alexandria, maintains that the Cephas of Gal. ii. 11 was not the apostle Peter (although he obviously was) but another Cephas, one of the Seventy (q.v.).

CERDO (III. 21; IV. 1). Bishop of Alexandria (and called such at IV. 1).

CERDO (IV. 10f.). Heretic who, according to Irenaeus, taught in Rome in the time of pope Hyginus: he opposed the God of the Old Testament to the Father of Jesus Christ, was docetic and rejected the resurrection of the body. Irenaeus presents him as the precursor of Marcion.

CERINTHUS (III. 28; IV. 14; VIII. 25). Eusebius presents Cerinthus simply as a chiliast, indeed one who presented the coming kingdom of Christ on earth as a time of sensuous indulgence. (Dionysius mentions that some ascribed the Revelation of John to Cerinthus.) Irenaeus, however, saw Cerinthus as a Gnostic and an Ebionite, a heretic peculiarly opposed to Johannine Christianity, against whom John wrote his Gospel. According to Epiphanius, the *Alogi* (q.v.) ascribed both the Gospel and the Revelation to Cerinthus.

CHAEREMON (VI. 19). Stoic philosopher from Alexandria (first century A.D.).

CHAEREMON (VI. 42). Bishop of Nilopolis who fled during the Decian persecution.

CHAEREMON (VII. 11). Deacon, companion of Dionysius of Alexandria.

CHILIASM. The belief that at the second coming Christ will reign on earth for a thousand years (also called millenarianism). Most orthodox (non-Gnostic) Christians in the second century seem to have upheld it (cf. Rev. xx). It was anathema to Eusebius, and it is possibly because of his staunch chiliasm that Papias is regarded by Eusebius as being so simple-minded.

CHRESTUS (X. 5). Bishop of Syracuse, ordered by Constantine to attend the synod of Arles (314).

CHRYSOPHORA (IV. 23). Recipient of letter from Dionysius of Alexandria.

CLARUS (V. 25). Bishop of Ptolemais, late second century.

CLAUDIUS (II. 8, 11, 19). Tiberius Claudius Nero Germanicus, Emperor 41–54.

CLAUDIUS (VII. 28). Marcus Aurelius Claudius (Gothicus), Emperor 268–70, later claimed by Constantine as his ancestor.

CLEMENT OF ALEXANDRIA (I. 12; II. 1, 9, 15; III. 23, 29f, 34; IV. 26; V. 11, 28; VI. 6, 11, 13). Early Christian philosopher–theologian who taught in Alexandria at the end of the second century. His work, much of which survives, presents Christianity under an elegant guise, drawing on classical philosophy and literature as well as the Scriptures. He left Alexandria as a result of the persecution there (202), and we hear nothing of him again unless Eusebius' report (VI. 11) is to be trusted, which has him *c.* 211 carrying a letter for his friend Alexander from Cappadocia to Antioch (from the letter he appears to have been ordained presbyter). Eusebius quotes a good deal from his writings. E. F. Osborn, *The Philosophy of Clement of Alexandria* (Cambridge, 1957).

CLEMENT OF ROME (III. 4, 15, 16, 21, 38f.; IV. 22f.; V. 6; VI. 25). Third bishop of Rome, whom Eusebius (following Origen) identifies with the Clement of Phil. iv. 3. Eusebius mentions and quotes from the letter he 'wrote in the name of the Roman Church' to the church of Corinth, and reports that from the beginning it was read in Christian Churches. He knows of the so-called Second Epistle, but is reserved about its attribution to Clement. The Clementine Homilies he regards as spurious. Eusebius is quite favourably disposed to the idea that the Epistle to the Hebrews was composed by Paul in Hebrew and translated into Greek by Clement. For the *I Clement*, see *Early Christian Writings*, pp. 19–51.

CLEOBIUS (IV. 22). Otherwise unknown heretic.

CLEOPATRA (I. 5). Last of the Ptolemaic rulers of Egypt, reigned 51–30 B.C.

CLOPAS (III. 11; IV. 22). The disciple mentioned in the Gospels (Luke xxiv. 18, John xix. 25). According to Hegesippus he was the brother of Joseph, the foster-father of Jesus; his son, Symeon, succeeded James the Just as bishop of Jerusalem.

COLON (VI. 46). Bishop of Hermopolis, who received a letter from Dionysius of Alexandria on the subject of repentance, of which a fragment survives.

COMMODUS (IV. 26; V. 9, 21f., 26; VI. 6). Lucius Aelius Aurelius Commodus, elder son of Marcus Aurelius; sole Emperor 180–92 (when he changed his name to Marcus Aurelius Commodus Antoninus).

CONFESSORS. Those Christians who suffered during persecution without actually being killed: in this sense it is to be distinguished from the term 'martyr' (cf. V. 2.3), though sometimes the term 'martyr' is used more generally to cover the term confessor. In a more specific sense, the 'Confessors' refers to a group well-known from Cyprian's correspondence. They comprised two presbyters, Moses and Maximus, two deacons, Nicostratus and Rufinus, and four laymen, Celerinus, Sidonius, Urban and Macarius. All were imprisoned at Rome during the Decian persecution. Celerinus, apparently the first Confessor during the persecution at Rome, was examined by Decius himself, released and returned to Carthage. The rest were imprisoned after the martyrdom of Fabian. Moses, certainly, and Rufinus, probably, died in prison; the rest were released and for a time supported Novatian. They all, however, returned to the allegiance of pope Cornelius.

CONSTANTINE THE GREAT (VIII. 13, 17; IX. 9, 11; X. 5–9). Flavius Valerius Constantinus, born at Naïssus *c.* 285, he was proclaimed Augustus at York in 306, and became a Christian (in some sense) as a result of his victory over Maxentius at the Milvian Bridge outside Rome in 312, a victory that made him sole Emperor of the West. From then on he supported the Christian Church with gifts, legal exemptions for its clergy, etc. Eusebius tells us relatively little about Constantine in *The History of the Church*: his account of the battle of the Milvian Bridge is very low-key. His *Life of Constantine* (still unfinished when he died in

339) has a much more elaborate account, supposedly based on the Emperor's own memories.

CONSTANTIUS CHLORUS (VIII. 13, appendix). Flavius Valerius Constantius, father of Constantine the Great. He became Western Caesar in 293, and senior Augustus after Diocletian's abdication in 305. Although not a Christian himself, he was lenient to Christians during the Great Persecution.

COPONIUS (I. 5). First Prefect of Judaea, A.D. 6–9.

CORACION (VII. 24). Leader of the chiliasts in the Fayûm, who were convinced of their error by their bishop, Dionysius of Alexandria.

CORNELIUS (IV. 20). Bishop of Antioch.

CORNELIUS (VI. 39, 43, 46; VII. 2). Bishop of Rome 251–3. Elected pope April 251, when, owing to the Decian persecution and the martyrdom of Fabian, the see had been vacant for fourteen months. He found himself opposed by the Novatianists, but was supported by synods in both Rome and Carthage. He was banished to Centumcellae (Città Vecchia) by the Emperor Gallus, June 253, and died there.

CORNUTUS (VI. 19). Lucius Annaeus Cornutus, teacher of rhetoric and philosophy in Rome (first century, A.D.).

CRESCENS (III. 4). Associate of Paul the apostle.

CRESCENS (IV. 16). The philosopher who opposed Justin Martyr. He is described as a 'Cynic', the name given to a school of philosophy that despised conventions; it also means 'dog'.

CRISPUS (X. 9). The eldest son of Constantine. He was put to death by Constantine in 326, apparently on a charge of treason, and consequently there is no mention of him in the corresponding passage of the *Life of Constantine*, or in the Syriac version of *The History of the Church*.

CRONION (VI. 41). Martyred at Alexandria during Decian persecution; commemorated by the Church under his nickname, Eunus ('Goodfellow').

CRONIUS (VI. 19). Pythagorean philosopher, second century.

CULCIANUS (IX. 11). According to Eusebius, a friend of Maximin

Daia, appointed by him Prefect of Egypt and executed after his downfall. But there was a Clodius Culcianus whom we know from papyri to have been Prefect of Egypt in February 303 (too early to have been appointed by Maximin) and still there in May 306. It was he who condemned Phileas and Philoromus to death, apparently in February 307. For the Acts of Phileas, see Musurillo, pp. 328–53.

CYPRIAN (VI. 43; VII. 3). The great bishop of Carthage, *c*. 248–58. Eusebius seems not to have known very much about him, apart from his support for Cornelius over the Novatianist schism and his views on the rebaptism of heretics (which Eusebius regarded as an innovation). Many of his works survive, and an extensive correspondence.

CYRIL (VII. 32). Bishop of Antioch, a 'contemporary' of Eusebius. He was bishop when the Great Persecution broke out and was banished to Pannonia, where after three years, according to the *Passion of the Quatuor Coronati* (the Quattro Coronati, or the 'four crowned ones', to whom an ancient basilica on the Celian Hill in Rome is dedicated), he died of grief on hearing of the deaths of these four Pannonian martyrs.

DAMAS (III. 36). Bishop of Magnesia on the Maeander, mentioned by Ignatius.

DECIUS (VI. 39–41; VII. 1, 11, 22; VIII. 4). Gaius Messius Quintus Decius, Emperor 249–51. He instigated the first fully imperial persecution of the Christians. Eusebius says it was because of hatred of Philip, whom he overthrew and whom Eusebius says was a Christian. Rather the persecution was the inevitable consequence of his attempt to remedy the ailing condition of the Empire by requiring everyone to sacrifice to the traditional gods (the extant *libelli* – certificates of having sacrificed – make it clear that everyone was required to sacrifice, including pagans who could be under no suspicion of being Christians: see *A New Eusebius*, no. 200, pp. 228f.). Many Christians sacrificed, or otherwise acquired *libelli*, thereby provoking a crisis in the Church as it sought to deal with such mass apostasy.

DEMETRIAN (VI. 46; VII. 5, 14, 27, 30). Bishop of Antioch.

DEMETRIUS (V. 22; VI. 2f., 8, 14, 19, 26, 29). Bishop of Alexandria 189–231/2. He appointed Origen head of the Catechetical School in Alexandria *c.* 203 (and may have founded the school then). Later he fell out with Origen and in 231 at a synod banished him from Alexandria. Eusebius represents the quarrel between the two as concerned with disciplinary matters (Origen's preaching although a layman, and then his being ordained priest irregularly at Caesarea); it is possible the quarrel involved theological matters.

DEMETRIUS (VI. 13). Hellenistic Jew quoted by Clement of Alexandria, who compiled a brief chronological history of Israel *c.* 220–204 B.C. Schürer, III, pp. 513–17.

DEMETRIUS (VII. 11). Presbyter of Alexandria during Decian persecution.

DEMETRIUS (VII. 13). One of the bishops (presumably in Egypt) addressed in Gallienus' toleration edict.

DESPOSYNI (I. 7; III. 11, 9, 32). Name given to the relatives of Jesus (= 'belonging to the Lord'). Eusebius regards them as step-relations, relations of Joseph, Jesus' foster-father. James 'the Lord's brother' (q.v.), according to Eusebius Joseph's son, was the most famous of the *desposyni*: he became first bishop of Jerusalem, and was succeeded by Symeon (q.v.), another *desposynus*.

DIOCLETIAN (VIII 30; VIII. 2, 5, 13, appendix; IX. 9a, 10). Gaius Aurelius Valerius Diocletianus, Emperor 284–305. In 293 he reorganized the Empire by establishing his famous 'tetrarchy', with himself as Augustus in the East, Galerius being his Caesar, and his old comrade, Maximian, as Augustus in the West, Constantius Chlorus being his Caesar. In 303 he began a persecution of the Christians, the so-called 'Great Persecution', possibly at the instigation of Galerius. There were four edicts: the first ordered the closing of churches, the handing over of the Scriptures, and deprived the better classes who were Christians of their civil rights; the second ordered the imprisonment of the clergy; the third decreed torture and death for the clergy; and the fourth (in 304) required all to sacrifice to the gods. These edicts were unevenly enforced: much less strictly in the West than the East. After various vicissitudes the persecution came to a temporary halt with the edict of Galerius (311), but flared up again in the East and only came to an end with the so-called 'edict of Milan' (313) after Constantine's victory over Maxentius and conversion to Christianity. Meanwhile Diocletian and Maximian abdicated as Augusti in 305. Diocletian died probably in 311 (rather than the traditional later dates of 313 or even 316).

DIONYSIA (VI. 41). Christian mother martyred at Alexandria during the Decian persecution.

DIONYSIUS (II. 25; III. 4; IV. 21, 23). Bishop of Corinth, an important late second-century figure.

DIONYSIUS (III. 4; IV. 23). Paul's Athenian convert (Acts xvii. 34), who, according to Dionysius of Corinth, became the first bishop of Athens. At the end of the fifth or beginning of the sixth century, some works composed by a Syrian monk (*Celestial Hierarchy*, *Ecclesiastical Hierarchy*, *Divine Names*, *Mystical Theology*, and nine letters) were attributed to him: they were destined to be very influential. Later tradition also made him first bishop of Paris, and patron of France.

DIONYSIUS (VII. 5, 7–9, 13(?), 27, 30). Bishop of Rome, 260–68. Little is known about him apart from his correspondence with his namesake of Alexandria. (Eusebius mistakenly dates his reign 266–75.)

DIONYSIUS OF ALEXANDRIA (III. 28; VI. 29, 35, 40–46; VII. 0, 1f., 4–7, 9–11, 13(?), 20–8, 30, 32). Bishop of Alexandria 247–*c*. 264. We know little for certain about him before he became bishop. Eusebius says he was head of the Catechetical School after Heraclas (from *c*. 233), and a pupil of Origen's. But his own exceptional rhetorical and philosophical culture, together with what seems a reference to a distinguished civil career (see VI. 11, 18), perhaps suggests that he was a late convert to Christianity who received his intellectual formation as a pagan. Eusebius devotes almost as much attention to him as to Origen, and it is perhaps his devotion to Origen that leads him to represent Dionysius as Origen's disciple. As bishop he had to deal with the Decian persecution (during which he fled) and the mass apostasy it occasioned: he was indulgent towards repentant apostates. In 251 he immediately supported Cornelius in Rome against the anti-pope, Novatian. Later he supported pope Stephen against Cyprian over the question of the rebaptism of heretics. We also learn from him about civil war and plague in Alexandria, apparently after the persecution under Valerian in which he was banished from Alexandria. An episode Eusebius does not tell us about concerns the correspondence with his namesake of Rome about the doctrine of the Trinity, in which Dionysius of Rome accused him of tritheism. He was invited *c.* 264 to a synod in Antioch to deal with the problem of Paul of Samosata, but could not go because of ill-health and must have died about that time. He opposed chiliastic interpretations of the Revelation, which he argued was not by the apostle, but by another John, perhaps John the presbyter (q.v.).

DIOSCURUS (VI. 41; VII. 11). A boy who was tortured during the Decian persecution.

DIUS (VI. 10). Said to have been appointed bishop of Jerusalem in succession to Narcissus during his absence (temporary, according to Eusebius' account).

DIUS (VIII. 13). Alexandrian presbyter, martyred in the Great Persecution.

DOCETISTS (VI. 12). Heretics who denied that Christ had a real humanity (so he only seemed – Greek: *dokein* – to be human). A common heresy in the early centuries, especially amongst Gnostics.

DOLICHIAN (V. 12). Twelfth Gentile bishop of Jerusalem.

DOMITIAN (III. 13–20, 32). Titus Flavius Domitianus, son of the Emperor Vespasian; Emperor 81–96. Towards the end of his reign, he became more and more ruthless, until it degenerated into a Terror (93–6). It is very likely that Christians suffered along with everyone else, less clear that there was a specific persecution of Christians as Eusebius alleges.

DOMITILLA (III. 18). Niece of Domitian and husband of Flavius Clemens (not his niece, as Eusebius claims). They were charged with atheism (probably Judaism, or sympathy with Judaism): Flavius Clemens was executed, Domitilla exiled to Pandateria.

Eusebius treats her as a Christian martyr, and the existence of the (Christian) Cemetery of Domitilla in Rome was for long held to support this. But the cemetery itself proves no more than that from about 150 onwards, the Christians constructed a cemetery on land that had belonged to Domitilla fifty years before.

DOMITIUS AND DIDYMUS (VII. 11, 20). Recipients of a letter from Dionysius of Alexandria. It refers to events belonging to the Decian persecution, though Eusebius misplaces it and has it referring to the persecution under Valerian.

DOMNINA (VIII. 12). Martyred at Antioch during the Great Persecution. We learn her name from St John Chrysostom: her two daughters were called Bernice and Prosdoce.

DOMNUS (VI. 12). Christian of Antioch who lapsed into Judaism because of persecution, and to whom Serapion wrote.

DOMNUS (VII. 14). Bishop of Caesarea, 257/8.

DOMNUS (VII. 30, 32). Bishop of Antioch, son of Demetrian, elected to succeed Paul of Samosata (Demetrian's successor).

DONATISTS. A schismatic body in the North African Church that rejected the consecration of Caecilian as bishop of Carthage, on the grounds that he had been consecrated by one who had been a *traditor* during the Great Persecution. They elected Majorinus as bishop of Carthage, who was soon succeeded by Donatus, from whom they are called. They were particularly strong in Numidia. Eusebius never mentions them by the name Donatists, but knows of them, alludes to them (V. 2), and preserves important documents relating to the beginning of the Donatist schism (X. 5.15–7.2). W. H. C. Frend, *The Donatist Church* (Oxford, 1952).

DOROTHEA (VIII. 14). Exiled at Alexandria after refusing the advances of the Emperor Maximin (we learn her name from Rufinus' Latin translation of *The History of the Church*).

DOROTHEUS (VII. 32). Learned presbyter of Antioch, about whom we know nothing more than Eusebius tells us; late third century.

DOROTHEUS (VIII. 6). Member of the imperial household, martyred in the Great Persecution.

DOSITHEUS (IV. 22). A Samaritan, the founder, apparently, of a messianic sect, about whom we know virtually nothing; second century.

EASTER. The yearly festival of the Resurrection of Christ, along with Sunday, the weekly anniversary of the Resurrection, the oldest festival of the Christian Church. The Greek name (*pascha*) is the same word as that used for the Jewish Passover. It is to be noticed that there was no commemoration of the Passion of Christ apart from Easter: the Passion and Resurrection of Christ were observed as a single liturgical event.

The celebration of Easter has given rise to several controversies. The first was over the question whether Easter was the Christian Passover, to be celebrated a the same time as the Jews celebrated Passover, or whether, as the feast of the Resurrection, it must always be celebrated on a Sunday. Those who celebrated Easter on the Jewish Passover were called *Quartodecimans* (q.v.). Quartodecimanism was, though only by implication, condemned at the Council of Nicaea (325), where the immediate issue about Easter seems to have been a conflict between different ways of calculating the date of the Paschal full moon. According to Jewish methods (followed by the church of Antioch), the Paschal full moon could occur either before or after the Vernal Equinox (which had simply to fall in the month Nisan); according to Christian methods (followed at both Alexandria and Rome, though otherwise these methods were not identical), Easter (and therefore the Paschal full moon) had to fall *after* the Vernal Equinox. The Council of Nicaea seems to have forbidden Christians to celebrate Easter 'with the Jews', i.e., to follow their methods of calculation, but does not seem to have further specified how to calculate the date of Easter.

Eusebius is interested in methods of calculating the date of Easter. It was inconvenient simply to wait until the full moon after the Vernal Equinox and then celebrate Easter on the following Sunday: it allowed no time for preparation. So various schemes were devised. Eusebius tells us of Hippolytus' sixteen-year (really, double eight-year) cycle (VI. 22), Dionysius of Alexandria's eight-year cycle (VII. 20), and Anatolius' nineteen-year cycle, which is the one still in use.

EBIONITE (III. 27; V. 8; VI. 17). The word is derived from a Hebrew word meaning 'the poor': this may indicate that the original Ebionites were materially poor, or that they thought of themselves as the 'poor ones' who depend utterly on the grace of God (cf. the figure of the poor in the Psalms, e.g., Ps. xl. 17, and the first Beatitude, Matt. v. 3, Luke, vi. 20). The derivations Eusebius gives (both derived from Origen) – that they have a poor or mean idea of Christ in thinking him merely a man, or display poverty of intelligence in rejecting the pre-existence of the Reason (or Word) of God – are both derogatory. They seem to have been Jewish Christians, who respected Christ, but could not conceive of his relationship to God as anything other than that of a man inspired by God (like one of the prophets). Eusebius is scornful of Jewish Christianity, and knows little about it anyway: it seems to have been much more important in the early centuries of Christianity than appears from *The History of the Church*.

ELAGABALUS (VI. 21). Varius Avitus Bassianus, Emperor 218–22 (he took the name Elagabalus, the name of the sun-god of Emesa, whose hereditary priest he was, when he became Emperor).

ELEUTHERUS (IV. 11, 22; V. 0, 3, 4, 6, 22). Bishop of Rome *c*. 174–89, during the beginning of the Montanist crisis.

ELKASAITES. Called by Eusebius Helkasaites (q.v.).

ELPISTUS (IV. 23). Corinthian Christian in the time of Dionysius of Corinth.

ENCRATITES (IV. 28f.). From the Greek *enkrateia*, 'self-control'. Encratites were ascetics, who abstained from wine and meat, and frequently from marriage as well. Many early Christians manifest Encratite tendencies, especially in the Syrian Church. Those who rejected Encratism accused them of calling in question the doctrine of creation (as those who were Gnostics certainly did). Eusebius suggests that Tatian was the founder of Encratism, but the tendency seems too widespread for that to be plausible.

EPHRES (IV. 5). Thirteenth bishop of Jerusalem.

EPIMACHUS (VI. 41). Martyred at Alexandria in the Decian persecution. He is commemorated with Alexander on 12 December, which suggests that the 'long imprisonment' may have lasted from February to December.

EROS (IV. 20). Bishop of Antioch.

ESSENES (IV. 22). One of the seven Jewish sects listed by Hegesippus; also one of the four sects mentioned by Josephus (*Ant.* xviii. 1, 2, 6). They were an ascetic group and formed themselves into religious communities: the community at Qumran was probably Essene, and Eusebius' *Therapeutae* (not Christians, as he thought) are very like Essenes. Schürer, II, pp. 555–74, 583–90.

EUELPIUS (VI. 19). A layman who preached in Laranda at the invitation of the bishop, Neon.

EUETHIUS (VIII. 5). The name, probably, of the man who tore down Diocletian's Edict of Persecution and thus suffered martyrdom. Eusebius does not give his name, but according to the Syriac martyrology a Euethius suffered martyrdom at Nicomedia on 24 February, the day the edict was published. Tradition identified him with St George (of England).

EUMENES (IV. 5, 11). Bishop of Alexandria (not called bishop).

EUPHRANOR (VII. 26). Recipient of a letter from Dionysius of Alexandria on temptation.

EUPOLEMUS (VI. 13). Hellenistic Jew quoted by Clement of Alexandria, who wrote a colourful account of the history of the Jews, embellished with midrashic tales (second half of second century B.C.). Schürer, III, pp. 517–21.

EUPORUS (VII. 26). Recipient of letter from Dionysius of Alexandria.

EUSEBIUS (VII. 11, 32). Deacon who had visited the confessors in Alexandria during the Decian persecution, and shared the sufferings of Dionysius under Valerian. Bishop of Laodicea in Syria, prob. *c.* 264–9.

EUSEBIUS (X. 4). The Church Historian himself, modestly styled as 'one of the moderately capable'. Bishop of Caesarea, *c.* 313–39.

EUTYCHIAN (VII. 32). Bishop of Rome, 4 January 274/3 January 275–7 December 282/3: therefore, nine years (not ten months, as Eusebius has it).

EUTYCHIUS (VII. 30). Member of the synod that condemned Paul of Samosata.

EVARESTUS (III. 34; IV. 1; V. 6). Bishop of Rome, *c.* 100–*c.* 109.

EVODIUS (III. 22). First bishop of Antioch.

EZRA (V. 8). Jewish priest (fourth/fifth century B.C.) who played a major role in the restoration of Judaism in Jerusalem after the return from Exile. Jewish tradition attributed to him the miraculous recreation of the Jewish Scriptures (see 2 Esdras xiv), a story alluded to by Irenaeus.

FABIAN (VI. 29, 36, 39). Bishop of Rome 10 January 236–20 January 250, when he suffered martyrdom in the Decian persecution. An election of a successor was impossible until Decius had left Rome on his expedition against the Goths: Cornelius was elected after a vacancy in the see of fourteen months.

FABIUS (VI. 39, 41, 43f., 46; VII. 14). Bishop of Antioch, who was inclined to support Novatian after the Decian Persecution, and to whom Dionysius, Cornelius and Cyprian wrote to prevent him.

FADUS (II. 11). Cuspius Fadus, Procurator of Judaea, 44–?46.

FAUSTINUS (VII. 11). Alexandrian presbyter (probably) mentioned in Dionysius' letter to Domitius and Didymus.

FAUSTUS (VI. 40; VII. 11; VIII. 13). A deacon who shared Dionysius' sufferings in Alexandria under Decius and Valerian, and later in the Great Persecution suffered martyrdom as a presbyter. (It is possible that there are two Fausti involved.)

FELIX (II. 19–20). Procurator of Judaea *c.* 52–?60 (cf. Acts xxiii–xxiv).

FELIX (VII. 30, 32). Bishop of Rome 269–273/4 (Eusebius mistakenly implies 275–80).

FESTUS (II. 22). Procurator of Judaea ?60–62 (cf. Acts xxiv. 27–xxv. 27).

FIRMILIAN (VI. 27, 46; VII. 5, 14, 28, 30). Bishop of Caesarea in Cappadocia, *c.* 230–268. An influential churchman and an admirer of Origen, whom he visited at Caesarea and who spent several years with him in Cappadocia. He attended the synod at Iconium *c*. 230, which concerned itself with the Montanist schism, and took part in the Novatianist controversy at Antioch in 252. He supported Cyprian of Carthage against Stephen of Rome over the question of the rebaptism of heretics (his only extant writing is a letter to Cyprian). He was president of the first synod of Antioch called to examine the question of Paul of Samosata, and died at Tarsus on his way to the final synod in 268.

FLAVIUS (VII. 20). Recipient of one of Dionysius of Alexandria's festal letters.

FLAVIUS CLEMENS (III. 18). Husband – not uncle – of Domitilla (q.v.).

FLORINUS (V. 15, 20). Roman presbyter who became a heretic, and later embraced Valentinianism. Irenaeus wrote a letter and a treatise, *The Ogdoad*, against him.

FLORUS (II. 26). Procurator of Judaea, 64–6.

FRONTINUS (V. 18). Aemilius Frontinus, Proconsul at Ephesus, who tried the Montanist 'martyr', Alexander. Otherwise unknown.

GAIUS (II. 4–8). See Caligula.

GAIUS (II. 25; III. 28, 31; VI. 20). A churchman of Rome of the early third century for whose learning Eusebius had the greatest admiration. He composed a *Dialogue* against the Montanist Proclus during the time of pope Zephyrinus. In this he attacks Cerinthus for his chiliastic beliefs (for Cerinthus the coming kingdom of Christ would be a time of riotous sensual indulgence). It is possible that Eusebius' enthusiasm for anti-chiliasm has got the better of him. Elsewhere it appears that Gaius was a heretic whom Hippolytus opposed, and that his anti-chiliasm was but part of his total rejection of the Johannine corpus (both Revelation and the Gospel), which he ascribed to Cerinthus (the passage quoted at III. 28.2 is probably meant to imply that Cerinthus was the author of Revelation, though Eusebius clearly did not so understand it). All this makes Gaius look like one of the *Alogi* (q.v.), and would fit with the hypothesis that he wrote the *Little Labyrinth* (q.v.), a hypothesis that is, however, unproven.

GAIUS (V. 12). The name of the sixth and the eighth Gentile bishops of Jerusalem.

GAIUS (V. 16). Martyr from Eumenia in Phrygia who suffered at Apamea.

GAIUS (VI. 40; VII. 11). Christian who shared Dionysius' sufferings during the Decian Persecution.

GAIUS (VII. 32). Bishop of Rome, 16/17 December 282/3–22 April 295/6, one of Eusebius' 'contemporaries'.

GALEN (V. 28). The famous physician, A.D. 129–?199.

GALERIUS (VIII. 5, 16f., appendix). Gaius Galerius Valerius Maximianus, chosen by Diocletian as Caesar of the East in 293, he became Augustus of the East on Diocletian's abdication in 305. He is thought to have been behind the Great Persecution. Falling ill in 311 he relented and issued an edict of partial toleration (VIII. 17), and died a gruesome death shortly afterwards, which Eusebius describes with grim delight, relishing the parallels with the fates of other tyrants: Herod the Great (*The Jewish War*, p. 117), Herod Agrippa I (Acts xii. 20–3 and Josephus, *Antiquities*, XIX. 8) and Antiochus I (2 Maccabees ix. 5–29).

GALILEANS (IV. 22). One of the seven sects of the Jews listed in Hegesippus, probably the same as the fourth of Josephus' Jewish 'philosophies', the more recent sect founded by Judas the Galilean or Gaulonite.

GALLIENUS (VII. 10, 11, 13, 22, 23, 28). Publius Cornelius Egnatius Gallienus, son of Valerian, appointed Augustus with him in 253. After the capture of his father by the Persians (260), Gallienus faced various revolts, including that of Aemilian in Alexandria. He established himself in the East, but had tacitly to accept the rule of Postumus in the West. He quickly put an end to his father's persecution of the Christians, and issued an edict of toleration that recognized the Church's right to places of worship (rescript summarizing edict: VII. 13). He was murdered 20 March 268.

GALLUS (VII. 1, 10). Gaius Vibius Trebonianus Gallus, succeeded Decius after his death, Emperor 251–3. Towards the end of his reign he banished pope Cornelius in Centumcellae, but it is not clear that there was a renewal of persecution in his reign.

GERMANICUS (IV. 15). Martyred in Smyrna shortly before Polycarp.

GERMANION (VI. 10). One of the bishops appointed to succeed Narcissus, during his absence from Jerusalem.

GERMANUS (VI. 40; VII. 11). Bishop who accused Dionysius of Alexandria of cowardice for fleeing in the Decian persecution, to whom Dionysius wrote a long response.

GNOSTICS A name given to dualist heretics prominent in the second century. Their beliefs vary widely, but almost all agreed that the creator of the world was not the true God whom Jesus had revealed. Eusebius seems to regard Carpocrates as the founder of Gnosticism (IV. 7): more commonly it was Simon Magus (q.v.) who was so regarded.

GORDIAN (VI. 29, 34). Antonius Gordianus, Emperor 238–44. Eusebius passes over the complicated events of 238. In that year Marcus Antonius Gordianus, then aged seventy-nine, was invited by some nobles to become Emperor in succession to Maximin. He made his son, Gordian II, his colleague. In the struggle against those loyal to Maximin, Gordian II was killed, and Gordian I committed suicide after a reign of twenty-two days. Balbinus and Pupienus Maximus were appointed Emperors, Gordian III (the Gordian Eusebius mentions) being Caesar. After Maximin's murder, Balbinus and Pupienus were also murdered, and the boy Gordian (he was thirteen) became sole Emperor. Power was first in the hands of his mother, Maecia Faustina, daughter of Gordian I, then passed to the Praetorian Prefect Timesitheus, and eventually into the hands of Philip the Arab, who had Gordian murdered and succeeded him in 244.

GORDIUS (VI. 10). One of the bishops appointed to succeed Narcissus, bishop of Jerusalem, during his absence.

GORGONIUS (VIII. 6). Member of imperial household martyred under Diocletian.

GORTHAEUS (IV. 22). Heresiarch, of whom nothing is known.

GRATUS (V. 16). Proconsul of Syria during the early stages of Montanist crisis, otherwise unknown.

GREGORY (VI. 30; VII. 14, 28). Gregory Thaumaturgus ('miracle-worker', though Eusebius does not use this name), also called Theodore. He and his brother, Athenodore, were born of pagan parents in Neocaesarea in Pontus, and studied rhetoric, before going to Caesarea where they were converted to Christianity by Origen and became his pupils. After studying with Origen, they went back to Pontus, Gregory becoming bishop of Neocaesarea, and converted the pagan population. When Gregory left Origen, he composed a fine panegyric on Origen, which contains a splendid account of Origen as a teacher. In 253–4 he witnessed the Goths devastating Pontus, something he describes in his 'Canonical Letter'. He also took part in the first synod of Antioch (264/5) called to deal with Paul of Samosata. He died *c.* 270. See Lane Fox, pp. 517–42.

HADRIAN (IV. 3–10; V. 5, 11). Publius Aelius Hadrianus, Emperor 117–38. His rebuilding of Jerusalem as Colonia Aelia Capitolina with a shrine to Jupiter Capitolinus on the site of the Temple provoked the Jewish revolt of 132–5. After the suppression of the revolt, Jews were banned from Aelia Capitolina (therefore from this date the succession of *Gentile* bishops of Jerusalem begins), and Judaea became Syria Palaestina, under a Consular Legate with two legions.

HEBREWS, Epistle to (III. 3, 38; VI. 13f., 20, 25, 41). Eusebius includes this among the epistles of Paul the apostle, but is well aware that there was dispute about this attribution, especially at Rome (Gaius is mentioned as denying its Pauline authorship). Eusebius also knows of a compromise position: that Paul wrote an epistle to the Hebrews in Hebrew, and that the epistle we have is a translation of it into Greek, either by Luke the Evangelist or (as Eusebius thinks more likely) by Clement of Rome (III, 38). It is now generally accepted that the Epistle is not by Paul.

HEBREWS, *Gospel of the* (III. 25, 27, 39; IV. 22). A gospel that found especial favour with Jewish Christians (i.e., Jews who had become Christians). Eusebius includes it among the 'disputed' books of the New Testament (probably among the spurious ones), but does not regard it as heretical (cf. III. 25). This *Gospel of the Hebrews* is the Jewish–Christian gospel most often mentioned by the Fathers (others being the *Gospel of the Nazarenes*, which was written in Aramaic or Syriac, to which Eusebius refers as known to Hegesippus – IV. 22 – and the *Gospel of the Ebionites*, which seems to have been definitely heretical). A few fragments remain: it seems to have no special relationship to the Canonical Gospels, and gave some prominence to the appearance of the Risen Lord to James 'the Lord's brother'. Eusebius knows a fragment about a woman 'falsely accused before the Lord of many sins': this could be the passage that appears in our Bibles as John vii. 53–viii. 11, which is omitted by most manuscripts or included after Luke xxi. See James, pp. 1–10 and Hennecke and Schneemelcher, I, pp. 117–65.

HEGESIPPUS (II. 23; III. 11f., 16, 19f., 32; IV. 7, 8, 11, 21f.). A converted Jew (a 'Jewish Christian'), probably a native of Palestine, who wrote his 'Memoirs' in five books, a work directed against the Gnostics. Though they now survive only in fragments (mainly preserved by Eusebius), the work is said to have existed entire in some libraries until the sixteenth or seventeenth century. He is one of Eusebius' principal sources for the early history of Jerusalem. Eusebius places him in the first half of the second century.

HELEN (II. 12). Mother of Izates, king of Adiabene (beyond the Tigris, near ancient Nineveh). She and her whole family had converted to Judaism in the first century A.D.

HELENUS (VI. 46; VII. 5, 28, 30). Bishop of Tarsus, who apparently convened a synod at Antioch to gather support for Novatian (who had won the support of Fabius, bishop of Antioch) (VI. 46). He attended the synods of Antioch that condemned Paul of Samosata, at the latter of which he presided instead of the recently deceased Firmilian.

HELIODORUS (VII. 5). Bishop of Laodicea in Syria.

HELKESAITES (VI. 38). A Jewish–Christian sect which arose early in the second century in the Jordan valley and which took its name from their sacred writing, the *Book of Elkesai*, in which Elkesai wrote down the revelation he had received from an angel of enormous stature, who was the Son of God, and who had been accompanied by a female of similar dimensions, who was the Holy Spirit. They rejected the authority of Paul the apostle, in common with many Jewish–Christian sects, and laid great emphasis on the forgiveness of sins in baptism. We know more about them from Hippolytus and Epiphanius (who call them Elkesaites) than from Eusebius, who is mistaken both as to their date (not as late as *c.* 140) and as to their duration. Far from being short-lived, there seems evidence of them as late as the tenth century. They seem, too, to have provided the background in which Mani was nurtured.

HEMEROBAPTISTS (IV. 22). One of the seven Jewish sects mentioned by Hegesippus, who practised daily ablutions. From other (Christian) sources, it seems that their beliefs were similar to those of the Pharisees, except that they denied the doctrine of the resurrection of the body.

HERACLAS (VI. 3, 15, 19, 26, 29, 31, 35; VII. 7, 9). An older man than Origen, who had attended the classes of Ammonius Saccas for five years before Origen began to do so. Converted by Origen, he was closely associated with him in the Catechetical School, and succeeded Origen as head when he left Alexandria *c.* 231. He soon succeeded Demetrius as bishop of Alexandria (*c.* 232) and remained bishop until 247. According to Africanus (VI. 31), he had a great intellectual reputation, and was probably less in the shadow of Origen than Eusebius seems to imply. (Called 'pope' at VII. 7: a common and early title for the bishop of Alexandria.)

HERACLIDES (VI. 4). Pupil of Origen's at the Catechetical School, martyred while still a catechumen.

HERACLIDES (X. 6). Procurator (chief financial officer) of Africa under Anulinus.

HERACLITUS (V. 27). Christian writer who composed a work on the Pauline epistles, otherwise unknown.

HERAIS (VI. 4). A woman, a pupil of Origen's, who was martyred ('received the baptism of fire', and so was still a catechumen).

HERMAMMON (VII. 1, 10, 22). Recipient of letter from Dionysius of Alexandria.

HERMAS (III. 3; V. 8). Author of *The Shepherd*, an early Christian work of visions and moral exhortation (usually reckoned as one of the 'Apostolic Fathers') that was accorded nearly canonical status in some circles of the early Church (it appears after the books of the New Testament in the fourth-century *Codex Sinaiticus* (now in the British Library), and is quoted as Scripture by Irenaeus, as Eusebius reports: V. 8). The Muratorian Canon (and the Liberian Catalogue) identifies him as a brother of Pius, bishop of Rome *c.* 140–55, and says he wrote during his reign. Hermas himself refers to Clement as his contemporary, which would suggest a late first-century date. There is no consensus as to which date is correct. See Lane Fox, pp. 381–90.

HERMO (VII. 32). Last of the bishops of Jerusalem 'up to the persecution of my time'.

HERMOPHILUS (V. 28). Otherwise unknown, presumably disciple of Theodotus (q.v.), the cobbler or the banker.

HERO (III. 36; IV. 20). Bishop of Antioch in succession to Ignatius.

HERO (VI. 4). Pupil of Origen's, martyred just after his baptism.

HERO (VI. 41). An Egyptian (i.e., a Copt) martyred during the Decian persecution at Alexandria.

HEROD (I 6, 8f.). 'The Great'. Appointed king of the Jews by the Romans in 40 B.C. and reigned 37–4 B.C. It was during his reign that Christ was born.

HEROD (IV. 15). Chief of police who took Polycarp to the arena in Smyrna to be martyred. (It is possible that his name is an embellishment, to bring out the parallel between Polycarp's martyrdom and Christ's crucifixion; or it may have been recorded for that reason.)

HERODIAS (I. 11; II. 4). Daughter of Aristobulus IV, one of Herod's sons, who married first another of his sons, Herod, and then Herod's brother, Antipas. The marriage of Antipas and

Herodias provoked the condemnation of John the Baptist, and Herodias' resentment eventually secured John's death.

HESYCHIUS (VIII. 13). An Egyptian bishop, imprisoned with Phileas during the Great Persecution, and martyred.

HIERAX (VII. 21, 30). An Egyptian bishop, recipient of letter from Dionysius of Alexandria and member of the final Antiochene synod (268) that condemned Paul of Samosata.

HIPPOCRATES (X. 4). The great Greek physician, quoted (not by name) in Eusebius' festal oration addressed to Paulinus of Tyre.

HIPPOLYTUS (VI. 20, 22). Great Roman theologian and writer, and probably the first anti-pope. We know very little about him, and Eusebius seems to know even less. A man of enormous learning, he wrote extensively against the Gnostics and particularly opposed Sabellianism. He was also a rigorist in the matter of the Church's penitential discipline. Both these seem to have led to his sustained opposition to the popes of his day, and during the reign of Callistus he seems to have become anti-pope (hence (?) Eusebius' ignorance of his see). During the reign of the Emperor Maximin, both he and the pope (Pontian) were exiled to Sardinia, where they were apparently reconciled. In 1551 the torso of a statue was discovered at Rome, the base of which is inscribed with an Easter table and a list of works, much like what we know Hippolytus to have written (not much like Eusebius' admittedly incomplete list). It was taken to be a statue of Hippolytus, and thus restored (it now stands in the entrance-hall of the Vatican Library). It seems, however, to be the statue of a female figure (perhaps representing the Church, and commemorating the achievement of one of her theologians?). Apart from his Scriptural commentaries, his most important work (known to Eusebius) is his *Refutation of all Heresies*, most of which was discovered in a manuscript on Mount Athos in the last century. The important *Apostolic Tradition* (in the list on the statue) with its account of the Church's liturgy at the beginning of the third century has also survived (though not in its original form).

HIPPOLYTUS (VI. 46). Bearer of Dionysius of Alexandria's letter to the Romans.

HOSIUS (X. 6). (So in Greek sources, meaning 'pious': properly Ossius) Bishop of Cordova from *c.* 296, from early in the fourth century he appears as Constantine's ecclesiastical adviser. He was sent by Constantine to investigate the Arian controversy and played an important role at the Council of Nicaea. He lived to a great age, and suffered considerably during the later stages of the Arian controversy.

HYGINUS (IV. 10f.; V. 6, 24). Bishop of Rome 136–40.

HYMENAEUS (VII. 14, 28, 30, 32). Bishop of Jerusalem, one of Eusebius' 'contemporaries'. Participated in the synods at Antioch that dealt with the problem of Paul of Samosata.

IGNATIUS (III. 22, 36, 38f.; V. 8). Bishop of Antioch who was arrested there and sent under guard to Rome, where he was martyred in the reign of the Emperor Trajan. During the journey he wrote letters to various churches in Asia Minor and to the church at Rome, encouraging the Christians in their faith and combating those Jewish Christians who seemed to him to be restricting the meaning and practice of the Christian Gospel, and others (maybe the same) who could not accept the reality of Christ's Incarnation and his sufferings, and inclined to docetism. He speaks with great enthusiasm of his coming martyrdom. See *Early Christian Writings*, pp. 53–112.

INGENUUS (VI. 41). Soldier, martyred at Alexandria in the Decian persecution.

IRENAEUS (II. 13; III. 18, 23, 26, 28, 36, 39; IV. 7, 10, 11, 18, 21f., 25, 29; V. 4, 7f., 20, 23, 26, 28; VI. 13). The greatest theologian of the second century, he was bishop of Lyons in succession to Pothinus who died in the persecution at Lyons and Vienne in 177, the account of which Eusebius preserves (V. 1). Two of this works have survived: *Against Heresies*, which survives complete in a Latin translation, and the *Demonstration of the Apostolic Preaching*, which survives in an Armenian version discovered in the last century. In addition, Eusebius mentions several letters, a treatise called the *Ogdoad*, a brief apologetic treatise and a collection of homilies. His *Demonstration* is an exposition of the Church's Rule of Faith (or

Rule of Truth), the creed-like summary of the Christian faith that Irenaeus (in common with other second- and third-century writers) refers to several times. *Against Heresies* is a lengthy attack on Gnosticism, especially Valentinianism in its various forms. Against their speculations, dualistic opposition of the Old and New Testaments, and appeal to a secret apostolic tradition, he lays emphasis on a faith available to all, even the simplest, the identity of the God of the Old Testament and the Father preached by Jesus, and the unity of the two Testaments, and the public, and demonstrable, nature of the Church's tradition, to which the succession lists of the principal sees of the Christian Church (especially that of Rome) bear witness. A native of Asia Minor, he was fond of recalling his acquaintance with Polycarp, bishop of Smyrna, himself a disciple of John, the Beloved Disciple, and during the Quartodeciman controversy Irenaeus mediated between Rome and the Quartodecimans of Asia Minor. By tradition he died a martyr, but this tradition has no confirmation.

ISCHYRION (VI. 42). Martyred at Alexandria in Decian persecution.

ISIDORE (VI. 41). An Egyptian (i.e., a Copt) martyred at Alexandria in the Decian persecution.

JAMES (I. 12; II. 1, 23; III. 5, 11; IV, 5, 22; VII. 19). 'The Lord's Brother', also 'the Righteous' or 'the Just'. Eusebius, along with most early tradition, regards James as a son of Joseph, Jesus' foster-father, and therefore really a step-brother (from Jerome onwards, the Western tradition thought of him as a cousin of Jesus). The Risen Lord appeared to him (1 Cor. xv. 7), and this may have convinced his doubting brother (cf. John vii. 5). He became a leader of the Church in Jerusalem, while remaining devoutly Jewish. According to Hegesippus, he was a Nazirite and wore the linen clothes of a priest (and according to Epiphanius, in a passage from Hegesippus omitted by Eusebius, he wore the *petalon*, the sacerdotal plate, or perhaps mitre, as did John, the Beloved Disciple: see III. 31). He entered the Sanctuary of the Temple (reserved for priests), and spent much time there in prayer. He was martyred in 62, of which martyrdom Eusebius preserves two accounts: one from Hegesippus, and a much briefer one from Josephus. Eusebius records that the *Epistle of James* is ascribed to him, but records, too, that some doubt it. He was the first bishop of Jerusalem or, as Eusebius puts it, the first to be elected to the 'episcopal throne' of Jerusalem. He regularly refers to the 'episcopal throne' of Jerusalem (and of nowhere else), and tells us that it still existed in his day (VII. 19).

JAMES THE APOSTLE (II. 9; III. 5, 39; V. 11). 'The Great', the brother of John, the first of the apostles to be martyred (Acts xii. 2).

JESUS (III. 8). A Jew (son of Ananias) who, according to the account of Josephus that Eusebius cites, was handed over to the Roman authorities by the Jewish authorities in Jerusalem for his preaching of doom: a fate oddly similar to that of Jesus Christ. He was released, and went on proclaiming woe to Jerusalem, until he was finally killed by a stone from a siege-engine in the early stages of the siege of Jerusalem (66).

JESUS CHRIST (I. 13; VII. 18). The ever-present subject of Eusebius's narrative. Two events are more specific. There is the story of His correspondence with king Abgar of Edessa (q.v.). There is also the account of a statue of Jesus, erected in gratitude by the woman cured of haemorrhaging (Mark v. 25–34) in Caesarea Philippi, who was herself commemorated in another statue facing it. Eusebius says that he himself had seen it, and does not seem at all censorious, though he describes it as a 'Gentile custom'. This is all the more odd in that, later, when Constantine's sister, Constantina, requested of Eusebius a portrait of Jesus, he replied very negatively, underlining the theological impossibility of any such depiction of Christ.

JOHN THE APOSTLE (III. 1, 18, 20, 23–5, 28f., 31, 39; IV. 14, 18, 24; V. 8, 11, 18, 20, 24; VI. 14, 25; VII. 10, 24f.) The 'beloved disciple', to whom are traditionally ascribed the fourth Gospel, the Epistles of John and the Revelation. Eusebius admits to doubts about his authorship of 2 and 3 John and of Revelation. The Passion Narrative in the fourth Gospel seems to suggest that John was known to the high priest (John xviii. 15), even though John was a Galilean fisherman, the son of Zebedee. Polycrates tells us that he wore the *petalon* (like James the Lord's brother, q.v.), which perhaps suggests that he belonged to one of the priestly families. Eusebius tells us that John was exiled to Patmos during the reign of Domitian, and returned to Ephesus after his death (in 96). On Patmos he received the revelations recorded in the book of Revelation. He died in the reign of Trajan (98–117) and was buried at Ephesus. John's Gospel was, according to Eusebius, the last of the canonical Gospels to be written and had the special aim of proclaiming Christ's divinity. Eusebius notices the discrepancy between John's Gospel and the others over the length of Christ's ministry, and explains it (unconvincingly) by saying that the synoptic Gospels record only the last year of the ministry, from the imprisonment of John the Baptist, while John covers the events of Jesus' ministry that preceded it (III. 24; cf. I. 10). Eusebius also knows of the *Acts of John*, which he regards as heretical: a good deal of it survives, and it is Gnostic (see James, pp. 228–70 and Hennecke and Schneemelcher, II, pp. 188–259).

JOHN THE BAPTIST (II. 9; III. 24). The Jewish prophet of repentance, put to death by Antipas, regarded by Christians as the forerunner of Christ.

JOHN 'THE PRESBYTER' (III. 39; cf. VII. 25). The writer of 2 and 3 John calls himself 'the presbyter' (though he does not give his name), and in a famous passage of Papias there is mention of 'the presbyter John', a disciple of the Lord, whom Eusebius takes to be distinct from John the apostle, so that there were two prominent Christians called John in Asia in the first century, both buried in Ephesus (the tradition of the two tombs of John in Ephesus is referred to twice). Eusebius is inclined to attribute the Revelation to John the presbyter, if it is felt that it cannot be attributed to the evangelist (as Dionysius of Alexandria argued with great force: VII. 25). It has to be said that it is not at all clear from the passage quoted from Papias that he is referring to two Johns. Nevertheless, John the presbyter had proved a tantalizing figure; some modern scholars have wanted to attribute the whole of the Johannine corpus to him, and indeed have seen in John the presbyter an important, though shadowy, figure in the beginnings of the Church in Asia Minor (see, e.g., B. H. Streeter, *The Primitive Church* (London, 1929), pp. 89–97).

JOHN (IV. 5). Seventh bishop of Jerusalem.

JOSEPH (I. 7, 8; II. 1; III. 11). The husband of Mary, the Mother of Jesus, and therefore foster-father of Jesus. According to Eusebius, it is his sons by a former wife who are known as the 'brothers of the Lord', Mary having remained a virgin and having had no children other than Jesus.

JOSEPH (IV. 5). Fourteenth Jewish bishop of Jerusalem.

JOSEPHUS (I. 5f., 8–11; II. 4–6, 10, 20f., 23, 26; III. 5f., 8, 9f.; VI, 13; VII. 32). The great Jewish historian, who lived *c.* 37–*c.* 100. Joseph, son of Matthias, as he is properly called, a priest from Jerusalem, was born in Palestine. He became a Pharisee, took part in the Jewish War, and was taken prisoner by Vespasian, whose favour he won by prophesying that he would become Emperor. When that prophecy was fulfilled in 69, Josephus was set free and took the name 'Flavius'. His first work, the *Jewish War*, was an account of that uprising and its suppression by the Romans. His other great work was the *Antiquities of the Jews*. He wrote a response to criticisms of his *Antiquities*, usually called *Against Apion*. Eusebius knows and mentions all these (III. 9), and regards the *Life*, from which he quotes, as an appendix to the *Antiquities*. However, he ascribes to him incorrectly the book known as *4 Maccabees* (for which see Charlesworth, II, pp. 531–64). In listing Josephus' works, Eusebius quotes a passage in which Josephus summarizes the Hebrew canon of Scripture – twenty-two books, divided into the familiar Law, Prophets (including the history books) and the Writings (comprising, it seems, Psalms, Proverbs, Ecclesiastes, and the Song of Songs) – a passage that many modern scholars find curiously anachronistic (cf. Origen's list: VI. 25). The passage quoted also insists on the inviolability of the text of Scripture in a way that is similarly held to be anachronistic.

Josephus is Eusebius' main source for the history of the first century A.D. Eusebius is also fond of showing how Josephus supports the history presupposed by the writings of the New Testament. These citations raise various problems. At I. 11. 7f., Eusebius quotes *Antiquities*, XVIII. 3. 3, a passage that refers to Christ as 'a very gifted man – if indeed it is right to call him a man'. All the manuscripts we have of the *Antiquities* agree with Eusebius' reading here: but it is hard not to think that it has been subject to some Christian interpolation. (A similar problem arises with passages in the *Jewish War* found only in the Slavonic version: see the Penguin Classics edition, pp. 470f.) At II. 23. 20, Eusebius quotes a passage from Josephus about the fall of Jerusalem being a punishment to the Jews for the stoning of James the Righteous (and including a reference to 'Jesus known as Christ'). This passage is nowhere found in the manuscripts of Josephus known to us, though Origen (*Contra Celsum* I. 47) quotes the same passage as from Josephus. Again, it is difficult not to think it a Christian embellishment. Another problem raised by Eusebius' citations of Josephus has to do with his very desire to show how they support the biblical record (in this context, principally Luke's *Acts of the Apostles*). Luke's account of the death of Agrippa I (called by him, quite correctly, Herod) has an angel smiting the king (see Acts xii. 21–3). Eusebius' citation from Josephus also has an angel, but Josephus' text in the manuscripts has an *owl*, which is described as a messenger (*angelos*) of death. Here Luke's version (to which Eusebius assimilates his quotation from the much fuller Josephus) may be the more authentic, and Josephus the one who has embellished the account. A more crucial example is Eusebius' citing Josephus' account of Theudas' rebellion in support of Luke's account of Gamaliel's speech (Acts v. 35–9), which also mentions an impostor named Theudas. But Josephus places the rebellion of Theudas in the procuratorship of Fadus, and Fadus became procurator in 44, more than a decade later than the date of Gamaliel's speech in Acts, so Gamaliel can hardly be referring to Josephus' Theudas.

JOSHUA (I. 2). Moses' successor as leader of the people of Israel (in Greek: Jesus).

JUDAS (I. 5). 'The Gaulonite or Galilean', who led a Jewish revolt *c.* A.D. 6, which is referred to by both Luke and Josephus. (Eusebius seems unaware that such a date, which is meant to be the date of the registration referred to in Luke's Infancy Narrative as taking place at the time of Christ's birth, poses problems for his chronology.)

JUDAS (I. 12; II. 1; V. 16). 'Iscariot', the disciple who betrayed Jesus. Eusebius shows no interest in Judas: in particular he does not preserve what Papias had to say about Judas' death (fragment 3).

JUDAS (IV. 5). Fifteenth and last Jewish bishop of Jerusalem; he must therefore have been bishop at the time of Bar Cochba's revolt.

JUDAS (V. 17). Christian prophet (cf. Acts xv. 32).

JUDE (III. 19f, 32; VI. 14). The brother of Jesus, presumably his step-brother (see James the Lord's brother). Supposed author of the *Epistle of Jude*. According to Hegesippus, his grandsons were brought before the Emperor Domitian, because they belonged to the royal line of David, but were dismissed as constituting no threat to his authority. Eusebius says that having been released they became leaders in the Church, both because they had borne witness (as martyrs or confessors) and because they were the Lord's kin (see *Desposyni*.)

JUDE (VI. 7). The Christian author of what would seem to be some kind of apocalypse, early third century.

JULIAN (V. 9, 22; VI. 2). Bishop of Alexandria.

JULIAN (V. 11). Name of the fifth and ninth Gentile bishops of Jerusalem.

JULIAN (V. 16). Bishop of Apamea, opponent of Montanism.

JULIAN (VI. 41). Martyred at Alexandria in the Decian persecution.

JULIANA (VI. 17). A woman from whom Origen received the notes (or commentary) on the Gospel of Matthew by Symmachus, the translator of the Hebrew Bible. According in Palladius (in the *Lausiac History*, 64), this Juliana was a Christian virgin in Caesarea in Cappadocia, with whom Origen stayed after he left Alexandria (*c.* 235). He says that he himself saw the volume of notes by

Symmachus, and says that it was inscribed in Origen's own hand to the effect that he had found the book with Juliana who had herself received it from Symmachus.

JUSTIN MARTYR (II. 13; III. 26; IV. 8f., 11, 16–18, 29; V. 8, 28). The greatest of the second-century apologists. He had studied as a philosopher before he became a Christian, and as a Christian continued to wear the robe of a philosopher (IV. 11), and thus taught Christianity as the true philosophy. Of his works only the first and second *Apologies* and the *Dialogue with Trypho the Jew* survive: Eusebius knew of other works. His *Apologies* are defences of the Christian faith against persecution, and the suspicions that seemed to justify such persecution; his *Dialogue with Trypho* is a long, and rather stylized, discussion of the interpretation of Scripture, in which Justin justifies the Christian 'prophetic' interpretation of the Scriptures against the arguments of Trypho. His other works were directed against heretics, notably Marcion and the Gnostics, and seem to have included some philosophical treatises. He was deeply influenced by the Platonic philosophy of his day, in which he saw many parallels to Christianity. He was martyred sometime between 162 and 168: the account of his martyrdom survives (see Musurillo, pp. 42–61). H. Chadwick, 'Justin Martyr's Defence of Christianity' in *Bulletin of the John Rylands Library* 47 (1965), pp. 275–97, reprinted in his *History and Thought of the Early Church* (London, 1982).

JUSTUS (III. 35; IV. 5). Name of third and eleventh bishops of Jerusalem.

JUSTUS (IV. 4). Bishop of Alexandria (not called bishop).

LAETUS (VI. 2). Quintus Maecius Laetus, Prefect of Egypt 200–203.

LATRONIAN (X. 5). 'Corrector' (i.e., governor) of Sicily under Constantine. Chrestus, bishop of Syracuse, is referred to him for transport for himself and his entourage to Arles.

LEONIDES (VI. 1). The 'father of Origen', as Eusebius says he is usually called; martyred at the beginning of the third century.

LEVI (IV. 5). Twelfth Jewish bishop of Jerusalem.

LICINIUS (VIII. 13, 17; IX. 9–11; X. 5, 8f.). Valerius Licinianus, born of peasant stock in (new) Dacia, he became a comrade of Galerius, and in 308 was made Augustus of the West to succeed Severus, who had been killed by Maxentius. In 312 he married Constantine's sister, Constantina, and after Constantine's victory over Maxentius, himself defeated Maximin (313). He began to fall out with Constantine, fought and lost an indecisive war (316), and *c.* 320 renewed the persecution of the Christians in the region under his control (the East). Constantine attacked and defeated him in 324, and sent him into retirement in Thessalonica, where he had him put to death. The treatment of Licinius in *The History of the Church* reveals evidence of different stages in its composition. In Book IX he appears as Constantine's friend and ally. When the end of Book X was added, which gives an account of the victory over Licinius, references to him in Book IX are touched up with mention of his 'coming madness' (IX. 9. 1, 12), and in some MSS references to him are deleted (notably, the closing sentence of book IX).

LINUS (III. 2, 4; III. 13, 21; V. 6). First bishop of Rome (conventional dates: 64–76).

LITTLE LABYRINTH (V. 28). The name given by Theodoret to the treatise, from which Eusebius quotes, directed against adoptionism. Eusebius says it concerns Artemon and his heresy, but the passages he quotes refer only to Theodotus the Cobbler and his disciples. The *Little Labyrinth* attacks what it regards as a highly rationalistic form of Christianity, which owes more to Euclid, Aristotle and Galen than to the Scriptures, and is much given to heavy-handed textual emendation of the Scriptures. Theodoret ascribed the *Little Labyrinth* to Origen, which is certainly wrong; Photius, the learned ninth-century Patriarch of Constantinople, seems to ascribe it to Gaius (q.v.). Gaius seems to have shared the views of the *Alogi* (q.v.) mentioned by Epiphanius (who denied that John had written the fourth Gospel or Revelation, and ascribed them to Cerinthus); the anti-rationalist sentiments of the author of the *Little Labyrinth* might well have been shared by the *Alogi*. The favoured opinion is, however, that its author was

Hippolytus, a noted hunter of heretics, especially in Rome, about the same time as the heretics mentioned in the *Little Labyrinth* (though it seems to show more respect for pope Zephyrinus than Hippolytus did).

LONGINUS (VI. 19). Cassius Longinus (*c.* 213–73), rhetorician and philosopher; pupil of Ammonius Saccas and teacher of Porphyry in Athens. Later he became adviser to the rulers of Palmyra, Odenathus and Zenobia, and was executed after their downfall.

LUCIAN (VII. 9). The subject of a letter on baptism sent by Dionysius of Alexandria to his namesake of Rome. Lawlor wonders whether this Lucian could be the presbyter who caused Cyprian to write a letter to Quintus on the rebaptism of heretics (Ep. 71).

LUCIAN (VIII. 13; IX. 6). Lucian of Antioch, born in Samosata, who studied in Edessa under one Macarius, and finally settled in Antioch where he became a renowned teacher. He was ordained presbyter, possibly by Paul of Samosata. He was a considerable biblical scholar and revised the text of the Greek Bible. He was also noted for his great sanctity. His pupils played a major role in the Arian controversy in support of their fellow-pupil, Arius. Alexander, bishop of Alexandria, accused Lucian of having followed Paul of Samosata in his heretical opinions and of having been 'out of communion with three bishops for many years'. It is difficult to know what credence to give to this accusation. Lucian died a martyr's death in 313, having earlier been imprisoned at Nicomedia at the beginning of the Great Persecution in 303.

LUCIUS (IV. 12, 14; V. 5). Lucius Aurelius Verus, adopted son of Antoninus Pius (whose other adopted son was Marcus Aurelius). On Pius' death in 161, Verus (as he is properly called) was made Augustus alongside Marcus Aurelius (q.v.), and remained co-Emperor until his death in 169. (Eusebius usually calls him Lucius; at V. 5, however, he seems to call him Marcus Aurelius Caesar: the Antoninus must be Marcus Aurelius).

LUCIUS (IV. 17). 'Voluntary' martyr, whose death is recorded by Justin.

LUCIUS (VII. 2). Bishop of Rome, 26 June 253–5 March 254.

LUCIUS (VII. 11, 30). Presbyter of Alexandria who went underground during the Decian persecution, and attended the synod that condemned Paul of Samosata.

LUCUAS (IV. 2). Leader of revolt of Jews in Cyrene in the reign of Trajan.

LUKE (II. 22; III.4, 24, 31, 38; V. 8; VI. 14, 25). Companion of Paul the apostle and author of the gospel that bears his name and the Acts of the Apostles. Eusebius lays great stress on his reliability.

LUPUS (IV. 2). Marcus Rutilius Lupus, Prefect of Egypt 113–17.

LUSIUS (IV. 2). Lusius Quietus, a Moorish general who distinguished himself in the Parthian war.

LYSANIAS (I. 9). Tetrarch of Abila (Luke iii. 1: Abilene), at some period before A.D. 37.

MACAR (VI. 41). Martyred at Alexandria in the Decian persecution.

MACRIAN (VII. 10, 23). Fulvius Macrianus, staff officer of Valerian's, who, according to Dionysius (who is exceptionally vitriolic about him), incited Valerian to persecute the Christians and then after Valerian's capture by the Persians, sought to make his sons, Macrian and Quietus, Emperors. They quickly perished in battle and Gallienus became Emperor.

MACRINUS (VI. 21). Praetorian Prefect under Caracalla, who contrived his assassination and succeeded him in 217. In little more than a year his luck had turned, and he was defeated and put to death by Bassianus, who succeeded him as Elagabalus.

MALCHION (VII. 29, 30). Head of school of rhetoric at Antioch and presbyter. He was chosen to interrogate Paul of Samosata at the synod of Antioch (fragments of his dialogue with Paul survive), and, according to Jerome, himself composed the synodical letter (much of it preserved in VII. 30) that condemned him.

MALCHUS (VII. 12). Martyred at Caesarea under Valerian.

MAMAEA (VI. 21). Julia Avita Mamaea, mother of the Emperor (Severus) Alexander. Having heard of Origen's fame, she sent for him and had an interview with him at Antioch (probably 231–3, not 218 as often supposed, when she was not yet the Emperor's mother).

MANI (VII. 31). Eusebius has a short and vitriolic section on Mani (216–276/277), the founder of the religion called after him, Manichaeism, which was a threat to the Church for many centuries. It was a kind of extremely dualistic Gnosticism, preached by Mani in Persia from 240 onwards. He was exiled to India, and finally condemned to a long and horrible death at Ctesiphon. It was a powerfully missionary faith. Eusebius tells us little about it, though his few statements of fact are not altogether false. See S. N. C. Lieu, *Manichaeism* (Manchester, 1985).

MARCELLA (VI. 5). Martyred with her daughter, Potamiaena, at beginning of the third century in Alexandria.

MARCELLINUS (VII. 32). Last bishop of Rome whose reign Eusebius notes, and said by him to have been martyred in the Great Persecution. It seems, however, that he lapsed, handing over Scriptures and offering incense to the gods.

MARCELLUS (VII. 11). A Christian from Rome who was with Dionysius when he appeared before the prefect in the Valerian persecution.

MARCIAN (VI. 12). Apparently the leader of the Docetists at Rhossus; otherwise unknown.

MARCION (IV. 10f., 14f., 18, 22–5, 29f.; V.8, 13, 16; VII. 12). A native of Sinope in Pontus and a wealthy shipowner, and said by Hippolytus to have been the son of a bishop who excommunicated him for immorality, he was the founder of the sect that formed the most effective challenge to Christianity in the early centuries. He began to form his sect in Rome from the 140s. The essence of his teaching was a sharp sense of the newness of the Christian Gospel and its contrast with Judaism, a contrast so great that he rejected the Old Testament, regarding the God of the Old Testament, the creator God, as altogether different from the God proclaimed by Jesus Christ. He held that only Paul had understood the radical nature of Jesus' teaching, and accepted as Christian Scriptures only Paul's Epistles and the Gospel of Luke (both of which he claimed had been interpolated by Christians who had not grasped the radical break implied by the Christian gospel). His sect was well organized with recognized clergy, and high (indeed severe) moral standards: they boasted of martyrs ('an immense number of Christian martyrs': cf. V. 16), two of whom Eusebius records in *The History of the Church* (Metrodorus: IV. 15, and an unnamed woman; VII. 12. He mentions another martyr, a bishop, Asclepius, in *Martyrs of Palestine*). Eusebius tells us nothing about Marcion's teaching, only that he took further the error of his teacher, Cerdo, but he reveals how serious a challenge it was felt to be in the number of writers he mentions attacking Marcion: Justin, Dionysius of Corinth, Irenaeus, Theophilus of Antioch, Philip of Gortyna, Modestus, Rhodo, Bardaisan (he is ignorant of the most extensive attack on Marcion to have survived: Tertullian's *Against Marcion*). The most important book on Marcion is A. von Harnack, *Marcion. Das Evangelium vom fremden Gott* (Leipzig, 1921; 2nd edn, 1924).

MARCIUS TURBO (IV. 2). Prefect of Egypt January–August 117.

MARCUS (IV. 11). Gnostic heretic (his followers were called Marcosians) who flourished in the Rhône Valley in the middle of the second century. Irenaeus is our sole source for them: they seem to have believed in a trinity consisting of the Father, the Mother (Truth) and the One who descended on Jesus.

MARCUS AURELIUS (IV. 12–14, 18; V. 0, 2, 5, 9). Born Marcus Annius Verus, he was nicknamed Verissimus by Hadrian, who decreed that he should succeed Antoninus Pius as Emperor, from whom, on his adoption, he acquired the name Antoninus. Marcus Aurelius Antoninus became Emperor at Pius' death and ruled 161–180. He made Lucius Verus co-Emperor, who like Aurelius had also been adopted by Antoninus Pius at Hadrian's instruction. Aurelius' son, Commodus, was appointed his successor. As well as being an effective Emperor, he was a philosopher whose *Meditations* (in the original Greek called 'To himself') have been cherished throughout the centuries as a 'breviary for contemplatives' (E. R. Dodds).

Eusebius, however, is deeply confused by the names of the Antonine Emperors: he calls Aurelius by his full name only once

('Marcus Aurelius Verus (also Antoninus)': IV. 14) and on one occasion Aurelius is confused with Lucius Verus (V. 5). Eusebius commonly calls him 'Antoninus' and so invites confusion with Antoninus Pius, Aurelius' predecessor as Emperor. This confusion is central to an understanding of the rescript at IV. 13. Eusebius' text ascribes it to Marcus Aurelius, whilst simultaneously claiming that its author is 'the same emperor' as the author of the rescript immediately preceding at IV. 12: this rescript is written by Antoninus Pius. Moreover, Eusebius seems to wish to give the impression that Antoninus Pius was a 'good' Emperor who did not persecute Christians and Marcus Aurelius was a 'bad' one who did. This simplistic contrast is unsustainable if the rescript at IV. 13, which includes a defence of Christians against persecution ('if anyone persists in starting legal proceedings against one of these people simply because he is one of them, the accused shall be acquitted of the charge'), were written by Aurelius. Elsewhere, Eusebius allots to the reign of Aurelius the martyrdoms of Polycarp (very likely wrongly), Metrodorus, Pionius (certainly wrongly), Ptolemy and Lucius (probably wrongly), Justin, the martyrs of Lyons and Vienne and many others. If the rescript is authentic (and although there are doubters it has notable defenders, e.g., Harnack), then it appears that Eusebius has confused the identity of the imperial author in line with his preconceptions about the 'good' and 'bad' reigns of two Emperors who, although neither was particularly personally sympathetic to Christians, did not pursue any imperial persecution.

MARINUS (VII. 5). Bishop of Tyre. He was not successor to Alexander: the parenthesis should come after the mention of Mazabanes.

MARINUS (VII. 15). Soldier in the *legio X Fretensis*, martyred at Caesarea (note that Theotecnus, the bishop of Caesarea, presents him with a simple choice between the Gospel and the sword).

MARINUS (X. 5). Bishop of Arles, ordered by Constantine to investigate the Donatist complaints against Caecilian, bishop of Carthage. He presided at the Council of Arles (314).

MARK (II. 15f., 24; III. 24, 39; V. 8; VI. 14, 25). The traditions

Eusebius knows present Mark as a disciple of Peter the apostle, who wrote his Gospel from what he had heard from Peter's teaching. It was the second to be written (Matthew's being the first), and was composed during the lifetime of the apostle (though Irenaeus, cited V. 8, thinks it was after his death), presumably at Rome (cf. VI. 14). Papias remarks that Mark did not put down the events in order. (In contrast modern scholarship regards Mark's as the first to have been written, in the late 60s.) Eusebius also records the tradition that Mark brought Christianity to Egypt and estabished and governed the Church in Alexandria. (He is not called bishop, but apart from Cerdo few of the early leaders of the Church in Alexandria are.)

MARK (IV. 6; V. 12). First Gentile bishop of Jerusalem.

MARK (IV. 11). Bishop of Alexandria (not called bishop).

MARK (X. 5). Addressed, along with pope Miltiades, in one of Constantine's letters. Conceivably he was pope Sylvester's successor in 336.

MARTYRS. The name (meaning 'witness') is the name given to those who have died rather than abjure their Christian faith; sometimes it is used more loosely of those who have suffered, but have not been killed (though more often these were distinguished as 'confessors'). Martyrdom, because it was a signally close following of the way of Christ Himself, was quickly seen as the ideal goal of the Christian life (the word Eusebius habitually uses to describe the martyr's death means to 'fulfil', 'accomplish', 'perfect', 'finish', 'consecrate': the Penguin Classics translation usually uses 'fulfil'): the martyr was one who had been filled with Christ's Spirit; his words were prophetic, his intercession powerful. The *Acts of the Martyrs* – sometimes records of the trial, sometimes accounts written from one church to another telling of another 'fulfilment' – were treasured by the churches (and soon embellished), and read at the celebrations of the Eucharist in honour of the martyrs at the places where they were buried (their remains were treasured as relics, and soon shrines were built to house them) on the anniversary of the martyrdom (his, or her, 'heavenly birthday': see IV. 15.40–4). The martyrs thus became archetypal saints. For martyrs and martyrdom, see Lane Fox, pp. 419–92. For the *Acts of the Martyrs*, see H. Musurillo, *The Acts of the Christian Martyrs*.

MARY (I. 7; II. 1; III. 27; V. 8). Mary, the mother of Jesus.

MARY (III. 6). A woman from Bathezor, who was driven to infanticide and cannibalism during the siege of Jerusalem.

MARY (III. 32). Wife of Clopas, whose son was Symeon, second bishop of Jerusalem. Eusebius identifies her with the woman who stood with Mary, the mother of Jesus, and the other women at the foot of the cross (John xix. 25).

MASBOTHEANS (IV. 22). Listed by Hegesippus as both a (Christian) heresy and as one of the seven Jewish sects. The *Apostolic Constitutions* also mentions them, saying that they deny providence and the immortality of the soul. Otherwise unknown.

MATERNUS (X. 5). Bishop of Cologne, ordered by Constantine to investigate Donatist complaints against Caecilian, bishop of Carthage.

MATTHEW (III. 24, 39; V. 8, 10; VI. 17, 25). The apostle, thought by Eusebius to have written the first Gospel, in Hebrew or Aramaic, the Greek version being a translation. Eusebius says that the Gospel of Matthew was taken to India by Bartholomew, who preached the Gospel there. (Modern scholars have largely abandoned the idea that the Gospel of Matthew which we have had a Semitic original, and it is generally held that Matthew's Gospel is dependent on Mark's, rather than being the first.)

MATTHIAS (I. 12; II. 1; III. 25, 29). The disciple, originally one of the Seventy, who was elected to succeed Judas Iscariot as an apostle. Eusebius mentions a gospel of Matthias as one of the heretical scriptures (III. 25). Clement preserves several sayings of the apostle, one of which Eusebius gives us (III. 29). But the gospel is lost, and it is not clear from where Clement derived his traditions of Matthias (see Hennecke and Schneemelcher, I, pp. 308–13).

MATTHIAS (IV. 5). Eighth Jewish bishop of Jerusalem.

MATURUS (V. 1). Recently baptized Christian, martyred in the persecution at Lyons and Vienne.

MAXENTIUS (VIII. 14; IX. 9; X. 8). Marcus Aurelius Valerius Maxentius, son of Maximian, he was passed over when Diocletian and Maximian abdicated in 305. When Constantius died in 306 and Constantine was declared Emperor at York by the army, he was declared Emperor by the Praetorian Guard and the city of Rome. He called his father from retirement to help him, and for some years established himself. Initially, he was favourable to the Christians under him, but later, according to Eusebius, he initiated a reign of terror (it is not clear how true this is). In 312 Constantine invaded Italy and Maxentius was destroyed at the battle of the Milvian Bridge.

MAXIMIAN (VIII. 13, appendix; IX. 9a, 10). A soldier, born of peasant parents, who became Diocletian's Caesar in 285. With the inauguration of the tetrarchy, he became Augustus of the West. In his regions (Rome and North Africa) the Great Persecution was enforced with some severity from 303–5. In 305, he abdicated together with Diocletian. The next year, when his son Maxentius was declared Emperor in Rome, he came out of retirement to support him, initially with some success. He then won over Constantine, who married his daughter, Fausta. In 307 after the failure of Galerius to seize Rome, he tried to depose his son, but failed and fled to Gaul, and was again forced to abdicate (308). He was involved in a revolt against Constantine, was captured and committed suicide (310). He was the subject of a *damnatio memoriae* (311), from grief at which, it is alleged, Diocletian died; though it was later ignored and Maximian regarded as an ancestor of the Constantinian dynasty.

MAXIMILLA (V. 14, 16, 18). One of the two original Montanist prophetesses.

MAXIMIN (IV. 24; V. 19). Bishop of Antioch.

MAXIMIN (VI. 28f.). Gaius Julius Verus Maximinus, Emperor 235–8.

MAXIMIN (VIII,. 13f.; IX. 1f., 4, 6–11; X. 8). Gaius Galerius Valerius Maximinus (also called Daia or Daza), who became Caesar to his father, Galerius, when Galerius became Augustus of the East on the abdication of Diocletian and Maximian (305). He governed Syria, Egypt and south of Asia Minor. He was an enthusiastic persecutor of Christians (Eusebius regularly refers to him as the 'tyrant'), and renewed persecution after the death of Galerius in 311 (Galerius had issued an edict of toleration in 311: oddly Maximin's name is not included in the edict as Eusebius gives it: VIII. 17). He resented Licinius' elevation to Augustus in 310 (he refused the title of 'son of Augustus'), and allied himself with Maxentius. He was defeated by Licinius, and died, a fugitive, in 313 after he had issued an edict of toleration and turned on the pagan priests he had supported previously to such little effect (cf. IX. 10). Eusebius portrays his death as the typical death of a tyrant (cf. his account of the death of Galerius: IX. 16); Lactantius says that he died slowly from poison he had given himself.

MAXIMUS (V. 12). Fourth Gentile bishop of Jerusalem.

MAXIMUS (V. 27). Author of two brief works mentioned by Eusebius, apparently a contemporary of Irenaeus. In his *Preparation of the Gospel* Eusebius quotes a long passage from *On matter*. This passage appears in the *Philocalia*, as if Origen were the author, in a work by 'Adamantius' (thought to be by Origen from the fourth century), and in *On Free Will* by Methodius, a contemporary of Eusebius. The solution of the enigma thus posed is not at all clear.

MAXIMUS (VI. 43). One of the Confessors (q.v.).

MAXIMUS (VII. 11, 28, 30, 32). Presbyter of Alexandria who succeeded Dionysius as bishop.

MAXIMUS (VII. 28, 30) Bishop of Bostra, who attended the synod that condemned Paul of Samosata.

MAZABANES (VI. 39; VII. 5, 14). Bishop of Jerusalem, who succeeded Alexander.

MELETIUS (VII. 32). Metropolitan of Pontus, early fourth century.

MELITO (IV. 13, 21, 26; V. 24, 28; VI. 13). A notable second-century Christian who was bishop of Sardis. He apparently made a pilgrimage to the Holy Land and was interested in Jewish traditions (he gives a list of the books of the Old Testament, which corresponds with the Hebrew rather than the Greek canon, though the order is not Jewish). Polycrates, Irenaeus and the *Little Labyrinth* all refer to him as a pillar of orthodoxy. He was apparently a celibate. He also supported the Quartodecimans in the Quartodeciman controversy (q.v.). Eusebius lists many of his works, and quotes a few passages, but they are all lost save for a few fragments. In 1940, however, a work was published which survives in papyri, which claims to be Melito's *On the Passover* (or *Easter Festival*). It is a homily, rather than a treatise, and it seems unlikely that it is the work Eusebius refers to. It may, nevertheless, be by Melito of Sardis. Although there is nothing unmistakably Quartodeciman about it (and references to the *Easter Festival* rather suggest that the work Eusebius knew was), it is clearly a product of Jewish Christianity, where the Quartodecimans would have been at home. See *Melito of Sardis: On Pascha and Fragments*, ed. and tr. by S. G. Hall (Oxford Early Christian Texts, 1979).

MENANDER (III. 26; IV. 7, 22). Gnostic heretic, claimed by Eusebius, as by other Fathers, to be successor to Simon Magus, and like him a Samaritan. He seems to have claimed that he himself was the Saviour, come to redeem mankind from invisible aeons (the supernatural angelic powers, who govern and often created the world, that play a prominent role in Gnosticism).

MERCURIA (VI. 41). An old lady martyred at Alexandria in the Decian persecution.

MERUZANES (VI. 46). Bishop of Armenia (Armenia Minor? 250–64 would seem too early for a bishop in Armenia, q.v.). Recipient of letter on repentance from Dionysius of Alexandria.

METRAS (VI. 41). An old man martyred at Alexandria in the Decian persecution.

METRODORUS (IV. 15). Marcionite presbyter, martyred together with Pionius (q.v.).

MILTIADES (V. 16). Leader of the Montanists in Pentapolis: the 'Anonymous' says that the sect was named after him (i.e., 'Miltiadians' rather than 'Montanists').

MILTIADES (V. 17, 28). A man widely known as a supporter of orthodoxy: though an Asian, both Tertullian the African and

Hippolytus the Roman knew of him. In addition to the works Eusebius mentions, he evidently wrote a treatise against Montanism (known to the 'Anonymous') and one against Valentinianism (known to Tertullian). (At V. 17 he seems to be called 'Alcibiades': cf. what is probably the reverse slip at V. 3.)

MILTIADES (X. 5). Bishop of Rome, 310/11–314. Only mentioned in a document cited in *The History of the Church*, and not formally included.

MINUCIUS FUNDANUS (IV. 8f., 26). Consul suffect in 107, Proconsul of Asia, *c.* 124–5, to whom Hadrian addressed his rescript on the treatment of Christians.

MODERATUS (VI. 19). Late first-century Pythagorean philosopher.

MODESTUS (IV. 21, 25). Early Christian writer, whose work against Marcion wins Eusebius' especial praise. Nothing of his survives.

MONTANUS (IV. 27; V. 3, 14–18). Founder of heretical movement in Phrygia in the latter half of the second century (called, therefore, Cataphrygians, or the Phrygian heresy, as well as Montanists). They called themselves the 'New Prophecy' and claimed that God spoke to his Church through ecstatic prophets (and prophetesses), whose authority was to be heeded rather than that of the bishops. Montanus, a recent convert, was the first such prophet (he called himself the Paraclete: cf. John xiv. 16, 26, etc.), and Maximilla and Priscilla (or Prisca) notable prophetesses. They claimed many martyrs for their sect, though their opponents dispute this (martyrs seem to have been rare in late second-century Phrygia), and looked for the imminent coming of Christ at Pepuza in Phrygia (renamed Jerusalem by Montanus). The movement was opposed by many bishops in Asia Minor. It spread to Rome where it encountered further opposition, and to North Africa where it won the allegiance of Tertullian. Eusebius is our only source for evidence about the sect in Phrygia: he mentions works against Montanism by Apolinarius and Serapion of Antioch, but relies mainly on two sources, one by an author whose name he does not give (called, therefore, the 'Anonymous') and the other by Apollonius. Montanism as Tertullian knew it was orthodox in doctrine and ascetic in practice: with a severe penitential discipline and a ban of second marriages, it laid great emphasis on fasting and eagerly looked forward to martyrdom. It is not clear that Phrygian Montanism was quite like this. It is claimed that Phrygian Montanism was Sabellian (q.v.): Maximilla's utterance, 'I am word and spirit and power' (V. 16. 17), certainly sounds Sabellian. Tertullian, however, was an avowed opponent of Sabellianism, and linked Sabellianism with the rejection of the New Prophecy (cf. *Against Praxeas*, 1). Opinions vary, too, as to the real nature of Montanism: whether it was the resurgence of a dying tradition of Christian prophecy in the face of a growing institutionalization of the Church, or (as seems more likely) an early instance of the apocalyptic movements that have emerged from time to time in Christian history. See Lane Fox, pp. 404–10.

MOSES (I. 2f.; VII. 32). The ancient leader of the people of Israel.

MOSES (VI. 43). One of the Confessors (q.v.).

MUSAEUS (VII. 32). Mentioned by Anatolius: presumably (from context) a learned Jewish writer, but quite unknown.

MUSANUS (IV. 21, 28). Unknown Christian writer aginst Encratism.

NARCISSUS (V. 12, 22f., 25; VI. 8–11). Fifteenth Gentile bishop of Jerusalem (and, Eusebius adds, the thirtieth from the apostles in unbroken succession). He seems to be the first bishop of Jerusalem about whom Eusebius knows anything since James and Symeon. The episcopal list he cites at V. 12 (like the one he cites at IV. 5) seems to be derived from Hegesippus (he has missed out two names in V. 12: from the *Chronicle* it appears that after Capito there should be a second Maximus, and Antoninus): they have not excited much scholarly confidence. Narcissus was clearly an important figure in the second century. Together with Theophilus, bishop of Caesarea, he called a synod in Palestine to discuss the Quartodeciman problem: this fact suggests that, even at this early date, Jerusalem and Caesarea were acquiring a certain metropolitan status amongst the churches of Palestine (later confirmed at the

Council of Nicaea: see canon 7). He had a reputation as a wonder-worker. At some stage he seems to have been absent from Jerusalem and a succession of bishops appointed in his stead, but he then returned and took over the government of his see again. He lived to a great age (he was 116 years old at some time between 212 and 216): in his later years (*c.* 212) Alexander was appointed to be bishop together with him, and to succeed him (what is called a co-adjutor bishop).

NATALIUS (V. 28). Mentioned in the *Little Labyrinth* as a disciple of the adoptionists, Asclepiodotus and Theodore the banker, whom they persuaded to be their bishop. If he really was a bishop, he would have a claim to be the first known 'anti-pope'.

NEMESION (VI. 41). Martyred, after being arrested on a false charge, in Alexandria during the Decian persecution. Like Christ, he died between two criminals.

NEON (VI. 19). Bishop of Laranda.

NEPOS (VII. 24). An Egyptian bishop, noted for his piety and the hymns he had composed, who embraced chiliasm and expounded it in a treatise that Dionysius went to the trouble of refuting.

NERO (II. 20, 22, 24–6; III. 1, 5, 32; IV. 26). Nero Claudius Caesar, Emperor 54–68. In 64 a fire half-destroyed Rome and rumours circulated that Nero had instigated it and recited his own poems over the burning city. Nero tried to make the Christians scapegoats for the fire (see Tacitus, *Annals* XV. 44. 2–8; Suetonius, *Life of Nero* XVI. 2). It was in the Neronian persecution that the apostles Peter and Paul died.

NERVA (III. 20f.). Marcus Cocceius Nerva, Emperor 96–8.

NICETES (IV. 15). Father of Herod, the chief of police, who met Polycarp after his arrest, and persuaded the Governor not to let the Christians have his dead body. His sister, Alce, was a Christian.

NICOLAUS (III. 29). Of the sect of Nicolaitans; we know no more than can be inferred from Rev. ii. 6, 15. It is quite uncertain whether they had any connexion with the Nicolaus of Acts vi. 5, though Eusebius is not alone among the Fathers in asserting this. Eusebius says the sect was short-lived: there is no trace of it after 200.

NICOMACHUS (VI. 19). An arithmetician and Neopythagorean from Gerasa (between A.D. 50 and 150).

NICOMAS (VII. 28, 30). Bishop of Iconium who attended the synod that condemned Paul of Samosata.

NILUS (VIII. 13). Egyptian bishop, martyred in the Great Persecution.

NOVATIAN (VI. 43, 45f.; VII. 4. 7f.). A learned Roman presbyter, the author of various works, the most important being *On the Trinity*. He seems to have been the spokesman for (some of) the Roman presbyters, and was disappointed in the election of a pope after the Decian persecution, when Cornelius was preferred. Against Cornelius, he took a rigorist line over the treatment of those who had lapsed in the persecution. He became an anti-pope (probably against his will), and according to Socrates the Church historian he suffered martyrdom in the Valerian persecution. He gained support for his rigorist position (e.g., from Fabius, bishop of Antioch), and the sect of Novatianists survived for several centuries. (Eusebius always calls him Novatus – except when quoting Dionysius' letter to Novatian, who gets his name right – but he is not to be confused with Novatus, who led the opposition to Cyprian in North Africa. Subsequent Greek writers follow Eusebius' practice.)

NOVATUS. Eusebius' name for Novatian (q.v.): the North African Novatus is not mentioned by Eusebius.

NUMENIUS (VI. 19). Leading Neopythagorean, native of Apamea (second century).

NUMERIAN (VII. 30). Marcus Aurelius Numerianus, younger son of Carus, he was appointed Caesar in 282 and succeeded his father as Emperor after his death in 283. The following year he died in mysterious circumstances and was succeeded by Diocletian, who killed Aper, the Praetorian Prefect and Numerian's father-in-law, suggesting that he was Numerian's murderer.

ONESIMUS (III. 36). 'Pastor' of the Church in Ephesus. He was there when Ignatius wrote to the Ephesians, and Ignatius certainly calls him a bishop (see, *Eph.* 1).

ONESIMUS (IV. 26). The person to whom Melito addressed his *Extracts*.

ORIGEN (III. 1; VI. 1–39, 46; VII. 1). The great theologian, ascetic and biblical scholar of the third century. Book VI of *The History of the Church* is more or less a biography of Origen, based on the *Apology for Origen*, on which Eusebius collaborated with his revered master, Pamphilus. Origen, who studied under the philosopher Ammonius Saccas in Alexandria, was one of the most learned of early Christian theologians. When still very young he was put in charge of the Catechetical School at Alexandria (a place for teaching catechumens about the Christian faith) by the bishop, Demetrius. Later he confined his attentions to more advanced teaching and handed over the elementary teaching to Heraclas. He eventually fell out with his bishop, Demetrius, and left Alexandria. He set up a School (or an academy) in Caesarea with the help of his wealthy patron, Ambrose. Eusebius represents the quarrel with Demetrius as being a matter of discipline (Origen had preached in the presence of bishops, though only a layman, and had been ordained by other bishops, though as a eunuch he could not be ordained): it is possible that already there was anxiety about Origen's orthodoxy. (The story about his self-emasculation is not above suspicion: Eusebius seems to be relying on hearsay.) Origen's output was phenomenal, but much of it has been lost, as from the sixth century onwards he has been regarded as a heretic (he was condemned at the fifth Ecumenical Council in 553). Several of his works had been translated into Latin (by Jerome, who later turned against Origen, and by Rufinus), and many more of these have survived. The Origenist controversy, an almost endemic feature of desert monasticism from the late fourth century onwards, which led to his condemnation, was certainly inspired by Origen's ideas but developed them with a confidence that went beyond Origen's intentions (the real master-mind of 'Origenism' was Evagrius, a great philosopher of the monastic life, who died in the Egyptian desert in 399). During the persecution of Decius, Origen was imprisoned and cruelly tortured; he died of his sufferings a few years later. See H. Crouzel S.J., *Origen* (Eng. tr. Edinburgh, 1989).

OSSIUS. See Hosius.

PACHYMIUS (VIII. 13). Egyptian bishop martyred in the Great Persecution.

PALMAS (IV. 23; V. 23). Bishop of Amastris, who called a synod (apparently as metropolitan of Pontus) to discuss the Quartodeciman problem.

PAMPHILUS (VII. 32; VIII. 13). Eusebius' friend and mentor, whose name Eusebius took (he called himself Eusebius Pamphili). Born *c.* 250 in Berytus (Beirut) of noble parents, he was well educated and embarked on a secular career. But as a still young man, he gave away all his wealth and devoted himself to theology and the study of the Scriptures, living in poverty. He studied at Alexandria under Pierius (known as 'Origen the Younger'), and there conceived his great reverence for Origen. He then went to Caesarea, revived Origen's academy, and replenished the library. There he became a presbyter, and there he met Eusebius, who became one of his pupils. Pamphilus and his pupils were devoted to the memory of Origen and collected his works in the library at Caesarea. They also worked on the text of the Greek Bible. In 308 Pamphilus was arrested, tortured and committed to prison. In prison, with the help of Eusebius, he composed the first five books of his *Apology for Origen*, a defence of Origen against accusations of his unorthodoxy that were already current. He was martyred on 16 February 310 (the account of his martyrdom is found in the *Martyrs of Palestine*, 11), and after his death Eusebius wrote the last book of the *Apology*. The *Apology* seems to have formed the basis for Book VI of *The History of the Church*: the original Greek is lost, but Book I survives in Rufinus' translation. Eusebius also wrote a *Life of Pamphilus*, which is lost.

PANTAENUS (V. 10f.; VI. 6, 13f., 19). Born in Sicily, he was a convert from paganism to Christianity. According to Eusebius, he undertook a missionary journey to India. From *c.* 180, he settled in Alexandria and taught there (as first head of the Catechetical School, Eusebius says, but more probably as a private teacher, like

Justin in Rome). His pupils included Clement and Alexander of Jerusalem. He died probably before the end of the second century.

PAPIAS (II. 15; III. 36, 39). Bishop of Hierapolis at the beginning of the second century, author of a work in five books, *The Sayings of the Lord Explained*, of which only fragments survive, preserved mainly by Irenaeus and Eusebius. Eusebius has a very low opinion of Papias' intelligence, perhaps because he so deplores Papias' chiliasm.

PAPIRIUS (V. 24). Eminent Quartodeciman mentioned by Polycrates; apparently Polycarp's successor as bishop of Smyrna.

PAPYLUS (IV. 15). Martyr, the account of whose martyrdom survives: see Musurillo, pp. 22–37.

PATRICIUS (X. 6). Vicar of the diocese of Africa, *c.* 313.

PAUL (II. 1, 3, 12, 21–3, 25; III. 1–4, 23f., 30f.; IV. 1, 29; V. 6, 8, 11; VI. 14, 25, 41; VII. 18). The converted Pharisee who became an apostle, and preached the Gospel throughout most of the Mediterranean world. According to Eusebius, he was martyred at Rome under Nero. Eusebius accepts all fourteen epistles as genuine, but knows about doubts as to the authenticity of the Epistle to the Hebrews (q.v.). He also knows of the so-called *Acts of Paul*, which he regards as inauthentic, though not heretical; fragments of this work survive (see James, pp. 270–99, and Hennecke and Schneemelcher, II, pp. 322–90). Eusebius regards Luke's Gospel as in some sense 'Paul's', and mentions the idea that when Paul referred to 'my gospel' he meant the Gospel according to Luke (III. 4. 7). Eusebius also refers to the existence of a portrait in colour of Paul, seemingly without any scepticism (VII. 18).

PAUL (VI. 2). A heretic, an Antiochene by birth, patronized by the lady with whom Origen stayed as a young man.

PAUL (VI. 40; VII. 11). Companion of Dionysius of Alexandria during the Decian persecution.

PAUL (VII. 27–30). Paul, bishop of Antioch, a native of Samosata, condemned for heresy at two synods of Antioch, in 264 and 268/9, but only deposed after the congregation of the church in Antioch had appealed to the (pagan) Roman Emperor. Eusebius tells us little directly about his heresy, but from the long synodical letter he quotes (VII. 30 and elsewhere) it would appear that he was an adoptionist, who believed that Jesus was a man inspired by God, a man 'from below' and not in any serious sense the Word of God made flesh.

PAUL (VII. 30). Member of the synod of Antioch that condemned Paul of Samosata.

PAULINUS (VI. 19). Lay Christian allowed to preach in his presence by Celsus, bishop of Iconium.

PAULINUS (X. 1, 4). Bishop of Tyre from at least 313; later, after Eustathius' deposition in 326, he was bishop of Antioch for six months. Eusebius had great admiration for him, and dedicated to him not only Book X of *The History of the Church*, but also his *Onomasticon* (a gazetteer of biblical sites). He was one of the Eastern bishops mentioned by Arius in his letter to Eusebius of Nicomedia as having been anathematized (by Alexander of Alexandria?) for denying the eternity of the Son of God, but seems (from a letter addressed to him by Eusebius of Nicomedia) to have been somewhat lukewarm in his support for Arius. He is praised quite extravagantly in Eusebius' oration for the rededication of the church in Tyre, which forms the bulk of Book X.

PELEUS (VIII. 13). Egyptian bishop martyred in the Great Persecution.

PERENNIUS (V. 21). Tigidius (?) Perennis (so correctly), Praetorian Prefect at Rome 183–5.

PERTINAX (V. 26). Proclaimed Emperor by the Praetorian Guard on 1 January 193, following the assassination of Commodus. He reigned scarcely three months, before being overthrown and killed.

PETER (I. 12; II. 1, 3, 9, 13–15, 17, 25; III. 1–4, 30f., 39; IV. 1; V. 6, 8, 11, 28; VI. 12, 14, 25; VII. 18). The leader among the disciples of Jesus, and the principal apostle, who died a martyr in Rome under Nero (upside-down, according to a tradition of which Eusebius is the first witness). According to Eusebius (who seems to deduce this from 1 Peter i. 1), Peter preached to the Jews of the Dispersion (or the Diaspora) in Asia Minor. Eusebius accepts 1 Peter as authentic, but regards 2 Peter as not by the apostle. He knows, and regards as spurious, various other works ascribed to the apostle: a gospel (which he regards as heretical), an *Acts of Peter*, the *Preaching of Peter*, and the *Revelation of Peter*. In VI. 12, he records that Serapion of Antioch composed a work exposing the so-called *Gospel of Peter* (for which see Hennecke and Schneemelcher, I, pp. 179–87); fragments of the *Acts of Peter* survive (see ibid., II, pp. 259–322 and James, 300–36); the *Preaching of Peter* (to be distinguished from the *Preachings of Peter*) was known to Clement of Alexandria, who quotes from it and regards it as authentic, it seems to have been transitional between early Christian missionary preaching and second-century apologetic (see Hennecke and Schneemelcher, II, pp. 94–102); the *Revelation of Peter* was also known to Clement, who seems to have regarded it as canonical (cf. VI. 14), it, too, survives in fragments (see ibid., II, pp. 663–83 and James, 505–24). Eusebius also records that a portrait in colour of Peter was known to exist, and that he had seen it (VII. 18).

PETER (VI. 40; VII. 11). Companion of Dionysius of Alexandria during the Decian persecution.

PETER (VII. 32; VIII. 13; IX. 6). The last bishop of Alexandria recorded by Eusebius, martyred in the Great Persecution (24 November, 312). Several fragments of his writings survive, which reveal him as an opponent of Origenist ideas.

PETER (VIII. 6). Servant of the Imperial household, tortured to death at the beginning of the Great Persecution.

PEUCETIUS (IX. 11). An otherwise unknown consul and friend of Maximin Daia, executed after his death.

PHARISEES (IV. 22). One of the seven sects of the Jews mentioned by Hegesippus, and one of the four 'philosophies' mentioned by Josephus (*Antiquities* xviii. 1. 3). They were zealous upholders of the Law, or Torah, and resisted attempts to dissolve the identity of Judaism in some overall Hellenism. They are represented in the Gospels as opponents of Jesus; this probably reflects the experience of the Church late in the first century, when the Pharisees took the lead in defining Judaism – against, among other things, the newly emerging Christian movement. See Schürer, II, pp. 381–403.

PHILEAS (VIII. 9f., 13). Bishop of Thmuis, martyred in the Great Persecution (306). Accounts of his martyrdom survive: a Latin account which includes the martyrdom of Philoromus, and a Greek account, preserved in the virtually contemporary Bodmer papyrus, which tells of Phileas alone (see Musurillo, pp. 328–53).

PHILEMON (VII. 5, 7). Roman presbyter, to whom Dionysius of Alexandria wrote about the controversy over rebaptism of heretics.

PHILETUS (VI. 21, 23). Bishop of Antioch.

PHILIP (II. 1; III. 30f., 39; V. 17, 24). Eusebius (or his sources) confuse Philip, one of the twelve apostles, and Philip, one of the seven deacons whose appointment is recorded in Acts vi, who was also called an Evangelist (cf. Acts xxi. 8). Philip the evangelist had four daughters: according to Gaius and the 'Anonymous', they were prophetesses; according to Clement of Alexandria some married; according to Polycrates two remained virgins. Philip is mentioned by Polycrates as a Quartodeciman, and said by him to be buried at Hierapolis.

PHILIP (I. 9). Son of Herod the Great, tetrarch of the northern part of his kingdom, from 4 B.C. to A.D. 34.

PHILIP (IV. 5). Ninth Jewish bishop of Jerusalem.

PHILIP (IV. 15). Philip the Asiarch, mentioned in the account of the martyrdom of Polycarp. The full text calls him (in an appendix) 'Philip of Tralles, high-priest'. A Caius Iulius Philippus of Tralles is attested as an Asiarch (the exact status of which is unknown) for September 149.

PHILIP (IV. 21, 23). Bishop of Gortyna in Crete, a writer whose works are lost (late second century).

PHILIP (VI. 34–6, 39). Julius Verus Philippus, Emperor 244–9 ('the Arab'). Succeeded Timesitheus as Praetorian Prefect, and connived at Gordian's assassination, whom he then succeeded as Emperor. The end of the 240s saw pretenders arise in the Balkans and the East, and Decius, having been appointed to the Danubian command was acclaimed Emperor by the troops. In an ensuing civil war (which Dionysius of Alexandria seems to refer to, though the main theatre of the civil war was a long way from Alexandria; VI. 41. 7), Philip was killed and Decius succeeded him. Eusebius says that Philip was a Christian (VI. 34: see under Babylas); but this is certainly false.

PHILO (II. 4–6, 17f.; VI. 13; VII. 32). The great Jewish philosopher and exegete (*c.* 20 B.C.–*c.* A.D 50). He belonged to a wealthy Jewish family in Alexandria, and in 39 he took part in an embassy to Rome to plead the rights of the Jews before the Emperor Caligula (described in his *Embassy to Gaius*, which survives: Eusebius evidently knew a much longer work in 5 books, cf. II. 5). He wrote very prolifically mainly in the form of commentary on passages from Genesis and Exodus: Eusebius is aware of more than has survived (cf. II. 18). In his works he essayed a massive synthesis of Jewish Scriptures and Hellenistic philosophy, which was very attractive to Christian theologians, especially in Alexandria (Clement, Origen and Anatolius). Later theologians such as Ambrose, fourth-century bishop of Milan, and Gregory, fourth-century bishop of Nyssa, were deeply indebted to him. Many of his works have been preserved, but by Christians rather than Jews, and indeed his thought has more affinity with second- and third-century Christian thought, than with Rabbinic theology. Nonetheless, Eusebius is wrong in taking Philo's account of the Therapeutae (q.v.) to be an account of early Christian monasticism. See Schürer, III, pp. 809–89.

PHILOROMUS (VIII. 9). Roman tribune martyred together with Phileas (q.v.).

PHILUMENE (V. 13). A prophetess who spoke in ecstasy (a 'clairvoyante'?), with whom Apelles associated, and from whose prophecies he claimed his authority.

PIERIUS (VII. 32). Presbyter and teacher in Alexandria. The fifth-century Philip of Side (followed by Photius) says that he was head of the Catechetical School in Alexandria, but Eusebius' silence on the matter renders it doubtful. Pamphilus studied with him, and probably picked up from him his enthusiasm for Origen (Jerome

called Pierius 'Origen the Younger'). He suffered as a confessor in
the Great Persecution, and afterwards retired to Rome, where he
died. He was a prolific writer, but only fragments survive.

PILATE (I. 9; II. 2, 6f.; V. 7; IX. 5). Pontius Pilatus, Prefect of
Judaea 26–36, when he was removed from his office by Lucius
Vitellius, Governor of Syria, for misgovernment. It was during his
prefecture that Jesus was crucified. According to Eusebius, he
eventually committed suicide, a tradition that may well be correct.
Eusebius mentions a work called the *Memoranda* of Pilate, saying
that they were a forgery of recent date: very likely they were part
of the anti-Christian propaganda put about by Maximin Daia in
the Great Persecution *c*. 311. The extant *Acts of Pilate* are conceivably a Christian response to such propaganda (see Hennecke
and Schneemelcher, I, pp. 444–84). The *Acts of Pilate* provide
further evidence for the Resurrection of Christ, building on the
tradition (referred to by Eusebius: cf. II. 2) that Pilate knew of the
Resurrection and of the claims that Christ was divine, and reported
them to the Emperor Tiberius. Tertullian even regarded Pilate as
'in his heart a Christian' (*pro sua conscientia Christianus: Defence*, 21.
24) in his report of this tradition; in the Coptic Church, Pilate was
eventually venerated as a saint.

PINNAS (VII. 13). One of the bishops addressed in Gallienus' edict
of toleration.

PINYTUS (IV. 21, 23). Bishop of Cnossus in Crete, mentioned by
Eusebius as a writer. Nothing of his survives.

PIONIUS (IV. 15). Martyred at Smyrna on the anniversary of the
martyrdom of Polycarp, actually a century later than Eusebius
says. The *Acts* of his martyrdom survive: see Musurillo, pp. 136–
67. See also Lane Fox, pp. 460–92.

PIUS (IV. 11; V. 6, 24). Bishop of Rome 140–55.

PLATO (II. 4; IV. 8). The great Greek philosopher, *c*. 429–347 B.C.

PLINY (III. 33). Gaius Plinius Caecilius Secundus, *c*. 61–*c*. 112
('Pliny the Younger'). In *c*. 110 he was sent by the Emperor Trajan
as *legatus Augusti* to reorganize the disorderly province of
Bithynia–Pontus. Among his problems there was what to do with

Christians, about which he wrote to Trajan, who replied. The letters survive; Eusebius knows of them only from Tertullian's *Defence* (or *Apology*), which he knew in a Greek translation.

PLUTARCH (VI. 3f.). The brother of Heraclas, converted by Origen. He was martyred at the beginning of the third century.

POLYBIUS (III. 36). Bishop (according to Ignatius) of Tralles (Eusebius' language is less definite).

POLYCARP (III. 28, 36, 39; IV. 14f.; V. 5, 20, 24). Bishop of Smyrna, a disciple of John the apostle and evangelist. Polycarp, who had deeply impressed the young Irenaeus, was venerated as a living witness to the apostolic age throughout the first half of the second century. He lived to a great age, claiming to have served Christ for eighty-six years at his trial (which probably means that he was baptized in infancy). He was martyred probably 155–6 (or even 157–9), but not during the reign of Marcus Aurelius, where Eusebius places it. The account of his martyrdom (which takes the form of an encyclical letter from the church of Smyrna) survives: Eusebius summarizes the first part and quotes the rest. See Musurillo, pp. 2–21. See also *Early Christian Writings*, pp. 115–35.

POLYCRATES (III. 31; V. 22, 24). Bishop of Ephesus *c.* 190, a Quartodeciman, whose letter to pope Victor is quoted in long excerpts by Eusebius.

POMPEY (I. 6). Gnaeus Pompeius, 106–48 B.C. One of the 'Triumvirate', mentioned only (in a summary of Josephus) for his violation of the Temple sanctuary (63 B.C.).

PONTIAN (VI. 23, 29). Bishop of Rome 22 August 230–29 October 235. He as banished by the Emperor Maximin to Sardinia in 235, with Hippolytus, where they both died, reconciled with each other.

PONTICUS (V. 1) A fifteen-year-old boy martyred in the persecution at Lyons and Vienne.

PONTIUS (V. 19; VI. 12). Correspondent of Serapion of Antioch.

PORPHYRY (VI. 19). Neoplatonist philosopher, pupil and biographer of Plotinus, 232/3–*c.* 305. Porphyry was an opponent of Christianity, and composed a work in fifteen books *Against the*

Christians. This work, which was ordered to be burnt in 448, only survives in fragments cited by others. Not only were his *Preparation of the Gospel* and *Demonstration of the Gospel* directed against it, Eusebius also wrote a refutation of Porphyry which is, alas, lost. Porphyry's work also attracted works written in refutation of it from Apollinaris of Laodicea and the Arian Church historian, Philostorgius. Eusebius quotes a passage from the third book of *Against the Christians* which concerns Origen. It reveals Porphyry's exasperated admiration for the Christian scholar.

POTAMIAENA (VI. 5). Christian virgin martyred at the beginning of the third century. Another account of her martyrdom is found in Palladius' *Lausiac History* (chap. 3): the story there (said to have been told by Antony the Great to Isidore, who told it to Palladius) places her martyrdom under the Emperor Maximian. The name of the Prefect concerned, Aquila, confirms Eusebius' date.

POTHINUS (V. 1, 5). Bishop of Lyons, who perished in the persecution at Lyons and Vienne in 177.

POTITUS (V. 13). An otherwise unknown disciple of Marcion.

PRIMUS (IV. 1, 4). Bishop of Alexandria.

PRIMUS (IV. 22). Bishop of Corinth in the middle of the second century.

PRISCILLA (V. 14, 18f.). One of the two original Montanist prophetesses (also known as Prisca).

PRISCUS (VII. 12). Martyred at Caesarea under Valerian.

PRISCUS (VII. 32). Presbyter of Alexander under Theonas.

PROBUS (VII. 30). Marcus Aurelius Probus, Emperor 276–82. After his murder in 275, Aurelian was succeeded by Marcus Claudius Tacitus who was in turn murdered *c.* June 276. His Praetorian Prefect, Marcus Annius Florianus (Florian) proclaimed himself Emperor and was recognized except in Syria and Egypt, which set up Probus. Probus outmanoeuvred him at Tarsus, where he was killed by his own troops in the autumn 276, and Probus became sole Emperor. Although successful in his attempts to consolidate the frontiers of the Empire, he made himself unpopular with the army. The troops in Raetia proclaimed Carus

Emperor in 282; Probus was deserted and killed by his own troops. (Eusebius skips Tacitus and Florian in his account of the Emperors.)

PROCLUS (II. 25; III. 31; VI. 20). A leader of the Montanists, against whom Gaius wrote his *Dialogue*.

PROCLUS (VII. 30). Member of the synod that condemned Paul of Samosata.

PROTOCTETUS (VI. 28). Presbyter of Caesarea (otherwise unknown), to whom (along with Ambrose) Origen dedicated his *Exhortation to Martyrdom*.

PROTOGENES (VII. 30). Member of synod that condemned Paul of Samosata.

PTOLEMY (IV. 17). Christian catechist martyred in Rome. The account of his martyrdom is given in Justin's *Apology*, which Eusebius quotes. Very likely he was a friend of Justin's.

PTOLEMY (V. 8; VII. 32). Ptolemy I Soter, friend and biographer of Alexander the Great, king of Egypt, 304–282 B.C. Irenaeus (quoted V. 8) places the translation of the Septuagint in his reign, probably owing to a misunderstanding of the *Letter of Aristeas*, which places the translation in the reign of his son, Ptolemy II Philadelphus.

PTOLEMY (VI. 41). A soldier martyred in Alexandria in the Decian persecution.

PTOLEMY PHILADELPHUS (VII. 32). Ptolemy II Philadelphus, second of the Macedonian kings of Egypt. It was during his reign, according to the *Letter of Aristeas*, that the Septuagint was translated. Made joint-ruler with his father in 285 B.C., he succeeded to the throne 283/2, and died 246. He built the Pharos, the Museum, the Library and many other edifices and institutions of Alexandria.

PUBLIUS (IV. 23). Bishop of Athens, who, according to Dionysius of Corinth, died a martyr's death. Dionysius may also imply that he was the successor of Paul's convert, Dionysius the Areopagite.

PUBLIUS (V. 12). Third Gentile bishop of Jerusalem.

PUBLIUS (V. 19). Aelius Publius Julius, bishop of Develtum in Thrace, one of the signatories of Serapion of Antioch's (synodical?) letter to Caricus and Pontius which condemned Montanism.

PYTHAGORAS (II. 4; IV. 7; VI. 19). Ancient philosopher (sixth/ fifth century B.C.) from Samos who migrated to Southern Italy *c.* 531. He believed that mathematical (or numerical) laws determined nature, and believed also in metempsychosis (transmigration of souls).

QUADRATUS (III. 37; IV. 3, 23; V. 17). Eusebius mentions a Quadratus in three different contexts. First, there is Quadratus the evangelist and Christian prophet: he is mentioned as last of a succession of prophets and compared to Philip's daughters, and perhaps came from Asia Minor (III. 37; V. 17). Secondly, there is Quadratus the first Christian apologist, who addressed his apology to the Emperor Hadrian (perhaps when Hadrian was in Asia Minor in 123/4 or 129). A third Quadratus is mentioned by Dionysius of Corinth as the third bishop of Athens. Jerome identified the apologist and the bishop, and it is chronologically possible for the bishop, apologist and evangelist/prophet to be the same, though such identification is by no means certain. It would be odd for the bishop of Athens to have come from Asia Minor, and Jerome's identification may be no more than a guess.

QUARTODECIMANS (V. 23–5). The early Christians seem to have followed two distinct traditions about the celebration of Easter (q.v.): some celebrated Easter at the same time as the Jews celebrated Passover, i.e., on the day of the full moon in the first month of the year, viz., 14 Nisan [the first (lunar) month of the Jewish Year was the month in which the Vernal Equinox fell]; other Christians always celebrated Easter, the feast of the Resurrection of Christ, on a Sunday, the Sunday following the Passover full moon. Those who stuck to 14 Nisan, whatever day of the week it was, were called *Quartodecimans* (from the Latin for fourteen). The Christians of Asia Minor were mainly Quartodecimans, while the tradition that restricted Easter to a Sunday was followed at Rome. The controversy that Eusebius records (from an anti-Quartodeciman point of view) seems to have begun with the Church of Rome attempting to achieve uniformity of practice amongst Christians. Under Anicetus (whom Polycarp visited not long before his death), the Romans and the Asians agreed to differ. Later, under Victor, the bishop of Rome tried to impose the Roman practice by excommunicating the Quartodecimans. Gradually the anti-Quartodeciman practice became virtually universal (it was, though only implicitly, endorsed at the Council of Nicaea in 325), though, according to Epiphanius, there were still groups of Quartodecimans in the latter half of the fourth century.

QUINTA (VI. 41). Martyred at Alexandria in Decian persecution.

QUINTUS (IV. 15). A Phrygian who offered himself too eagerly for martyrdom at Smyrna, and then took fright and lapsed. The mention that he was from Phrygia may be significant: it may be meant to imply that he was a Montanist, and express official disapproval of their enthusiasm for 'voluntary martyrdom'. (The *Martyrdom* takes the form of a letter to the church in Philomelium, in Phrygia.)

QUIRINIUS (I. 5). Publius Sulpicius Quirinius, Governor of Syria, A.D. 6–21. One of his first tasks was to supervise the assessment of Judaea when that territory was annexed after the death of Archelaus. This 'registration' Eusebius, following Luke (ii. 2), identifies with the registration at the time of Jesus' birth. But that took place during the reign of Herod the Great, who died 4 B.C. The other dating of the birth of Our Lord given by Eusebius in I. 5 ('forty-second year of Augustus' reign, and the twenty-eighth after the subjugation of Egypt and the deaths of Antony and Cleopatra') yields 3 B.C.: too late for the birth of Jesus, and too early for the registration under Quirinius.

RECHAB (II. 23). In the account of the martyrdom of James the 'Lord's brother' that Eusebius reproduces from Hegesippus, it is said that 'one of the descendants of Rechab the son of Rachabim' tried to stop the stoning. 'Rachabim' is simply transliterated from the Hebrew in the Septuagint of Jer. xxxv. 2 as if it were a proper name: it is a plural, meaning 'Rechabites'. So here it means 'one of the Rechabites', a foreign tribe who had intermarried with the Levites and so acquired priestly status. However, Epiphanius, when he quotes this passage from Hegesippus, puts the speech here attributed to one of the Rechabites into the mouth of Symeon (q.v.), the cousin of James (*On Heresies*, 78.14).

RETICIUS (X. 5). Bishop of Autun, ordered by Constantine to investigate Donatist complaints against Caecilian of Carthage together with Militiades.

RHODO (V. 13). A pupil of Tatian, who attacked the heresy of Marcion, and engaged in a dialogue with Apelles. He also wrote a commentary, *The Six Days of Creation*.

RUFUS (IV. 6). Quintus Tineius Rufus, governor of Judaea at the time of the Bar Cochba (q.v.) revolt (132–5).

SABELLIANS (VII. 6, 26). The name given to those Christians who thought that the unity of God entailed that 'Father', 'Son' and 'Holy Spirit' were simply the names for successive modes or operations of God. They are also called 'modalist Monarchians' and 'Patripassians' (those who say that the Father suffered). Sabellians were named after Sabellius, about whom we know very little, except that he was condemned at Rome *c.* 220 by Callistus. Dionysius of Alexandria (q.v.) was troubled by Sabellians (thus called) in Pentapolis. What Eusebius does not record is that these Sabellians appealed to Rome against Dionysius, and that a synod in Rome having considered the matter wrote to Dionysius asking him to explain what seemed to them heretical expressions in his own teaching. Dionysius replied to the pope, his namesake, Dionysius of Rome. The controversy caused embarrassment among the supporters of the Council of Nicaea in the next century, as the Arians were able to cite Dionysius' reluctance to use the word *homoousios* of the relationship of the Son to the Father. Consequently a good deal of the correspondence between the two Dionysii has been preserved in discussions of the episode in the next century. See C. L. Feltoe, *The Letters and Other Remains of Dionysius of Alexandria* (Cambridge Patristic Texts, 1904), pp. 165–98; *A New Eusebius*, nos. 235f. (pp. 268–71).

SABINUS (VI. 40; VII. 11). Aurelius Appius Sabinus, Prefect of Egypt, 249–50.

SABINUS (IX. 1, 9a). Praetorian Prefect (of Maximin Daia) 311–12.

SADDUCEES (IV. 22). One of the seven Jewish sects mentioned by Hegesippus, one of the four Jewish 'philosophies' mentioned by Josephus (*Antiquities*, XVIII. 1. 4). They were the priestly aristocracy, and did not survive the destruction of the Temple in A.D. 70.

SAGARIS (IV. 26; V. 24). Bishop and martyr, buried at Laodicea. (At IV. 26 it is unclear what is meant by 'at the time Sagaris died a martyr's death': it could mean that Sagaris died under Servillius (*sic*) Paulus (q.v.), or that an argument arose in Laodicea about the date of Easter at the time of year when Sagaris died, which probably means he died at Easter. The latter interpretation is more likely.)

SAMARITANS (IV. 22). One of the seven Jewish sects mentioned by Hegesippus. According to Jewish tradition, the descendants of those who were resettled in the northern kingdom of Israel by the Assyrians after they had conquered it in 721 B.C. (cf. 2 Kings XVII, xviii. 9–12). In fact they must have been the result of intermarriage between the Jews who were left behind and the Gentile settlers. At some stage they became a religious sect with a temple on Mt Gerizim; they accepted as Scripture the Pentateuch (the Torah) alone.

SANCTUS (V. 1). The deacon from Vienne, martyred in the persecution at Lyons and Vienne. (The fact that he is designated as from Vienne may imply that the persecution took place in Lyons.)

SATURNINUS (IV. 7, 22, 29). Gnostic heretic, a disciple, with Basilides, of Menander. He taught that an unknown Father made the angelic realm; while seven angels made man and the world, which was feeble without a spark of life from above. His understanding of Christ was Docetic, and his practice extremely ascetic; he condemned marriage and procreation. Not implausibly, then, Irenaeus traced the origins of Encratism back to him. (Eusebius calls him 'Satorninos' and his followers 'Satornilians': Latinized in the translation as 'Saturninus' and 'Saturnilians'. Greek sources usually have 'Satornilos', Latin sources 'Saturninus', possibly deliberately associating him with the dark god, Saturn.)

SEJANUS (II. 5). Lucius Aelius Seianus, Praetorian Prefect under the Emperor Tiberius, executed for suspected treason in A.D. 31. Noted (especially from Philo) for his hostility to the Jews.

SENECA (IV. 5). Tenth Jewish bishop of Jerusalem.

SEPTUAGINT. The name given to the earliest Greek translation of the Hebrew Bible, which became the version of the Old Testament used by Greek-speaking Christians. Its name derives from the legend, preserved in the *Letter of Aristeas* (q.v.), according to which it was translated at the command of Ptolemy II Philadelphus (q.v.) by seventy-two Jewish scholars in seventy-two days (*septuaginta* is the Latin for seventy). The legend is right in suggesting an Alexandrian origin for the Septuagint, but it is probably to be dated later, perhaps 200–150 B.C.

SERAPION (V. 19, 22; VI. 11f.). Bishop of Antioch from 199. Evidently an important theologian of the early third century, we know little about him apart from what Eusebius tells us. He was an opponent of Montanism, and exposed the 'Gospel of Peter' as Docetic.

SERAPION (VI. 41). Martyred at Alexandria in the Decian persecution.

SERAPION (VI. 44). An old man who lapsed in the Decian persecution at Alexandria, but was given communion on his death-bed (by his grandson).

SERENNIUS GRANIANUS (IV. 8f.). Quintus Licinius Silvanus Granianus, Consul suffect in 106, Proconsul of Asia in *c.* 123–4, who wrote to Hadrian to ask about the treatment of Christians. Hadrian's reply went to his successor, Minucius Fundanus. (Eusebius gets his name wrong: it is not Serennius but Silvanus.)

SERENUS (VI. 4). The name of two of Origen's pupils at the Catechetical School who were martyred at the beginning of the third century.

SERVILLIUS PAULUS (IV. 26). According to Rufinus, his name was Sergius Paulus. If so, he was probably Lucius Sergius Paulus, who was Consul for the second time in 168. He could have been proconsul of Asia 166/7.

SEVENTY (I. 10, 12f.; II. 1). The seventy disciples, distinct from the twelve who became apostles, whom Jesus sent out in pairs (Luke x. 1). According to Eusebius, there was no list, but he gives the names of several: Barnabas, Sosthenes, Cephas(?), Matthias, Barsabas, Thaddaeus.

SEVERA (VI. 36). Wife of the Emperor Philip, to whom Origen is said to have addressed a letter.

SEVERUS (IV. 29). The name of an otherwise unknown Encratite, whose followers were called 'Severians'.

SEVERUS (V. 26; VI. 1, 6–8). Lucius Septimius Severus, Emperor 193–211. There were persecutions of Christians in several places throughout the Empire at the end of the second and beginning of the third century. Eusebius dwells most on the persecution in Alexandria (VI. 1–5). But Alexander was imprisoned in Cappadocia (cf. VI. 11. 5); there was additional persecution at Antioch (cf. VI. 11. 4: Bishop Asclepiades martyred; VI. 12. 1: Domnus converted to Judaism because of persecution), Rome (according to Hippolytus), Corinth possibly (cf. Palladius, *Lausiac History* 65: as the story comes from Hippolytus, it may belong to this period), and Carthage, where Perpetua, Felicity and their companions were martyred (the dramatic account of their sufferings survives, though Eusebius seems not to have known of it: see Musurillo, pp. 106–31). Eusebius sees this as evidence of a Severian persecution, instigated by the Emperor (cf. VI. 1), and has been followed in this by many. But it is most unlikely that there was such an 'imperial' persecution at this stage: it is unclear what led to such an apparently widespread persecution.

SEXTUS (V. 27). Otherwise unknown author of a treatise on the Resurrection (contemporary of Irenaeus).

SICARII (II. 20f.). Jewish terrorists who sought to overthrow Roman rule. In the Jewish War they defended Masada to the bitter end.

SIDONIUS (VI. 43). One of the Confessors (q.v.).

SILAS (V. 17). Early Christian prophet (cf. Acts xv. 32), who accompanied Paul the apostle on his 'second' missionary journey (Acts xv. 40–xviii. 5).

SILVANUS (VIII. 13; IX. 6). Bishop of Emesa, martyred in the Great Persecution under Maximin (312).

SILVANUS (VIII. 13). Bishop of Gaza, martyred in the Great Persecution.

SIMON MAGUS (II. 1, 13f.; III. 26; IV. 7, 22). Simon Magus ('the magician') was the Samaritan who was converted by Philip's teaching, and then disastrously confronted Peter the apostle over his desire to possess the spiritual powers the apostles had (Acts viii. 9–24). He was regarded by the Fathers as the father of all heresy: the great heresiologists of the second and third century (Irenaeus, Hippolytus) trace all heresy (principally Gnosticism) back to him. Part of the reason for this is doubtless the desire to see the fount of all heresy decisively defeated at the beginning by the principal apostle. Justin tells us, in a passage reproduced by Eusebius (II. 13. 3f.), that he worked his magic in Rome and was commemorated by a statue there. The base of the statue was discovered in 1574, but the inscription reads SEMONI SANCO DEO etc. Semo Sancus was a Sabine deity; Justin or his informant had evidently misread the inscription. Simon seems to have regarded himself as a saviour-figure: he led about with him a woman he had saved from prostitution, whom he called Helen and regarded as Ennoia (= 'thought'), the first emanation, whose downfall led to the existence of the world. There seems to have existed a sect of Simonians at the end of the second century.

SOCRATES (IV. 16). The great Greek philosopher, who died 399 B.C. (The 'precept' which Eusebius strangely omits is: 'A man is not to be reverenced more than the truth'.)

SOCRATES (VII. 32). Bishop of Laodicea, succeeded by Eusebius c. 264.

SOPHRONIA (VIII. 14). A martyr (Eusebius gives no name, but Rufinus calls her Sophronia), who died by her own hand rather than yield to the advances of the Emperor Maxentius.

SOSTHENES (I. 12). One of the Seventy, associated with Paul the apostle in his greeting to the Corinthians (cf. 1 Corinthians i. 1).

SOTAS (V. 19). A Christian (? bishop) from Anchialus (on the Black Sea coast, in Thrace), an opponent of Montanism.

SOTER (IV. 19, 22f., 30; V. 0, 6, 24). Bishop of Rome 166–74.

STEPHEN (II. 1; III. 5, 29). One of the seven deacons appointed by the apostles (Acts vi. 1–6), the first Christian martyr (cf. Acts vi. 8–viii. 3). By chance his name in Greek means 'crown': Eusebius, and many following him (especially those who have composed texts for the liturgy on his feast day), have not been able to resist the pun between his name and the 'crown of martyrdom'.

STEPHEN (VII. 2f., 5). Bishop of Rome 12 March 254–2 August 257. He was engaged in controversy with Cyprian over the question of the rebaptism of heretics, and also over his right, as bishop of Rome, to intervene in the affairs of other dioceses. He seems to have been the first pope to base the papal claims on his status as the successor of Peter the apostle, to whom the Lord had given the power of the keys (cf. Matt. xvi. 17–19).

STEPHEN (VII. 32). Bishop of Laodicea, 'the last before the persecution'. He lapsed in the Great Persecution.

SYMEON (III. 11, 22, 32, 35; IV. 5, 22). Bishop of Jerusalem after James 'the Lord's brother'. His father, Clopas, was Joseph's brother, so he was called a cousin of Jesus. He suffered martyrdom at the age of 120 at a date which would seem to be *c.* 106/7.

SYMMACHUS (V. 12). Seventh Gentile bishop of Jerusalem.

SYMMACHUS (VI. 16f.). The translator of the Hebrew Bible into Greek, whose version occupied the fourth column of Origen's *Hexapla*. Eusebius states (probably rightly) that he was an Ebionite, but Epiphanius says he was a Samaritan who became a Jewish proselyte. He seems to have lived towards the end of the second century. It seems, too, that he wrote a collection of hostile notes on Matthew's Gospel, which he gave to a Christian virgin Juliana, who later passed them on to Origen.

SYNEROS (V. 13). An otherwise unknown follower of Marcion, who deviated from his master's teaching in postulating three ultimate principles.

TATIAN (IV. 16, 29; V. 13, 28; VI. 13). A native of 'Assyria' (i.e., east of the Euphrates, Adiabene) and born of pagan parents, he received a Hellenistic education, and at Rome became a Christian and a disciple of Justin Martyr. Like him he was one of the apologists, and his *Apology* (addressed 'to the Greeks' generally) has survived. Later, probably 172, he returned to the East. His greatest work, the *Diatessaron*, was a harmony of the four Gospels (*dia tessaron* = through or from four). He composed it, perhaps while still in Rome, in Syriac and it was widely used in the Syriac-speaking churches for centuries. Curiously there is no trace of his name in the Syriac tradition, and it has been conjectured that the tradition about their 'apostle' Addai preserved the memory of him (see Thaddaeus). The *Little Labyrinth* includes his name in a list of orthodox theologians, but Irenaeus (and following him, Eusebius) say that he lapsed from orthodoxy and founded Encratism. Part of his heresy, apparently, was to deny the salvation of Adam. Early Syriac Christianity was strongly ascetic, so Tatian would have found himself at home there. See *Tatian: Oratio ad Graecos and Fragments*, ed. and trans. by Molly Whittaker (Oxford Early Christian Texts, 1982).

TELESPHORUS (IV. 5, 10; V. 6, 24). Bishop of Rome 125–36, the first to suffer martyrdom (so Eusebius understands Irenaeus. It is possible that Irenaeus simply meant that he was a confessor).

TELESPHORUS (VII. 26). One of Dionysius of Alexandria's correspondents.

TERTULLIAN (II. 2, 25; III. 20, 33; V. 5). The first great Latin theologian. As is the case with much in the West, Eusebius knows very little about him. He identifies him, probably wrongly, with the Roman jurist, and of his many writings (most of which have survived) he knows only his *Apology*. So he knows nothing of Tertullian's attack on the laxity of the penitential discipline in the Church of his day, nor of his vigorous defence of orthodox Christian teaching against Gnosticism, Marcionism, Sabellianism, nor of his growing sympathy with Montanism, and his ultimate abrogation of the Catholic Church in favour of that sect. Tertullian seems to have been born *c.* 160 and brought up in

Carthage a pagan. He became a Christian *c.* 197, and wrote most of his works in the next twenty-five years. He must have died in the mid-220s.

THADDAEUS (I. 12f.; II. 1). One of the Seventy, after Jesus' death, sent by the apostle Thomas to preach the Gospel in Edessa. Thaddaeus is named as one of the twelve apostles in the lists in Matthew and Mark (cf. Matt. x. 2–4; Mark iii. 16–19) and he is called an apostle in the account of Thaddaeus' mission (I. 13. 11). In the other lists of apostles in the New Testament (Luke vi. 13–16; Acts i. 13), the name of 'Judas the son of James' seems to be substituted for 'Thaddaeus'. A further confusion of identity occurs in the account of Thaddaeus' mission, in which the apostle Thomas is also called Judas – 'Judas known as Thomas' (I. 13. 11), and Thomas simply means 'twin'. In the Syriac tradition Thomas is generally known as Judas Thomas (the Gnostic *Acts of Judas Thomas* go back to a Syriac original, which must be one of the earliest pieces of Christian Syriac literature: there Judas Thomas is the twin brother of Jesus). According to Syriac tradition, Christianity was brought to Edessa by Addai the apostle, identified with the Thaddaeus of the Gospels ('Addai' could also be derived from 'Judas'). It is quite unclear what lies behind all these traditions. The question seems further confused when it is noticed that Mani's two disciples were called Addai and Thomas. The great Syriac scholar Burkitt conjectured that behind the tradition of Addai lurked the memory of Tatian, who preached Christianity in Adiabene at the end of the second century. The summary of Christian belief about Jesus that Thaddaeus gives to king Abgar contains one point of interest: the assertion that Jesus 'descended into Hades'. This forms part of the Apostles' Creed and it is a late addition there. It seems to have found its way into western Creeds (but not eastern ones) from Syriac-speaking Christianity, where it is widely attested. See J. N. D. Kelly, *Early Christian Creeds* (London, 3rd edn, 1972), pp. 378–83.

THEBUTHIS (IV. 22). Disappointed in not being chosen to succeed James, the 'Lord's brother', as bishop of Jerusalem, he is said by Hegesippus to have introduced heresy into the Church, thereby corrupting her 'virginity'.

THELYMIDRES (VI. 46; VII. 5). Bishop of Laodicea, correspondent of Dionysius over the problem of repentance (of the lapsed).

THEMISO (V. 16, 18). Montanist, who prevented orthodox bishops from intervening over manifestations of the spirit; accused of being a phoney confessor by Apollonius.

THEOCTISTUS (VI. 8, 19, 27, 46; VII. 5, 14). Bishop of Caesarea, and an important churchman in the first part of the third century. He was a friend of Alexander and a supporter of Origen: the two Palestinian bishops ordained him priest. (He seems to have been bishop for a long time: c. 215–257/9.)

THEODORE (VI. 19). Layman allowed to preach in his presence by Atticus, bishop of Synnada.

THEODORE (VII. 30). Member of the synod that condemned Paul of Samosata.

THEODORE (VIII. 13). Egyptian bishop, martyred in the Great Persecution.

THEODOTION (V. 8; VI. 16). Late second-century Jewish proselyte from Ephesus, who produced a translation into Greek of the Hebrew Bible (probably revising earlier Greek versions, including the Septuagint), which occupied the sixth, and last, column of Origen's *Hexapla*.

THEODOTUS (V. 3, 16). Montanist, he seems to have been a kind of treasurer for the sect.

THEODOTUS (V. 28). The cobbler (or shoemaker). Founder of an adoptionist (or 'dynamic monarchian') sect in Rome; attacked in the *Little Labyrinth*. According to Hippolytus, he was a native of Byzantium.

THEODOTUS (V. 28). The banker. A disciple of Theodotus the cobbler, also attacked in the *Little Labyrinth*. According to Hippolytus, he founded the sect of the 'Melchizedekians', who held that Melchizedek was greater than Christ.

THEODOTUS (VII. 32). Appointed bishop of Laodicea after Stephen's apostasy. He was a close friend of Eusebius who dedicated to him his *Preparation of the Gospel* and his *Demonstration of the Gospel*. According to Arius he was condemned, with Eusebius and several others, by Alexander for denying the eternity of the Son of God, but he acquiesced in the condemnation of Arius at the council of Nicaea. He had a long episcopate: he was present at the council of Seleucia in 359.

THEONAS (VII. 32). Bishop of Alexandria.

THEOPHILUS (IV. 20, 24). Bishop of Antioch. One of the apologists. Of the works that Eusebius mentions only his apology (*To Autolycus*) survives. His lost work, *Against Hermogenes*, was probably used by Tertullian in his treatise of the same name: Hermogenes rejected the idea that God created the world out of nothing. For his apology, see *Theophilus of Antioch: Ad Autolycum*, text and trans. by R. M. Grant (Oxford Early Christian Texts, 1970).

THEOPHILUS (V. 22f., 25). Bishop of Caesarea (*c.* 190) who, together with Narcissus of Jerusalem, presided over a synod in Palestine to settle the Quartodeciman controversy.

THEOPHILUS (VI. 41). An old man martyred at Alexandria in the Decian persecution.

THEOPHILUS (VII. 32). Member of the synod that condemned Paul of Samosata.

THEOPHRASTUS (V. 28). Pupil and successor of Aristotle (*c.* 370–288/7 B.C.).

THEOTECNUS (VII. 14f., 28, 30, 32). One of Eusebius' 'contemporaries', a pupil of Origen's, bishop of Caesarea from *c.* 260 until about the end of the century. He consecrated Anatolius as his coadjutor, who became bishop of Laodicea nevertheless. He was a member of the synod that condemned Paul of Samosata.

THEOTECNUS (IX. 2–4, 11). Curator ('city sheriff') of Antioch during Maximin Daia's renewed persecution (winter, 311/12), of which he was a zealous agent. For his zeal he became Governor (probably of Coele Syria), but was executed by Licinius after Maximin's downfall.

THERAPEUTAE (II. 7). The Therapeutae (and Therapeutrides) were a Jewish community in Alexandria described by Philo in his *On the Contemplative Life*. They seem somewhat similar to the Essenes.

Eusebius is quite wrong in thinking of them as a Christian community, foreshadowing the monastic movement of his day (about which he is otherwise silent). Two things are striking about Eusebius' account. First, he regards such an ascetic, celibate life not as at all separate from normal Christian practice but a development of it. Second, he describes it as the 'philosophic life', seeing such ascetics as true philosophers: something found again in his account of Origen and his pupils (cf. VI. 3). Such an identification of the monastic and the philosophical was already traditional by the time of Eusebius, and remained so (especially in the Greek Church).

THEUDAS (II. 11). False prophet. Eusebius records Josephus' account of him, and identifies him with the Theudas referred to by Gamaliel (Acts v. 34–9), which is historically impossible (see Josephus). But Luke says that Theudas' revolt happened *before* Judas' rebellion (*c.* A.D. 6), so he may have intended to refer to another, otherwise unknown Theudas.

THOMAS (I. 13; II. 1; III. 1, 25, 39). One of the twelve apostles. According to Eusebius, he preached the Gospel to the Parthians; according to a tradition preserved among the Syrians (in, e.g., the Gnostic *Acts of Thomas*) he took Christianity to India, a tradition defended to this day by the Syrian Christians of Malabar (who call themselves the 'Christians of St Thomas'). Eusebius knows of a spurious, and heretical, *Gospel of Thomas*. A copy of this gospel has been discovered amongst the Gnostic library of Nag Hammadi (II. 2; see *The Nag Hammadi Library*, ed. J. M. Robinson, Leiden, 1984, pp. 117–30). It seems to have been known to Mani. See Hennecke and Schneemelcher, I, pp. 278–307. (For Thomas' involvement in the Abgar legend, see Thaddaeus.)

THRASEAS (V. 18, 24). Bishop and martyr from Eumenia, buried in Smyrna, counted by Polycrates among the Quartodecimans.

THUNDERING LEGION (V. 5). During the Danubian campaigns of the Emperor Marcus Aurelius (172), a sudden thunderstorm saved the Roman Army from drought and defeat. Christians (Tertullian and, according to Eusebius, Apolinaris also) attributed this to the prayers of the Christian members of *Legio XII Fulminata*. The miracle is also referred to by pagan writers, e.g. Dio Cassius, though without reference to *Christian* prayers. By Eusebius' time, the legend has developed to the point where the enemy is hit by a thunderbolt. The name of the legion (*Fulminata* – 'thunderstruck': not quite what the story requires anyway) goes back to the time of Augustus, and can have had no connection originally with the event Eusebius describes.

TIBERIUS (I. 9; II. 2, 4, 6). Tiberius Julius Caesar Augustus, Emperor A.D. 14–37.

TIMAEUS (VII. 32). Bishop of Antioch.

TIMOTHY (III. 2, 4). One of Paul the apostle's fellow-workers (to whom the first two 'Pastoral' epistles are addressed); according to tradition, bishop of Ephesus.

TIMOTHY (VI. 40; VII. 26). One of Dionysius of Alexandria's 'boys' (either children or pupils or servants); Dionysius' treatise *On Nature* was addressed to him.

TITUS (III. 4). One of Paul the apostle's fellow-workers (to whom the last 'Pastoral' epistle is addressed); according to tradition, bishop of Crete.

TITUS (III. 5, 10, 13). Titus Flavius Vespasianus, elder son of Vespasian. He played an active part in the Jewish War, and in August 70 captured Jerusalem. He succeeded his father in 79 and died two years later.

TOBIAS (I. 13). The Edessene with whom Thaddaeus stayed, according to the Abgar legend.

TOBIAS (IV. 5). Fifth Jewish bishop of Jerusalem.

TRAJAN (III. 20f., 23, 31, 33; IV. 1, 3; V. 5). Marcus Ulpius Traianus, Emperor 98–117. It was to Trajan that Pliny wrote about the treatment of Christians: Trajan's rescript, with its advice that Christians were not to be sought out, was preserved by Christians. The end of his life saw revolts of Jews throughout the East, echoes of which reach the pages of *The History of the Church*.

TRYPHO (IV. 18). Justin's interlocutor in his *Dialogue against the Jews*, said by Eusebius to be a renowned Hebrew, but otherwise unknown. He may even be entirely fictitious.

TYRANNION (VIII. 13). Bishop of Tyre, martyred in Antioch in the Great Persecution.

TYRANNUS (VII. 32). Bishop of Antioch, appointed in 303 after his predecessor, Cyril, had been arrested and banished to Pannonia at the beginning of the Great Persecution.

URBAN (VI. 21, 23). Bishop of Rome 222–30.

URBAN (VI. 43). One of the Confessors (q.v.).

URBICIUS (IV. 17). Quintus Lollius Urbicius, who fought with Hadrian in the Jewish War, was later *legatus* in Britain, and ended his life as *Praefectus Urbi* (City Prefect in Rome) *c.* 160.

URSUS (X. 6). *Rationalis Africae* (finance minister for Africa), who was instructed by Constantine in spring 313 to make payments to Caecilian, Catholic bishop of Carthage. He was later *vicarius* (in the West) *c.* 314–15.

VALENS (V. 12). Eleventh Gentile bishop of Jerusalem.

VALENTINUS (IV. 10f., 14, 22, 29f.; V. 20; VI. 18). Gnostic heretic who taught in Rome *c.* 136–*c.* 165. Probably the most influential of the Gnostics, he taught belief in an elaborately structured *pleroma* (= fulness) of pairs of aeons (invisible heavenly beings), consisting initially of an ogdoad (a set of eight: Irenaeus composed a lost treatise with this title, cf. V. 20), which spawned yet more pairs. The existence of the visible world is a result of the fall of Sophia (= Wisdom), the last of the aeons. The redeemer, Jesus, saves men from the world by giving them saving knowledge (or *gnosis*). This *gnosis* is available only to the spiritual (*pneumatikoi*); 'natural' (*psychikoi* = soul-ly) men can attain some kind of salvation through faith and good works (by 'natural' men, Valentinus seems to mean ordinary members of the Church), while the rest of mankind, the *hylikoi* (*hyle* = matter), have no chance of redemption. Valentinus had many pupils, whose teaching represented variants of his own. His own teaching seems to have developed, as the *Gospel of Truth* (discovered at Nag Hammadi: I. 3; *The Nag Hammadi Library*, ed. J. M. Robinson, Leiden, 1984, pp. 37–49) seems much less elaborate than Patristic reports. See W. Foerster, *Gnosis*, I, Oxford, 1972, pp. 121–243.

VALERIAN (VII. 10–13; VIII. 4). Publius Licinius Valerianus, Emperor 253–60. His reign, with his son Gallienus, was much disturbed by raids from Goths and Persians. In 257 he issued edicts of persecution against the Christians, initially attacking the clergy and the corporate life of the Church, and then proceeding to actual persecution. In 260, in an expedition against the Persians, he was captured at Edessa; his subsequent fate is unknown.

VALERIUS GRATUS (I. 9). Prefect of Judaea A.D. 15–26.

VERONICA (VII. 18). Or Bernice. The name of the woman healed of a haemorrhage who, according to Eusebius, erected a bronze statue of Jesus and herself at Caesarea Philippi in her house. (Eusebius does not give her name: that is found in Macarius Magnes' account of the statue, which in other respects contradicts Eusebius – it is at Edessa, for instance.) The same name is given to the woman (also identified with the woman cured of a haemorrhage) who according to the *Acts of Pilate* healed the Emperor Tiberius with a miraculous portrait of Christ. This seems to be the origin of the Veronica known in the West, who offered her head-cloth to Christ to wipe the blood and sweat from his face on his way to Calvary: she received it back imprinted with the features of his face.

VESPASIAN (II. 23; III. 5, 7f.; V. 5). Titus Flavius Vespasianus, Emperor 69–79. In 67 he was appointed by Nero to suppress the Jewish rebellion.

VETTIUS EPAGATHUS (V. 1). Young man of rank who objected to the treatment of the Christians during the persecution at Lyons and Vienne. He was arrested and himself suffered martyrdom.

VETURIUS (VIII. 4). Military commander (in the East?) from 297. He initiated the persecution in the army that heralded the Great Persecution. (Eusebius disdains giving his name: it is found in Jerome's translation of the *Chronicle*.)

VICTOR (III. 31; V. 22–4, 28). Bishop of Rome 189–99. He attempted to solve the Quartodeciman problem by imposing Roman practice (Easter always on a Sunday), and excommunicating the Quartodecimans.

XYSTUS I (IV. 4f.; V. 6, 24). Bishop of Rome 115–25 (Also called Sixtus.)

XYSTUS II (VII. 5, 9, 14, 27). Bishop of Rome 20 August 257–6 August 258 (eleven months, not eleven years, as Eusebius has it). Unknown to Eusebius, he suffered martyrdom in the Valerian persecution, so that he was no longer alive (let alone pope) when referred to at VII. 14. (Also called Sixtus).

ZABDAS (VII. 32). Bishop of Jerusalem *c.* 298–300.

ZACCHAEUS (IV. 5). Fourth Jewish bishop of Jerusalem.

ZACHARIAS (V. 1). Father of John the Baptist, with whom Vettius Epagathus is compared.

ZEBENNUS (VI. 23, 29). Bishop of Antioch.

ZENOBIUS (VIII. 13). Presbyter of Sidon, martyred at Antioch during the Great Persecution.

ZEPHYRINUS (V. 28; VI. 14, 20f.). Bishop of Rome 199–217.

ZEUS (VI. 41). Soldier martyred at Alexandria in Decian persecution.

ZOTICUS (V. 16, 18). The 'Anonymous' (q.v.) mentions two people of this name, both opponents of Montanism. Zoticus of Otrus is his 'fellow-presbyter'; Zoticus of Cumane seems to be bishop of that place (conjectured to be near Apamea, perhaps Conana?). This second Zoticus is also mentioned by Apollonius.

Appendices

A. EMPERORS AND BISHOPS

EMPERORS	BISHOPS			
B.C.	*Rome*	*Alexandria*	*Jerusalem*	*Antioch*
44 Augustus				
A.D.				
14 Tiberius				
37 Gaius				
(Caligula)				
41 Claudius				
			James	(Peter)
54 Nero				
	(Paul, Peter)			
	Linus	Mark I		
		Annianus		Euodius
68 Galba				
69 Otho,				
Vespasian			Symeon	
79 Titus	Anencletus			
81 Domitian				
		Avilius		
	Clement			
96 Nerva				Ignatius
98 Trajan		Cerdo		
	Evarestus		Justus I	
	Alexander	Primus		
			Zacchaeus	
			Tobias	
			Benjamin	Hero (Heros)
117 Hadrian			John	
	Xystus I	Justus	Matthias	
			Philip	
			Seneca	
			Justus II	

428

EMPERORS		BISHOPS		
A.D.	*Rome*	*Alexandria*	*Jerusalem*	*Antioch*
	Telesphorus		Levi	
		Eumenes	Ephres	
			Joseph	
			Judas	
			Mark	Cornelius
138 Antoninus	Hyginus			
Pius	Pius		Cassian	
		Mark II		
			Publius	
			Maximus I	
			Julian I	Eros
		Celadion	Gaius I	
	Anicetus		Symmachus	
			Gaius II	
161 Marcus				
Aurelius	Soter	Agrippinus	Julian II	Theophilus
			Capito	
			Maximus II	
			Antoninus	
	Eleutherus		Valens	Maximin
			Dolichian	
180 Commodus		Julian	Narcissus	
				Serapion
	Victor			
		Demetrius		
192 Pertinax				
193 Severus				
	Zephyrinus			
211 Caracalla			Alexander	
				Asclepiades
217 Macrinus				
218 Elagabalus	Callistus			
222 Alexander	Urban			Philetus
	Pontian			Zebennus
		Heraclas		
235 Maximin				
238 Gordian	Anteros			
	Fabian			Babylas
244 Philip				
		Dionysius		

EMPERORS   BISHOPS

A.D.	Rome	Alexandria	Jerusalem	Antioch
249 Decius	Cornelius		Mazabanes	Fabius
251 Gallus				Demetrian
	Lucius			
253 Valerian and				
Gallienus	Stephen			
	Xystus II		Hymenaeus	Paul of
				Samosata
	Dionysius			
261 Gallienus		Maximus		
only				
268 Claudius				Domnus
	Felix			
270 Aurelian				
	Eutychian			
276 Probus			Zabdas	
282 Carus		Theonas		
	Gaius		Hermo	
284 Diocletian				Timaeus
286 Maximian also				
	Marcellinus			
		Peter		Cyril
				Tyrannus
305 Constantius,				
Galerius, and				
Maximin				
306 Galerius,				
Constantine,				
Maxentius,				
and Maximin				
308 Licinius also				
311 Galerius dies				
312 Maxentius dies				
313 Maximin dies				
324 Licinius dies				

B: ROMAN ADMINISTRATION

It is impossible in a few paragraphs adequately to summarize
Roman administration in the period covered by Eusebius' *The
History of the Church*, a period which stretches from the first
Roman Emperor, Augustus, to the first Christian Emperor, Con-

stantine, and thus covers more than three centuries and includes the major reorganization of the Empire under the Emperors Diocletian and Constantine. What follows concentrates on the officials who appear in the pages of Eusebius.

The Roman Empire inherited a provincial structure of government which had already existed under the Republic when the provinces had been governed, for a period of years at a time, by a member of the Roman Senate who had already held a Consulship or Praetorship. Under Augustus, these provinces were divided into 'senatorial' and 'imperial' provinces. The 'senatorial' provinces continued to be governed by the Senate, and their governors, who had already held the Consulship, were called Proconsuls; these were the more established and settled provinces on the shores of the Mediterranean, e.g., Asia and Africa. The 'imperial' provinces were governed by the Emperor himself through his *legati* (deputies), also senators, or in the case of Egypt and some of the smaller provinces (e.g., Judaea) a man of equestrian rank called either Prefect or Procurator (the latter was normally the name of the official, also of equestrian rank, in charge of collecting the imperial taxes); these provinces included those on the frontier that needed a standing army to defend it, e.g., Britain, Palestine, Egypt. The Governor was the principal magistrate of the province and alone could order the death penalty (hence his prominence in the *Acts of the Martyrs*). He held office sometimes for a year, sometimes for longer. Rome (and Italy) was governed by the Senate. In the time of Augustus, the post of *Praefectus Urbi* (City Prefect) was first established. He was a Senator of consular rank, appointed by the Emperor for a period of years (latterly, for about a year), with special responsibility for the city of Rome itself, including the urban cohorts. Latterly he undertook a great deal of jurisdiction there. The Praetorian Prefects (*Praefecti Praetorio*) were commanders of the imperial guard (about 10,000 men): there were two of them, and they often exercised powers second only to the Emperor.

During the third century, Senators ceased to be involved in provincial government: all these posts were undertaken by men of equestrian rank. With the reforms introduced by Diocletian, the

Empire was governed by four Emperors – two *Augusti*, under the patronage of the gods Jupiter and Hercules, and two Caesars – each Emperor having a Praetorian Prefect as a kind of second-in-command. Provinces were multiplied and grouped into dioceses, governed by a *vicarius* (a deputy of the relevant Praetorian Prefect). Originally the administration had united both civil and military functions: the Governor was supreme magistrate and commander-in-chief of his province (in both cases, under the Emperor, or the Senate), but under Diocletian and Constantine civil and military responsibilities were separated, though the old terminology continued to be used, so that, for instance, the Prefect of Egypt in the fourth century had no longer any military responsibilities, despite his title.

For further details for the later period (which is the period Eusebius himself knew personally), see A. H. M. Jones, *The Later Roman Empire 284–602*, (Oxford, 1964), Chaps. XI, XII, XVI, XVII.

C: THE CALENDAR

Eusebius himself hardly ever dates anything (we have seen in the Introduction that he is very little interested in events). His *Martyrs of Palestine*, however, dates the Great Persecution month by month: there he uses the Macedonian calendar, and equates the months of this calendar with corresponding months in the Roman (Julian) calendar, familiar to us as we still use them. The only example of this in *The History of the Church* occurs at VIII. 2, where he records that the first edict of the persecution was published in 'the month Dystrus, called March by the Romans' (this perhaps reveals the dependence of Book 8 on *Martyrs of Palestine*, because such dating is characteristic of the latter work but not of *The History of the Church*). In Book 7, in Anatolius' canons on the Easter Festival, Dystrus is again mentioned, and identified with the Roman March (VII. 32. 14). Twice in Book 3, Eusebius repeats dates given by Josephus. Josephus also used the Macedonian calendar, but he reflects an earlier stage in the development of the calendar. He makes the months of the Macedonian calendar correspond with those of the Jewish calendar. Xanthicus, for instance, is identified with Nisan, the first month of the Jewish year, which always included the Spring Equinox. The Jewish year was made up of lunar months, running from new moon to new moon, so Nisan (and Xanthicus identified with it) could sometimes begin as early as the end of February and, lasting twenty-nine or thirty days, sometimes end as late as towards the end of April. The other month mentioned in the passage from Josephus cited by Eusebius (III. 8) is the next month in the Macedonian calendar, Artemisius, which thus corresponds to Iyyar in the Jewish calendar (and so fell sometime between the end of March and the end of May).

D: CURRENCY AND OTHER MEASURES

The basic unit of currency mentioned by Eusebius is the Roman *denarius*. He also mentions the Greek *drachma* (and several times specifies the Attic, i.e., Athenian, drachma), which seems to have been of roughly equivalent value. It is impossible in times of unstable currency, such as our own (and indeed those of Eusebius), to give any real equivalent in modern money. Even if one could, it would be misleading, as the relative value of commodities is not the same now as it was then: a book, for instance, then would have been so costly as to be beyond most people's means, domestic service (usually in the form of slaves) was relatively cheap. In the parable of the labourers in the vineyard (Matt. xx. 1–16), the labourers are engaged for a *denarius* a day, so we may take it that in the first century a *denarius* represented a day's pay for a labourer at a pretty basic rate. At the other end of our period, after the enormous inflation of the third century, a legionary's *stipendium* of 600 *denarii* a year had become quite nominal, and even supplemented by donatives to the tune of perhaps 7,500 *denarii* a year, a legionary's pay still remained poor.

Other units of currency mentioned or referred to by Eusebius include the *obol*, which was a sixth of a *drachma* (so Origen lived on two thirds of a *drachma* a day, somewhat less than the labourers in the parable), the *follis*, which meant a bag (of gold), and in the early fourth century was the equivalent of 12,500 *denarii*, and the *sesterce* (implied in the term (*procurator*) *ducenarius*, meaning a Procurator with a salary of 200,000 sesterces a year), which was a quarter of a *denarius*.

Other measures are rare: Eusebius refers to the *plethron* (III. 20), a Greek unit of area roughly equivalent to a quarter of an acre, but used to represent the Latin *iugerum*, which was somewhat more than half an acre.

E: LATIN TERMS USED BY EUSEBIUS

Eusebius uses various Latin words, usually the names of Roman officials, which have not been translated.

beneficiarii (IX. 9a): a soldier granted special privileges; here, probably, the officers in the entourage of a provincial Governor.

confector (IV. 15): the official in the games whose duty it was to dispatch the fatally wounded.

corrector (X. 5): title introduced by Diocletian for the governor of certain old proconsular provinces (including Sicily), usually held by a man of senatorial rank. (From it derives the *corregidor* of Old Spain.)

ducenarius (VII. 30): a *procurator ducenarius* was a Procurator paid the large sum of 200,000 sesterces a year: it is with such a wealthy (and overbearing) official that Paul of Samosata, as a bishop, is compared.

dux (IX. 5): a commander of frontier troops, a military rank introduced by Diocletian, later to become very important. (The title *duke* derives from it.)

evocatus (III. 20): this term was used for a veteran of the Praetorian or Urban cohorts, and may mean that here. Rufinus, however, could make nothing of it, and in his translation took it to be a mistake for *Revocatus*, a personal name.

frumentarius (VI. 40): a member of a special corps of soldiers employed in various ways, here as a military policeman.

magistratus (VIII. 11): (here) the office of the *magister rei privatae*, the official who controlled all imperial property, either on a central or on a provincial basis.

praepositi (IX. 1): those in charge; senior officials.

repudium (IV. 17): divorce.

secretum (VII. 30): a magistrate's private chamber – part of the comparison of Paul of Samosata's behaviour as a bishop with that of a high-ranking Procurator.

vicarius (X. 6): literally 'deputy'. As a result of Diocletian's reform, provinces were grouped together into *dioceses*: a *vicarius* (the 'deputy' of the Praetorian Prefects) was in charge of a diocese.

Discover more about our forthcoming books through Penguin's FREE newspaper...

Penguin

It's packed with:

- exciting features
- author interviews
- previews & reviews
- books from your favourite films & TV series
- exclusive competitions & much, much more...

READ MORE IN PENGUIN

In every corner of the world, on every subject under the sun, Penguin represents quality and variety – the very best in publishing today.

For complete information about books available from Penguin – including Puffins, Penguin Classics and Arkana – and how to order them, write to us at the appropriate address below. Please note that for copyright reasons the selection of books varies from country to country.

In the United Kingdom: Please write to *Dept. JC, Penguin Books Ltd, FREEPOST, West Drayton, Middlesex UB7 OBR*

If you have any difficulty in obtaining a title, please send your order with the correct money, plus ten per cent for postage and packaging, to *PO Box No. 11, West Drayton, Middlesex UB7 OBR*

In the United States: Please write to *Penguin USA Inc., 375 Hudson Street, New York, NY 10014*

In Canada: Please write to *Penguin Books Canada Ltd, 10 Alcorn Avenue, Suite 300, Toronto, Ontario M4V 3B2*

In Australia: Please write to *Penguin Books Australia Ltd, 487 Maroondah Highway, Ringwood, Victoria 3134*

In New Zealand: Please write to *Penguin Books (NZ) Ltd, 182–190 Wairau Road, Private Bag, Takapuna, Auckland 9*

In India: Please write to *Penguin Books India Pvt Ltd, 706 Eros Apartments, 56 Nehru Place, New Delhi 110 019*

In the Netherlands: Please write to *Penguin Books Netherlands B.V., Keizersgracht 231 NL–1016 DV Amsterdam*

In Germany: Please write to *Penguin Books Deutschland GmbH, Friedrichstrasse 10–12, W–6000 Frankfurt/Main 1*

In Spain: Please write to *Penguin Books S. A., C. San Bernardo 117–6° E–28015 Madrid*

In Italy: Please write to *Penguin Italia s.r.l., Via Felice Casati 20, I–20124 Milano*

In France: Please write to *Penguin France S. A., 17 rue Lejeune, F–31000 Toulouse*

In Japan: Please write to *Penguin Books Japan, Ishikiribashi Building, 2–5–4, Suido, Bunkyo-ku, Tokyo 112*

In Greece: Please write to *Penguin Hellas Ltd, Dimocritou 3, GR–106 71 Athens*

In South Africa: Please write to *Longman Penguin Southern Africa (Pty) Ltd, Private Bag X08, Bertsham 2013*

READ MORE IN PENGUIN

A CHOICE OF CLASSICS

St Anselm	**The Prayers and Meditations**
St Augustine	**The Confessions**
Bede	**Ecclesiastical History of the English People**
Geoffrey Chaucer	**The Canterbury Tales**
	Love Visions
	Troilus and Criseyde
Marie de France	**The Lais of Marie de France**
Jean Froissart	**The Chronicles**
Geoffrey of Monmouth	**The History of the Kings of Britain**
Gerald of Wales	**History and Topography of Ireland**
	The Journey through Wales and **The Description of Wales**
Gregory of Tours	**The History of the Franks**
Robert Henryson	**The Testament of Cresseid and Other Poems**
Walter Hilton	**The Ladder of Perfection**
Julian of Norwich	**Revelations of Divine Love**
Thomas à Kempis	**The Imitation of Christ**
William Langland	**Piers the Ploughman**
Sir John Mandeville	**The Travels of Sir John Mandeville**
Marguerite de Navarre	**The Heptameron**
Christine de Pisan	**The Treasure of the City of Ladies**
Chrétien de Troyes	**Arthurian Romances**
Marco Polo	**The Travels**
Richard Rolle	**The Fire of Love**
François Villon	**Selected Poems**